The Ethiopian Orthodox Täwahïdo Church

AFROASIATIC STUDIES

NUMBER 1

INSTITUTE OF SEMITIC STUDIES (ISS)
PRINCETON, NJ

SERIES EDITORS
EPHRAIM ISAAC AND GIRMA A. DEMEKE

Isaac, Ephraim. *The Ethiopian Orthodox Täwahïdo Church*. 2012.

The
Ethiopian Orthodox
Täwahïdo Church

EPHRAIM ISAAC

THE RED SEA PRESS

TRENTON | LONDON | NEW DELHI | CAPE TOWN | NAIROBI | ADDIS ABABA | ASMARA | IBADAN

THE RED SEA PRESS
541 West Ingham Avenue | Suite B
Trenton, New Jersey 08638

Book and cover design: Saverance Publishing Services

Library of Congress Cataloging-in-Publication Data

Isaac, Ephraim.
  The Ethiopian Orthodox Täwahïdo Church / Ephraim Isaac.
     p. cm.
  ISBN 978-1-56902-369-3 (pbk. -13) -- ISBN 978-1-56902-368-6 (hardcover
- 13)
  1. Ya'Ityopya 'ortodoks tawahedo béta kerestiyan. 2. Ethiopia--Church history.
I. Title.
  BX146.3.I83 2012
  281.75--dc23
                            2012013621

Table of Contents

❖

Preface

"Our own church is as ancient as our faith, and her history is replete with accounts of the unswerving faith of our people, the inspiring heroism of our martyrs, the Holiness of our Saints. The history of our nation has always been closely related to the history of our church, and the church has been both the rallying point and the inspirer of our national unity. Christianity has flourished in our country, keeping its original features and character through the centuries. As a nation we have a great debt to the church for our cultural heritage."[1]

- His Imperial Majesty Haile Selassie I

Ancient monolithic churches carved out of the solid rock of the Ethiopian mountains symbolize the enduring faith, culture, and freedom of one of the oldest civilizations in the world. In both its theology and Jewish practices, the Ethiopian Orthodox Tăwahïdo Church can be said to be the most ancient Christian Church outside of the first century church of Jerusalem—what some scholars call the Church of Peter and James. Judaic contact with Ethiopia itself is even pre-Christian. It goes back to at least the 10th century B.C. to the time of the visit of the Queen of Sheba. According to Ethiopic tradition, the Queen, called Negest Saba or Makïda in Ethiopic, travelled from her palace in Axum to the royal court of King Solomon.[2] Her mission was to gain wisdom from the great King. During her visit she also adopted King Solomon's religion (Judaism) and conceived his child to whom she gave birth after her return to Ethiopia. The son, named Menelik, is said to have later visited his father in Jerusalem and returned to Axum with a host of priests' and nobles' first-born sons, carrying the Holy Ark of the Covenant.[3] Tradition attributes Ethiopia's defense against

---

1   *Emperor of Ethiopia.* 1892, Miscellanea I: English Version of His Imperial Majesty's Inaugural Address to the Conference of Heads of Oriental Orthodox Churches (60).

2   I. Kings, 10:1ff

3   Pankhurst, Richard. *Historic Images of Ethiopia.* Shama Books, Addis Ababa, Ethiopia, 2005 (23-30).

attacks from Judaism, Islam, and other Christian sects to the royal Solomonic blood of Ethiopia's kings; the presence and guardianship of the Holy Ark; and the devout faith of her people. As the only country on the continent to defeat European colonization, Ethiopia has been a beacon of light for Africa and its Diaspora during the dark centuries of the Trans-Atlantic slave trade, the European "scramble for Africa", and the subsequent centuries of oppression. The Solomonic Dynasty extended up until 1974, when Emperor Haile Sellassie I was deposed.

Following the monarchy, the authoritarian military regime of President Mengistu Haile Mariam (1974 - 1991) committed great atrocities against its own people that gave Ethiopia a modern-day reputation as a desolate and impoverished land of famine and orphans. Westerners may be surprised to learn that their ancestors regarded Ethiopia as a home of a superior civilization. Homer, Aeschylus, and Herodotus described the people as just and courageous, gentle and hospitable. The ancient Israelites had no less regard for them: their great leader Moses married an "Ethiopian" woman.[4] Ethiopia's age-old alphabet, calendar, manuscripts, architecture, and systems of church education speak to its cultural sophistication since antiquity. The modern European realization of Ethiopic literary riches has caused scholars to increasingly turn to the study of such important works as the Book of Enoch and the Book of Jubilees, which are extant in full manuscript only in Ge'ez. These books shed light on the religious and intellectual environment in which Jesus lived and in which the earliest Church developed. In this context, the manuscripts and the traditions of Ethiopic texts are of great significance to world civilization.

The advent of the twentieth century, when modern warfare and modern communications affected every nation, stirred Ethiopia to take its place with the rest of the world, and provide additional leadership in the development of Africa. Today Addis Ababa has become the headquarters of the United Nations Economic Commission for Africa and the Organization for African Unity. Ethiopia is one of the richest countries in Africa naturally. Not only does it possess gold and other minerals, but also it has every potential for becoming "the breadbasket of Africa and the Middle East". It possesses numerous large rivers and streams, heavy rainfall in many parts of the country, amazingly fertile soil, healthy and vigorous climate, and great landscape. The wide variations in soil content, climate, and rainfall contribute to the everlasting fertility of Ethiopia; sixty percent of its 400,000 square miles is cultivable land. In vast areas of Western provinces, the topsoil is so deep and so rich that coffee, originating in Ethiopia, still grows wild. Substantial mineral resources offer further possibilities for economic growth. Although the land is rich, her people are certainly not. The widespread poverty that now prevails can only be overcome through

---

4   Numbers 12:1.

education to a wiser use of Ethiopia's abundant spiritual, cultural, and natural resources. With the development of its potential, Ethiopia, occupying the favored place in the horn of Africa, at the crossroads of the two largest continents, will no doubt re-emerge as a leading nation.

In conclusion I would like to emphasize that this work is a modest attempt to give a brief and purely objective description of the interesting history of the Ethiopian Church, its beliefs and practices. Nothing in the book is intended to express my personal views or opinions on the Ethiopian Church or State. I alone am responsible for factual mistakes that might have escaped my attention.

It is a nice thought to hope that you, who turn the pages of this book, will be able to think of it personally; it is a symbol of your contribution to support a worthwhile cause which is endeavoring in a small way to make this world a better place for fellow man to live in.

My first book on the Ethiopian Church was a small coffee table book published in 1968 when I was a graduate student at Harvard University. It was written to promote literacy in Ethiopia. Proceeds from its purchase were also donated to famine relief. It is interesting and a pleasure to reprint here below the foreword from that book at the beginning of this new endeavor and our new Millennium ("isra mi'it.) The late Dr. George Williams, Hollis Professor of Divinity at Harvard Divinity School and one of my thesis advisors, penned it and his words reflect the extent to which the times have changed since that book was published in 1968. I offer it to you as reminder of the continual making of history as well as a call to continued scholarship on a fascinating and ever changing culture.

It is interesting to note that the Ethiopian New Millennium, New Year, Maskaram 1, 2000, fell on September 12, 2007. The eve of that same day was also the first day of the Jewish New Year (Rosh Hashanah) and the first day of the Muslim Ramadan. The opening of this new Ethiopian Millennium thus epitomizes the long historical co-existence of the three great religions, Judaism, Christianity, and Islam in Ethiopia. It is an auspicious symbol for peace in the Horn of Africa and the Middle East!

Personal Note and Acknowledgement

❖

Some might ask why a Jewish person should write a book about the *Ethiopian Orthodox Täwahïdo Church*. From my first year at Harvard University, when I became the first Ethiopian student of the famous Divinity School, studying comparative religions, I began to realize that the *Ethiopian Orthodox Täwahïdo Church* is the most Jewish of all Christian churches. In this regard, any Jewish person must be naturally interested in knowing the history of the Ethiopian Orthodox Täwahïdo Church as many past western Jewish scholars have done, let alone an Ethiopian native and nationalist like me, who has developed a great respect for the tradition of *Ethiopian Orthodox Täwahïdo Church*.

The *Ethiopian Orthodox Täwahïdo Church* had roots in the early church of Jerusalem and contributed much to the preservation of Judaeo-Christian literature, such as the famous *Mashafa Henok, Book of Enoch* (which I had myself translated into English, <u>Old Testament Pseudepigrapha</u>, vol. I, Doubleday, 1983) and *Mashafa Kufale*, the *Book of Jubilees*. In this regard, all scholars of Semitic languages and cultures and Christian beginnings and of Classical Ethiopic literature, as I am also, must be interested in this important Church and its contribution to world civilization.

When I was growing up in my small town of Nedjio, Wallaga, *Ethiopian Orthodox Täwahïdo Church* priests used to visit my father. They looked upon him as a member of the beloved Children of Israel, and used to sing his praises. I still remember one priest who used to say to my father the Israelites are the greatest in the eyes of the Almighty, "you Yishaq are baptized in fire, I, a humble priest, only in water." Much later, when I was visiting Axum and Lalibala doing research on the history of Ethiopic/Ge'ez literature, I experienced the same love and respect for the people of Israel by practically all the priests whom I met. They made me feel very at home saying that I was one of them, because they too are Israelites. When I visited those churches with American friends, the priests would take me aside, sing the praises of the children of Israel to me, and even show me religious artifacts they said they would not show to others.

As a student at the University College, now Addis Ababa University, 1954-56, I was fortunate to meet and know His Holiness, the late beloved and respected Patriarch Abuna Tewoflos and befriend him. Abuna Tewoflos was then the Archbishop of Harrar and lived in a house across from the University College Arat Kilo campus. A relative of the Archbishop from Gojjam, who happened to be a close friend of mine from high school days, told the Archbishop, who was apparently interested in learning Hebrew, about me and brought me over to his residence one evening. Subsequently, I began to teach the great Archbishop reading Hebrew on a weekly basis for a year. From that time until his brutal murder, I kept a close relationship with him, even after he became a famous Patriarch. The epitome of my friendship with His Holiness was in 1971. In view to my interest in the history of writing in Ethiopia, Patriarch Tewoflos invited me to give a formal lecture on the origin and history of the Ethiopic/Ge'ez alphabet at the Trinity Cathedral one Sunday morning after the end of the liturgical service. If I remember correctly, almost all the Archbishops were there, as well as a large number of priests and the faithful and students of the Trinity Theological College. The chapter in this book on writing is partly based on that lecture. As the then Director General of the National Literacy Campaign of Ethiopia, I once suggested to His Grace to kindly give a press statement supporting the Literacy Campaign, calling upon all Ethiopians to learn reading and writing the alphabet. He generously consented to do so, for which I was deeply grateful. In January 1972, if I remember correctly, Patriarch Pimen of Russian was visiting Ethiopia and attended the Timqat festival ceremony. I happened to be in Ethiopia myself and came to observe the celebration. The great Patriarch spotted me in the audience, and to my surprise, sent a deacon to invite me to come to the front. As a humble person by nature, I only reluctantly agreed to come forward near him and the Russian Prelate to whom he generously introduced me. When His Holiness came to the USA, to receive an honorary degree from Boston University, he made it a point to invite me personally to attend the ceremony at the University. He also invited me to his suite for tea and to discuss religious matters. I can never forget all the generosity of His Holiness and a great deal that I learnt from him about *Ethiopian Orthodox Täwahïdo Church.*

Over the years, many distinguished Archbishops have been dear friends of mine. I can humbly claim that almost all the Holy Archbishops of the *Ethiopian Orthodox Täwahïdo Church* of the past fifty years, including, in particular, the late Abuna Mathewos, Abuna Matyas, Abuna Atenatewos, Abuna Gabriel, Abuna Melchisedeq, Abuna Timothewos, the late Abuna Yishaq, the late Abuna Merha Kristos, and the present Patriarch Abuna Pawlos, have been close personal friends.

In 1973-74, when I was a Visiting Professor at the Hebrew University of Jerusalem, His Grace the late Archbishop Mathewos (of blessed memory), the then Ethiopian Archbishop of Jerusalem invited me to help organize the Classical Ethiopic manuscripts in Deir Sultan Monastery ("Ethiopian Manuscripts in the Monasteries of Ethiopian Patriarchate, Jerusalem", <u>Rassegna di Studi Etiopici</u>, XXX, Rome, 1984-86, 53-80.) His venerable successors, the warm and kind hearted spiritual leaders, His Grace Archbishop Matyas and His Grace Archbishop Atenatewos, who remain great friends of mine to this day, encouraged me to continue the work and supported my effort to help establish a study group for the monks in Jerusalem. His Grace the late Archbishop Yishaq (of blessed memory) of the Western Hemisphere, a humble and wonderful human being, became a close friend when he was Archbishop of the Western Hemisphere. Every year 1983-1995, he invited me to be his special guest and keynote speaker to his faithful followers in Bronx and the West Indies. When a new church was inaugurated in Bermuda, he invited me to be the keynote speaker at the festive dedication attended by the Governor of Bermuda. I was his scholar-in-residence for one week, lecturing on the culture and history of Ethiopia to various groups and large audiences in Bermuda. My distinguished friend, the late Honorable Dejazmatch Zewde Gebre Selassie, and I were the two major reviewers of his book on the Ethiopian Church. During that time he was working on the book, he regularly visited me in Princeton seeking my comments and suggestions about his book. In 2004, the Addis Ababa University, invited by then President Endrias, former close collaborator on the Literacy Campaign, honored me. I decided to give my acceptance speech in Ethiopia/Ge'ez, and I needed a Church scholar to read and review it. My friend, Liqa Ma'ameran Demetros, introduced me to His Grace the late Archbishop Merha Kristos (of blessed memory) who graciously offered to read it. That sealed our friendship and I subsequently invited him to be a member of venerable Ethiopian Elders Coalition which he graciously accepted and to which he contributed his wisdom. His Grace Abuna Salama of Axum has succeeded him as one of our spiritual advisers. My collaboration with all these great spiritual leaders has enriched my knowledge of the *Ethiopian Orthodox Täwahïdo Church.*

In 1984, Ethiopian Calendar (1992) a conflict arose among the Fathers, the Archbishops of the *Ethiopian Orthodox Täwahïdo Church* regarding Church administration. His Grace Abuna Gabriel, His Grace Archbishop Timothewoas, His Grace Archbishop Melchisedq (whom I befriended when he was attending the Holy Cross Greek Orthodox Seminary in the Boston area when I was at Harvard), and His Grace Abuna Zena Marqos (with whom I shared a seat as observer at the conference for Peace and Democracy when the Transitional Government was formed in 1991) were so far-sighted and kindhearted to accept the humble invitation of Ethiopian Elders that I chaired to resolve the dispute and attain reconciliation. In the teleconference that ensued, they invited six other Archbishops within Ethiopia as well as the Archbishop of Jerusalem and Archbishop of North America *(see attached letter on page xvi). The manner in which these distinguished Archbishops pursued peace and reconciliation was a great lesson for me in understanding the spirituality of the Church.

In short, from my area of the study of ancient Semitic languages and literature and history of comparative religions, my close association with all the venerable fathers, not only have I come to learn a great deal about the church but also to respect its venerable history. I look forward to the day when great *Ethiopian Orthodox Church* scholars will write an even more definitive work on the history of this important Church.

I am most grateful to the late Professor George H. Williams of Harvard Divinity School, who first encouraged me to write the shorter version of this book. I thank Liqa Ma'amran Dimetros, Dr. Girma A. Demeke, Dr. Brook Abdu who have read this manuscript and given me their important comments. I am especially grateful to Dr. Girma for his generous time and energy in not only editing this work but also for his commitment to its speedy publication. I am deeply indebted to Kassahun Checole not only for his great contribution in publishing many important and needed books on Africa but also for his warm personality and friendship. I thank many wonderful fellow Ethiopians like Ato Gedlu Metafaria, St. Louis Ethiopian Community Chair who was also one of my strong Literacy Campaign friends, Dr. Irqu Yimar, Chicago Ethiopian Community leader, Dr. Mogus Gebre-Mariam of Baltimore, Woiz. Saba Meskel Gebre, and Woiz. Alitash Kebede of Los Angeles Ethiopian Community leaders, Presidents of the Ethiopian Students Association International who invited me from time to time to lecture on Ethiopian religious and spiritual culture, helping me thereby to review my knowledge of the subject. I also thank my research assistant Ms. Camille Coates, Princeton University, 2007, for her valuable assistance. I thank all my Ethiopian friends who at one time or another have participated in a discussion about religion in Ethiopia during the last thirty years. I beg forgiveness from those who had helped me but I have not been able to mention here.

Finally, yet importantly, I want to highlight the fact that the Ethiopian Orthodox Tewahedo Church and the Eritrean Orthodox Täwahïdo Church are identical in every respect. It is very well-known that the traditions of the Ethiopian Orthodox Täwahïdo Church is rooted in the civilization of the Axumite Empire, which is also the ancestor of the present day state of Eritrea. Hence, what is written in this book is also true for the great Eritrean Orthodox Täwahïdo Church. Indeed, I am most grateful to the Eritrean Orthodox Bishop, His Grace Abuna Makarios, who read this mauscript and gave me many valuable suggestions. I am deeply indebted to him and another Eritrean scholar, Dr. Gebre Yesus Walde Mikael (Dr. Mikael) of the University of Hamburg, both close friends whom I first met at the Hebrew University of Jerusalem from where they received their Master and Doctorate degrees respectively. They contributed to my inspiration to study the Ethiopic Ge'ez literature. I 1971, I travelled on foot with Bishop Makarios (then Abba Petros) to Dabra Bizen, one of the oldest and most venerable Ethio-Eritrean monasteries. Abuna Makarios and Dr. Mikael spent a year at Harvard University, assisting me as teaching fellows in my courses on African Religions and Ethiopian Orthodox Christian Literature in the Department of Afro-American (now African and African American) Studies of which I am one of the founders and the first professor. These two Eritrean brothers continue to contribute to my appreciation of the Ethiopian Orthodox and the Eritrean Orthodox Täwahïdo Churches.

በሰሜን አሜሪካ የኢትዮጵያ አርቶዶክስ ተዋህዶ ቤተ ክርስቲያን ሊቀጳጳስ
ETHIOPIAN ORTHODOX CHURCH IN THE UNITED STATES AMERICA
ARCRBISOP
3010 EARL PL.N.E.WASHNGTON, DC 20018

ለክብር ፕሮፌሰር ኤፍሬም ይስሐቅ
9 GROUEV AVE.
PRINCETON,NJ 08540

ክቡር ፕሮፌሰር ኤፍሬም

ከሁሉ በፊት ዘወትር የእግዚአብሔር ጸጋ እንዲበዛልዎ የዘወትር ደሎቴ መሆኑን በአክብሮት እገልጻለሁ

አንደ አ ጀሸ አቆጣጠር በ1984 ዓ ም በኢትዮጵያ ቤተ ክርስቲያኒ አባቶች ማለት በሊቃነ ጳጳሳቱ መካከል በተከስተው የአስተዳደር ልዩነት በዕርቅ እንዲፈታ በማሰብ በዚያ በዕመኒ ሕማማት ሚያዝያ ሰኞ 12 ቀን እና ሮብ 14 1284 ዓም ከዚህ ከሰሜን አሜሪካ ሆነው እኛን ካለንበት በቴሌፎን በመጥራት ቴሌ ኮፈረስን በማዘጋጀት ሰባት ሰአት የፈጀ የቴሌኮንፈረስ ውይይት ከፍተው ከኢትዮጵኡ ስድስት ጳጳሳት ከኢየሩሳሌም አንድ ሊተዳጰስ ከአሜሪካ ጳጳ ሳትና
ምሁራን ኢትዮጵያውያን የተከስተውን መለያየት በውይይት እንዲፈታ በመመኘት እንድነዋያይ ያደረጉት የተቀደሰ ተግባር የማይረሳ ነው በቤተ ክርስቲያን ታሪክም ዘወትር ሲዘከር ሊወሳ)የሚኖና ሕያው ሥራ መሆኑን እንመሰክራለን

"የሚያስታርቁ ብፁአን ናቸው" ሲል ጌታችን ኢየሱስ ክርስቶስ ያስተማረውን በመጥቀስ ማቴ.5.8 እርስዎ በብፁአን አባቶች መካከል ዕርቅና ሰላም እንዲፈጠር ከፍተኛ ጥረት በማድረግም ከልብ እናመሰግኗዎታለን በተጠቀሰው ወርና ቀንም በእርስዎ ጥረት በተደረገው ቴሌኮንፈረስ እንዲሁም በአካል ወደ ኢትዮጵያ መተተው ከሊቀት ምሁራን ጋር ሆነው ባደረጋችሁት ጥረት ተለያይተው የነበሩት ብፁአን ጳሳሳት ሊታረቁና አንድ ሊሆኑ ችለዋል
ስለዚህ ሐዋርያው ቅዱስ ጳውሎስ ይህንን ስለ መሰለው ጉዳይ ሲጽፍ ሃነ (መልካም) ሥራ ለሚያደርጉት ሁሉ ምስጋናና ክበር ሰላምም ይጣኛቸዋል በማለት ተናገርአል (ሮሜ2ፎ10)
በመሆኑም እርስዎ ኢትዮጵያን ሀገርዎን ከልብ የሚወዱ የሰላምና የፍቅር ሰው ስለሆኑ እግዚአብሔር በህይወትና በመልካም ጤንነት ይጠብቅዎት ዘንድ የዘወትር ጸሎቴ መሆኑን በአክብሮት ስገልጽም እጅግ ደስ እያለኝ ነው

" የሰላም አምላክ እግዚአብሔር
ሰላሙን ያብዛልን"

አባ ገብርኤል ሊቀ ጳጳስ
የኢትዮጵያ አርቶዶክስ ትዉሐዶ
ቤተክዜሐቲያን ትዱስ ሲኖዶስ አባል

Ethiopian Orthodox Church in the United States of America - Archbishop
3010 Earl Pl. N.E. Washington DC 20018

Professor Ephraim Isaac
9 Grover Avenue, Princeton, NJ 08540

Dear Professor Ephraim,

First of all, I extend to you respectfully my good wishes and let you know it is my prayer that abundant grace be unto you from the Lord.

In 1984 Ethiopian Calendar (1992), a conflict arose among the Fathers, that is to say, the Archbishops of the Ethiopian Orthodox Church, regarding the administration of the Church. You took the initiative to resolve the disputes peacefully through dialogues. During Passion Week, specifically on Monday Miyazia 12 (April 6) and Wednesday Miyazia 14 (April 8), you organized international teleconferences which took over 7 (seven) hours in which we participated. In the teleconferences, six (6) leading Archbishops locally in Ethiopia, the Archbishop of Jerusalem, the Archbisho: of North America, several other Ethiopian church leaders and educators of North Amerce took part. I testify that your sincere determination to resolve our dispute through calm dialogues and your action to bring us together led to our accord that wil never ever be forgotten. This holy deed of yours is recorded for posterity in the history of our Church and will be chronicled forever as living testimony to which I myself am a witness.

I quote the teaching of Our Lord Jesus Christ, "Blessed are the peacemakers" (Mathew 5:8), and extend to you our deep gratitude for making a tremendous effort t(build peace and reconciliation among our Holy Fathers. It is on account of your hard work and deeds that it became possible for the Archbishops who were alienated from each other to be compliant and agree to come together as one body for a synodic meeting at the specified date and time. Moreover, your coming in person to Ethiopia yourself to appear at our meeting together with your colleagues whom you recruited united us further.

St Paul writes about such deeds saying, "renown, honor and peace will come to everyone who does good deed" (Romans 2:10.)

You are a person of love and peace who loves and respects his country and people sincerely, so I want you to know respectfully and with great joy that I shall pray for you always that the Lord shall protect and preserve you and give you long life.

"May the Lord God of Peace increase peace for us"

(Signed) Archbishop Abba Gabriel *(TRANSLATION FROM AMHARIC ORIGINAL)*
Former Archbishop, Ethiopian Orthodox Church, Jerusalem
Member of the Synod of the Ethiopian Orthodox Church

Foreword

BY GEORGE HUNTSTON WILLIAMS
The Late Hollis Professor of Divinity
Harvard University

Within the emerging global civilization of the jet and the atom bomb and while the United Nations – the world's last hope – still halts between national passion and compassion, the Emperor Haile Sellassie of Ethiopia is, for most of the older people who will peruse the pleasant pages of the following book, an extraordinary symbol of continuity amid globally revolutionary change, the resolute reminder of the failure of the League of Nations to act betimes and efficaciously against aggression. It is a marvel that the slight, bearded monarch looks today scarcely older than during his memorable appeal to the nations in Geneva in 1936 while his people were in the throes of premeditated assault.

For younger readers the Ethiopia of Haile Sellassie is more likely the symbol of orderly and creative continuity amid sometimes violent change on a continent which in but a few years has passed from tribalism to modernity, from colonialism into a congeries of now largely independent black powers, whose views and votes are at long last heeded on the floor of the world parliament of nations. The capital of Ethiopia is also the headquarters of both the United Nations mission to the continent and of the indigenous continental Organization for African Unity.

For readers of this book who are themselves Ethiopians, either students and others in the commercial and academic Diaspora or at home in their native land, admiring a book on them and on their Church printed in their interest abroad, their Church in a period of rapid social change must more than ever be a precious symbol of continuity in their native land and of national identity among the African states.

In brief, an ecclesiastical and dynastic tradition that has long drawn upon the sanctions of peace, hospitality, and wisdom in the line of biblical King

Solomon, is a symbol of continuity, order, and resoluteness alike for the community of nations, for the continent of Africa, and for the church and citizenry of Ethiopia itself. The Emperor is also the Defender of the Faith of the Church of his land and of both its Patriarch and its *Itchege* (Archabbot).

The following essay on the Ethiopian Church sketches the history of Christianity in Ethiopia and provides the cultural context of the remarkable pictures with which the book is ornamented. The Defender of this Church, however, as the Emperor of the whole nation, is in a unique position with respect to the other religions besides Christianity professed by his subjects. As is clearly shown in the historical essay to follow, not only are there strongly Biblical-Hebraic and even Jewish elements in the theology, political theory, and liturgical calendar of the Ethiopian Church but also there are "Cushite" Jews, Bete Israel or Ethiopian Jews (called also *Falasha* by the Christians), living in large concentrations in one region of the country. And besides these Ethiopian Jews and, of course, the Orthodox Ethiopians and a few Roman Catholic Ethiopian Christians, there are in Ethiopia also very large numbers of Moslems and Animists of various native cults. Nowhere else in today's world does a Christian ruler have direct (as distinguished from nominal or ceremonial) responsibilities for an established Church while still governing in peace and justice the devotees of several other widely recognized religions.

Thus Ethiopia is again unique, not only in the antiquity of her continuous religious and political history, but also in the ever accelerating involvement of the nation in the problems and the promises of a society where religious belief, while remaining powerful and pervasive at all levels, is nevertheless more radically diversified in cultus and conviction and more regionalized in ethnic sectors and enclaves of the country than in any other unified nation except possibly India. (And in the latter no religion is the official religion as Christianity is in Ethiopia.) The world will therefore be very attentive to the way in which the Emperor, the Patriarch, and the *Itchege* lead their Church into cultural and technological modernity while remaining tolerant and constructive – in an ecumenical age – toward the spokesmen and institutions of the other forms of religion that also have a long history in their land.

In order to preserve the religious substance of Ethiopian society and conserve those Christian insights and institutions best adapted to the people and yet to recast this tradition in modes appropriate to the present restless and parlous age, the extension of literacy among all classes is requisite. Rendering all classes independently competent in the religious and social teachings of their own people past and present is of urgent concern for Ethiopians and for fellow Africans and for all world citizens who rejoice in the orderly changes that are proceeding in Ethiopia for the good of all. To strengthen the grasp of the ordinary Ethiopian on his past and hence on his own future among the nations the proceeds of the sale of the present volume of text and pictures, a labor of international philanthropy and inter-confessional faith, will be devoted to the continuance of that literacy campaign in Ethiopia, for which one of the indefatigable participants in the volume has been the prime mover in his organization's winning both the UNESCO Award (1967) and the Haile Sellassie Prize (1967) and for which both the philanthropic Editor and the Illustrator of the volume have alike made important contributions.

May this imaginative enterprise in its attractiveness and aim show by its success what another voluntary printer, another radiologist, and another doctoral student – in other words, what citizens in various walks of life and with various skills and concerns – can do when creatively banded together for some worthy cause.

Chapter 1

Origins of Ethiopian Civilization[1]

O ne of the most enigmatic inquiries in Ethiopian history concerns the
nature and extent of Ethiopian-South Arabian relations. Several centuries ago, the Greek grammarian Stephanus of Byzantium (6th cent.) stated that
the Ethiopians, together with the Sabaeans and the Hadramawti, form three
Arabian tribes. But Stephanus was neither a historian nor a geographer; he
was simply a linguistic compiler who brought material together from diverse
sources.

Among historians, in the 17th century Ludolphus Hiob first posited the
hypothesis that the founders of Ethiopian culture were foreign immigrants. But
it was not until late in the nineteenth century that the South Arabian origin of
the Ethiopian civilization hypothesis got a seemingly firm foundation from the
discovery and decipherment of Sabaean inscriptions. Since then, the subsequent
study of Semitic languages and civilizations and research in ancient history both
appeared to give it strong credence. In particular, the works of Halevy, Muller,
Bent, Glazer, Conti Rossini, Littmann, et. al. in Northern Ethiopia and Southern Arabia respectively during the nineteenth and early twentieth centuries
confirmed an indisputable Ethiopian-South Arabian tie.

The first detailed European reconstruction of South Arabian and early
Ethiopian histories by E. Glaser and Conti Rossini appeared to be definitive of
South Arabian influence on Ethiopian culture. Both of these scholars attached
special significance to the name "hbst" which appeared in a number of Sabaean
texts. The obvious similarity between "hbst" and the Arabic "al-habasa" (Abyssinia) was believed to be explicit proof of the Sabaean origins of Ethiopian civilization. As one critic interprets it, "By a process of conquest or absorption the

1   A previous version of this chapter appeared in 1988 as "Reflections on the Origin of Ethio-
     pian civilization," in the *Proceedings of the International Conference of Ethiopian Studies.*
     AAU Press: Addis Ababa.

habashat merged with the local native Hamitic population and became 'African-ized'. From this arose the proto-Ethiopian civilization and the proto-Ethiopic texts of Ethiopia. It thus came to be widely accepted that "hbst" referred to a South Arabian tribe, which some time before the fifth pre-Christian century crossed the Red Sea and settled in northern Ethiopia.

Since the days of Conti Rossini, little, if any, scholarly doubt has been expressed concerning what came to be accepted as a fact of South Arabian origin and/or influence on Ethiopian culture. Instead the new theory of large popula-tion movement from South Arabia to Ethiopia was accepted by historians as a matter of fact and promoted vigorously.

Taken in the context of post-eighteenth century historiography, the racial-ist overtones of this theory cannot be ignored. As with ancient Egypt, Benin, or Zimbabwe, a clear attempt was made to "Caucasianize" a major African civi-lization. Ethiopian civilization has been attributed to a core group of superior Semitic colonists. Even those who later came to have a lingering doubt about a large population movement from South Arabia to Ethiopia would not think of questioning the superior nature of the non-African founders of the Ethiopian civilization. There is little doubt that there was a strong relationship between Ethiopia and South Arabia during the first millennium BCE and in early Chris-tian times. It is also clear that the two shores of the southern end of the Red Sea share a veritable linguistic, literary, religious and historical tradition, attested in ancient historical and geographic writings, as well as in modern archaeological discoveries.

Nonetheless, there is an essential difference between historical and cultural ties and the concept of cultural domination directly or indirectly. In the case of Ethiopian-South Arabian relations, the former is a demonstrable fact, the latter, however, an unproven hypothesis containing erroneous historical, linguistic, and archaeological assumptions. The hypothesis reflects a Hegelian Euro-cen-tric philosophical perspective of history, as it presumes that no Semitic language is indigenous to Ethiopia, that Proto-Ethiopic inscriptions were brought to Ethiopia from South Arabia, and that no indigenous high culture developed in Africa. Although we are not yet able to sift legend from history and scientifically demonstrate the historical roots of Ethiopian culture, we are in a position to question the bases of the old.

Firstly, it can no longer be taken for granted that Semitic languages neces-sarily originated in the Near East. Various attempts at placing the ultimate origin of the Semitic languages in the Fertile Crescent or in Arabia have not altogether proven successful. Contrary to some older assumptions, it cannot be shown that "Semitic" is a major language family like Indo-European; rather, it is like Indo-European sub-families like "Slavic" or "Germanic," a smaller subdivision of a major family of languages that we call Afroasiatic. The debate on the origin of

"Semitic" continues. Meanwhile, however, many serious scholars accept the view that it is a branch of a major language family called Hamito-Semitic or Afro-Asiatic. It is now further thought by some that Proto-Hamito-Semitic originates in Africa rather than in the Near East. The well-known Russian Assyriologist, Diakonoff, for instance, proposes Proto-Hamito-Semitic to be a language spoken in the eastern Sahara somewhere around present day Chad, about six thousand years ago. However, he does not question the fact that Proto-Semitic developed in the Near East after it branched off of Proto-Hamito-Semitic, or that the original Semitic language(s) of Ethiopia come from there. On the other hand, Murtonen has gone as far as proposing the Horn of Africa in which Ethiopia is centrally embedded as the original home of Proto-Semitic.

It is hence not impossible that some forms of Semitic languages are indigenous to Ethiopia. Nonetheless, it is not our task here to demonstrate the veracity of such a theory, nor to argue for or against one or another theory concerning the origin of Semitic languages. It is enough to point out that the premise of a South Arabian origin of Ethiopian Semitic language(s) is undermined by the facts that there remain lingering problems as to the origin of Semitic languages and that no scholar has yet fully demonstrated scientifically the origin of Ethiopian Semitic languages, or how exactly the first Semitic language(s) arrived in Ethiopia from South Arabia, if they did so.

Secondly, there is a historical problem with the chronology proposed for the migration of South Arabian tribes to Ethiopia. The author of the *Periplus of the Erythraean Sea* already noted in his pre-third century work that the two shores of the Red Sea spoke different languages. If tribes had migrated to Ethiopia so recently during the first millennium BCE, one would naturally expect the peoples of the Ethiopian side of the Red Sea to speak the linguistic dialect of the dominating colonists of South Arabia at least up to the third century. Furthermore, scholars believe that "hbst" is the name of (one of) the principal South Arabian tribe(s) which migrated to Ethiopia. But A.J. Drewes has pointed out that this name, found in Sabaean inscriptions in South Arabia, does not appear in the Ethiopian ones at least until Santa's time about 350.[2] It is equally significant that none of the inscriptions on either side had any information about any extensive migrations from South Arabia to Ethiopia.

Clearly, the identification of the "hbst" as the South Arabian precursors of the Ethiopian civilization is at best a guess. At least one scholar has suggested that "hbst" refers not to a South Arabian tribe, but to a region around Axum. Using Albert Jamme's contributions to the study of Sabaean inscriptions in South Arabia, A.K. Irvine has cogently argued in his "The Identity of the Habashat", that the term "hbst" is the nomenclature of a geographical region, not of a tribe. He argues that "hbst" is grammatically not a form of a tribe's

---

2   Inscriptions de l'Ethiopie Antique, 1962.

name, apart from the fact that there is no mention of such a tribe in the inscriptions. He concludes:

> [t]here is little or no reason to suppose that any case of Habasat or Habasa refers to a South Arabian tribe or district... Whenever Habasat occurs in a context, which permits identification, it is reasonable to suppose that it refers to Abyssinia... It would not therefore be legitimate to accord the Habasat with certainty the honor of having laid the foundations of a civilization which is at least eight centuries older than their first apparent mention in the country.[3]

Irvine's suggested identification of "hbst" with the Axumite region is far from certain. In particular, his theory fails to explain the reasons why the name "hbst" is absent from the earliest Ethiopian inscriptions, as opposed to the South Arabian ones. Nevertheless, Irvine is doubtless correct in challenging the unsubstantiated theories of earlier scholars.

We shall here allude in passing to the presence of the title *mkrb* in Ethiopia in the post-fifth century BCE inscriptions. Some have suggested that this word, believed to be the pre-fifth century BCE title of the king of Saba in South Arabia, indicates South Arabian origin of early Ethiopian state and royal tradition. This is a meaningless assertion based on a secondary inference rather than on tangible evidence. It neither warrants a conclusion that the Ethiopian political state is of South Arabian origin nor that the title was a necessary loan from outside. At best it indicates that the early Ethiopians and South Arabians shared a common or similar political structure, perhaps originating from a single earlier civilization on both banks of the Red Sea.

Thirdly, after examining the Sabaean inscriptions more closely, we find certain revealing facts. In most cases, the earliest Sabaean inscriptions found in Northern Ethiopia (before c. 400 BCE) cannot be distinguished from those found in South Arabia both in style and content. Asras Yanesaw (1943) rejects the South Arabia theory of linguistic origin, saying that South Arabia was a part of Ethiopia, and the inscriptions found there were the works of Ethiopian emperors.[4] Jacqueline Pirenne (1987) wrote that the Axumite inscriptions are as old as, and perhaps older, than the South Arabian ones.[5] In any case, the inscriptions are monumental and elegant in character and resemble the standard South Arabic inscriptions in their form of dedications. Yet, the inscriptions of Ethio-

---

3   Irvine, A.K. "On the Identity of the Habashat in the South Arabian Inscriptions." *Journal of Semitic Studies,* Vol. 10, 1965. Edited by C.F. Beckingham, Manchester University Press (p. 178).

4   Bekerie, Ayele. *Ethiopic: An African Writing System.* 1997 (11).

5   Bekerie, Ayele. *Ethiopic: An African Writing System.* 1997 (11).

pia are no mere imitations of the South Arabian ones; they manifest a certain degree of independence and initiative. Drewes's division of the inscriptions into two groups is indeed as enlightening. Nonetheless, it is not clear on what grounds he claims the first type to be of direct South Arabian provenance.

During the succeeding centuries from c. 400 BCE to late first century BCE, Ethiopian inscriptions reflect even more independence in epigraphic execution, the study and interpretation of ancient inscriptions, despite what some scholars call the continuing South Arabian influence upon them. As a result of internal evolution, changes in style and syntactical structure begin to take place. The writing becomes less geometrical, and the monumental form of inscriptions begins to disappear by the end of the fourth century BCE.

Numerous inscriptions may be adduced to show Ethiopian independent epigraphic development of indigenous authorship. The cultural ties between Ethiopia and South Arabia should not be used as precedent to show a one-way flow of influence. The Ethiopians neither copied nor imitated the South Arabians but freely produced these proto-Ethiopic texts, the major body of Sabaean epigraphic literature.

We must underline here again that there can be no doubt about the significant contact and interaction between the South Arabians and the Ethiopians by the fifth century BCE. But facts such as that the monumental script appears in Ethiopian inscriptions only later (in the fifth and fourth centuries BCE) are at this stage of our knowledge of Ethiopian inscriptions not adequate proof of the South Arabian ethnic origin of the Ethiopian people or of Ethiopian civilization let alone of a dominance and expansion. At most what they show is a common cultural heritage.

Fourthly, scholars had conjectured at different times since the seventeenth century the origin of the Ethiopic alphabet to be Samaritan (Ludolphus, Silvestre), Syriac (Kopp), or Sabaean (Glazer, Hommel, Conti Rossini). But we now know that Ethiopic is a cursive form of monumental Sabaean, hence, the immediate southern branch of Sinaitic or the first known alphabet from which also comes the Phoenician (Canaanite / Hebrew) script.

Some scholars trace the origin of writing to the ancient Near East, in general, and to Mesopotamia, in particular, where they believe the first system of writing was invented by the Sumerians about 3500 BCE. Others, however, consider Egypt the home of the first system of writing dating back to the end of the pre-historic times, or roughly about the same time as in Mesopotamia. Not only did the Egyptians develop a systematic pictographic and ideogrammic a written character symbolizing the idea of a thing without indicating the sounds used to say it, e.g., numerals and Chinese characters, form of writing but also a whole series of unilateral symbols, in fact a system of an entire proto-alphabet of 24 characters, which some scholars believe might have inspired the invention of the ingenious device of symbols of sounds which we call the alphabet.

By whom and when the alphabetic system was invented is still a matter of conjecture, but the earliest known examples of it, the Proto-Sinaitic, have so far come from about twenty-five inscriptions in the Sinai Peninsula, discovered in 1906 in Egyptian turquoise mines by the English archaeologist Flinders Petrie. Proto-Sinaitic, a linear consonantal script alphabet that developed from hiero-glyphs or pictographic writing on the acrophonic principle, evolved into Sinaitic during the second half of the second millennium BCE. Sabaean (which can be called Proto-Ethiopic), like Phoenician / Hebrew, derived from Sinaitic, and is one of the oldest alphabetic forms of writing. It has preserved many of the original forms and shapes of the Sinaitic (or Proto-Sinaitic).

A monograph incised on a sherd in South Arabia has been dated to the 8th century BCE by the radiocarbon method, and some earlier inscriptions have been dated to the end of the second or early first millennium BCE on paleo-graphic (the study of ancient writing systems and the deciphering and dating of historical manuscripts) grounds. But when and how Sinaitic first reached the southern end of the Red Sea (Ethiopia or Yemen?) is still unknown; it could not have been much before the beginning of the first millennium BCE.

The fact that the earliest Sabaean inscriptions so far found in Ethiopia are not dated much before the fifth century BCE does not warrant a conclusion that the alphabet came to Ethiopia through South Arabia. Such a conclusion awaits an exhaustive survey and definitive study of ancient inscriptions in Ethiopia.

In conclusion, however, we should note that only in Ethiopia significantly did the Sinaitic-Sabaean script become fully exploited and developed. Not only did the Ethiopians quite early modify the script from the graphic monumen-tal into a less symmetrical style, but also over the centuries they developed a new order of the letters, completely different from Phoenician. Moreover, they became the first to innovate and vocalize the script of a Semitic language, change and standardize the direction of its writing, and use it in manuscripts and lit-erature. It is equally significant that the South Arabians, on the contrary, never developed Sabaean much beyond its earliest form, nor were able to adapt it to literature as the Ethiopians did. (It was not until after the rise of Islam that they produced local manuscripts in borrowed Arabic script.) The manner, in which the Ethiopians used Sabaean, with freedom and originality, hardly betrays the behavior of borrowers.

Fifthly, historians have used ancient literary references to the Sabaeans, in particular the Biblical story of the Queen of Sheba, as proof for the precedence of South Arabia over Ethiopia. The origin of the people whom we call Sabaeans is shrouded in mystery. The earliest known literary source that mentions them is believed to be Gen. 10:7 (cf. I Chr. 1:9) where we find Sheba and Seba listed as descendants of Ham through Cush. In this and other biblical sources, Sheba is associated with Egypt and Nubia (cf. also Is. 43:3). On the other hand in Gen. 10:28 (cf. I Chr. 1:22) Sheba is listed among the sons of Shem. According to another source in Gen. 25:3 (1 Chr. 1:32), Sheba is a descendant of Abraham and of a Keturah. In these latter respects the Sabaeans would be regarded as a group related to the peoples of the Fertile Crescent and Arabia. At any rate, "the genealogical references indicate that the Israelites thought that the Sabaeans were related to the peoples of the Fertile Crescent—including themselves—on the one hand, and to the peoples of Africa on the other."

When the Deuteronomic redactor, who functioned some time between 620 and 610 BCE in Judea, decided to insert the short story about the Queen of Sheba (I Kings 10:1-10, 13) into his larger narrative of I Kings, little did he know that he was initiating a controversy of no small historical significance. The Queen of Sheba story is actually incidental to the redactor; a tradition about her is merely pressed into service in I Kings 10 in order to aid the writer's own theological design. His primary purpose in using the story about the Queen of Sheba is to dramatize his consistent theological claim that the God of Israel rewards those who obey the Deuteronomic laws (I Kings 3:12). In this respect, he focuses upon the wisdom and glory of Solomon as loyal and obedient leader of the people of God. Yet, despite this intended focus for the earliest biblical account about the Queen of Sheba, a wide variety of interpretations have been spawned by certain problematic features of the I Kings 10:1-10,13 story.

The text of I Kings 10:1-10,13, essentially repeated nearly 300 years later by the author of II Chronicles, indicates that the Queen who visited Solomon in Jerusalem hailed from a place called Sheba. A major problem caused by such a designation is the paucity of biblical evidence, which would help one identify more precisely the geographical location of this land of Sheba and the ethnic identity of the Queen. Do we have here a reference to a Cushite/Ethiopian Queen of ancient Africa or is this a Queen of Arabia? For centuries Ethiopians have insisted on the former and have named her Saba Makeda. Some modern scholars have insisted on the latter. In accordance with the various claims, the story of the Queen of Sheba has undergone extensive Arabian, Ethiopian, Jewish and other elaborations and has become the subject of one of the most ubiquitous and fertile cycles of legends in the Middle East.

Before turning to some of these expansions and re-interpretations of the original Old Testament story about the Queen of Sheba, a word needs to be said about the rationale for considering this topic important within the context of Ethiopian history. Modern western scholarship generally insists that the Sheba mentioned in I Kings 10:1 is to be located in Arabia. The implication is that the Queen of Sheba was in no sense an African. In order to dispel this possible implication, we wish to argue three points. First, the biblical evidence is noticeably silent or confusing regarding the location of Sheba and the racial identity of the Queen. Secondly, the non-biblical evidence that would place Sheba in Arabia is drawn from cuneiform (Assyrian) inscriptions that are in a number of respects problematic in themselves. Thirdly, to place the Queen of Sheba in the southern part of the Arabian Peninsula still leaves open the question of her ethnic identity, given the close relations between Cush and ancient Sheba--wherever it was. The curious persistent testimonies of Josephus, Origen, Jerome and the Ethiopians themselves, who all considered the Queen of Sheba to be an Ethiopian woman ruling Axum, the capital of the powerful Axumite Empire of northern Ethiopia (1st-7th centuries) may throw light upon the third point. As mentioned elsewhere, the Queen, also named Makeda in Ethiopia, bore the first King of Ethiopia by Solomon. The basis of their belief may offer for us an opportunity to discern a certain historical basis beneath the legend of the Queen of Sheba, which also illustrates the long historical relationship that existed between ancient Israel and Ethiopia.

What, then, are the more significant biblical passages that appear to be of some assistance in identifying the geographical location of ancient Sheba? Our attention is first directed to the famous Table of Nations in Genesis 10. According to this account Noah's son Ham gave birth to both Cush and Misraim whose descendants respectively inhabited Ethiopia and the land of the Nile Valley. His third son, Put (Punt), also is thought to have inhabited part of the lands of the Horn of Africa. Moreover, according to the late distinguished Biblical archeologist William Foxwell Albright, the two rivers of the Garden of Eden in Genesis 2, Gihon and Pishon, can be identified with the lands of Cush, Ethiopia, and Hawila, Eritrea.[6] Genesis 2:13 states, "A river watering the garden flowed from Eden; from there it was separated into four headwaters. The name of the first is the Pishon; it winds through the entire land of Hawilah, where there is gold... The name of the second river is the Gihon; it winds through the entire land of Cush." The Gihon, considered the source of the Nile, is only a few hours away by car from the ancient Axumite capital.

In the Table of Nations in Genesis 10, set forth as part of the descendants of Noah, are also three references to Sheba. At a glance, Genesis 10 seems to be a single listing of the descendants of Noah; but on close inspection, with the aid of the source, form, and redaction critics, it becomes clear that, in Genesis 10, we have an older so-called (J) list synthesized by a priest redactor who has his own separate so-called (P) list. The conflation of these two lists may account for the fact that a son of Cush, son of Ham, is named Seba (Sb') and a grandson of Cush is named Sheba (Sba') on the one hand, whereas in Gen. 10:28, Sheba (Sb') is also mentioned as a descendant of Shem. Assuming that the Queen of Sheba would be associated with one of these persons is of little consequence, when it is

---

6   "Where Was the Garden of Eden Loated?", *Journal of Hebrew Studies*.

virtually impossible to determine which is the correct person. Nonetheless, it is plausible to assume that this confusion arises from attributing the same name to one location, albeit from different genealogical lines. This location is Ethiopia, including Yemen an Ethiopian domain over two thousand years ago.

Any conclusions to be safely drawn from this passage in Genesis 10 must be modest. The Table of Nations presents not so much an objective historical account of genealogies as a theologically motivated collection. The names are listed to some extent without regard for consistency of detail, which would be of interest to the student of geography and ethnography. Despite this, we may further infer that in the midst of the Babylonian exile, Deutero-Isaiah's image of the most remote nations claims that wherever Sheba was, it was not the same place as Cush (Meroitic Ethiopia) or Egypt. Yet, Genesis 10 has informed us that two of Cush's descendants were called Sheba. This fact may serve to show how very close ancient Sheba was to the land of the Cushites. Thus, Sheba was either somewhere else in Africa or quite near the African coast.

Having drawn attention to the sense in which general biblical references to Sheba are somewhat limited, we must further now examine the larger context of I Kings 10 in order to discover other clues about the land of Sheba. One need not look beyond I Kings 10:15. Here, following the Queen of Sheba story, the Deuteronomic redactor resumes his narrative. In 10:14 the reader is told about the 666 talents of gold, which Solomon received in one year. Then in v. 15 the reader is told that all that was brought by all the kings of Arabia augmented this wealth.

This expression, "all the kings of Arabia" is also found in Jeremiah 25:24 as a description of one of the groups which is to drink the cup of death. Since Jeremiah's oracles are part of the *Zeitgeist* for understanding the Deuteronomic Reforms of Josiah (621 BCE) and their aftermath, the use of the phrase, "all the kings of Arabia," appears not to be coincidental. Indeed, Jeremiah and the editor responsible for I Kings 10:15 in their use of this phrase may be informing us rather intentionally that in the land which they understood to be Arabia, kings ruled not queens.

Just as Sheba has been shown not to be in the land of Cush, the use of the phrase, "all the kings of Arabia," by Jeremiah and the first editor of I Kings may demonstrate that Sheba was not considered to be part of Arabia. The most frequently cited non-biblical evidences appealed to by scholars are the cuneiform inscriptions of Tiglath-Pileser II (744-727 BCE) and Sargon II (721-705 BCE).

While these inscriptions do attest to the fact that there were queens in North Arabia in the eighth century, they tell us nothing about the tenth century reign of Solomon (962-922 BCE), nor do they tell us anything about queens in Arabia during the time in which I Kings 10:1-10,13 was written. Moreover, we have the testimony of Jeremiah and the redactor of I Kings 10, who explicitly distinguish between the Queen of Sheba and "all the kings of Arabia." Therefore, it seems reasonable to conclude that, whatever had been the case a century earlier, at the time of the I Kings redactor and Jeremiah, Sheba was not considered part of Arabia, for Arabia at that time may not have had any queens.

As far as we know, no inscriptions from South Arabia indicate that there ever was a queen ruler of the Sabaeans. We apparently have priest-kings before about the fifth century BCE. Besides that, all that we possess would be silence and conjecture regarding South Arabia of the Solomonic reign. Regrettably, the situation is scarcely better with Cushite history. The period between the eleventh and eighth centuries is shrouded in obscurity with regard to Egyptian-Cushite relations. If, then, we have no biblical or non-biblical hard data by which the story of the Queen of Sheba can emerge from the realm of legend into the full light of history, why have Josephus, a number of the Church Fathers, and the Ethiopians themselves maintained that the Queen of Sheba was an African woman? Flavius Josephus calls her "the Queen of Egypt and Ethiopia" as he amplifies considerably the text of I Kings 10:1-10,13. The most striking feature of the Josephus rendition of the Queen of Sheba story is that it is faithful to the text of I Kings 10:1-13, even though it provides much more detail. The immediate issue, which this fact might raise, is the nature of Josephus's source. Does he have a specific source or two in much the same manner as the first redactor of the I Kings 10 story, or is Josephus's report otherwise motivated? Quite possibly, an answer to this question may help explain why some early Christian writers thought the Queen of Sheba to be an African.

As a point of departure, let us postulate the thesis that Josephus, who claims to be writing from "his own books", does in fact have a version of the *Acts of Solomon* mentioned as a source for the original story in I Kings 11:41. There are a number of factors that catapult such a thesis into the realm of possibility. First, the most significant discrepancy between Josephus's account and that of I Kings 10 and II Chronicles 9 is that Josephus never refers to the royal visitor as the Queen of Sheba. Rather, Josephus insists that "his own books" inform him that after Pharaoh, the father-in-law of Solomon, no other king of Egypt was called Pharaoh. Clearly, Josephus has ignored the Old Testament record on this point, in favor of "his own books." The crucial issue is not that the Old Testament disputes Josephus's source and therefore Josephus is simply wrong. Rather, the central issue is this: Why would Josephus prefer his own source, when he was probably aware of Old Testament citations that contradicted his source? One explanation would be that one of "his own books" was treasured precisely because it was a copy of the very ancient *Acts of Solomon,* a document that may not have used the term Sheba at all.

A second factor is that, while Josephus twice describes Solomon's visitor as the Queen of Egypt and Ethiopia, his final designation for her is simply the Queen of Ethiopia. Josephus may not only be aware of the 25th Egyptian Dynasty established by an Ethiopian, which ruled Egypt for many years, but his source may antedate this period, going back to the time in which Egypt exercised an hegemony over Ethiopia.

A third and most persuasive factor is that Josephus's story may be an indication that, within segments of first century Jewish communities, there was an awareness of a larger story that focused on the Queen more than on Solomon. As one author says, "the way in which [Josephus] tells the story no doubt reflected the state of contemporary interpretation..." [33]. If this is true, then for some first century Jews, the Queen of Sheba was an African.

If there were any merit in our thesis that Josephus may have had an ancient source (which knew of a Queen of Egypt and Ethiopia instead of a Queen of Sheba), the suspicion of quite a few theologians would be confirmed, if we briefly consider the pertinent New Testament passages. Matthew 12:42 and Luke 11:31 make mention of a Queen of the South who has an eschatological function. This image preserved in the Synoptic Gospels immediately called to mind, for some, the Queen of Sheba as a person who knew how to respond to God's initiative among his people. Luke (Acts 8:27ff.) also provides a story about another queen and specifically refers to her as Candace, Queen of the Ethiopians, and it was inevitable that not a few would identify the Queen of the South with the Queen of the Ethiopians. It is clear that there was, of course, no relation between the two. Certainly, any careful student of biblical history would have to discriminate between the vastly different periods of time in which the Queen of Sheba, i.e., Queen of the South, and the one-eyed Queen Candace were alive. This fact aside, insisting that there is no relation between the two queens may be overstating the case. If both queens were of African lineage and related to Ethiopia, and both ruled the ancient Ethiopian empire of Axum, there certainly would be a relationship here and a most significant one at that.

Unfortunately, no definitive conclusion can be drawn which would establish the certainty of the African descent of the Queen of the South. What can be certainly established is that early Christian scholars like Origen and Jerome, much like the historian Josephus, who claimed that she introduced the balsam plant to the land of Israel,[7] believed her to be of African ancestry and built some of their exegetical opinion upon the idea about which they never expressed any doubt. Any assertion that the Queen of Sheba was South Arabian instead of Ethiopian must therefore begin from a defensible criticism of some of the most notable historians and biblical scholars of two thousand years ago.

The ambivalent picture of the location of the tribes of Sheba that we get in the Bible is ironically similar to that which we find about the people called

---

7   Antiquities viii, 6:5-6.

"Ethiopians" in some classical literature. The term "Ethiopians" is used through-out Classical literature to refer in a general way to Black people who inhabited Africa, South of Egypt; occasionally the expression is used to refer to specific African peoples like the Nubians or the Cushites. Nevertheless, in some Greek textual sources the expression refers to a people who inhabited the two shores of the Red Sea. The poetry of Aeschylus reads:

> There, the sacred waters of the Erythraean Sea break upon a bright red strand, and at no great distance from the ocean lies a copper-tinted lake – the lake that is the jewel of Ethiopia, where the all-pervading Sun returns again and again to plunge his immortal form, and finds a solace for his weary round in gentle ripples that are but a warm caress...[8]

Other Greeks spoke in similar favor of the land of the Ethiopians. The Iliad refers to Zeus departing to join 'the virtuous Ethiopians' at a feast.[9] Homer's narration of Neptune's journey through the world describes, "At the end of the world, and to the remote people of Ethiopia divided in two/ where the rising and setting sun shoots its oblique rays."[10] Diodorus said Egypt derived its worship of kings from the Ethiopians, and that the Egyptian hieroglyphics, sculpture, and conservation of royal sepulcher take their origin from Ethiopia. Diodorus also considered Ethiopians the first inhabitants of the Earth.[11]

Other Greeks described Ethiopia after extensive travels and studies. Geographer Erastosthenes refers to Lake Tana as "Psebo" or "Koloe" and an island called "Dak." Agatharchides describes cave-dwellers in Ethiopia; Artemidones gave details about the coastal configuration and desert regions of the Dankali lakes, describing them as dense in foliage and laden with incense. Yet it was only after Alexander the Great that the route to 'Punt' was opened to the Greeks. Ptolemy II wrote in hieroglyphics at Pithom about the trade of products and animals, between 269 and 264 BCE on the Erythraean Coast.[12] In far more ancient times, the Egyptian empire had extensive contact with the Ethiopian empire. Around 2400 BCE, an expedition was sent to Punt by Pepi II. Queen Hatshepsut (1520-1484 BCE) acquired goods from Ethiopia, and described

---

8   Quoted in John Doresse's *ETHIOPIA*. Translated from the French by Elsa Coult. London, ELEK Books. 1959 (p. 7).

9   Ibid, (p. 19).

10   Teklehaymanot, Abba Ayele. *Miscellanea Aethiopica*. Capuchin Franciscan Institute of Philosophy and Theology, Desktop Publishing, Addis Ababa (12).

11   Ibid, (12).

12   Doresse, John. ETHIOPIA. Translated from the French by Elsa Coult. London, ELEK Books. 1959 (p. 19).

the details of her voyage to Punt on the walls of her temple at Deir el Bahari. Other Egyptian expeditions were sent by Seti I, Ramses III, and Ramses IV.[13]

By the beginning of the 2nd century BCE, when Strabo lived, the Sabaeans had come to be known as a distinct Arabian people; and Strabo identifies them as such without questioning. In this regard, Strabo (Book 15:4:2) quotes Eratosthenes (276-194 BCE) saying that the extreme southern corner of Arabia, facing Ethiopia, is inhabited by four Arabian peoples: the Minaeans on the Red Sea, whose capital town is Qarna; the Sabaeans, whose capital is Mariaba; the Qatabanians near the Straits of Bab-el-Mandab, whose capital is Tamna; and the Hadramawti (Chatramotitae), whose capital is Sabota. He also gives a description of their trade of myrrh (Hadramuti) and frankincense (Qataban). Additionally, Strabo quotes Agatharchides (c.120 BCE) who speaks of the Sabaeans in South Arabia.

On the other hand, Strabo comments extensively and revealingly on a subject that seemed to fascinate him, the location of the people called Ethiopians. In Book I, he opens the discussion of the subject saying "It is incredible that [Homer] mentioned Ethiopia ... and the fact that the Ethiopians are 'sundered in twain' but did not know what was well-known ... What is the meaning of "the Ethiopians sundered in twain"? The cynic philosopher Crates (c. 325 BCE) had interpreted the phrase from Homer saying that the Ethiopians stretch along both shores of Oceanus from the rising to the setting of the sun" (1:2:24). In agreement with Aristarches (c. 320 BCE), Strabo rejects the hypothesis of Crates. Nonetheless, Strabo also rejects Aristarches's own hypothesis that the meaning of the Ethiopians "sundered in twain" may mean the division of Ethiopia by a river into east and west by the Nile, like Egypt.

Strabo in this way examines the various interpretations of Homer, including those of Aeschylus (525-456 BCE), Euripides (480-406 BCE), Ephorus (4th cent. BCE), and then proceeds to investigate various possible ways in which Ethiopia may be said to be "sundered in twain." (1, 2:25-28). He finally draws his own conclusions based on various points made by his forerunners, more importantly, from those who made coasting-voyages on the ocean along the shores of Libya and in the Red Sea. From such a basis Strabo concludes that Oceanus must be understood in a more general sense: "a body of water that extends along the entire southern belt" and Ethiopians, "the people along the same extent." Ethiopia, according to Strabo, stretches from the south of Egypt all the way to Asia from east to west. "Sundered in twain," means nothing but divided into two by the Red Sea. So Strabo argues over and over again saying "I contend in the case of the Ethiopians that "sundered in twain" [means] ... [they] extend along the whole sea-board of Oceanus ... For the Ethiopians that are spoken of in this sense are "sundered in twain" naturally by the Arabian Gulf

---

13   Doresse, John. Ibid, 1959 (p. 8).

[the Red Sea] ... as by a river [like Egypt by the Nile]" (1, 2:28). He goes on to say that the Arabian Gulf is a natural boundary of division in the manner the other geographers divide Africa from Asia.

Furthermore, Strabo still goes on to say that probably rightly "Homer divides the Ethiopians into two groups ... not because he knew that the Indians were physically similar to the Ethiopians (for Homer probably did not know of the Indians at all....), but rather on the basis of the division of which I have spoken above" (11 3.8) that in the Ethiopians that border on Egypt are themselves, also, divided into two groups; for some of them live in Asia, others in Libya [Africa] though they differ in no respect from each other [!]" (11:3:8) Strabo examines the question of a people that straddle the Red Sea with profound interest. The picture that he draws of the Ethiopians who inhabit both Africa and Asia calls to mind the biblical genealogies of the two Shebas. It is indeed interesting to note that two such diverging witnesses draw an almost identical picture of the location of the Sabaeans and the Ethiopians respectively.

In the first century A.D., a Graeco-Egyptian wrote the *Periplus of the Erythraean Sea*, in which he described Zoscales or Zahagale, King of Axum, as "the most miserly of men, too much given to storing up great wealth, but in other respects able, with an excellent knowledge of Greek literature."[14] Certainly the ancient empires of Egypt, Greece, and Ethiopia influenced and interacted with one another in knowledge and trade.

In conclusion, serious methodological questions must be raised concerning theories that seek to reconstruct the origins of the Ethiopian civilization from South Arabia. In general any idea of cultural influence should not be taken at face value, in particular, since such a concept often tends to be a complicated, if not a simplistic, one.

In every case where cultural influence is discussed, the complex issues often do not warrant an easy solution. Thus in the present case, it is possible to reverse the argument and demonstrate Ethiopian influence on the South Arabians. Gus van Beek, while not questioning the old hypothesis of a South Arabian origin of Ethiopia, has nonetheless argued that certain South Arabian pre-Christian pottery, perhaps as early as about 8th BCE, shows Ethiopian influence. Moreover, there is hardly any period in Ethiopian history during which time can be demonstrated that South Arabia directly governed Ethiopia or dominated it politically and militarily. In other words, no single evidence for direct South Arabian rule in Ethiopia has been demonstrated, despite Conti Rossini's conjectures. For it can be shown that South Arabia was under actual Ethiopian domination several times during its history, in particular, from about 335 to

---

14   Quoted in John Doresse's ETHIOPIA. Translated from the French by Elsa Coult. London, ELEK Books. 1959 (p. 28).

370 and from about 525 to 575 of this era.[15] During the first period, Christianity was introduced in the 4th century from Ethiopia to South Arabia, apparently through the active missionary work of one called Theophilus the Ethiopian or Indian.[16]

During the second period, Abraha extended Christian missionary religious activity in South Arabia and used it as a launching region for the Christianization of the Arabian Peninsula. During this latter period, the northern slice of the great dam of Marib was constructed with protruding headers beyond the wall face. Gus van Beek has rightly argued "[t]his technique has no construction antecedents in South Arabian architecture. In Ethiopian architecture, on the other hand, the ends of wooden joists frequently protruded beyond the face of the building and often done also in stone. In view of the fact that Ethiopians dominated Sabaeans throughout much of this period, it seems likely that they are also responsible for such architectural forms, this technique should probably be interpreted as cultural influence coming from Ethiopia to South Arabia."

Were one to attempt a demonstration of an Ethiopian origin of South Arabian culture, there is no reason why such examples, expanded and exaggerated like the former hypothesis about Ethiopian origins, cannot be used to show the opposite. For our part, however, we wish to pass no such judgment at this stage of international scholarship on the subject. For the time being, however, we would prefer to view, at least hypothetically, South Arabia as a common cultural sphere with Ethiopia from prehistoric times, and nothing more.

---

15   Carlo Conti Rossini, Storia de Ethiopia; Yuri M. Kobishchanov, Axum, 1979; A. Jeffrey, "The Foreign Vocabulary of the Qur'an", 1938, Gaekwad's Oriental Series No. LXXIX;

16   Philostorgius, Ecclesiastical History, Epitome of Book IV, Chapter 7.

Chapter 2

Brief History of the Ethiopian Orthodox Täwahïdo Church

"Christianity has been the most important cultural factor in the lives of the Ethiopians; it lay at the root of the social order, the religion of church and state being such that it was almost feudal; it was the sole repository of traditional learning, maintaining village and monastic schools, and entered fully into the lives of its adherents in the observance of feast and fast from birth to death."[1]

Tradition traces Ethiopian Christianity back to the time of the Apostles. Some trace its origins to the meeting of Philip the Deacon with the Ethiopian eunuch of Queen Candace' Axumite court, and the eunuch's subsequent baptism, as recorded in Acts of the Apostles viii: 26-40 of the Bible. Other stories say that on the day of Pentecost when Peter preached to the mixed crowd in Jerusalem, Ethiopian Jewish pilgrims, who had come for the Passover, heard of the new religion and were converted (Acts 2). Saint John Chrysostom's Homily on Pentecost attests to the presence of Ethiopian.[2] Since the pilgrims spoke their native Ge'ez, the ancient Semitic language of Ethiopia, they understood the sermon of Peter in Hebrew (Aramaic) as it was made clear to them by the Holy Spirit. These converts then returned to Ethiopia as missionaries. Still other stories tell that the disciple Matthew traveled to Axum to preach Christianity, which thereafter spread throughout the land.

---

1   Trimingham, J. Spencer. *The Christian Church and Missions in Ethiopia*. WORLD DOMINION PRESS, London, 1950 (p. 6).

2   *Homily on the Acts of the Apostles*; Ethiopian Orthodox Church, *The Church of Ethiopia: A Panorama of History and Spiritual Life*. Addis Ababa, 1997 (3).

All these traditions contain some truth about the relation of Ethiopian Christianity to the early days of the Church; for some form of Christianity must have come to the country as early as the first century with the well-known Red Sea traders. Merchants from the Roman Empire settled in Axum and Adulis, and established prayer houses where they openly practiced Christianity.[3] However, no Ethiopian or foreign historical records regarding the presence of Christianity in Ethiopia lead us further back than third century CE.

The church historian Rufinus (410 CE) reports the story of the Ethiopian state's conversion to Christianity. Around 330 CE, two Syrian Christian boys from Tyre, Aedesius and Frumentius, appeared in Emperor Ella Amida's court at Axum. Shipwreck victims of a Syrian merchant vessel that had been attacked and killed, the young survivors' display of integrity, piety, and wisdom found favor in the sight of the Emperor, whose will freed them from slavery. The Emperor's widow asked the Syrian sages to become her advisor until her infant son, Ezana, was old enough to replace her as regent. During these years, Frumentius encouraged the development of churches and helped Christian merchants spread the gospel.[4] Aedesius went back to Tyre, where he became a priest, and reported the Ethiopian incident. Frumentius succeeded in converting the first Ethiopian imperial family to Christianity.

When Ezana became king, Frumentius traveled to Alexandria to request a bishop for Ethiopia from Athanasius, the 20th Patriarch. Athanasius, "having carefully weighed and considered the words and deeds of Frumentius" (339-340), declared in a council of priests: "What other man can we find than you, who have already carried out such works?"[5] Frumentius was consecrated, returned to Axum as the first Bishop of Ethiopia, and was named by the people of Axum, "Abuna Salama, Kassate Berhan" (Father of Peace, Revealer of Light).[6] He built the first Christian church in Axum:

> ...dedicated to the *Holy Virgin Mary of Seyon*, which is the name of the holy mountain of Jerusalem where there was the Temple preserving the Ark of the Covenant, confirmed the Ethiopian traditions that considered Axum as the second Jerusalem which have the privilege of hosting the Ark of the Covenant.[7]

3   Ibid, 3.

4   Marcus, Harold. *A History of Ethiopia.* University of California Press, London, 1994 (7).

5   Pankhurst, Richard. *Historic Images of Ethiopia.* Shama Books, Addis Ababa, Ethiopia, 2005 (40).

6   Ethiopian Orthodox Church, *The Church of Ethiopia: A Panorama of History and Spiritual Life.* Addis Ababa, 1997 (5).

7   Teklehaymanot, Abba Ayele. *Ethiopian Review of Cultures: Miscellanea Aethiopica.* Capuchin Franciscan Institute of Philosophy and Theology. Senait Worku, Addis Ababa (20).

The name of the first Ethiopian church, "Mariam Seyon," built following inter-national recognition of Ethiopia's adoption of Christianity by the Patriarch of Alexandria, serves as a reminder of Axum's status as a "holy city," home to the Ark of the Covenant.

Ezana collaborated with Abuna Salama in completing the evangelization of the country, facilitated by the fact that Christianity had already begun to take root among the people. Ezana is among the greatest of Ethiopian emperors of antiquity. Ezana replaced the ancient Axumite symbol of sun and moon on the coin currency with that of the Cross of Christ.[8] Ethiopia was one of the first countries in the world to coin the Cross.[9] After the change (around 340 CE), a list of Christian kings names began to be printed on the coinage: Ouazebas, MHDYS, Eon, Ebana, Nezana and Nezool, Ouras, Kaleb, WZB, Alla Amidas, Wazena, Ella Gabaz, Ioel, Hataz, Esrael, Gersem, Armah. These coins provide the names of twenty Axumite rulers not known from any other sources. They feature the rulers' effigies, crowns, headgear, and some clothing.[10] Many of the coins also feature Christian mottos and good wishes, such as "Mercy and Peace," "Joy and Peace to the People," "By the Grace of God," "Thanks be to God," and "He Conquers Through Christ."[11] Christianity was not only the official religion of Ethiopia, but it was also firmly rooted in the national conscience and cur-rency.

King Ezana was titled "King of Axum, Himyar, Raydan, Habasat, Saba, Salhen, Seyamo, Kasu, and the Beja tribes, king of kings."[12] During battles and efforts to secure Ethiopian trade, he raised stellae, some trilingual,[13] to give thanks to the Christian God for success and protection:

> I set up a throne here in Shado by the might of the Lord of Heaven, who has helped me and given me sovereignty. May the Lord of Heaven make my kingdom strong! And as He has this day con-quered my enemy may He conquer for me wherever I go. As He has this day conquered for me, and overthrown my enemy, I will rule the people with righteousness and justice, and will not oppress them. And may they preserve this throne, which I have set up for the

---

8   Pankhurst, Richard. *Historic Images of Ethiopia*. Shama Books, Addis Ababa, Ethiopia, 2005 (32).

9   Ibid.

10   Pankhurst, Richard. *Historic Images of Ethiopia*. Shama Books, Addis Ababa, Ethiopia, 2005 (35).

11   Pankhurst, Richard. *Historic Images of Ethiopia*. Shama Books, Addis Ababa, Ethiopia, 2005 (36).

12   Encyclopaedia Aethiopica, 174.

13   Encyclopaedia Aethiopica, 176.

Lord of Heaven, who has made me King, and the land upon which it lies. And if there shall be anyone who shall remove it, destroy it, or overthrow it, he and his kinsfolk shall be rooted out and removed from the land. I have set up this throne by the might of the Lord of Heaven.[14]

Other inscriptions of Ezana's speak of "the Lord of the Heaven and the Earth." One reads, "In the faith of God and the Power of the Father, the Son, and the Holy Ghost."[15] In the late third century CE, the prophet Mani listed Axum as one of the four kingdoms in the world, along with Rome, Persia, and Sileos.[16]

During this period, Ethiopia is believed to have been ruled by governor-high priests (mukarib) like the Melchisedek of the Bible (Genesis 14:18 ff.), then by *malkanas* (kings); the kings later probably adopted the title *negashi* (originally "treasurer" or "tax collector," which came to mean simply "king" or "ruler"); the imperial title "king of kings" (*Neguse negast*), still used by the rulers of Ethiopia, makes first appearance probably in the second century.

As far as we know, since the church was established, no substantial doctrinal change took place after Ezana. It can, in this respect, be said that the theology of the Ethiopian Church today is the theology of the first three major councils of Christendom—all of which took place before 451. The important fourth council at Chalcedon (451), which held to the doctrine of the two natures of Christ, was rejected by both the Ethiopian Church and the Coptic Church, as well as by the Armenians, Syrians, and the Indian Malabar churches. This decision had little effect on the people of Ethiopia. The doctrinal position held by Ethiopians and Copts at the Council of Chalcedon is generally known by western scholars as Monophysitism—the doctrine that in the person of the incarnate Christ there was but a single, divine nature. Interestingly, however, the Ethiopian Church, in conformity with the decision of the Council of Chalcedon, condemned Eutyches, the archimandrite of a monastery near Constantinople, who had made the real formulation of this doctrine, as a heretic. It should be clear that the Ethiopian Orthodox Church is not Eutychians: It teaches the "true man, true God" theory. Still it regarded as a saint, Dioscorus, the Patriarch of Alexandria, who was the chief exponent of Monophysitism at the Council of Chalcedon and who was also banished as a heretic (Dioscorus, the 25th patriarch, is still commemorated in the Ethiopian liturgical calendar on September 4th and October 14th).

---

14 Pankhurst, Richard. *Historic Images of Ethiopia*. Shama Books, Addis Ababa, Ethiopia, 2005 (37, 38).

15 Ethiopian Orthodox Church, *The Church of Ethiopia: A Panorama of History and Spiritual Life*. Addis Ababa, 1997 (5).

16 Encyclopaedia Aethiopica, 174.

The most important development that occurred after Ezana's reign was the introduction of monasticism into Ethiopia around 480 by a party of nine monks arriving in Ethiopia mainly from Syria.[17] Traditionally known as the "Nine Saints," these holy men established monasteries in Axum and the northern province of Tigre. They were well-received by Emperor Ella Amida, and soon became well-versed in the language and customs of the Ethiopians.[18] They established traditions of Christian education, and translated the bible from Greek (including Books of Enoch and Jubilees), into Ge'ez.[19] The translation work had been started under Frumentius, but the monks, who were acquainted with both Syriac and Greek, achieved the complete biblical translation. The nine saints also translated dogmatical treatises and homilies of the church fathers from Syriac into Ge'ez.[20]

Headed by Abba Za-Mikael Aregawi Manfasawi ("the Spiritual Elder"), a disciple of the Coptic abbot Pachomius, the monks founded monasteries throughout Ethiopia. Abba Liqanos and Abba Pantalewon remained near Axum, while Za-Mikael Aregawi established a monastery on the cliffs of Dabre Damo, which is still accessible to men by rope today. Aregawi's church is the oldest existing example of Christian architecture in Ethiopia, as the raids of Ahmed "the Left-Handed," Queen Yodit, or the Italian fascists never destroyed it. Other saints, Abba Pantalewon and Abba Afse Yeha, turned pagan temples into churches.[21] These monks and other saints flocked into Ethiopia in the fifth and sixth centuries, contributing to the monastic tradition, which is still strong in the Ethiopian Church.

By the sixth century, the schism in Eastern Christendom over the two natures of Christ, as defined by the imperial Council of Chalcedon, had led to severe persecution of Miaphysites. The Orthodox Emperors of Byzantium, especially Justin I the Elder (518-527), led the persecutions. It was in the Ethiopian Church that many of these persecuted Miaphysite saints found refuge and rehabilitation during two centuries. The Byzantine Emperors, however, maintained friendly relations with distant Ethiopia, possibly because it lay beyond the boundary of the Byzantine Empire. Because of the exception they had made, Justin I and his nephew Justinian 1, the Great (527-565), indeed sided with

---

17   Before them came to the country st. Libanus, his name is Mata, but they call him Met'a'.

18   Ethiopian Orthodox Church, *The Church of Ethiopia: A Panorama of History and Spiritual Life*. Addis Ababa, 1997 (7).

19   Pankhurst, Richard. *Historic Images of Ethiopia*. Shama Books, Addis Ababa, Ethiopia, 2005 (41).

20   Ethiopian Orthodox Church, *The Church of Ethiopia: A Panorama of History and Spiritual Life*. Addis Ababa, 1997 (7).

21   Ethiopian Orthodox Church, *The Church of Ethiopia: A Panorama of History and Spiritual Life*. Addis Ababa, 1997 (9).

Ethiopia in fighting opposition from another quarter, a Jewish king of Yemen[22] named Dhu Nawwas, called Phinhas in Ethiopic 9cf. Heb. who was reported to be in conflict with the Christians of South Arabia. Upon the intercession of Emperor Justinian on behalf of the latter who had appealed to him, the Ethiopian Emperor Caleb (514-543) crossed the Red Sea and waged war against Dhu Nawwas and his company. In 525 the army of Dhu Nawwas was completely suppressed under the leadership of the Emperor Caleb (or Elasbah), who later was made a saint of the Ethiopian Church. Under his other name, Elasbah, Caleb is still honored in the Roman calendar on October 27th. According to *Kebra Nagast* (see below) Emperor Caleb of Ethiopia and Emperor Justinian of Rome (Byzantium) were destined by God to meet in Jerusalem and divide the earth between them—Rome and Ethiopia. For seventy years the Ethiopian Church had jurisdiction over the Christians of South Arabia. Abraha, Caleb's successor in South Arabia, had a plan to convert all of Arabia to Christianity, but after having successfully reached Mecca in 570 (year of Mohammed's birth) riding on an elephant, his army succumbed to a smallpox epidemic and his campaign failed (compare the Moslem story of *am-al-fil*—Year of the Elephant).[23] After the reign of Caleb and his son Atse Gabre Mäsqäl (c. 550-580), the Ethiopian Church entered upon a gradual decline. The eclipse became complete with the rise of Islam. The constant threats against the church caused it to turn inward and break its ties with the world body of Christianity. Ethiopia became "a Christian island," as Atse (King) Menelik II described it, holding out against Islam to the east and eventually the north, and against paganism to the south. From the beginning of the seventh century to the end of the thirteenth, very little is known of the history of the Ethiopian Orthodox Täwahïdo Church.

However, two developments from this obscure era are upheld by elaborate oral and literary traditions, one from Ethiopia itself, the other from Europe. The Ethiopian tradition is quite detailed in accounts of the religious and political conflicts caused by the rise of the so-called "Non Solomonic" Zagwe Dynasty (c. 1137-1270). According to one tradition, a Jewish queen, called Yodit, founded this Dynasty. Heretofore, tradition holds, an uninterrupted line of kings descending from King Solomon and the Queen of Sheba (cf. I Kings 10:1 ff.) ruled in Ethiopia. The elaborate story of the visit of the Queen of Sheba to King Solomon is told in a sacred book of the Ethiopian Church, called the Kebra Nagast (Glory of the Kings). As alluded to above, the Kebra Negast relates how the Queen of Sheba was married to King Solomon and gave birth to a son, Menelik (cf. Ben-Malak Son of the King) who became the founder of the Solomonic Royal Dynasty (c. 900 BCE). Moreover, tradition holds that Menelik also brought to

---

22   Encyclopaedia Aethiopica, 175.

23   Doresse, John. ETHIOPIA. Translated from the French by Elsa Court. London. Elek Books, 1959 (8).

Ethiopia the religion of Israel, which was later to shape the form of Ethiopian Christianity.

Though this powerful national saga cannot furnish historical proof for the existence of a Solomonic Royal House antedating the Zagwe Dynasty, its use in religio-political propaganda by the leading Ethiopian churchman, Tekle Haymanot, who later became probably the first *Itchege* (see below), did prove to be highly effective in the circumstances that led both to the overthrow of the Zagwe Dynasty and the acension or restoration of the supposedly Solomonic Dynasty, under Emperor Yekuno Amlak (1270-1285). With the restoration of the Solomonic Dynasty, the total fusion of Church and State was achieved. The Zagwe line itself ruled from the tenth century to the end of the thirteenth. There is a tradition that the Zagwe contenders also actually descended from King Solomon but through the line of Queen of Sheba's royal handmaid. It was probably during this period that the famous monolithic churches of Ethiopia, the best examples of which are attributed to King Lalibala (c. 1167-1207), were built.

The other clue to Ethiopian history during this period of eclipse comes from European legendary literature. One of the widespread stories in Europe from the twelfth to fourteenth century was the legend of a Christian Emperor, Prester John. At a period when the failure of the crusades had brought European Christianity to a state of depression, the rumor of a powerful Christian Emperor in an eastern land helped sustain European hope that Christianity would someday triumph over Islam. In 1165, Latin and Franciscan monks tried to penetrate Ethiopia to explore this legendary figure, yet it was Venetian merchants in the 14th century who wrote that the town now known as Asmara and Axum had "fine basilica whose interior was completely overlaid with gold" and explained, "It is in this city that all the kings who serve Prester John are crowned."[24] Some Ethiopian words were added to their writings. The manuscript mentions Shoa, and says that his people called Prester John "David." In fact a King David did reign in Ethiopia from 1382-1411.[25]

The legend of Prester John and the search for his Empire inspired other explorations in the Age of Discovery and ended the isolation of Ethiopia. In 1431, the Pope tried to establish a link to Ethiopia through the Ethiopian monks in Jerusalem. He sought Ethiopian assistance in delivering Egypt from the Muslims.[26] In 1439, Ethiopia sent delegates to the Council of Florence. Following these first envoys, other Ethiopian pilgrims visited the Holy See, and some even settled in Rome, providing Europeans with further information about their Christian country. The Ethiopian pilgrims from Jerusalem became such familiar

---

24   Ibid, 8.

25   Ibid, 8.

26   Ibid, 8.

visitors in Rome; they were given a hospice behind St. Peter's church.[27] In 1450, Alfonso of Aragon tried to create an alliance with Negus Zär'a Ya'aqob through a marriage exchange, but did not succeed. In 1459, Duke Francois Sforza wrote a personal letter to Zär'a Ya'aqob, requesting that if he happened to have preserved any works of "his ancestor Solomon" that were unknown to Europe, he send them so they could be translated into Latin. Apparently nothing came of this. Yet Portuguese envoys were received in the Ethiopian Court. The Portuguese ambassador Pedro de Covilham arrived in Shoa in 1493, and died there thirty years later.[28] Other international explorers, ambassadors, soldiers and Roman Catholic missionaries flowed in for more than two centuries. Portugal's Canon Alvarez published "An Authentic Report on the Lands of Prester John" in 1540, which was at once translated into all the languages of the west.[29]

Portuguese-Ethiopian relations (1520-1632) revolved about two important religious developments in Ethiopia. The first was occasioned by the invasion of Ethiopia and the harassment of its established Church by the Moslem warrior Ahmed ibn Ibrahim el Ghazi, the Amir of Harar, nicknamed Gragn, that is, the left-handed (died 1544). His chronicle "Futuh al-Habasha" (the Conquest of the Abyssinians) conveys his aim of destroying the Ethiopian Church.[30] Upon the plea of Emperor Lebna-Dengel (1508-1540) to Christian Portugal for help, a contingent of Portuguese fighters arrived in Ethiopia in 1541, led by Dom Christoph da Gama, but perhaps too late. Between 1528 and 1544, the Ethiopian Church lost not only many of its great teachers, writers, and leaders but also many of its treasures of literature, gold, and art. Countless churches and monasteries were sacked and destroyed. A description of the attack and plunder of the island monasteries of Hayq reads:

> They carried off the gold... there were crucifixes of gold in great quantity, books with cases and biddings of gold, and countless idols of gold; each Muslim took 300 ounces; each man had sufficient gold plate to satisfy three men. They also took a vast quantity of cloth and silk... The next morning (the Muslim chief) sent the Imam three rafts loaded with gold, silver and silk; there were only five men on board, two in front and three at the back, the rest of the raft being covered with riches thought it could have carried 150 persons. The cargo was unloaded in front of the Imam who marveled at it... the treasure, which he had seen before. The rafts returned to the island

---

27   Ibid, 8.

28   Ibid, 10.

29   Ethiopian Orthodox Church, *The Church of Ethiopia: A Panorama of History and Spiritual Life*. Addis Ababa, 1997 (27).

30   Ethiopian Orthodox Church, *The Church of Ethiopia: A Panorama of History and Spiritual Life*. Addis Ababa, 1997 (28).

were a second time loaded with riches. They came three times, on each occasion loaded; they then returned to the island and the men went on board to return to the mainland. On the following day Ahmad partitioned the spoil; he gave one part to the Arabs and... one to the troops who had gone on the water; the rest he divided among the Muslims...[31]

The churches of Lalibala survived destruction solely because of Ahmed the Left-handed's awe at witnessing them. It was this second phase of Moslem onslaught that brought the golden age of monastic life in Ethiopia to a close. Once again, as it came to pass after Islamic pressure of the seventh century the Ethiopian Church sank into an eclipse. It was a time of internal instability and religious controversy. Many Ethiopians were forced to renounce Christianity and adopt Islam.[32]

The second development of the period of Portuguese-Catholic penetration and Moslem challenge is related to the first. By the seventeenth century Portuguese influence had found a foothold in the controversy over monasticism and Christology and added fuel to the fire. The Portuguese Jesuit missionaries were so popular for a time that they succeeded in converting many of the people including Emperor Susenyos (1607-1632) to Roman Catholic obedience (although upon falling terminally ill, Susenyos revoked Catholicism and went to live in an Ethiopian Täwahïdo monastery). In 1626 the Portuguese almost succeeded in converting the whole royal family. The masses of the people, however, would not forsake their ancient religion. Under the able leadership of Emperor Fasiledes (1632-1667), the son of Emperor Susenyos, the Portuguese were expelled in 1632.[33] The Ethiopian Church regained internal stability and went through a period of literary and intellectual revival in the kingdom's new capital of Gondar. From then on, Täwahïdo reemerged from controversy and foreign penetration as the symbol of national unity even during subsequent periods of political upheaval and foreign assault.

In the nineteenth century the flow of Western missionaries resumed, including, this time, Protestants from Germany. But the Ethiopian Orthodox Täwahïdo Church has remained basically undisturbed in its liturgy and theology from its origin to the present. All the intermittent events and controversies have not changed the basic characteristics of the Church. It has always sought to establish good relations with other Christian churches from its inception,

---

31 Ethiopian Orthodox Church, *The Church of Ethiopia: A Panorama of History and Spiritual Life*. Addis Ababa, 1997 (28).

32 Ethiopian Orthodox Church, *The Church of Ethiopia: A Panorama of History and Spiritual Life*. Addis Ababa, 1997 (29).

33 Ibid, 29.

in particular with the Syrian and Coptic Orthodox Churches in the early days. In the year of 1439, it sent a delegation to the famous Council of Florence to explore the proposed ecumenical Christian unity concept of the time. Under completely indigenous leadership since 1954 due to the persistent efforts of Emperor Haile Sellassie, the Ethiopian Orthodox Täwahïdo Church moved into the era of fresh ecumenical contacts on the basis, at once, of full autonomy and Christian irenicism. It became a founding member of the World Council of Churches in 1948 when it was officially established, (originally proposed in 1937), and was represented by observers at the Second Vatican Council (1962-65). One of the Ethiopian observer is my friend, the present Archbishop Maqarios (formerly Abba Petros). It is also a founding member of the All African Council of Churches in 1963 (proposed in 1958). Its relations with nationals under the jurisdiction of Rome and adherents to Protestant faiths are gradually broadening on a line of new dialogue that may lead to further ecumenical developments.

Chapter 3

The Judaic Character of the Ethiopian Orthodox Church

The Jewish molding of Ethiopian Christianity, specifically its affect on praxis and teachings, has been a subject of great ecumenical curiosity, at least since the time of the Armenian writer, Abu Salih, in the middle Ages. In recent times, the subject has developed into an intense discussion and broad speculation among students of Ethiopian languages and civilization. The question of the Jewish molding of Ethiopian culture, and the scholarly debates surrounding it, have for the most part focused upon comparative cultural studies with emphasis on the similarities between customs or common practices of Jews and Ethiopian Christians. In particular, the debates have involved such practices as dietary regulations, circumcision, the worship of Saturday Sabbath, the worship of the *taabot* or Ark of the Covenant, certain features of ecclesiastical music and dance, liturgy, and elements of religio-magic and language.

In comparative cultural studies, exaggerations and mistaken analogies are unavoidable. Nonetheless, it is significant that even an elementary examination of Ethiopian culture reveals a striking set of common Ethiopian Christian and Jewish practices. Every scholar who has undertaken research in Ethiopian history in modern times, including Dillmann, Noldeke, Conti Rossini, Guidi, Littmann, Rodinson, Ullendorff, and Hammerschmidt, has had to deal with this apparent Jewish molding of Ethiopian culture, which is indicative of the importance of the subject.

Many Ethiopian folkways reflect biblical customs and traditions that are still quite common among Jews. Probably the most universal custom of both peoples is circumcision, which is still limited to eighth day after birth, as decreed in Genesis 17. Another important set of Ethiopian customs consists of food regulations and dietary laws. The Ethiopians recognize that the crucial distinction they make between "clean" and "unclean" food is biblically inspired. They obey the food laws of the Pentateuch, strictly following the proscriptions of Leviticus 11 (cf. Deutronomy 14) regarding mammals and birds, and also Genesis 32:33 concerning the forbidden sinew. The sanction for these food regulations is explicitly Hebraic. In *Fetha-Nagast* (Legislation of the Kings), the dietary laws are attended by the following order: "Remember what God has commanded thee by the mouth of Moses." Ethiopia, like most Christian nations accepts, respects, and follows the teachings of St. Paul in principle, but de facto rejects the traditional doctrine of Pauline thought that biblical law lost its binding force at the coming of Jesus. In this regard, the Church agrees more with the teachings that faith must be combined with good works of the Epistle of St James (that Martin Luther had called the Epistle of the straw). This is perhaps because of its ancient roots worshiping the Old Testament and its guardianship of the Holy Ark of the Covenant.

The Judaic influence on the customs associated with holiday celebrations is perhaps less obvious, but equally important. Scholars do not know exactly when the observance of the Saturday Sabbath was introduced to Christians in Ethiopia, but almost all of them maintain that the strictness with which many Ethiopians keep the Sabbath indicates a Jewish origin.

More significant is the celebration of the Ethiopian New Year, September 11th (leap year12[th]). Edward Ullendorf contends that "the New Year feast is undoubtedly of Jewish origin and [that] its date, as well as that of Maskal [Festival of the finding of the true crossand dedication of the church of the Holy Sepulcher which takes place about 15 days after the New Year] corresponds closely to the Hebrew season of the most holy season, *Yamim nora'im*. In the Jewish practice the High Priest prepared himself for Yom Kippur by a ritual immersion in water, then by laying his hands upon, and subsequently slaughtering, a bullock" (Yoma 3: 4 f, 4: 2 f). Ullendorff sees in these rituals a reflection of the general Ethiopian custom of the purification bath and the animal sacrifice, both of which are associated with the period of the celebration of the New Year.[1] Finally, the holiday of Fasika, the Ethiopian festival of resurrection, has definite overtones of the Jewish Pesah, both in its name and in the nature of its observance. It is quite probable that the Ethiopians used to keep Fasika on the 14th of Nisan, following the Jewish practice (Ex 12:6), like the Quartodecimans. The author of *Mäs'hafä Bǝrhan* expresses anger at those who say that the Passover does not occur on the different days of the week, calling them "stupid." He affirms, "Let us understand the reckoning of Passover day, and let us not make the mistake that it takes place on another day except during the week when the Feast of the Leavened Bread occurs at midnight on the fourteenth [of Nisan]."[2]

---

1   Ullendorf, E. Ethiopia and the Bible.

2   *E. Isaac, A New-Text Critical Introduction to Mäs'hafä Berhan* (E. J. Brill, 1973)

The New Year falls under the season of the "*addäy abäba*", which blooms only at this period of time and is a decoration of celebration on the grounds of many homes and shops.

Ethiopians build their churches with the three-fold division, which characterized the Tabernacle and the Temple of Solomon (Ex 26: 33, 1 Kings 6). The innermost of the three concentric circles is referred to as "*qïdustä qïddusan*"—the "Holy of Holies." It contains the altar and the ark, and none but kings and priests and deacons are allowed to enter it. The ark, known as the *Tabot* containing the *s'ilat* or the Tablets, is the most sacred object in the Ethiopian house of worship. Without it, no religious service can be conducted. According to sacred tradition, the original Tablets of Moses, on which God wrote the Ten Commandments at Sinai, were stolen with the Ark of the Covenant by Eleazer (the oldest son of the Jewish High Priest in Solomon's time) and Menelik (the son of the Queen of Sheba by Solomon), and brought to Ethiopia. The tradition holds that they are located today in the chapel of the Cathedral of Axum, the holiest of all Ethiopian sanctuaries, which only one monk is allowed to enter. He spends his entire life guarding the Ark in this sanctuary, until death. The Tabot in other churches are generally believed to be replicas of this original Ark of the Covenant. As one Ethiopian author explains, "A church is considered but an empty shell without the presence of the Tabot, the essential element that bestows religious significance to the physical structure of the church." Scholar Ayele Bekerie writes, "(Täwahïdo) is a church that defines *Tabot*, or *Tsilat*, or the Ark of the Covenant, as its central tenet together with Mäsqäl or the Cross."[3] The *Tabot* represents the blend of old and new faith that makes the Ethiopian Täwahïdo ("United") Church so unique.[4]

On various holidays, including the Feast of Immersion, the *Tabot* is taken down from its normal position in each church, and carried by the priest in a great seven-fold procession of singing, dancing in colorful ceremonial dress. This is done to the accompaniment of musical instruments, some of which may be counterparts to the instruments mentioned in II Samuel 6:5—harps, psalteries, tumbrels, sitar, and cymbals. One is struck by the resemblance of this ceremony to the scene described in II Samuel 6: 14-15: "And David danced before the Lord.... David and all the house of Israel brought up the ark of the Lord with shouting, and with the sound of the horn." In the march from Sinai, and at the crossing of the Jordan, the Ark preceded the Israelites and was the signal of their advance (Num. 10: 33, Joshua 3: 3-6). The descending of the people to a river and the symbolic crossing of it by priests carrying the Ark at the Feast of Immersion, both in form and in the texts chosen to be read (e.g. Psalm 113), are intended to repeat the drama of the crossing of the river Jordan.

3   Bekerie, Ayele. *Ethiopic: An African Writing System*. 1997 (p. 22).

4   Bekerie, Ayele. *Ethiopic: An African Writing System*. 1997 (p. 22).

The liturgy of the Ethiopian service is largely biblical in content. This of course is true of all the liturgies of other Christian churches; but the Ethiopian emphasis on the Old Testament is very significant. The reading of sacred texts, as in the synagogue, and as distinguished from the custom in most Christian traditions, plays a very central role. The basic text of the Ethiopian morning service is the Book of Psalms, supplemented by a collection of nine odes, all but one coming from the Old Testament and the Apocrypha. They include the Red Sea Song (Exodus 15), the Song of Moses (Deuteronomy 32), the Prayer of Hannah (I Samuel 2), and the Prayer of Jonah (Jonah 2).

In contrast to the religion of the country, the Ethiopian constitution and law reflect the Hebraic influence not so much in their formal aspects as in the traditional legends and folkways. According to the *Kebra Nagast* (Glory of Kings), one of the most important of the Ethiopian sacred books, Makeda, the Queen of Sheba visited Solomon in Jerusalem, and was converted to his religion (cf. I Kings 10:1-13 and II Chronicles 9:1-12). She returned to her country and bore him a son, who was named Menelik, a corrupted form of the Hebrew *ben-melech* ("son of the king" Arabic *al-malik*) or Arabic *Ibn Hakim ("Son of the Wise")*. Grown to manhood, Menelik went to visit Solomon and he returned to Ethiopia with the original Ark of the Covenant and the sons of Israel's highest state officials. He then established the "Solomonic Dynasty," shortly usurped by the Zagwes before being restored in the year 1270. From then to 1974, when Emperor Haile Sellassie I was dethroned, there existed an unbroken line of emperors claiming descent from Solomon and styling themselves the "Conquering Lion of the Tribe of Judah, Elect of God, King of Kings of Ethiopia," and "successors of the House of David."

The belief that the Emperor was of the line of David, strongly supported by the Church, has a great hold on the people. It is the sanction of the Emperor's legitimacy, his throne and attributes, and his claim to allegiance. Each Emperor keeps the manuscript of *Kebra Nagast,* which tells the story of the founding of the Solomonic Dynasty, as a proof of his sacredness. In 1868, the British forces that attacked Maqdala, the citadel of Emperor Theodore (1855-1868), under Sir Robert Napier, had run away with an important copy of *Kebra Nagast.* Several years later, Emperor Yohannes IV (1872-1889) succeeded in retrieving it from the trustees of the British Museum, after having written a plea to Lord Granville: "Again there is a book called *Kebra Nagast....* I pray you will find out who has got this book and send it to me, for in my country my people will not obey my orders without it." The Kebra Nagast was a crucial tool of maintaining justice and order.

Ethiopian justice is another fine example of biblical customs preserved in folkways. The administration of local justice is the most important part of the legal system. The impromptu court, which meets in the market place or in some outdoor center such as under a tree, carries the same weight among the people of the community as it did in Israel during the period of the Judges. Two men who have a dispute find a party, sometimes among members of their own respective families, to act as judge between them. No man may refuse to perform this duty. The judge, or *dañña* (a Semitic word, like the Hebrew *din* or "lawsuit"), gathers witnesses, hears the case and gives his judgment. There are also "permanent" local *daññas,* usually priests or learned elders of the community, who act as judges and advisors. They give relevant interpretations of the existing laws in difficult cases. In this way, a body of interpretations accumulates, with local variations expounded by the respected elders of the different regions, and gradually becomes custom. The voluntary and spontaneous form of administering justice becomes a daily practice, and law art is an integral part of the lives of the masses, as in Biblical times.

As far as we know, the official religion of Ethiopia since 330 has been Christianity, but it is Christianity far removed in content from that of the Mediterranean world. There is but little systematic theology in the Ethiopian Church. Belief is not as important as practice. The formal aspects of Ethiopian religion, especially the place, manners, and content of worship, show strong Biblical-Hebraic influences that have a greater effect on the people than do many aspects of Christian dogma.

While there is thus no doubt in the mind of any serious scholar that virtually every phase of Ethiopian life has been significantly affected by the Biblical-Hebraic impulse, a great deal of uncertainty prevails concerning when and how this component entered the main body of Ethiopian Christianity. Some scholars maintain that what appears Hebraic in Ethiopian culture is no more than a part of the (biblical) legacy left to all Christians. They deny any pre-Christian contact between Jews and Ethiopians, which could have molded Ethiopian customs along Hebraic lines. For example, it is argued by Conti Rossini that the "Hebraic" traits of Ethiopian Christianity result from the reforms instituted by Zär'a Ya'aqob in the fifteenth century.[5] It is surmised that his zeal for reform might have caused him to reestablish primitive Christianity, which was closer to Biblical Judaism than the contemporary forms.

Maxime Rodinson, a leading French Semiticist, also proposed a similar "non-contact" theory. He argues that the great dynamic of Ethiopian Christian culture has been *l'imitation d'Israel.* This principle has had a significant effect in many Christian milieux, leading, at times, even to conversion. All Christians venerate the Old Testament, especially the Decalogue, but some sects or communities have gone farther than simple veneration in their imitation of Israel. The Puritans, like the Afrikaners, called themselves by Hebrew names, conceived of themselves as the chosen people, and in some cases replaced English (or Dutch)

---

5   C. Conti Rossini & L. Ricci, *Mäs'hafä Berhan* in CSCO, Scriptores Aethiopic XLVII.

practices, even laws, by those of the Bible. Christian Sabbatarianism is widely documented from the sixteenth century leading to the emergence of Seventh Day Adventists who keep the Jewish Sabbath. Recently, an entire village, San Nicandro of Italy, converted to Judaism under the influence of a local Christian "prophet"[6]. The source of Ethiopian-Hebraic practices might well be analogous, and could have arisen without external Jewish contact.

These "non-contact" theories, however, are not convincing, for they leave several matters unexplained. Zär'a Ya'aqob's reforms did not essentially introduce new customs, but modified already existing ones. Indeed, his zeal for Miaphysite Christianity in conformity with the regnant Christian "orthodoxy" in Muslim Egypt led him to suppress several customs of possibly Biblical and post-Biblical Jewish origin. And the argument for *l'imitation d'Israel*, almost entirely an argument from analogy, fails to account fully for the fact that the Hebraic impulse in Ethiopia has persisted throughout the nation for many centuries, permeating every aspect of life.

To be sure, few scholars would rule out the possibility that there has been cultural contact between Jews and Ethiopians at some point in history. And surely we cannot dismiss out of hand the hypothesis that some meeting took place between the Ethiopians and the ancient Israelites, and later the Jews of South Arabia. There is indeed strong evidence that Jewish Christianity of Aramaic speech entered Ethiopia early through Red Sea travelers who were very active during the first centuries of the Christian era. The Ethiopian Church teaches that some of the disciples of Jesus came to preach in Ethiopia, and that an Ethiopian eunuch, of Queen Candace's court in Axum, was converted by Philip and subsequently baptized. Acts 8 of the Bible recorded this 'first baptism' as follows:

> Now when they had testified and spoken the word of the Lord, they returned to Jerusalem, preaching the gospel to many villages of the Samaritans.
> But an angel of the Lord said to Philip, "Rise and go toward the south to the road that goes down from Jerusalem to Gaza." This is a desert road. And he rose and went. And behold, an Ethiopian, an eunuch, a minister of Candace the queen of the Ethiopians, in charge of all her treasure, had come to Jerusalem to worship and was returning; seated in his chariot, he was reading the prophet Isaiah. And the Spirit said Philip, "Go up and join this chariot." So Philip ran to him, and heard him reading Isaiah the prophet, and asked, "Do you understand what you are reading?" And he said, "How can I, unless some one guides me?" And he invited Philip to come

---

6   Cf. M. Rodinson, *SUR LA QUESTION DES "INFLUENCES JUIVES" EN ETHIOPIE.*

up and sit with him. Now the passage of the scripture that he was reading was this:

"As a sheep led to the slaughter
Or a lamb before its shearer is dumb,
So he opens not his mouth.
In his humiliation justice was denied him
Who can describe his generation?
For his life is taken up from the earth."

And the eunuch said to Philip, "About whom, pray, does the prophet say this, about himself or about some one else?"

Then Philip opened his mouth, and beginning with this scripture he told him the good news of Jesus. And as they went along the road they came to some water, and the eunuch said, "See here is water! What is to prevent my being baptized?" And he commanded the chariot to stop, and they both went down into the water, Philip and the eunuch, and he baptized him. And when they came up out of the water, the Spirit of the Lord caught up Philip; and the eunuch saw him no more, and went on his way rejoicing." (Acts 8:25 – 9:39).

It is believed that the eunuch returned to the Queen bringing the news of Christianity.

Since most scholars have spoken but in general terms about this cultural contact and the elements of cultural influence, they have not been able to deal with the specific characteristics of the group that became the channel of the Hebraic-Jewish molding of Ethiopian Christianity. Could it have been through the conduit of Biblical-Israelites, or through Jewish sectarians such as the Sadducees, the Pharisees, the Essenes, or the Hellenists, or some first-century sect of Jewish-Christians that both Biblical and post-Biblical Jewish elements entered Ethiopia?

First, we are certain that the Israelites of Biblical times had some contact with the people living south of Egypt, in the land called "*Cush*" in Hebrew ("*Ethiopia*" in Greek). Isaiah 18: 1 and Zephaniah 3:10 both refer to the land and people "beyond the rivers of Ethiopia." When the Assyrians attacked Judea, Judea received some military aid from "Cush" [11 Kings chaps. 18 and 19; Is. 19:2ff.]. But what contact those "Ethiopians" had with modern Ethiopia is still not understood. There is also archaeological and historical evidence of a possible meeting ground. There have been Israelite-Jewish colonies in both Egypt and South Arabia for 3000 and 2500 years, respectively. And the Ethiopians had contact with both the Egyptians and the South Arabians as early as 1500 BCE There is a sense in which, in fact, the Ethiopians may be said to be the cultural counterpart of, particularly, the Sabaeans of ancient South Arabia. The

Sabaeans apparently traded with Solomon and his successors through the Red Sea [I K. 10: 1-10; 14: 22; 16: 6]. Ullendorff seems to make much of the expression [11 Chron. 21: 16f] to establish an indirect Israel-Ethiopian tie through South Arabia. But except for pointing at the close proximity assumed in the phrase to exist between the (South) Arabians and the Cushites, there is no way of identifying the latter with the modern Ethiopians. But other indirect contacts between the Hebrews and the Ethiopians via South Arabia still may have existed and could be a likely explanation for the Biblical molding of Ethiopian culture. On the other hand, hints in the prophetic books of the Bible lead one to believe that there were Israelite-Jews among the immigrant traders and settlers who traveled to Ethiopia ("to the land beyond the Nile") before Christian times. They might have moved southward from Egypt, as did the Elephantine Colonizers. The temple practice of Elephantine Jewry at that time was highly syncretistic, and syncretism is, of course, an important characteristic of Ethiopian religion.

Second, contact might have originated in South Arabia, in the time when there was a Jewish colony there. Many cultural affinities between Ethiopia and Arabia, on opposite shores of the Arabian Gulf, were noted by ancient travelers. Apart from varieties of other contacts, we know that at least four Ethiopian military expeditions into South Arabia were made at a time when Jewish influence in that country was especially strong. Recent archaeological expeditions in Yemen have confirmed direct Ethiopian influence on Sabaean culture. In particular, the dates 335 CE - 370 CE and 525 CE-575 CE can be well established as periods of Ethiopian cultural superiority in South Arabia. In turn the early establishment of a Jewish community adhering to Rabbinic Judaism in Southern Arabia is now well established. A direct contact between Ethiopia and the Jews of South Arabia took place in 525 CE when Emperor Kaleb (523-540) defeated in battle Dhu Nuwwas called Phinhas in Ethiopia, the Himyarite king who fully adopted Judaism. It is thus possible to envisage that Hebraic-Jewish elements entered Ethiopia through South Arabia.

In the final analysis, however, there is no documentary confirmation that either the ancient Israelites or the later Jews of South Arabia influenced Ethiopia directly. Moreover, neither of the two separately can be regarded as a sufficient direct source for Hebraic-Jewish elements in Ethiopia, and in the absence of good evidences, we must seek a better hypothesis instead of the present ones which assume a double conversion, first to Judaism and then to Christianity.

Very little attention has so far been given the view that the most important conduit or channel of Hebraic-Jewish influence in Ethiopian culture was neither Biblical nor Rabbinic Judaism but Jewish Christianity. There were several sects among the followers of Jesus who for a while maintained their Judaism. It is believed in the Ethiopian Church that Matthew, Bartholomew, and other early

Jewish Christians made their way to Ethiopia. Furthermore, there were important Jewish-Christian elements in South Arabia at the time when the Ethiopians ruled over South Arabia and Yemen. These Jewish Christians accepted the authority of Mosaic Law and, when they could, frequented the Temple in Jerusalem. They retained circumcision, the Sabbath, and the dietary laws. There is no doubt that most of the practices of the Ethiopian Church are remarkably close to those of the early Jewish Christians, so that almost every aspect of the strong Hebraic-Jewish ingredient in Ethiopian Christianity can find its explanation on the basis of their influence.

Before we proceed, it is important to define more specifically what exactly we mean by Jewish Christianity. Perhaps under the influence of Acts 22:3 or Gal 2:15 and early Christian authors, such as Eusebius and Epiphanius, a great deal of present scholarly attention has been devoted to the study of heretical Jewish Christian sects such as, for instance, the Ebionites or the Nazarenes. Unfortunately, the early Christian writers have left us but only scanty information on the subject. As Shlomo Pines put it, perhaps "the heresiographical schemas of the patristic authors may be responsible for this fact." Yet, there is a sense in which all Christianity may be said to be "Jewish." In this respect, coming down even to our modern times, it can be argued that Calvinism, for example, is a more "Jewish" form of Protestantism than Lutheranism because comparatively it gives more weight to the Hebrew Bible (Old Testament). As to the early Catholic (Orthodox) Church itself, however, there is no doubt that serious scholarly research can lead to genuine discovery of Jewish Christian survivals in it.

However, for our understanding of Ethiopian Christianity, important though they are, neither the study of heretical Jewish sects, on the one hand, nor on the other the search for Jewish Christian survivals in the early Catholic (Orthodox) Church would by themselves alone enlighten us sufficiently. It may well be that we have in early Christianity a whole spectrum with fuzzy lines among those who adhere to the practices of the various aspects of the Jewish law. Therefore, it becomes indeed very difficult to know how to proceed from the general designation "Jewish Christianity" to more specific definitions. To analyze such a major problem is however far beyond the scope of the present book. What is indeed important for our present study may well be an understanding of the Jewish *Sitz im Leben* of the first centuries of the Christian era, to which reference has already been made. For there is no doubt that many early Jewish converts to Christianity must have come from varieties of sectarian backgrounds, and that there is no reason why one should expect more "theological" uniformity among them than in general among the Jews of the first centuries of the Christian era. On the contrary, there is indeed strong reason to believe that the experience of each Jewish Christian converts was molded by his respective sectarian background.

On the basis of what we have said thus far, it would be sufficient to make just a broad and general differentiation between two possible groups of Jewish Christians: originally Aramaic speaking (Palestinian) Jewish Christians and originally Greek-speaking Jewish Christians. As an example of the latter category we may cite the Hellenists of Acts 6:1 and 9:29. In Palestine itself, as elsewhere, it appears from Acts 6 and 7 that some tension might have existed between the Hellenists and the "Hebrews" who spoke Jewish Aramaic. It is thought that the tension between them might have intensified the problem of admitting the Gentiles to the church, as reflected in Acts 15 and Gal. 1 and 2. Outside Palestine itself, there is no doubt that a sizable number of Christians consisted of converted Hellenistic Jews, in places like Rome, Antioch, or North Africa as well as in Alexandria where a large number of thoroughly Hellenized Jews were living.

In the light of our discussion above and what follows hereafter, it should be clear that Hellenistic Jewish Christians played much less of a role, if any, than Aramaic-speaking Jewish Christians in the creation and shaping of Ethiopian Christianity. Aramaic-speaking Jews were some of the earliest converts to Christianity and must have constituted an important segment of the Church in Jerusalem. They must have shared many common beliefs with the "Hellenist" and the other Jewish Christian groups, and might have manifested slight differences among themselves, depending upon the Jewish sectarian backgrounds they originated from. Nevertheless, as a more or less distinguishable class, the Aramaic-speaking Jewish Christians must have differed from the others not only in their important linguistic characteristics, but also in their excelling loyalty to the Torah and to the Tannaitic rabbinic Jewish practices and traditions of Palestine (cf. Acts 13:15). Important among their religious literature, the Aramaic-speaking Jewish Christians, not unlike other Jewish sects such as the Essenes, possessed, particularly, such apocalyptic works as the *Book of Enoch* and *Jubilees*, which they used for edification and enlightenment, and often quoted like scripture (e.g. Jude 14-15). Many church historians have thought it since antiquity that the Jewish Christians of the early Church of Jerusalem had fled north, particularly to Syria, after the destruction of Jerusalem in 70 CE. It would be only natural for Aramaic-speaking Jewish Christians who would come to Syria not only to be exposed to the Syriac language as well as to the Septuagint, the Bible of Hellenistic Jewry, but also, in due time, to become Syriac-speakers as well as users of the Septuagint, while retaining strong Jewish Aramaic traditions. If some of them had eventually become missionaries there is no doubt that they would have, therefore, taken with them their multiple Jewish-Syria-Christian cultural heritage to distant lands.

Whatever may have happened to the early Christian community of Palestinian Jewish culture, when we use the expression "Jewish Christianity" in this book, we are constantly keeping in mind that a Jewish Aramaic-speaking Christian group, or one identical with it, eventually established direct or indirect contact with Ethiopia. It is by no mere accident that the practices, beliefs, sacred literature, and important religious expressions of the Ethiopian church and of that community came to be so completely identical.

It is beyond question that many Christians, who flocked to Ethiopia, particularly from the fourth to sixth centuries, and perhaps from earlier times, came from Syria. On the other hand, as said above, there is reason to believe that Syria became a haven for Jewish Christians after the destruction of Jerusalem in 70 CE Antioch, especially, became the center for Palestinian Jewish Christians. Many of the early church manuals such as the *Didascalia* (and some Apocryphal New Testament writings), which became favorites in the Ethiopian Church, originated among these Jewish Christians. Moreover, in this connection, Jewish Apocalyptic works, especially the books of *Enoch* and *Jubilees* possessed by early Jewish Christians, survived *in toto* only in the Ge'ez version in Ethiopia where they exercised an authority equal to that of the Bible. The *Ascension of Isaiah,* a work believed to be genuinely Jewish Christian, survives in its entirety only in Ge'ez. Furthermore, we know from established historical sources that merchants converted the Ethiopian royal family to Christianity from Syria around 320.[7] It goes without saying that by the time Christianity was an established religion in Ethiopia, there was undoubtedly a sizable community of "Christians from Syria" in the country.

Now, who these "Syrian" Christians were and what form of Christianity they brought with them is not known for certain. They had strong Jewish Christian tendencies. More important still is the stamp of their language, which the "Syrian" Christians left for posterity on Ge'ez, the classical language of Ethiopian literature. Ge'ez is a Semitic language as Aramaic, but scholars can still distingush common Semitic word from loan words. Such expressions as *Orit* (Torah, Law), *haymanot* (faith), *qurban* (oblation, sacrifice, Eucharist), *s'alot* (prayer), *s'om* (fast), *mäqdas* (sanctuary) are Syriac imprints on the Ge'ez language. Still more important, however, are words like *ta'ot* (idol), *gähannäm* (hell), *Fasika* (Easter), *mäswa'ït* (alms, cf. Commandments), *atarra* (to purify) and *Tabot* (the Ark) that are believed to be Aramaic forms with specifically Jewish connotation.

Noldeke says, "*meswat* alone would suffice to demonstrate Jewish religious influence among the Abyssinians." Ullendorff, who also quotes Noldeke on this point, says: "Those terms were in pre-Christian times, but survived after the introduction of Christianity with slight shifts in meaning and substance." I, however, contend that they were brought over by Jewish Christians from Syria. Ethiopian *'arb* for Friday, corresponding to *'erev* connotating *'Erev Shabbath*

---

7   Frumentius who later became Abba Salama and the first Ethiopian Archbishop c.325.

must also originate from a Jewish circle; there is no other word in Ethiopic or modern Amharic for Friday. Professor H.J. Polotsky has shown conclusively that the whole group of religious terminology must come from Jewish Aramaic.[8] He states, "In the light of the linguistic evidence it seems hardly possible that the Aramaic words should have been introduced by Syriac speaking missionaries or Bible translators: some of the words are characteristically non-Syriac, while none of them is characteristically and exclusively Syriac." The formal linguistic evidence is paralleled and supported by the semantic evidence. None of these words is distinctively Christian in meaning. What they denote belongs to the Jewish leaven in Christianity. It is perhaps remarkable that perfectly good indigenous words were found for notions like "baptism," "savior," and "cross," "resurrection." The interpretations of these linguistic facts in terms of history may be left to those who are better qualified than I am. As regards the supposed textual evidence for Syriac-speaking Bible-translators, I hope that at least some of it rests on mere verbal misunderstanding.

When we accept these conclusions of Polotsky, then all the remaining problems can be solved, provided we concede that Jewish Christians who came from Syria, and who established first the oral tradition and then collaborated with the translators of the Bible influenced the earliest form of Christianity in Ethiopia. Future research on the history of the Ethiopian church must take this into consideration.

At this point, we must consider the question of when the Ethiopian Church came to he mistakingly regarded "Miaphysite." As far as we know, Ethiopia was never represented at the Council of Chalcedon (451 CE). That many persecuted Miaphysites found refuge in Ethiopia is no surprise as Ethiopia has been a refuge for persecuted souls of many religious since ancient times: a classic example is the protection of the earliest disciples of Mohammed got in Ethiopia. Sir W. Muir, speaking of the "sympathy and hospitality as cordial as that afforded by the Abyssinian King" to them says, "If an Arab asylum had not at last offered itself at Medina, the prophet himself might have emigrated to Abyssinia...." The cordial relationship Emperor Kaleb (514-543) had with the Byzantine Emperors, Justin (518-527) and Justinian (527-565), great persecutors of Monophysitism, goes to show that the Ethiopians had normal relations with Chalcedonian Christians. In any case, Monophysitism is attributed wrongly to the Ethiopian Church primarily on the basis of its relationship with the Coptic Church. We should consider this assumption briefly.

Regardless of the contact Frumentius of Syria had with Athanasius, about whose conversations we know very little, and regardless of the influence of the earlier Egyptian monastic tradition in Ethiopia, it is clear that Christianity took

---

8   Th. Ndldeke, *Nan Btitrag ^*r stmtutbm Sprachmnsstnstbaft* (Strasbourg, 1910), pp. 32-46. See pp. j and 6 above. H.J. Polotsky,

shape in Ethiopia through the labors of "Syrian" Christians (whom we have suggested to be Jewish Christians). Ethiopian contact with the (Miaphysite) Coptic Church remained minimal until 1270. It is believed that, as an act of institutionalizing gratitude to Athanasius, Ethiopia received her Abunas from Alexandria, after 350. Pre-1270 Ethiopian and Coptic records on the relationship of the two churches are scanty and unreliable. Moreover, as we have said above, Guidi has shown that many early, foreign churchmen in Ethiopia credited as Copts were actually "Syrian" Christians. It is indeed very significant that Cosmas, an important early visitor to Ethiopia, and an Egyptian monk himself, does not by 525 mention the presence of any Coptic Abuna in Ethiopia, though he specifically states that Ethiopia was Christianized. Yet it is not impossible that after about 650, when the Red Sea was dominated by Muslim South Arabia and Egypt, and when Ethiopia was isolated from the rest of Christendom, that she retained some contact with Miaphysite monks in the Egyptian deserts. But the status of monastic Coptic/ Egyptian Abunas presiding over the Ethiopian Church was never fully regularized before the time of the churchman, monk, theologian, diplomat and revolutionary leader, Takla-Haymanot in 1270.[9] "He thought the procedure desirable, [and] gave it his sanction, since it would keep the Abyssinian Church cut off from the rest of Christendom... somewhat in touch with the outer world." It is now well known that the term of the agreement, which became the foundation for the traditional dependency of the Ethiopian Church on Coptic monastic leadership, was based on a fabricated canon of the Council of Nicea (the 42 Arabic Canons of Nicea), not on the Nicean canons which are only 20.

During the period of Ethiopian isolation from the rest of the Christian world, and probably during a time of some internal turmoil in the 10th century, it seems that the Copts had been given support and encouragement by the Fatimid Sultans of Egypt to make friendly overtures to Christian Ethiopia, ironically with the hope of encouraging the overthrow of the Christian establishment. The Ethiopians welcomed the overtures of "Christian friendship" but, because of the ulterior motives of the Copts and because of their participation in internal revolutionary plots, we hear, from the earliest records, of their frequent expulsion from Ethiopia. Trimingham says, "the Coptic Church ... sometimes took the side of Islam ... acting in collusion with the Muslim rulers of Egypt, the Church sometimes appointed Abunas who worked for the promotion of Islamic interests in Abyssinia...."[10] Jean Doresse writes: "There was another kind of pressure... from the Moslems in control at Cairo who in order to spread Islamic

---

9   Cf. E. Isaac, "An Obscure Component in Ethiopian Church History," *Le Muséon*, LXXXV (1-2), 1972, 225-258

10   Trimingham, J. Spencer. *Islam in Ethiopia*. London, Frank Cass and Co., Ltd. 1965 (63).

doctrine made use... of Coptic bishops on their official visits to Ethiopia."[11] No doubt, the Ethiopian church, with its predominately Jewish-Christian influence, also felt uncomfortable with the Miaphysites. Thus, in the first half of the ninth century, we hear of an Abuna who was expelled from Ethiopia on the grounds that he was uncircumcised. He was sent back from Egypt circumcised! Then we hear of Coptic intrigues to side with their favorite candidates for the throne. During most of the 10th century we hear of a long breach between the Patriarchate of Alexandria and the Ethiopian court.

The whole story of the intrigue of the Abunas cannot be told here, but a brief summary of the history of the Patriarchs of Alexandria during some of the early centuries will suffice. First, the earliest clear records that we have regarding Ethio-Coptic relations indicate that a certain Abuna Peter arrived in Ethiopia sometime about 925, after what was supposed to have been "one hundred years" of broken communications due to constant troubles and war. Peter is said to have been invited by Ethiopia; nonetheless, the records reveal that he actually perished in exile where he was banished due to a court intrigue he had played. At this time, we are also told that the Moslem authorities opened all letters coming from Ethiopia before being forwarded to the Patriarch. Secondly, the successor of Peter, Abuna Menas, was put to death in Ethiopia as an imposter; in retrospect Alexandria disavowed him. The succeeding Abuna was an Ethiopian appointee of the Emperor. The records of the Patriarchs say that he had requested to go to Egypt to obtain confirmation but that the Emperor refused absolutely. Following this, for about one hundred years, no Abunas from Egypt were allowed into Ethiopia.

Then about 1070, we find that the government of Bedr-el-Jamal "arrested" the Patriarch Christodolus and questioned him about the conduct of a certain Abuna of Ethiopia, called Cyril or Abdun. On the one hand, the question was why Cyril, who was on friendly terms with the Moslems of Ethiopia, served them wine at dinner. On the other, Christodolus, who claims that he had not consecrated any Abuna for Ethiopia, was ordered by Bedr to consecrate the same Cyril (!)[12] by sending a messenger to Ethiopia. Consequently, we discover that Christodolus was in reality on excellent terms with Bedr, to the extent that his successor was made to bless the palace of the *Caliph*. The inconsistencies of this story must reveal some deeper secret maneuverings. Then a little later, about 1080, an interesting incident took place. A young Coptic monk, Severus, who had befriended Bedr, promised the *wazir* that if the latter elected him to the see of Ethiopia, he, Severus, would not only build four mosques but would do everything possible to advance Moslem interests in Ethiopia. In the meantime,

---

11   Doresse, Jean. *Ethiopia*. Translated from the French by Elsa Coult. London, ELEK Books, 1959.

12   Patrologia Orientalis.

the former Abuna Cyril had fled Ethiopia, and had been executed upon his return to Egypt. Severus, who eventually got to Ethiopia, took time to establish himself before fulfilling his promises. He then built not only four but indeed seven mosques. The Ethiopians, to use Jean Doresse's phrase, "in righteous indignation" leveled the mosques and chained the Abuna.[13] The Patriarch then sent two more Abunas both of whom openly requested the rebuilding of the mosques, or that otherwise all the churches in Egypt would be thrown down. To this the Ethiopian Emperor YX gave a strong and final reply threatening that "If in Egypt one single stone of God's temples were touched, he would himself send to the court of Cairo every single brick and stone of Mecca ...but if one brick should be wanting he would supply its weight in gold."

With the coming of the Zagwe or Agaw Dynasty (1137-1270) into power, we begin to see more light. We hear at the outset of an Abuna Michael that he was was rejected by the first Zagwe King on the grounds that the former was too old. This incident lead to a severe conflict with the Patriarch of Alexandria who, because of the same reason, is thrown into prison by the *wazir* of Egypt. Later, during the reign of Lalibala (d.c. 1220) about 1200, another prelate who was sent to Ethiopia by Cairo, was overcome with nostalgia and fled the country on the grounds that he was persecuted.

The Coptic relationship with Ethiopia was indeed never secured until 1270. Then the Copts finally succeeded in identifying themselves with a dissident political group, led by a certain Yekuno Amlak who succeeded to overthrow the then established Ethiopian Zagwe Dynasty that he considered the usurpers of the earlier Solomonic Dynasty. He becomes the new Emperor (1270-1285) to whom the succeeding rulers of Ethiopia until Emperor Haile Sellassie traced their ancestry. Yekuno-Amlak's chief religio-political advisor was the monk Takle Haymanot. The Egyptians/Copts were ready to offer both moral support and a strong propaganda document, for they knew they stood to gain with a change of hands in Ethiopia.

It is likely that the most important contribution the Egyptian/Coptic Church made for the revolutionaries was making available the *Kebra Nagast* (Glory of Kings), a powerful religio-political legend that derived the Kings of Ethiopia from King Solomon and the Queen of Sheba. This legend became extremely important, both because of the immemorial Jewish Christian tradition in the land and because the then ruling dynasty had claimed ties with ancient Israel without specifying any descent from the House of David (or Solomon). (External legends and writings point toward this direction). An extraordinary Jewish legend of the 9th century, which told of the Kingdom of the Ten Tribes in the Ethiopian mountains, made its way to Europe. Sometime about 1200 an Armenian writer, Abu-Salih, compiled a valuable treatise on the

---

13   J. Doresse, *Ethiopia, Ancient Cities and Temples, 1959*

Coptic Church including information about Ethiopia. According to him the King who was then ruling in Ethiopia was a descendant of Moses (N.B. not of David) who sat on the throne of David. Internal legends concur with the outside ones. Finally it may be significant to note that the Beta-Israel or the Jews of Ethiopia are thought by some to be close relatives of the most indigenous people of Ethiopia - the Agaw stock.

In view of the fact of strong Jewish Christian influence in Ethiopian Christianity and in view of the fact that the early Christian founders of Ethiopia claimed descent from Israel, it is not surprising that Yekuno Amlak and the revolutionaries of 1270 found it highly useful to provide a political propaganda, such as the *Kebra Nagast*, to justify a claim that they descended from the House of David and Solomon, the legitimate rulers of Israel. Tekle-Haymanot (who also claimed descent from Zadok) saw to it that this propaganda sunk into the spirit of the church. He and the revolutionaries must have left in the legend that the former dynasty had ties with Israel only because they descended from Solomon through the maid of the Queen of Sheba. Later generations, which made Tekle-Haymanot a saint, attributed the fall of the Zagwe Dynasty not to a bloody revolution in which the last king seeking an asylum in the church was murdered (as it really happened), but to the spiritual intervention of Tekle-Haymanot who persuaded the King to abdicate joyfully to Yekun-Amlak of the House of Solomon!

There is, indeed, an Ethiopian legend that Tekle-Haymanot introduced Christianity into Ethiopia. Even if this is a far cry from historical reality, there is a sense in which it is true. Tekle-Haymanot may be said to be the first Ethiopian to be "converted" to Coptic Monophysitism and who thus became the main mediator for the Coptic alliance with the Ethiopian church. Ironically, in his time, Tekle-Haymanot functioned as an Abuna, the last such indigenous official prelate. This fact gives still more support to the belief that preceding Tekle-Haymanot there indeed must have been native Ethiopian Abunas. But he saw to it that the Copts inherited the right of the bishopric of the Ethiopian Church for posterity, perhaps to insure the continuity of Monophysitism. He opened the way to confirm a prerogative then claimed by the Church of Alexandria in respect to the nomination of the senior members of the clergy and the investiture of Ethiopian bishops. The anxious Coptic Church officials were only too ready to take advantage of the opportunities offered to them. Girded by their now canonically strengthened position, the Coptic Abunas saw to it that the Emperors of the New Dynasty, with whom occasional clashes did not cease to occur, allowed the people to absorb as much as possible the beliefs and the practices of the Coptic Church. This they achieved especially by causing a mass translation of their books of miracle-stories, canon laws and legends into the vernacular. It is even possible that the then extant Ethiopic Bible was replaced by a new translation from the Coptic or Arabic.

From *Mäs'hafä Berhan* we learn something about the culmination and the fruition of these new developments in Ethiopia: the succession of the Miaphysite tradition and the suppression, if not by conviction then by force, of the old Jewish Christian tradition in Ethiopia. To be sure, the church was split into two for many years. The Jewish Christian leaders or the traditionalists preferred to live in exile and to die keeping their old customs rather than to give in. Some, like Eustathius and his followers, fled into the mountains; others, like the Stephanites, skipped from one monastery to another. National uprising and unrest went on for two centuries.

The turmoil and struggle was brought to an end by the hardy Emperor Zär'a Ya'aqob (1434-68), a little less than two centuries after the rise of the Solomonic Dynasty. Zär'a Ya'aqob success cannot but be attributed to a determination he had after an unusual incident took place in his spiritual life. It appears that until that time, Jewish Christians or Jewish Christian oriented traditionalists still enjoyed some popularity even in the royal court, as, for instance, we see Gamaliel who seems to hold the position of advisorship to the Emperor. The psychological intensity and significance of the turnabout in the Emperor's life is reported in *Mäs'hafä Berhan* as follows:

> In the period of our reign, these Abunas that came from Egypt (are) the chosen, honorable exponents of books, men full of understanding and of upright (orthodox) faith: Abba Michael and Abba Gabriel who reached us in the month of Yakatit [February]. And after a brief while, when the Friday of the Crucifixion of our Lord Jesus Christ arrived, while we were in the church of our Lady Mary to celebrate the Crucifixion Day of our Redeemer, we asked the Abunas a question concerning the nature of the Trinity, in the presence of Amha Sion, Aqabe Sa'at, of Haiq. And those holy fathers of ours, the Abunas, replied in joy and gladness and they said to us: "We believe in three persons, three essences, and three hypostases, but in one divinity, one kingdom, one glory, and one authority." Then we asked them, "How is it then that there are among the Christians those who say the Father, the Son and the Spirit are one person (ahadu)?"And they said, "He who says such a thing is really not a Christian, but a Jew; and he should not come to the church." They then produced many proofs from the books of [canon] law concerning the Trinity.... And secondly they said, "was there not Sabellius... who said that the Father, the Son and the Holy Spirit are one person...? And Bishop Timothy of Alexandria... spoke to Sabellius... then he excommunicated him... and sent him away. O, our

beloved son, are we not the sons of Bishop Timothy... and believers in the Trinity...?

Now when we heard of this orthodox faith of our chosen and holy fathers Abba Michael and Abba Gabriel, we rejoiced with great joy in their faith which shined like the sun, and we embraced them on the Day of His Crucifixion, from the amplitude of excitement which filled our heart; for it is not meet to embrace on that day for it is the day of the passion, crucifixion and death of our Redeemer. But, we praised God who gave us those chosen Abunas... and all... Ethiopia rejoiced... Now at this time we say to you: O, people of Ethiopia, people of orthodox faith, let not the false teachers make you err, those who say the Father, the Son and the Holy Spirit are one person, in collaboration with the Jews...[14]

The emotional intensity that Zär'a Ya'aqob experienced on that day of Good Friday (expressing joy and excitement on the day when it is forbidden to do so) was probably what became the spark of the flame in the Emperor who, as his chronicler tells us, became a staunch persecutor of Jews and Jewish-Christians. Many of these Jewish Christians who refused to accept the new officially approved doctrinal line were dispersed by force until in reaction a number of them, including even one of his sons, went altogether to the side of the extreme group which found refuge among the Jews, they referred to as Felasha (exiles),[15] in the mountains, abandoning Christianity altogether. The manner in which Zär'a Ya'aqob generally treated his own family, his wife and children, could earn him the name "Herod the Great, Redivivus." But to his credit, perhaps due to the pressure of public opinion, Zär'a Ya'aqob's first method of appeasing Ethiopian Jewish Christianity was that of conviction and compromise. Such especially was his approach to the Eustathians, as we gather from *Mäs'hafä Berhan:*

Understand again, God, who is merciful and who finds cause of mercy for all people, how he revealed to our holy and honorable Fathers, Abuna Abba Michael and Abba Gabriel the [necessity of] keeping both Sabbaths which matter had not been [formerly] revealed to the other Abunas who had come over to Ethiopia before them. It happened on Yakattit 21 [February 28] on the Day of the Festival of our Lady Mary, while we were in Debre Metmaq, in the 16th year [i.e. 1450) *(of* our reign) since God had placed us on the throne of our father, David, King of Ethiopia, head of Kings: we

---

14   E. Isaac, *A New-Text Critical Introduction to Mäs'hafä Berhan* (E. J. Brill, 1973). The bishops mentionded in *Mäs'hafä Berhan are not known from Coptic sources.*

15   The term Felasha is derived from Ge'ez, felasi (felasiyan in plural)and in the Ethiopic-Ge'ez Bible refers to Jewish exiles. See Jermiah 29:4, 20, 22, 31; 40:1; 6:16, 21. In these passages it translated goloh. In Psalm 119:19 the same word falasian is from Hebrew ger.

said to our Fathers, Abunas Abba Michael and Abba Gabriel, "Why do people abolish the first Sabbath? We indeed do not find in the books that one should abolish her but to keep her: in the Orit, the prophets, the Gospels, and Apostles...."

Now when our Fathers the Abunas... heard this matter they at once came over to our side in the matter of keeping both Sabbaths and wrote down with their own hands the matter of honoring the Sabbaths. [They were made to sign?] Therefore, in this manner God destroyed the schism that was between us and between the Abunas - and between the Eustathians. All of us were united in the matter of keeping both Sabbaths.

Then, after that, we said to the Eustathians, 'behold we have got the cooperation of the Abunas in the matter of keeping both Sabbaths. Now what reason is there for you not to receive the priesthood? Where in the 81 books do you find that one called a lay-monk is a teacher [mamher] who is not a priest and who does not serve the church and her priests and all her sons? Now if you have a scriptural reason from the Law books, come on and tell us before this assembly.'

They gave a reply and said, "We have no argument for it from the 81 books of the Law concerning this matter; we shall accept priesthood. But we are not ready now to accept the priesthood because of our sins. Formerly we used to say that we shall not receive the priesthood according to the rules of our Fathers Absadi and Filipos, but this time we have no reason...."

So, they were overcome by the word of the Scriptures and by the power of God ... And the Abunas... made an anathema that they should not appoint a lay-monk ... And the Church [of Ethiopia] became one community of the Apostles.... After the Church which had been in schism for many years, God, by his manifold mercies brought us together in one orthodox faith, in the belief in the Trinity as well as the divine unity, in the honoring of the priesthood and in the keeping of both Sabbaths. Praise be to God... That of the Abunas is ended Amen.[16]

In this interpolated, but extremely useful royal ecclesiastical document, we see how the Eustathians were silenced by a compromise that was forced upon them. Note well that the author who had given earlier as the cause of the Eustathian schism the keeping of Saturday Sabbath and their refusal to accept priesthood, in his conclusions, he indicates the concept of the Trinity as being one of the causes cleared for Church unity, revealing another dimension of the Eustathanian ties with the Jewish Christians. That the Ethiopian Jewish Christians were also Quartodecimans is hinted at in *Mäs'hafä Berhan*. In the text it is clear

16   *A New-Text Critical Introduction to Mäs'hafä Berhan* (E. J. Brill, 1973).

that it was the Abunas who were made to agree to the old Ethiopian custom of keeping the Saturday Sabbath. It is inconceivable that if the custom of keeping Saturday Sabbath were not already a widespread national practice with which the reform program of the Abunas could not cope, they would give in so easily to the Eustathians.

The Abunas were not, however, always so ready to give up their objectives as the story above makes it seem. But neither were they traditionalists, for they continued their struggle under the leadership of the Stephanites. It is one thing to suppress a belief, a matter in which the Abunas succeeded; it is another to suppress an established practice, in which they failed. If it is difficult to suppress all existing customs, it is equally difficult to introduce a new one. Thus when it came to the new cult of Mary and the cross, which the Abunas were anxious to not let go, it required nothing less than the destruction of the Jewish Christians. For when conviction and compromise became impossible, the Emperor, in favor of the Abunas, resorted this time to force and to the extermination of the traditional adherents to Jewish Christianity. The final verdict, recorded for us in another interpolation in *Mäs'hafä Berhan* reads as follows:

> Regarding the Stephanites, *I* say unto you, O, Christian people, believers in Mary, the double fold Virgin: Everyone who receives or welcomes them, or has social intercourse with them, or puts them *up* in his house, or keeps them in his church or on his inherited land, if he be an official let him be fired and his house investigated; and let all his property and his inherited land be given to an alien. If chief-priests, burned, other church officials, and monks as well as the rest *of* the people welcome them ... let them lose their offices ... and let all their land ... [and] property ... be given to an alien.
>
> As for you Stephanites, you are truly Jews who refused to worship Mary the double fold Virgin and the cross of the one Son: the verdict you get is the sentence of death. Those who welcome them will be dealt with severely, but one must surely not kill them but bring them to the court in order that we shall hear their case and pass appropriate judgment on them. He who is found greeting a Stephanite, let his portion be with those who receive them.[17]

We know that even this verdict of extermination did not bring to an end the Jewish Christianity of Ethiopia. Exiled and persecuted, staunch leaders of the Stephanites continued to find refuge with dissident political groups even after the death of Zär'a Ya'aqob. Due to some skill in handcraft their leaders, such as Ezra, had acquired while abroad, in the Holy Land, the Stephanites became gradually not only tolerated, but even wanted in the royal court. If anything

---

17   *A New-Text Critical Introduction to Mäs'hafä Berhan* (E. J. Brill, 1973).

brought the end of Jewish Christianity in Ethiopia it was that the Jewish Christianity of Ezra and his friends, who were the remaining leaders of the community, yielded to palace popularity and comfort and became acculturated into the official religion. According to Taddesse Tamrat, Ezra used this position "as a means of clearing the name of Estifanos [sic] and bringing an end to the persecution of his beleaguered community."[18]

After that, many Stephanites could come to court and receive holy orders in public. But even this did not change the views of the official clergy, and anti-Stephanite persecution continued to resume. The public image of the Stephanite "heresy" created by the official religious propaganda for over two centuries was too deeply rooted in the minds of the people: "The stories of the miracles of Mary against them were part of the regular reading in every little church. It was part of the religious duty of every good Christian to persecute them," and only the common shock of the Ottoman Turkish conquest under Amir Ahmed ibn Ibrahim (Gran) (1527-42) could give the Stephanites a "real chance of re-integration with the official church."[19]

Thus in this manner the end of the old Ethiopian tradition of Jewish Christianity came to a close. But it left its impression on that church for posterity, and the notable Hebraic-Judaic features of the church, that we have described elsewhere in this work, survive to our time.

---

18   Taddesse Tamrat. *Church and state in Ethiopia, 1270-1527*, Oxford : Clarendon Press, 1972.

19   Ibid.

Chapter 4

Teachings of the Ethiopian Church

As stated above, the Ethiopian Orthodox Church is a unique strand of Christianity that was deeply influenced by its isolation from the rest of Christendom, its early and sustained contact with Judiasm, and its African context, among other variables. This uniqueness is also apparent in its particular teachings on things such as the person of Christ, the Law, salvation and good works. While its formulations and particular configurations of Christianity is unique, it still maintains a strong 'family resemblance' with other Christian communities located around the globe. The following will attempt to highlight some of the distinctive teachings of the Ethiopian Orthodox Church as well as its teachings that bring it into relation with other Christian communities.

The *Täwahïdo* Church accepts the teachings of the first three ecumenical councils of Christendom: Nicea (325), Constantinople (381), and Ephesus (431). Hence it adheres to the Nicene Creed and the Nicene formula of the Trinity—One in Three, Three in One. But it rejects, as we observed earlier, the Council of Chalcedon (451) in which both the Eastern and Western Churches formulated the concept of the two natures in the one Person of Christ—human and divine. The Ethiopian Church holds that there were, to be sure, two natures before the incarnation, but only one after the union: the humanity being absorbed in the divinity. Hence the Ethiopian Church is wrongly characterized along with the Coptic Church of Egypt and the Jacobite Church of Syria, and the Armenian Orthodox Church and a few others as Miaphysite, worshiping Christ as one Person and of one Nature.

The internal stability of the church's Miaphysite Christology was not interrupted until the coming of the Portuguese Jesuits in the sixteenth century. Their influence brought fresh controversies concerning Christology. Thus, though there is still one official doctrine, called *Täwahïdo* (Miaphysite), stating the concept of the perfect unity of the divine and the human Christ, other formulations are now strongly supported, the basis of such passages as Jn 1:14 (kaio lohos srax regeneto).

Two of these, *Qebat* (Anointing) and *Tsega* (Grace), are especially significant. The first, associated with the Gojjam (Province of Gojjam) teachers, states that Jesus became a perfect man and perfect Savior by the anointing of the Holy Spirit in the Jordan River. The other doctrine, associated with Gondar (the 17th-century capital founded by Emperor Fasiledes and nicknamed "town of forty-four churches") and other monastic centers, holds that Christ was human by nature until he was changed at Jordan through a special act of Divine Grace. In the circles of sophisticated churchmen, these formulations can become very important.

The other dogmatic principles of the Ethiopian Church may be briefly summarized as follows: God is the Eternal Creator and Ruler of the Universe. The world is created through the Son (God's Word). The original good creation was corrupted through the Fall: "Because of the sins of our Father Adam and our Mother Eve ... We believe that we take all their sins upon us." In actual practice, however, very little emphasis is put on the concept of original sin, and man is blamed for his own committed sins. God sent his Son into the world to save man from eternal condemnation. Yet, in reality, the Church insists, salvation primarily comes by keeping the Ten Commandments. Christ will come again in the last days to judge the living and the dead. The dead will be raised, and sinners will be punished according to their deeds. Like the Greek Orthodox, the Ethiopian Church does not believe in Purgatory, a place where those who have died in faith will receive proportional punishment until they are purged for their sins. The souls of the dead are believed to be confined in a separate place called *Seol* (the Scriptural *Sheol*). Intercession may be sought in prayer to the dead. Prayers offered by and to Mary, the saints, and the angels are believed to be potent.

As briefly mentioned before, one individual feature of Ethiopian Christianity, which scholars have considered to be a peculiar Judaic trait, is the veneration of the *Tabot* or Ark of the Covenant. Already in the thirteenth century, Abu Salih wrote, "the Abyssinians possess also the Ark of the Covenant, in which are the two tablets of stone, inscribed by the finger of God with the commandments which he ordained for the children of Israel." As was prophesized in King Solomon's dream the first night he spent with Queen of Sheba, the Holy Ark moved from Israel to Ethiopia during the journey of their son Menelik. During Menelik's visit to his father in Jerusalem, the High Priest, Zadok, gave his son Azariah money to purchase a golden box to hold the Ark; Azariah then secretly took the box to the Temple, where an angel opened the doors for him. He then replaced the box with the Ark, which was carried to Ethiopia by Menelik's caravan of first-born sons of the nobles, princes, and priests of Israel, along with 1,000 chosen people from each of the Twelve Tribes of Israel. King Solomon, upon hearing of the Ark's disappearance, rode to Egypt to search for the Ark, but was too late.[1] He warned those with him to never tell of the loss of the Ark, which is why nothing is known of its whereabouts outside of Ethiopia. The Holy Ark of the Covenant has been kept in the sanctuary of the church of Tsion Mariam at Axum, considered the holiest of Ethiopia's churches.

Until recently, scholars have been interested in the central role of the Ark in Ethiopian Church as simply just one other curious Ethiopian Christian feature of the imitation of ancient Israelites. In particular, the colorful ceremonies accompanying the Ark at certain festivals are seen as the reminiscences of King David's dancing before the Ark when it was brought up to Jerusalem (II Samuel 6:14). But the Ark has been thought by some scholars as one form of the ubiquitous alter of Christendom. Others have suggested that it is no more than "la table d'auteil chretienne" or a mere "*tabula quadrangularis oblongata*," or some kind of alter such as the one whose extensive and interesting description is given in Hammerschmidt-Graf-Euringer.

The Armenian Abu Salih is one of several medieval writers who, in the early 13th century, noted the Ark's importance in the Ethiopian church. He gave the following very accurate description of the Ark's role in the church:

> The Abyssinians [Ethiopians] possess also the Ark of the Covenant, in which are the two tables of stone, inscribed by the Finger of God with the commandments which he ordained for the children of Israel. The Ark of the Covenant is placed upon the altar, but is not so wide as the altar; it is as high as the knee of a man, and is overlaid with gold; and upon its upper cover there are crosses of gold; and there are five precious stones upon it, one at each of the four corners, and one in the middle. The liturgy is celebrated upon the Ark four times in the year, within the palace of the king; and a canopy is spread over it when it is taken out from its own church to the church which is in the palace of the king; namely on the feast of the great Nativity, on the feast of the glorious Baptism, on the feast of the holy Resurrection, and on the feast of the illuminating Cross. And the Ark is attended and carried by a large number of Israelites descended from the family of the prophet David ...

Almost all of these words, recorded about 800 years before the present, could have been written in 2001. They describe succinctly the practices still prevalent in the Ethiopian church to this very day, albeit with replicas substituted for the original ark.

The role of the *Tabot* in Ethiopian Church thought is more than a simple *imitatio Israel*. It can rightly be compared to the Jewish *luhot ha-brit* and seen as

---

1   Giday, Belai. *Ethiopian Civilization*. Addis Ababa, 1992 (13).

the guarantor of the legitimacy of the Ethiopian Church and royal dynasty. The many *Tabots* in the thousands of the churches of Ethiopia today are more than some architectural object. They may indeed not be the physical repository of the law or be a legitimate copy of the Ark of the Covenant as Ethiopian Christians believe; however, the *Tabot* is *par excellence* the symbol of the Law. Its veneration signifies the centrality of the law in the Ethiopian Church. Throughout Ethiopic literature we find it associated, actually and symbolically, with Moses, the *ba'ala heg*, the Law-Giver, and arch prophet. A story in *Gadla Uriel* "The Acts of Uriel" tells of the lions that met certain messengers carrying three *Tabots* from one bishop to another. The lions fell on their faces and confessed "Zion, the *Tabot* of the Law of God whom Moses saw you in the fashion of wood..." Thus, even a beast recognized its association with the law and Moses. The *Tabot* is par excellence God's *Tabot* given to Moses as the holy temple of the Law for all believers.

The central role of the *Tabot* within the church is equally supported by and contributes to the church's as well as culture's emphasis on the centrality of the Law. Ethiopian theological understanding of the role of the Law, like that of the Church of Peter and James in Jerusalem, and in contradiction from that of Paul and early gentile Christianity (cf. Acts 15:1ff.), is closer to that of Judaism. The Law (*Orit*) comprises, as in Judaism, the civil, social, criminal, and moral rules of conduct. It embraces every aspect of human activity, including the keeping of the Sabbath, circumcision, and the dietary prescription. The true believer must willingly submit to the whole range of these teachings and to the demands of the Law.

The Ethiopic term *Orit*, like the Hebrew *Torah* or Aramaic *Orayta*, denotes the whole range of the Law, specifically as grounded in the Pentateuch. But the Decalogue is thought to be the heart of the Law. This should not surprise us, for the Decalogue also has a special position in Judaism as well. It is one of the early pericopes of the Hebrew Bible to have been incorporated into the daily Jewish prayers (B. Ber. 12a; Jer. Ber. 1:3c). Even today when it is read in the synagogues, in the assigned Exodus *parasha* Yitro, it is intoned with a special lofty aura. The Decalogue is fundamental among the precepts of the torah. Its supreme importance is already expressed in the Bible, which speaks of its revelation in the midst of thunder and lightening, fire and smoke in the mountain and the sounding of the shofar. Philo regards the Decalogue as the general heading of the Law under which the specific commands given to Mosses are to be grouped. Although the Apostle Paul refers to the Decalogue separately (Rom. 2:20ff; 7:7; 13:8-10), in his general usage of *nomos* (vouos) he does not make any essential difference between it and the whole Jewish Torah (I Cor. 9:9; 24:21; 3:19; Rom. 7:22, 25; 8:7). But some early Palestinian and Syrian Christians attached special importance to the Decalogue as having a special divine revelation—the reason why it may have been dropped from the daily Jewish prayers. The same view is expressed in *Mäs'hafä Berhan*, according to which the Decalogue is assigned a special distinction in that it alone is written by the very hand of God.

The special place accorded to the Decalogue goes beyond its essential and intrinsic importance. Even its accidental and extrinsic form is significant. Each and every one of the Ten commandments is weighty both in respect to its inherent value as well as its external form, namely, the specific number of the letters of the alphabet in which it was and still is written. In *Mäs'hafä Berhan*, "The Book of Light," it is pointed out that over two-hundred letters of the alphabet were used in the command to keep the Sabbath. Using a well-known ancient Jewish exegetical method and philosophy the religious force of the law is brought out and underlined.

The special significance attached to the Decalogue in Ethiopian Church theology is consistent with mainstream Judaic thought. More significantly, however, is the importance attached to the whole (Pentateuch) Law. A 15th century Ethiopic mystico-theological work known as the *Book of the Mysteries of Heaven and Earth* makes the following explicit point:

> But we may marvel in this that all *the Laws (hegg) of our God shall abide forever* [emphasis mine] and they shall never be abrogated. Enoch says thus, "I saw fourteen trees which did not shed their leaves; but all the other trees were dry with fallen leaves. "Abba Bahyla Mikael asks, "What are these fourteen trees about which Enoch spoke?" The Holy Spirit [responds and] says, "They are the Decalogue of the Orit, the Covenant of Noah, the Circumcision of the Fathers, the Priesthood of Melchisedeq, and the Baptism of John.[2]

Many early Christian writers, especially Paul, give a generally inferior position to the Law (cf. Gal. 3:19; Heb. 2:2). Paul describes his view about it in various ways: the Law is paidagogos (Gal. 3:24); it is powerless (Rom. 3:20-21, 27-28; Gal. 3:16; Phil. 3:9); and it is tyrannical (Phil. 3:6). In contrast, the Ethiopic Church writings give the Law an undeniably basic and central role. They hold that the Law is equal to the Gospel in essence, and in its role in human life. This view is expressed in various places throughout Ethiopic literature, often by means of symbolic interpretations.

In an Ethiopic commentary on the Gospels, it is propounded that the Church is based upon two foundations: the *Iota* and the *Delta* of the Hebrew letter *yod*. The *Iota* is the Law; the *Delta* is the Gospel. *Yod*, the tenth letter of the alphabet is also the tenth letter in an old Ethiopic order of the alphabet; but

---

2   Mystery of Heaven and Earth.

in another equally old order of the Ethiopic alphabet, T is the tenth. *Yod*, whose numerical value is ten, symbolizes the Decalogue, in particular, and the whole law, in general, but T is the symbol of the cross, and, therefore, the Gospel.

According to *Mäs'hafä Berhan*, a 15th century Ethiopian theological work, the Law is not only equal to the Gospel in importance but, as in Judaic thought, it is the cornerstone of human conduct, indeed the *raison d'etre* of life. Furthermore, according to the *Book of Light* the Law is the *Iota* whose form is single and whose shape is unique. It is written and engraved by the hand of God, the hand of fire, upon stone tablets. It is therefore, changeless and endless. The Iota is not only a letter whose numerical value is ten but also the smallest letter of the alphabet. Hence, it symbolizes not only the Decalogue, but also at the same time both the importance of the minutest details of the law as well as its wholeness.

Paul emphasized the temporality and finiteness of the law. The dispensation of the Law was[3] at an end (Rom. 6:4; Gal. 3:13, 25) having ceased to be operative for those whom he claimed have died with Jesus (Gal. 2:19; Rom. 7:4; Col. 2:20) through Baptism (Gal. 2:21), and who share in Jesus' fulfillment of the Law (Rom. 3:31; cf. 8:34ff.). The Ethiopic exegesis of the letter *Iota* in the *Book of Light* and the ideas ensuing from it underlie a different theology. The doctrine that is made emphatically in *Mäs'hafä Berhan* is repeated in various ways throughout Ethiopic literature, in biblical commentaries, hagiographies, and theological work, which states that the law is infinite and eternal.

The view that the law is mediated by angels is found in the *Book of Jubilees*, but without any deviation from basic Jewish norm of its divine origin, nor from the claim, found also in *Mäs'hafä Berhan* that it was written by the very hand of God. On the other hand, Paul asserts the angelic origin of the Law as a means of emphasizing its inferiority (Gal. 3:19; II Cor. 3:3). He does so particularly when he relates it to the elemental spirits of the Universe (Gal. 4:3, 9; Col. 2:8, 20).

In general, the Pauline contentions are that the Law has been abolished, abrogated, or minimized (Rom. 3:21; 7:4-6), that it is weak and powerless (Rom. 3:20-21, 27-28; Gal. 3:116; Phil. 3:9), tyrannical (Phil. 3:6), and that it makes people sin more providing the occasion for it (Rom. 7:11) or enhances it (Rom. 7:5). If the Apostle indeed means what he says by these and similar pronouncements, then this particular understanding of the Law, while it has become part of the theological thinking of Western Christendom, is not part of the Ethiopian Church.

However, it must be said, that Paul is a very important figure in Ethiopian Christian theology. In fact, his views about the Law: that Jesus is the *telos* of the Law, the prototype of perfect obedience (Rom. 10:4), that the Law reveals sin as

---

3   Acts of St. Filimona, CSCO.

disobedience to God (Rom. 5:13ff; 3:20), and that it is the Law of God (Rom. 7:22, 25; 8:7) are wholly within the purview of Ethiopian theological thought. In short, Ethiopian theologians hold the apostle Paul and his writings in very high regard but without relinquishing views held in opposition to him.

The centrality of the Law in Ethiopian theological thought is expressed not only in its theoretical conception, but also in its practical functioning. Contrary to Paul (Gal. 3:2) and the above-mentioned generally accepted Western theological views, the Ethiopian Church specifically teaches that it is necessary and expedient to keep the Law. It holds that the final judgment will be evaluated on the basis of one's merit; and that salvation comes through good works as much as through faith. In the introduction to the Amharic theological treatises entitled *Mäs'hafä Haymanot Wämïgbar, The Book of Faith and Good Works* or *Nägära Haymanot, The Word of Faith* it is propounded that "Faith is the foundation, and good works is the building . . . faith without works and works without faith is useless . . . It is like a body without soul . . . good works and faith are one."[4] In Ethiopic theological thought, the formula "salvation through faith and good works" is unequivocal. Neither faith by itself nor good works by itself is adequate or sufficient for salvation. The Acts of St. Filimona (239-246) is equally assertive about the role of the Law and the Gospel. It says:

> From the single double Law, the Law of the Orit and the Word of
> the Gospel flows the wine of life--the life-giving wine—from which
> the prophets drank. The single double Law is the sea of spiritual
> milk which bears and nourishes the fruit of righteousness.

In Jewish *Mishnah* (*Pirqe Abot* 2:8), we read, "He who has acquired the words of the Torah has acquired for himself the life of the world to come." It is startling that we read an almost literal quotation of this in the Ethiopic *Mäs'hafä Milad*. In this work, we find, "those who read the Orit, the Prophets, Kings, and the Gospel in their life-time, inherit the Kingdom of God." Those who do not keep that which is written in the Law of Moses, "their lot will be in the fire of hell." The wise virgins (Mt. 22:1ff.) are those who, having believed and baptized, do good works; the foolish one are those who having believed and been baptized do not do good works. The Law gives spiritual sustenance and life for the flesh and the soul. Everyone who fulfills it fulfills all righteousness and overcomes sin.

A work called *Mäs'hafä Milad* (The Book of Generation) has the following interesting polemic against the anti-nomian view:

---

4   Mäs'hafä Milad.

Hear, o you apostate, if it is possible for you to desecrate the Sabbath, and say "I cannot believe in the One God the Father who wrote the Iota, which is the Decalogue, with his hands, because the Israelites worship (believe) it and believe in the faith of the Orit, and [because] they celebrate the Sabbath." Is it possible for you, therefore, to say that you do not wish to cooperate with the Jews because they believe in the One Father? We also ask you, were the Apostles not one with the Jews, and did they not also teach the Jews?[5]

In addition to its teachings on the Law, Christology, and the Tabot, the Ethiopian Church teaches and practices the seven sacraments, known as "mysteries." These sacraments do not work *ex opere operato*; they do not function miraculously regardless of the recipient's attitude as in the Roman Catholic Church. Whoever receives them must be worthy and have a worthy faith in their effectiveness. Among these, baptism, confirmation, and Eucharist are familiar to most Christians. In addition there are penance (confession of sin to the Church and repentance through fasting and humiliation); unction (for the sick or dying); holy orders (ordination of bishops and priests, deacons and other church officials); and holy matrimony (the covenant of marriage).

Baptism takes place forty days after birth in the case of boys and eighty days in the case of girls. According to tradition, these two periods of time before baptism correspond respectively to the time that lapsed before Adam and Eve received the Holy Spirit. However, the custom is more likely to be of Hebraic origin or sanction (cf. Leviticus 12:1-8.) During the performance of the rite, the priest first pronouncing a church name for the child; blows into its face in order to drive out evil spirits; then, he anoints it on the forehead, breast, shoulders and so on, traditionally on thirty-seven places; and finally, with the assistance of a deacon turning it to the east, he pours water over it from a vase and washes it with his other hand, while the godfather (or godmother if it is a girl) holds up the child's right thumb. In the case of an adult baptism, which is rare, it is performed with triple immersion.

The sacrament of confirmation is administered immediately following baptism. As before the baptismal washing, the child is again anointed with the holy chrism on his eyes, lips, nose, ears and so on. Then the priest is supposed to bestow the Holy Spirit by placing his hands upon the infant, then dressing it in a white garment, and placing a crown upon its head. Confirmation is concluded by giving the child communion. Before the parents are dismissed to hold a family feast, every infant is laced with a neck-cord of silk or cotton (mahtab) - the distinguishing mark of all Ethiopian Christians. The godfather (godmother for girls), generally referred to as "Christian father" (Kristina-abat), is impor-

---

5   Mäs'hafä Haymanot Wämïgbar, The Book of Faith and Good Works or Nägära Haymanot.

tant in Ethiopian culture; and, should a godfather die without an offspring his godson can become his legal heir.

The sacrament of the Eucharist, celebrated at daily services, is very elaborate, taking place in the solemn atmosphere of religious singing, dancing, ringing of bells, rattling of cymbals, and beating of drums. Communion itself is administered towards the end of the mass, at the ringing of bells under multicolored umbrellas. With the exception of priests, monks, children under the age of thirteen, and the aged, the laity seldom partake of the elements of the sacrament. Almost invariably the majority of the people pray outside the church and the few who want to worship inside (which is really the outer circle of the church building) must take off their shoes. The rules of the Ethiopian Church prescribe that each communicant must wash his mouth thoroughly before leaving the church; and he must refrain for a whole day from spitting, traveling, talking or making restless movements. Communion bread must be made from unleavened bread during Ba'al-Matslat ("Feast of the Leavened Bread" corresponding to Passion Week) and must always be kept in the Ark (see below).

The sacrament of unction is administered both to those in extremis as well as to those who are simply sick. The rite itself, which may take place at home or in a church, in the presence of generally seven priests (but before even one prist), is primarily a rite of anointing (with oil or water) preceded by a confession and absolution of the sick or dying person and followed by the administration of communion. Seven wicks are lighted respectively as tile prayers, consisting of seven parts, are said. If a person is dying, he makes a will given to the priests orally at the same time in the presence of witnesses. One may mention here also important Ethiopian customs of mourning: the shaving of the head, the sitting on the ground for a month, and the Memorial Banquets (tazkar) held in the churches in honor of the dead. The banquets occur on the thirtieth, fortieth, eightieth days and after the sixth and twelfth months of the funeral.

The sacrament of penance is an integral part of Ethiopian life. Each couple, upon marriage, chooses, preferably, a known family priest to serve as their "spiritual father" (näfs abbat). He visits them regularly and hears confessions, prescribes penance, blesses their house by sprinkling holy water, and serves as an advisor. Confession is demanded as a requisite for the sacrament of unction mentioned above, and those who fail to make a deathbed confession and receive absolution are denied burial in a churchyard. Though regular times of confession are not fixed, the Fast of Lent (Hudade) and Good Friday ("Siqlaät" - "Crucifixion") are appointed as special periods of confession. Specifically on the afternoon of Good Friday, universal confession, publicly and physically manifested in the form of repeated deep bows above the waist, is held in all churches: each confessor will approach a priest and utter a number - understanding that the number designates how many "bows of confession" or "prostrations" (sigdät) he wishes to make. The average is about forty by each penitent. The priest strikes the penitent over the shoulder with the branch of a special tree called wäyra as the sign that his sins are forgiven. To see a multitude bowing, prostrating and rising one by one at varying speeds is quite a spectacle. During regular services, confessions are made by saying a threefold *kyrie* each twelve times as counted with the right thumb on the twelve knuckles of the four fingers of the right hand.

Since 1959, the chief Ethiopian ecclesiastic is the Patriarch (Abuna), now a native Ethiopian appointed from among, and installed by, the bishops. The Patriarch in turn ordains the bishops and the priests. There are many religious leaders and functionaries in Ethiopia who do not receive ordination (see below).

Holy matrimony is the seventh sacrament and is solemnized with a mass. Since such consecrated weddings are considered perpetually binding, only priests and already married couples having long experienced happy union, solemnize their marriages in holy matrimony. For the rest, the church encourages, recommends, and blesses civil marriages that usually take place in the home of the bride in the presence of relatives, elders, and family priests.

Chapter 5

The Bible in Ethiopia

The translation of the *Mäṣaḥǝft Qǝddusat* or *Qǝddusat Mäṣaḥǝft* (hereafter Holy Scriptures) into the Ge'ez language — generally classified as a member of the southern branch of the family of ancient Semitic languages — was completed in early Christian times around the middle of the fourth century CE.[1] The Ge'ez canon includes the Hebrew Bible (the Christian Old Testament), late Second Temple Jewish literature (known as Apocrypha and Pseudepigrapha), and the Christian New Testament. The Ge'ez language, known among western scholars as Ethiopic, thus became one of the first seven languages of the ancient world to receive the Holy Scriptures. None of the European languages shares such a high distinction, with the exception of Greek and Latin.

The translation of the Holy Scriptures was of paramount importance in Ethiopian history. It gave rise to an extensive body of ancient Ethiopic literature and the evolution of a distinct Ethiopian culture. Today, Ge'ez/Ethiopic literature represents an invaluable source not only for the understanding of African civilization, but also for the study of the transmission of the biblical text, as well as the study of several of the major religions of the world: Judaism, Christianity, Islam and the traditional African religions.

Any glance at scholarly publications of the last five hundred years will reveal the high position Ge'ez holds among ancient languages as an important repository and nurturer of many ancient literary works. The large body of venerated works, such as hagiographies, chronicles, homilies, and calendaric and theological treatises, all offer insight into the history of early Christianity. To cite two examples, the Dominican Wansleben[2] in the late seventeenth

---

1   About a dozen South Semitic languages are still spoken in Ethiopia: Amharic, Tigrinya, Tigre, Gurage (several dialects), Harari, Argobba, Gafat, etc.

2   *Ludolf, Hiob*, *Lexicon Aethiopico-Latinum*, Ed. by J. M. Wansleben, London 1661; Nouvelle Relation En forme de Journal, D'vn Voyage Fait en Egypte. Par le P. Vansleb, R.D., en 1672 & 1673. Paris. chez Estienne Michallet, 1677.

century discovered the liturgical usage of the language when he came across the 'Apostolic Church Order' of Hippolytus of Rome (early third century).[3] Likewise, in his recent work on Ethiopian astronomy and calendars, the late and noted historian of mathematics Otto Neugebauer has shown that the Judaeo-Hellensitic calendar that served as the basis of the early Christian calendar is preserved only in the Ethiopic work known as *Mäs'hafä Hasab.*[4] Furthermore, the examination of Ethiopic literature may shed light not only on the history of early Christianity, but also on the Jewish legacy. There is a wellspring of Ethiopic works connected to early Jewish literature, as well as to the history of Jewish communities in Ethiopia and Southern Arabia. In my own study of *Mäs'hafä Berhan*, a fifteenth-century Sabbath homily, I have demonstrated the preservation of certain halachic gleanings in Ethiopic literature (that is, relating to legal parts of the Talmud).[5]

Finally, it is well known that Muhammad's earliest followers sought refuge in Ethiopia. The scholarly works of the last century have in fact shown that numerous fundamental terms found in Islamic literature (*mäs'haf, mänbar, tabot, ta'ot*) are originally classical Ethiopic biblical expressions. It is indeed not unlikely that future investigations and studies of Ethiopic literature may shed new light on the Christian and Jewish components of early Islamic theology.

The translation of the Holy Scriptures into Ge'ez so early would not have been possible were it not for the development of writing in Ethiopia in ancient times, and especially alphabetic writing. Since the seventeenth century, scholars have deliberated on the origin of the Ethiopic alphabet. Theories include a foundation in Samaritan (Ludolphus, Silvestre),[6] Syriac (Kopp),[7] or Sabaean (Glaser).[8] We know that Ethiopic is a cursive form of monumental Sabaean, and

---

3   The translation efforts continued in 1691 with Ludolf, who published fragments along with a Latin translation. Further fragments were published and translated in 1895 by Franz Xaver von Funk, in 1848 by Tattam, and in 1883 by Lagarde. The original text of the Church order has yet to be found, but all indications suggest that it was in Greek.

4   O. Neugebauer, *Ethiopic Astronomy and Computus* (Vienna: Verlag der Österreichischen Akademie der Wissenschaften, 1979).

5   E. Isaac, *A New Text-Critical Introduction to Mäs'hafä Berhan* (Leiden: Brill, 1973).

6   H. Ludolf, *A New History of Ethiopia. Being a Full and Accurate Description of the Kingdom of Abessinia, Vulgarly, though Erroneously called the Empire of Prester John* (London: Samuel Smith, 1682).

7   Silvestre de Sacy, *Mémoires d'histoire et de littérature orientales*, Paris, *1818; Mémoire de Acadademie des Inscriptiones.* vol. xlix),

8   E. Glaser, *Die Abessinier in Arabien und Afrika* (Munich: Franz, 1895). See also F. Hommel, *Süd-arabische Chrestomathie* (Munich: Franz, 1893); and C. C. Rossini, *Storia d'Etiopia* (Milano and Bergamo: Instituto Italiano D'Arti Grafiche, 1928). *Recent Research in Bible Lands: its progress and results,* ed.by Herman V. Hilprecht (Philadephia, J.D.Wattles & Co., 1898)

hence in the immediate southern branch of Proto-Sinaitic/Proto-Canaanite, the first known alphabet. In other words, it is the sister alphabet of the Phoenician (Canaanite) script. Proto-Ethiopic inscriptions were read from right to left or from top to bottom as well as in the boustrophedon manner (i.e., alternately from right to left and left to right), but owing to Christian influences, the Ethiopians standardized the direction of reading and writing from left to right, as is still the rule today. They also vocalized the alphabet, making it one of the first Semitic scripts to be so treated. This enabled the priests and the ordinary person to read the Bible with facility. The order of the letters of the alphabet was probably like that of Phoenician, but gradually a new order was created for reasons not yet fully known.

The Holy Scriptures of the Ethiopian Orthodox Täwahïdo Christian Church — the largest of the oriental Orthodox Christian churches; the name means 'being made one' or 'being one' — consist of eighty-one books: (a) the 'twenty-four' books of the Hebrew Bible, including the Torah, Nabi'im (the Prophets), and Ketubim (the Hagiographa or Writings), excluding only Lamentations; (b) the twenty-seven books of Christian New Testament; (c) the books known as apocryphal or deutrocanonical by the rest of Christendom; and (d) the *Masaheft Henoch* (the Book of Enoch) and *Mäs'hafä Kufale* (the Jubilees).[9] According to another tradition of the Ethiopian Orthodox *Täwahïdo* Church, the Holy Scriptures consist of eighty-two books, adding the work known as the *Synodos*, a compilation of the decisions and documents of the early Church councils, such as the Nicean Council with its explanation and interpretation of the Nicene Creed.

Today there are also numerous other versions of the *Mäs'haf Qïddus,* or the Holy Bible as it is known in the West, in modern Ethiopian vernaculars. Among these are the *Machafa Qulqulu* in Afaan Oromo, the most widely spoken languages of modern Ethiopia; the *Mäs'haf Qïddus* in Amharic, the Ethiopian official language; and *Mäs'haf Qïddus* in Tigrinya, the important language of northern Ethiopia and the official language of the state of Eritrea. Parts of the Bible are also found in translation in numerous other languages of Ethiopia and the Horn of Africa.

History of Translation: According to an accepted Ethiopian Orthodox Täwahïdo Church tradition, the Hebrew Bible had already been translated from into Ge'ez shortly after the visit of the Queen of Sheba to Jerusalem. The descendants of the Jews who came to Ethiopia with her son Menelik preserved the text

---

9   Direct numerical comparison between the contents of the Ethiopian and other scriptural canons is difficult, owing to the varying systems of sub-dividing books or collections of books. Traditionally, Hebrew Bible is said to consist of 24 books (5 of the Torah, 8 of the Prophets, 11 of the Writings), but these 'expand' to 39, when the sub-division of Samuel, Kings, Chronicles, Ezra-Nehemiah and the Minor Prophets is taken into account.

faithfully for centuries. This is in accordance with the belief that Ethiopia 'became Christian' a thousand years before Jesus Christ! The accepted tradition claims that 'Belief in One G-d, the G-d of Israel, and circumcision were introduced to Ethiopia by the Queen of Sheba, Baptism and the Eucharist by the Ethiopian eunuch. Subsequently, the New Testament was translated from the Greek language in early Christian times. However, another tradition of the *Tǎwahǐdo* Church, regarded by scholars as closer to the truth, holds that the Holy Scriptures were translated by *tǎsa'tu qǐddusat*, the Nine Saints, who came from Syria in the fifth century, seeking refuge from persecution. The mid-fourth century is the time of the Abuna Salama, the first Patriarch or Metropolitan of Ethiopia, who is credited with the conversion of the then Emperor Ezana and the Christianization of Ethiopia. Although Abuna Salama was of Syrian origin, the Patriarch Athanasius of Alexandria installed him as the Bishop of Ethiopia.

My belief is that the first rendering of the Holy Scriptures into the Ethiopic/ Ge'ez language began to be made sometime before the middle of the fourth century CE. Most scholars would agree that the translations and revisions were completed by the beginning of the sixth century. The period from the fourth to the sixth centuries is probably the most magnificent era of ancient Ethiopian culture, and the translation of the Holy Scriptures into the then official language is the major achievement of this African civilization. Critical scholarly textual editions of the western Holy Bible generally include variant readings of the Ge'ez/ Ethiopic Holy Scriptures, among less than a dozen early biblical versions.

Vorlage: During the last five hundred years, numerous heated disputes and conflicting theories developed among Ethiopic scholars regarding the Vorlage of the Holy Scriptures and the time and identity of the original translators. Prominent Ethiopists such as H. Ludolf (1624–1704), A. Dillmann (1823–94), T. Noldeke (1836–1930), and F. Praetorius (1847–1927), to mention a few, have offered their own divergent theories. There is a general consensus, however, that the Ge'ez Bible was translated from the Greek Septuagint used in Alexandria at the time of early Christianity. It is believed, too, that the New Testament was rendered from the Greek text about the same time. A spurious Ethiopic reference to an Arabic translation is found in the *Synaxarium* (a liturgical collection of saints' lives) for the twenty-first of the month of Nahese, but most likely this refers to a later revision from Arabic probably under the influence of the Coptic Abuna Salama of the fourteenth century.

Ludolf suggests that the translation was completed over a span of time, not just at the beginning of the Christian period in the fourth century.[10] The distin-

---

10   H. Ludolf, *Historia Aethiopica sive brevis et succincta descriptio regni Habessinorum* (Frankfurt, 1681), III, cap. 4, pp. 2–7, and H. Ludolf, *Commentarius ad suam Historiam Aethiopicam* (Frankfurt: Zunnerus, 1691), p. 295 ff.

guished Ethiopist scholar Dillmann[11] theorized the existence of at least three distinct groups of Ge'ez/Ethiopic manuscripts of the Hebrew Bible — those that depend on the original translation from the Septuagint; those subject to revision based on Hebrew; and those with later texts revised according to the Septuagint. He holds that the translators' Greek was not very good, which was the reason for a second version, produced with the help of Hebrew and other Semitic scholars, to correct errors of translation. Therefore, the Ge'ez biblical text follows the Hebrew but the language is faithful to the Septuagint, even down to the word order. I have myself argued elsewhere that the translators were Jewish Christians who spoke Jewish Aramaic, but used the Septuagint as their Vorlage.[12] Consequently, they imported several important Jewish Aramaic religious expressions into Ge'ez/Ethiopic in their work. A doctoral thesis by Dr. Mikael for the Hebrew University on the translation of the Holy Scripture to Ethiopic also argues for a Septuagint Vorlage, but with the possible use of an additional Hebrew Vorlage.[13] A. Rahlfs,[14] who is not an Ethiopist, assumes the influence of Alexandria on Ethiopia and holds the Ethiopic version to be dependent on the Hesychian recension, but this view is generally rejected. Regarding the New Testament, L. Hackspill,[15] although also not an Ethiopist, rightly theorizes that the Greek Vorlage has a Syrian, not Alexandrian, origin. He also believes that several translators made the translation around the year 500 AC. A. Voobus, on the basis of quotations found in Ethiopic literature, favors the Syriac Vorlage for the Ge'ez New Testament,[16] a view supported by F. C. Burkitt.[17]

Editions of the Ge'ez Bible: To date, there is no complete critical edition of the Ethiopic Holy Scriptures. Several printings of one part or another of them

---

11   A. Dillmann, *Biblia Veteris Testamenti Aethiopica*, 5 vols. (Leipzig: Vogel, 1853–94), II.1, p. 3 ff.) See also J. J. Herzog, *Realencyklopädie fur protestantische Theologie und Kirche,* 24 vols., 3rd ed. (Leipzig; Hinrichs, 1896–1913), III, p. 87 ff.

12   E. Isaac, 'An Obscure Component in Ethiopian Church History', *Le Muséon* 85 (1972), 225–258.

13   Gebre Yesus Gebre Mikael, PhD. The Basis of the Ge'ez Bible Translation, Unpublished Doctoral Thesis (in Hebrew), Hebrew University of Jerusalem, 1978.

14   A. Rahlfs, *Septuaginta-Studien I–III*, 2nd ed., enlarged by R. Hanhart (Gottingen: Vandenhoeck and Ruprecht, 1965), I, p. 87, and II, p. 235.

15   L. Hackspill, 'Die athiopische Evangelienubersetzung (Math. I–X), in *Zeitschrift fur Assyriologie* 11 (1896), pp. 117–96, 367–88.

16   See the two relevant works by A. Voobus, *Die Spuren eines alteren aethiopischen Evangelientextes im Lichte der literarischen Monumente* (Stockholm: Estonian Theological Society in Exile, 1951) and *Early Versions of the New Testament* (Stockholm: Estonian Theological Society in Exile, 1954).

17   F. C. Burkitt, 'Text and Versions', in *Encyclopedia Biblica,* ed. T. K. Cheyne and J. S. Black, 4 vols. (London: Black and New York: Macmillan, 1899–1907), IV, col. 5012.

have appeared since the Renaissance, however. These include the first printing of an Ethiopic biblical text, the 1513 Psalter, by Johannes Potken,[18] the Cologne German scholar and papal secretary. This was followed in 1701 by the first, more or less critical edition of Psalms, *Psalterium Davidis aethiopice et latine* by Hiob Ludolf.[19] Meanwhile, three Ethiopian monks had published the Ethiopic New Testament in 1548 in Rome.[20] Among them was the influential Tasfa Seyon or 'Petrus Aethiopus' who left an indelible mark in Europe in respect of Ethiopian culture. In the late nineteenth century, Augustus Dillmann, published the Octateuch, Samuel, Kings and the Apocrypha,[21] followed by Johann Bachmann, who published Isaiah, Lamentations, Obadiah and Malachi.[22] And early in the twentieth century, J. O. Boyd, published Genesis to Leviticus.[23] There is a useful four-volume Ge'ez Holy Scriptures published in 1926 by the Catholic Mission in Eritrea (under Coelestinus Catteneo, Apostolic Vicar to Eritrea), at the Franciscan Printing House. It is an eclectic edition, consisting of the Pentateuch (vol. I), Kings, Chronicles, Ezra and Nehemiah (vol. II), the Prophets and the Apocryphal books, 1–2 Maccabees (vol. III), and Tobit, Judith, Esther, Job, the Psalms, and 'Solomon's books' —Proverbs, Ecclesiastes, Song of Songs, Wisdom of Solomon, Wisdom of Sirach (vol. IV). The Bible Society published a New Testament text in Leipzig in 1907 (reprinted 1957). The Ethiopia Orthodox Täwahïdo Church has promised a critical edition of the whole Ge'ez Holy Scriptures, but to date it has put out only a general edition of the Octateuch, the Book of Enoch, and Jubilees. In 1996, Oscar Löfgren, who did a study of the Book of Daniel, proposed a critical edition at the Third International Conference of Ethiopian studies at Addis Ababa. So far, such a work has not appeared.[24]

---

18   J. Potken, *Alphabetum seu potius syllabarium literarum Chaldaearum. Psalterium Chaldaeum* (Rome, 1513).

19   H. Ludolf, *Psalterium Davidis aethiopice et latine cum duobus impressis et tribus MSStis codicibus diligenter collatum et emendatum* (Frankfurt: Zunner und Helwig, 1701).

20   *Testamentum Novum cum Epistola Pauli ad Hebraeos... quae omnia Frater Petrus Aethiops ... imprimi curavit* (Rome, 1548).

21   A. Dillman, *Biblia Veteris Testamenti Aethiopica*, 5 vols. (Leipzig: Vogel, 1853–94).

22   J. Bachmann, *Der Prophet Jesaia nach der aethiopischen Bibelubersetzung* (Berlin: Felber, 1893).

23   J. O. Boyd, *The Octateuch in Ethiopic, According to theText of the Paris Codex, with the Variants of Five Other MSS. In Bibliotheca Abessinica*, 2 vols. (Leiden and Princeton: Brill, 1909–11).

24   O. Löfgren, 'The Necessity of a Critical Edition of the Ethiopian Bible', in *Proceedings of the Third International Conference of Ethiopian Studies, Addis Ababa 1966* (Addis Ababa: Institute of Ethiopian Studies, 1969), pp. 161–7.

It may be noted that a large number of Ge'ez Ethiopic biblical manuscripts are in the British Library, the Paris Bibliothèque Nationale, the Vatican Library, the Ethnological Museum in Berlin and other German collections in Munich, Leiden and Bonn, the National Library of Russia in St. Petersburg, the Ethiopian Orthodox Täwahïdo Church Monastery, the Deir Sultan Monastery in Jerusalem, and the Princeton University Garrett Collection (catalogued by this author), among others. An important manuscript of the Ethiopic New Testament of the fourteenth century is in the Morgan Library in New York City. Nowadays we have large collections of microfilms of Ethiopian manuscripts worldwide, among which there are those in the Ethiopian Microfilm Manuscript Library (EMML), Addis Ababa, the Bayerische Staatsbibliothek in Munich, and the Smithsonian in Washington, DC, along with smaller collections in other libraries.

THE BOOKS OF ENOCH AND JUBILEES: Even more important is that Ethiopic preserved many ancient writings that have been lost in the original languages. The most distinguished examples of these, without doubt, are the Book of Enoch and the Book of Jubilees of the late Second Temple period. These works exist today in their entirety only in Ethiopic, and are still the subject of richly deserved worldwide scholarly attention. In fact, in the eighteenth century, when James Bruce first brought some manuscripts of the Book of Enoch to Europe, the impact it had on the scholarly world was like the excitement generated by the discovery of the Dead Sea scrolls in the twentieth century. Like the scrolls, the Book of Enoch offers valuable insight into the religious and cultural milieu of the time of Jesus and his first followers.

More than any other Ge'ez Bible books, the Book of Enoch and the Book of Jubilees are widely studied, edited and translated. Jubilees is an exposition on *Bereshit* (Genesis), considered by scholars as the first written *midrashic* work, a precursor of the Temple Scroll of Qumran that Yigal Yadin edited. The Book of Enoch, or as some scholars call it the 'Five Books of Enoch', is to a great extent an apocalyptic work containing Jewish religious and 'theological' thought of the late Second Temple period. It is named for Enoch, whom the Hebrew Bible (Gen. 5:18–24) describes as one who 'walked with G-d....'; some later generations of Jews believed that Enoch ascended into heaven (the first to do so and the prototype of Elijah and Jesus), where he saw all the mysteries of time and space and recorded them in a book.

The influence of the book is all over Jewish theological literature and thought. It surpasses all other extra canonical Jewish books, including the Apocrypha, other pseudepigraphic works, and Qumran literature, in being the most fundamental to our understanding of the late Second Temple Jewish religious worldview. The Essenes, in particular, used Enoch as scripture, as we learn from the Aramaic fragments of the book discovered at Kirbet Qumran. They incorporated its theology into their teachings, as did some Tannaitic rabbis. About 100 years ago, R. H. Charles, the Oxford scholar of Enoch, wrote: 'In fact the history of the development of the higher theology during the two centuries before the Christian era could not be written without the Book of Enoch.'[25] That higher theology is the foundation of later Judaism, Christianity, and Islam. The late Gershom Sholem of Hebrew University, in his *Major Trends in Jewish Mysticism*, claimed that the book is the basis for later Jewish mystical thought, and the Kabbalah.[26]

For Ethiopic literature, the Book of Enoch is like Pushkin for Russian literature and Shakespeare for English literature. The teachings and literary ideas of the book have left an indelible mark on *zenas* (chronicles), *gadles* (acts or great deeds of saints), *malks* (physiognomic poems and hymns), especially *gadles*, and on other Ethiopian literary traditions and cultural expressions, metaphors, and language as a whole. In other words, Enoch is *par excellence* the basic source of Ethiopian literary idioms. The Jews who came to Ethiopia must be among those who held Enoch as precious religious and spiritual work, and the Ethiopians inherited their legacy.[27]

The corpus of literature related to these the Books of Enoch and Jubilees is vast and numerous pages could be written about it. What is important is that Ethiopians consider the two works to be fully integral parts of the Holy Scriptures.

THE BIBLE IN MODERN ETHIOPIAN LANGUAGES: In the Amharic language, Asselin de Cherville, French consul at Cairo, produced the first translation of the Bible between 1810 and 1820; it appeared in 1840 (reprinted 1842).[28] A newer edition was published in three volumes in 1871–3 by the missionary J. L. Krapf, with the help of Ethiopian scholars. Another Amharic version of the Bible was published in 1962 by order of Emperor Haile Sellassie. More recently, in 1992–3, Hiruye Tsige and his wife Genet prepared for the Ethiopian Bible Society under Ato Kebede Mamo, the director, a computerized Amharic Bible. In Afaan Oromo, St Matthew's Gospel was published by Krapf in 1842.[29] Genesis

---

25   R. H. Charles, *Book of Enoch: Together with a Reprint of the Greek Fragments* (Oxford: Clarendon, 1912; repr. Whitefish, MT: Kessinger, 1995), p. x.

26   G. Scholem, *Major Trends in Jewish Mysticism* (New York: Schocken, 1961). See also his *Sabbatai Zevi, the Mystical Messiah, 1626–76* (Princeton, NJ: Princeton UP, 1973) and *On Kabbalah and its Symbolism* (New York: Schocken, 1965).

27   See Introduction, *The Book of Enoch: A New Translation from the Oldest known Manuscript, with Introduction and Notes in The Old Testament Pseudepigrapha* (J. Charlesworth, ed. Doubleday, 1983.)

28   For the fullest account refer to William Jowett's *Christian Researches in the Mediterranean from 1815 to 1820* (London: Seeley and Hatchard, 1822).

29   J. L. Krapf, *The Books of the Old Testament Translated into the Amharic Language by Abba Rukh ...*, 3 vols. (Basle: British and Foreign Bible Society, 1871–3).

and Psalms followed in 1873, and Exodus in 1877, issued by the Bible Society. The most important Afaan Oromo Bible translation in Ge'ez script was that of Onesimos Nesib, with the help of Aster Ganno, published in 1893. In Tigrinya, the missionary Samuel Gobat commissioned versions of the Gospels, the first of which began with John's Gospel in the 1830s. The whole New Testament was published in 1902 (with later editions) by the Swedish Evangelical Mission in Monkullo, Eritrea. The American Bible Society published another in 1953. There are also modern editions published in Eritrea, the most recent one appearing in 2000. In numerous other Ethiopian languages, one or another books of the Bible have been published by the Bible Society.

THE OVERALL CENTRALITY OF THE HOLY BIBLE: It is well known that no other known literary work has had such an impact upon world culture and literature and the great Abrahamic religions of Judaism and Islam as the Bible. The picture in Ethiopia is even more significant. The Holy Scriptures are not only influential, but they are foundational to its cultural, social and political structures. Pertinent questions and speculations concerning the biblical molding of Ethiopian culture have been subjects of intense discussion among observers and students of the life and teachings of the overall Ethiopian religious tradition. These questions and speculations, as well as criticisms and evaluations of them, have, for the most part, focused upon comparative cultural issues or emphasized the striking similarities between specific beliefs and practices of the ancient Israelites and Ethiopian Christians. They have concerned such matters as dietary laws, ritual cleanliness, circumcision, Saturday Sabbath, the role of the *tabot,* liturgy and music, and the like.

The shortcoming of past research, with occasional exaggerations and poor comparisons, has been the tendency to concentrate on a quasi-hermeneutical method, examining individual features of the Israelite characteristics of Ethiopian culture without considering the basic evidence of the uniting principal. This uniting principle is the centrality of the biblical Torah (Law) or *Orit* (Aramaic *Orayta*) in Ethiopic in the Ethiopian tradition. It is central to both belief and practice formally, and to the custom of the veneration of the Torah symbolically. Until the beginning of this century, the Holy Scriptures were used in the courts throughout Ethiopia for legal opinions and rulings. In short, the Ethiopian Church's understanding of the Torah/*Orit* is closer, in general, to that of the ancient Israelites than to Christianity (cf. Acts 15). As just alluded to, the supremacy of the Torah/*Orit* is symbolized in the veneration of the literal object associated with it, the *tabot* or the Ark of the Covenant (Hebrew *tebah*), believed to be the original *luhot ha-brit* (Tablets of the Covenant), the physical repository of the Law.

Some scholars have dismissed the Ethiopian *tabot* as some kind of a sacral object, its veneration by means of elaborate dance and music as nothing more than 'l'imitation de l'Ancien Testament', as Rodinson puts it.[30] Yet, we cannot overlook its association with Moses, who is called the *ba'ala hegg* (Law Giver, literally the Master/Owner of the Law; cf. *huq* in Hebrew) and arch-prophet. The *tabot* is par excellence G-d's *tabot 'enta westeta Orit* ('the tabot/ark wherein is the Orit/Law' or 'the tabot/ark that contains the Orit/Law'), given to Moses as the holy temple of the Law for all believers.[31] To relate the central role of the *tabot* in belief and ritual to the centrality of the Law in Ethiopian Church theology is regrettably something scholars have overlooked.

For the Ethiopians, the Torah/*Orit* comprises the civil, criminal, and moral laws to whose whole range of teaching the true believer must submit willingly. Until the early twentieth century, in the secular courts, legal precepts and precedents from the *Orit* or related oral guidelines bore upon juridical decisions. The *Orit* embraces every aspect of human activity – including the keeping of the Sabbath, ritual cleanliness, circumcision, and dietary prescriptions. It denotes the whole range of the Law, grounded in the Pentateuch, the Decalogue being thought to be its core. This should not surprise us, for the Decalogue does have a special position in Judaism as well, being one of the first pericopes of the Hebrew Bible to be included in the early Jewish prayer book. This is not the place to discuss why it was later removed.

The Torah/*Orit* is not only equal to the Gospels in importance. It is also the cornerstone of life here on earth and the path to the life to come. According to *Mäs'hafä Berhan* (the Book of Light), popularly attributed to the great Emperor Zär'a Ya'aqob (1434–68), the Decalogue is the *Iota* whose form is singular and whose shape is unique, written and engraved by the hand of G-d, the hand of fire, upon stone tablets. It is, therefore, changeless and endless. The letter *Iota*, along with the ideas ensuing from it, are meant to unfold the concept of the eternality of the Law as unequivocally as possible, as opposed to the general Christian view that the Torah is temporal and its dispensation has ceased to be operative (cf. Rom. 6:4; Gal. 3:13, 25).

Again according to *Mäs'hafä Berhan*, the *Iota* is not only a letter whose numerical value is ten, the number of the Ten Commandments, but is also the smallest letter of the alphabet. This has a double significance for the Law, in that it symbolizes not only the Decalogue but also the importance of the minutest details of the Law, as well as its wholeness. This point is made emphatically in *Mäs'hafä Berhan*, which asserts that even the number of each alphabetic letter in which a command is written is significant and must be counted, as I have

---

30   M. Rodinson, 'Sur la question des "influences juives" en Ethiopie, *Journal of Semitic Studies* 9 (1964), pp. 11–19.

31   See E. Isaac, *A New Text-Critical Introduction to Mäs'hafä Berhän* (Leiden: Brill, 1973), p.109.

demonstrated elsewhere.[32] This point is repeated throughout Ethiopic literature, in biblical commentaries, hagiographies, and theological works.

The Decalogue is fundamental among the precepts of the Torah, and its supreme importance is already expressed in the Bible, which tells us that is was revealed amid thunder and lightning, fire and smoke in the mountain, and the sounding of the *shofar*. The Ethiopian Church, likewise, attaches a special divine revelation to the Decalogue. This same view is expressed in *Mäs'hafä Berhan*, according to which the Decalogue is assigned a special distinction in that it is written by the very hand of G-d. Another important Ethiopic work, the fifteenth-century *Mäs'hafä Mist'irä Sämayat wä-Midir* (Book of Mysteries of the Heavens and the Earth) makes the following explicit point: 'But we may marvel in this that all the Laws (*hegg/huqqoth*) of our God shall abide forever; and they shall never be abrogated. Enoch says thus, "I saw fourteen trees which did not shed their leaves, but all the other trees were dry with fallen leaves." Abba Bahla Mika'el asks, "What are these fourteen trees about which Enoch spoke?" The Holy Spirit [responds and] says, "[they are] the Decalogue of the *Orit*, the Covenant of Noah, the Circumcision of the Fathers, and the Priesthood of Melchisedek, and the Baptism of John."

In general, in contrast to the inferior position given to the *Orit*/Law by the New Testament and Christendom, Ethiopian church theology gives it an undeniably central role. The church is founded upon the *Iota* (Law) and the *Delta* (Gospel). At Matt. 5:18 it is stressed: *yod* is the tenth letter of the Hebrew alphabet as *T* is in one Ethiopic tradition. The *yod*, the symbol of the Decalogue, stands for the *Orit*, as *T*, the symbol of the cross, stands for the Gospel. Therefore, the authors of *Mäs'hafä Berhan* argue, 'the Gospel, the cross-centered Law of Christ, cannot enter the man's heart apart from the *Orit* and the Prophets.'[33]

Even more significant in Ethiopian theological thought is not only the basic importance of the Law, but also the insistence that, as stated above, each and every one of the Ten Commandments is weighty both in respect to its inherent value and to its external form, namely, the specific number of letters of the alphabet in which it is written. In *Mäs'hafä Berhan*, for instance, it is spelled out that over two hundred letters of the alphabet were used in the command to keep the Sabbath, by way of bringing out the total strength of the Law as in the similar, well-known ancient Jewish exegetical method and philosophy.

The centrality of the Law in Ethiopic theology is not only in its essence and nature, but also in its function in human life. Contrary to the Pauline indifference towards keeping it (Gal. 2:3), the Ethiopic Church specifically teaches that it is necessary and expedient to keep the Law and that salvation comes through

---

32   *A New Text-Critical Introduction*, p. 50f.

33   *A New Text-Critical Introduction*, p. 108f.

faith and good works. In the introduction to the Amharic theological treatises called *Mäs'hafä Haymanot Wä-mïgbar* or *Nägärä Haymanot*, we read: 'Faith is the foundation, and good works is the building ... faith without good works and work without faith is useless ... it is like a body without a soul ... good works and faith are one ...'.[34] This same idea is expressed in various related works, such as the Jerusalem Ethiopic archbishopric manuscripts.[35] While the building metaphor can be found in the writings of John Chrysostom, and the dead body metaphor in the Epistle of James, the striking statement that faith without works is useless is clearly contradictory to Pauline Christian teachings.

In Ethiopic theology, the formula 'salvation through faith and good works' is indivisible.[36] From that single double law ensues the life-giving wine — from which the prophets drank. The single double Law is the sea of spiritual milk, which bears and nourishes the fruit of righteousness.[37] Those who read (study) the *Orit*, the Prophets, Kings, and the Gospel in their lifetime inherit the Kingdom of God.[38] This belief is almost identical to the Jewish teaching regarding the study (reading) of the Torah, for instance, 'He who has acquired the words of the Torah has acquired for himself the life of the world to come' (Mishnah: Pirkei Aboth 2:2; 2:8.). Those who do not keep that which is written in the Law of Moses will face eternal damnation (literally: '... their lot will be in the fire of hell ...')[39] The wise virgins of Mother Filimona are those who, having believed and having been baptized keep the Law; but the foolish are those who having believed and having been baptized do not (cf. Matt. 22). Everyone who fulfills the Law 'indeed fulfills all righteousness and overcomes sin.'[40] The Law gives spiritual sustenance and life of the flesh and the soul.[41]

---

34   See E. Isaac, *Ethiopic Manuscripts in American University and Private Collections*, American Philosophical Society, 1985. *This is a book-manuscript, a work sponsored by the American Philosophical Society. Copies of the ms are found in their library and a couple dozen libraries whose collections are described.*

35   See E. Isaac, "Ethiopian Manuscripts in the Monasteries of Ethiopian Patriarchate, Jerusalem, *Rassegna di Studi Etiopici*, XXX (Rome, 1984-86), 53-80.

36   Cf. James 2, *Collectio monastica*, ed. V. Arras, Corpus scriptorum christianorum orientalium 238–9, Scriptores aethiopici 45–6 (Leuven: Peeters 1963), p. 153.

37   *Gadla Filmona, Corpus Scriptorum Christianorum Orientalium, Scriptores Aethiopici, Tomus 35,* p.3.

38   K. WENDT, Das Mäs'hafä Milad (Liber Nativitatis) und Mäs'hafä Sellase(Liber Trinitatis) des Kaisers Zar'a Ya'qob, *Corpus Scriptorum Christianorum Orientalium, Scriptores Aethiopici,* Tomus 41, p.120.

39   Gadla Filmona, op. cit. p. 32. Cf. pp. 9, 63.

40   Isaac, *A New Text-Critical Introduction to Mäs'hafä Berhan*, p. 35.

41   Ibid, p. 38.

Chapter 6

The Role of Fasting
in the Ethiopian Church

❖

No one would question that food is central to human existence. The processes of eating, digesting, and nutrition represent fundamental biological necessities of life. These processes promote other related functions of life such as growth and movement. But food is not only an essential and basic biological or economic necessity. It is also a fundamental ingredient of religious life and human thought. For this reason food and the practice of fasting serves as an excellent socio-cultural phenomenon to study and illustrate the dynamics of the Ethiopian Orthodox Church.

From the view of many religions, food is the foremost, blessed gift of the creator for the sustenance of life. The Book of Genesis expresses this view simply stating that the creator gave people "every plant that yields seed that is upon the face of the earth and every tree with seed in its fruit" (Gn. 1.29). In biblical, as in many African traditions, religious life revolves around agriculture. The sacred seasons and the calendar are built around it. Tilling the ground and herding cattle are the two oldest professions mentioned in the Bible (Gn. 4.2). The Creator emerges par excellence as the first gardener who makes "every tree that is pleasant to the sight and good for food" to grow (Gn. 2.9). Most biblical gifts to friends as well as religious and political officials are solemn gifts of food. The Psalmist sings "[every creature, O Lord,] will look to you to give them their food in due season; when you give it to them, they gather it up; when you open your hand they are filled with good things" (Ps. 104.27-28). The song of the Psalmist echoes the hymn to the Aten, which is in perfect accordance with the well-known ancient Egyptian spiritual view of food.

Food is the essence of life, and sacrifice for the fertility of the earth is a cardinal element of Egyptian religion. According to the Memphite theology, food and the human soul, Ka, were among the first orders of creation. The Egyptians could not conceive of life, even after death, without food in the normal form. The tomb food offerings to the Ka and the burial of large numbers of utensils containing food and drink, a custom common among many African peoples, confirm this view.

For the Egyptians, agriculture, as well, could not prosper without divine supervision: "If you plough and there is growth in the field, God causes it to be plenty in your hand." Ptah made all and from Ptah "came forth foods, provisions, divine offerings, and all good things." From Ra flows "life, prosperity, health … bread, beer…." In a land where there was hardly any rain, the Nile—which brought the water upon which the agricultural life of the people, depended—played a dominant role in the religious thought and practice of the Egyptians. The fundamental unity of the Egyptian festivals sprang precisely from the religious character of the seasonal agricultural practices. The celebration of the fertility of the sod is a dimension of this, exemplified in the festival of the goddess Bast, whose feast at Bubastis—vividly described by Herodotus[1] was purportedly attended by about seven hundred thousand people.

The ancient Greeks inhibited the free citizen from performing the so-called menial tasks. In particular, after Greece became a slave society and native-born Greek gentlemen became landlords, the aristocratic philosophers, especially Plato and Aristotle, propounded the view that the tillers of the soil also should be slaves (Aristotle, Politics 30a.25ff. cf. Plato, The Republic 806.de). The earlier Greek traditions, however, attest to the fact that agricultural work, a basic economic activity, was regarded highly. Hesiod even claimed that farmers receive the favor of the gods.

For the ancient Israelites, food was an essential component of the bond of true fellowship with divine and human beings, and the refusal to eat at someone's table signified hostility. According to some scholars, the rejection of the pig's flesh (Lv. 11.7) by the Israelites resulted from the sacrificial use of that animal by their Canaanite enemies. A meal was not only an expression of social fellowship but also a sign of moral and spiritual union. Such was the case when Moses and the elders ate and drank as they beheld God (Ex. 24.11; cf. Gn. 19.3); when the pact between Jacob and Laban was accompanied by a ceremonial meal (Gn. 31.54; cf. 26.30); and the Israelite-Gibeonite alliance was concluded with a similar meal (Jos. 9.3-15).

The wearing of special garments at certain meals (Is. 61.3; Eccl. 19.18), the obligation to say blessings over wine and bread before a meal or grace after it, as well as the respective blessings over other foodstuff (Berakhot 6.1; Berakhot 48b; Sotah 10a) and similar other customs, point to the communal moral and spiritual values of food and meals. It has even been suggested that the root of

---

1   Hist. 2.60.

the Hebrew brit (covenant) is *barah* (to eat); and Ge'ez *mesah* (meal, lunch) has definite etymological relation to *maseha,* (to anoint), a religious royal function (cf. Ps. 23.5). *Malah* (salt), which makes food tasty, symbolizes permanent covenant (Nm. 18. 19; 2 Chr. 13.5; Ez. 4.14).

The religious significance of food among the peoples of Ethiopia is widely recognized by those who have studied the cultures of the various nationalities. C. R. Hallpike, an anthropologist who worked among the Cushitic Konso, correctly observes that food has such an important religious significance for them that "[the bestowal of food is] a symbol of blessing between the physical order of society and the social order itself." Moreover, beer is "the prime substance used in libations" and other religious rituals. Hallpike further notes that as among the ancient Israelites, "refusing to eat with, or to accept food from, a class of persons is a clear indication of social and ritual distance ... Commensuality is an indication of social and ritual equality."[2] For most Ethiopian peoples, whether they are speakers of the Cushitic or Semitic languages, these observations hold true, as they do for ancient Jews and other peoples. In Ethiopia, people of different faiths such as the Christians and the Moslems would not touch any meat not slaughtered by a fellow believer. And the real sign of intimacy among members of the same household or circle of friends is direct mutual hand feeding or *gursha,* the giving or acceptance of food from the hand of one directly to the mouth of another respectively. Even the round shape of the common meal table called *masob,* similar to the ancient Jewish dining table, indicates solidarity among the dining family members or guests.

The sanctity of food among the various Ethiopian peoples is further exemplified by the attitude toward cattle among the Nilotic Nuer. In refuting those who have intimated that the cow is venerated by the Nuer, E. E. Evans-Pritchard rightly agrees that:

> ...there is ... no evidence at all that cattle are venerated or in themselves are in any way regarded as guardian spirits, and in so far as it may be true to say that Nuer religion "is centered in the cow" or that their attachment to cattle *"May* also be called religious," in so far, that is, that we may legitimately speak ... of "die sakrale Stellung des Rindes," it is for a different reason.

But this different reason is not only because of the sacrificial role of cattle, as he intimates, but also because cattle constitute the main source of the food of the people, the milk on which they depend for sustenance.

The various forms of religious rituals and liturgies, including Jewish and Christian ones, have their origin in the practice of sacrifice. The Passover Seder

---

2   Hallpike, C.R. (291, 292).

(Mishnah, *Pesah* 10), the commemoration of the Israelite liberty from Egyptian slavery, as well as the sacred meal of the Qumran covenant community (I Q Sa 2.17.22), the symbol of hope and longing for the coming Heavenly Kingdom, and the Christian Eucharist (*anaphora*, "offering" in Eastern Christendom), related to the Passover as a meal of redemption *(Mk.* 14.22ff.), acquire their theological significance from the ancient Hebraic-biblical sacrificial meals.

Food in Hebraic-biblical thought finds its ultimate expression in the apocalyptic idea of the eschatological meal or the messianic banquet, the feast in the coming Kingdom of Heaven (Is. 25.6, 55.1-5, 65.13; Ps. 22 (23). 5; Prv. 9.1-6; 3 Ex 62.14, 2 Bar. 29.5-8; Mishnah Avot 3.20). In the beginning of creation, paradise was the Garden of Eden, full of delightful edible fruit trees and plants, including the Tree of the Knowledge of Good and Evil; and at the end of time the Kingdom of Heaven will be the banquet hall of eternal meal "a feast of fat things" (Is. 25.6). The grandiose nature of this banquet is envisioned in the type of food reserved for the occasion: whereas fruits, legumes, milk, honey, lamb, beef, bread, and wine are most frequently mentioned as popular foods in the Bible, the huge creatures behemoth and leviathan are given in the Pseudepigrapha (3 En. 60.7; 2 Bar. 29.4; 4 Ezr. 6.52).

In the Ethiopian church, as in all other Christian churches, the Eucharist has come to take on purely spiritual meanings, losing its original physical *Sitz im Leben* of the communal meal (*koinonia*, 1 Cor. 10.16). Nevertheless, the Ethiopian church does retain what resembles an observance of communal meals held in the church courtyards after regular worship service. At one time, such a meal, served on both Saturdays and Sundays, was set forth as a liturgical banquet. It involved the formal blessings over the wine and the bread, which the people consumed, as in a Passover meal, and not unlike the Essene or early Christian eschatological meal. In the fifteenth century the emperor Zär'a Ya'aqob (1434-1464) restricted or prohibited such a formal ritual meal, but the ceremonial meals survive still today in many traditional churches.

Food is a special divine gift. Its absence, therefore, in the form of hunger, drought, and famine represent unusual and severe divine punishment (Is. 51.19; Jer. 14.13-18; Am. 4.6) especially during the apocalyptic woes of the end of time (Mk. 13.8). The destruction of crops by blight or locust (Am. 4.9), the ravaging of the land by warfare (Is. 1.7, 3.1,7), and particularly the absence of rain signal the withdrawal of divine favor (Hg. 1.10-11) or manifest direct divine punishment.

The earth yields food because of rain. Hence, its absence calls for a solemn occasion of prayers and fasting in both biblical and rabbinic Judaism (Jgs. 10.26; I Kgs. 18.12ff. Neb. 9.1; 11.1, 13, 2.12, Zee. 7.5; Mishnah, Ta'anit). According to *Ta'anit*, if no rain has fallen on or before Marcheswan 17, a light fast of three days accompanied by washing and anointing, is ordered. Continued drought calls for prayers and fasts of higher intensity, ashes to be sprinkled on public streets, on the ark, and on the head of the Nasi and Ab-beth din.

Food has been regarded as central in the religious thinking of diverse peoples since time immemorial. It represents not only the present sustenance of life but also the very meal of eternal life. So, why is fasting, the negation of food, also part of the religious tradition of so many peoples?

Some historians of religion think that fasting inevitably and naturally grew out of the custom of leaving food and drink for the dead, so that they, and not the living, might make use of them. This hypothesis does not seem to be very convincing, and requires a clear proof that there is not enough food for the living and the dead to share. Furthermore, it overlooks the fact that since time immemorial people feasted, not fasted, at burial ceremonies and held other memorial feasts (for instance, the Ethiopian *tazkar* and the Jewish *zikaron* meals) in honor of the dead. Religious fasts also precede, not follow, funeral sacrifices. The longest period of fasting in the Ethiopian Church is that preceding the death of Jesus Christ (Fasika).

Other historians of religion hold the view that fasting grew "out of the desire in primitive man to bring on at will certain abnormal nervous conditions favorable to the seeing of visions and dream believed to give direct access to the spiritual world."[3] This view dates from the seventeenth century, when Jesuit missionaries who worked in "New France" claimed that the natives fasted because they believed that "fasting makes their sights extraordinarily acute" and enables them to see distant or absent things, and that dreams helped them to see the whereabouts of the elks or enemies that they sought. Following these missionaries, Levy Bruhl argues that "when a dream was desired, fasting was the ordinary means of supplication" and that "if the Huron does not succeed in seeing in dreams a herd of elks or deer, it is because, in spite of his fasting, the mystic essence of these animals remains hostile to him."[4]

The problem with this hypothesis is that people do see dreams not only when the body is exhausted by hunger but also when it is fully satiated. Numerous visions seen by the prophets in the biblical books do not seem to have occurred in the context of fasting. Unusual dreams also take place after overeating, and certain foods and herbs and believed equally to induce extraordinary visions, not unlike modern-day consciousness-expanding drugs and hallucinogens. According to the Ethiopian tradition found in the *Kebra Nagast*, the night King Solomon slept with the Queen of Sheba after an elaborate spicy meal, he

---

3   "Food and Religion: The Nature and Objective of Fasting in the Ethiopian Church," in *Asceticism..*, ed. V. Wimbush *et. al.* (Oxford Univ. Press, 1995).

4   *La mentalité primitive* (1922), translated as *Primitive Mentality* (1923).

saw in a dream how the glory of ancient Israel departed for the land of Ethiopia in the form of the sun.

A third hypothesis has it that fasting is "nothing more than a preparation for the sacramental eating of holy flesh." Such an assertion of a preparatory formula is somewhat far-fetched, but the view deserves a closer examination. The great Jewish fast of Yom Kippur was accompanied by sacrificial rites (Lv. 16.1-34). The abstention from eating certain foods at *Pesah* (Passover) may have a similar provenance. In the Christian tradition of the pre-Easter Lent, there is a connotation of a sacrificial feast preceded by fasting; in the Ethiopian church, the *gahad* of Christmas and the *gahad* of Epiphany, held on the eves of the feasts respectively; the fast of the Dormition of Mary; and others. The most notable feasts and fasts of the Ethiopian church in the established calendar are determined in relation to the time of the Jewish *Pesah* or the Christian Easter, both of which carry sacrificial significance. A case can easily be made for the rhythmic cycle of fasts and feasts.

The historian of religion, Gerardus van der Leeuw, wrongly attaches too much significance to mystical and divinatory origins to feasts; but he is right in asserting that festivals are not intended to be merely recreational. The origin of feasts must be in the solemn seasons of sacrificial rites and the eating of ritual meals. They may be associated with certain events in the experience of the individual, from birth to death (birth, Gn. 40.20; marriage, Jub. 14.10) or the life of the society, from agriculture to warfare and victory (sowing and harvesting Jgs. 9.27; Ru. 2.14; 1 Sm. 13.23; sheep shearing, I Sm 25.11). They may also be associated with certain cosmic occurrences such as the beginning and end of the rainy seasons. Fasting was associated with the religious festival of Isis (Herodotus, Hist. 2.40).

However, the eating of holy flesh or sacrificial meals, and the common fast-feast rhythmic counterpoint do not adequately or fully explain the origin of fasting. Certain fasts happen to be expressions of mourning and calamity (Ezr. 8.21-23; Neb. 1.4; 4 Esd. 3.6; 1 Mc. 3.47; 2 Mc. 13.2; Dn. 9.3); certain others of repentance and sorrow (11. 1. 14, 2.12; Jn. 3.5); and still certain others of discipline, piety, and meritorious life (Ps. 35.13, 69.10; Tb. 12.8; Testaments of the Twelve Patriarchs: Rb. 1.10; Sm. 3.4; Jd. 15.4). Neither can one explain the origins of the pious fasts on Mondays and Thursdays (*Ta'anit* 12a; Lk. 18.12; Judith 8.6) or on Wednesdays and Fridays for the early Christians (*Didache* 8.1) and present day Ethiopian Christians (cf. the Friday abstinence in Eastern and Catholic churches) on the ground of the fast-feast cycle.

The difficulty in understanding the ultimate purpose and origin of fasting arises out of the complexities of understanding the religious world-view. By its very nature, the religious world-view contains an internal dichotomization or contradiction. It works like a pendulum that swings from one extreme end to the other about a central focal point. Is religion a system of divine obligation with service orientation (relegare, "to bind," following Lactantius) or the state of a reflective and contemplative relationship with the divine and a total detachment from the world (relegere, "to gather," following Cicero)?

Whichever it is, religion has a force which, at one end of the pendulum, can divine the realm of phenomena into two mutually irreducible polar elements, such as the division of reality into matter and mind with their attendant spacio-temporal and subsistence forms (metaphysical/ ontological dualism), or the division of the universe into two opposing forces or principles, one good and one evil (Zoroastrian/ cosmic dualism). At the other extreme, the form of religion can unite the sacred and the profane into one single reality or creator-creation, combining the laws of humanity and nature into one single harmonious principle (as in the Hebrew Bible and certain African monistic traditions).

These positions are essentially variations on or expressions of the human attempt at understanding the world and ultimate reality—all of the great religions of the world manifest pendulating characteristics from one polarity to the other. But generally different religions tend to pull habitually toward one or the other end of the pendulum.

Hebraic and certain African traditional religions, including ancient Egypt, are in general homo-socio-centric and put emphasis on the unity between the divinity and creation (the material world). They make little or no distinction between the sacred and the secular, but this is not to be confused with pantheistic thought. All things are sacred and all aspects of cultural and social life are permeated by religious ideas. On the other hand, Hindu/Buddhist and ancient Greek philosophical thought in general tend to divorce the sacred from the secular, the material world from the spiritual, unity being achieved either by the abnegation of matter or its absorption into the mind. For the former, the needs of both the soul and the body are spiritual; hence food and procreation are aspects of the religious panorama. The latter, however, idealize asceticism and regard animal food and procreation as inherently evil, if at all possible to be avoided.

Asceticism is based on *a priori* assumption that sensuous, bodily, and worldly matters, contrasted with spiritual ones, are either non-real, the source of evil, or simply evil itself. Eastern asceticism teaches self-denial to achieve liberation from the body through spiritual life (*moksa*) ultimately ending in total freedom from worldly existence and rebirth in the knowledge of Brahma or through the annihilation of the passion that attracts karma, a subtle form of matter, to free the soul from bondage (Jainism). Western asceticism teaches liberation through the life of reason and philosophy (Plato); through an austere life (Neo-Platonism); or through a total repression of fleshly desires and renouncing the world through mental (gnosis) and spiritual life (Gnosticism).

From the point of view of biblical and certain African religions, material food is central to the physical and spiritual life equally. The future/life after death itself becomes an eternal banquet with God. From the point of view of Eastern religions, however, material food is secondary to human existence: for the essence of a person, the soul does not need it. The end or ultimate goal of life is pure spiritual existence, a nirvana or state of nonbeing.

Buddha considered the body evil, but rejected extreme asceticism. However, his idea of the renunciation of the world led his disciples directly into instituting various rules of fasting (more severe for the monks than for the laity). The Mahayana considers fasting as means of rebirth in higher grades. In the West, even before the time of Plato, the Pythagoreans of the sixth century BCE criticized excessive bodily desires and recommended their repression to free the soul in search of knowledge, or virtue, as the Cynics put it several centuries later. The Dionysian or Orphic cults also taught the avoidance of animal food and practice of self-maceration. It is interesting to note the irony whereby Epicureanism has come to be equated in popular minds with sensuous eating: in fact, "eat, drink, and be merry, for tomorrow you shall die" was an ascetic maxim. Even the somewhat socially conscious Stoics were not free from elements of ascetic thinking. They too considered emotion an accomplice of what they termed "irrational desire" (an idea that still plagues the Western mind). The maxim "Man is an alien in his own world" succinctly summarizes the anti-materialistic philosophy of life of the Hellenistic world.

The early church inherited the ascetic philosophy of life either directly through Greek philosophical ideas or indirectly from oriental religions through syncretistic Manichaeaism or Gnosticism. Many early church leaders like Athanasius, Chrysostom, Gregory of Nyssa, Augustine, and Ambrose, considered bodily desire low and recommended its suppression as much as possible to achieve Christian virtues. Some of the heroes of the early church like Anthony, the anchorite founder of Christian asceticism, Pachomius, the father of organized monasticism, Black Moses, and other desert monks believed that their way of life was good and virtuous and pleasing to God. The extremist Simeon the Stylite would rather sit on his desert pillar contemplating and enjoying the worms eating his wounds caused by the ropes by which he tormented himself rather than eating victuals himself.

Fasting in the early church was no doubt associated with these early ascetic tendencies, and with the belief that it exalted the spiritual faculties at the expense of the lower bodily ones. In his treatise, *De jejuniis* (of Fasting) Tertullian propounded the ascetic concept that fasting originated in the command given by God in the Garden of Eden not to eat certain fruit trees, "*Acceperunt Adam Deo legem non gustandi do arbore agnitionis boni et mah, morituris si gustasset.*"... in reference to the fasting of forty days and forty nights by Jesus in the desert, when he was tempted by Satan to make bread from stone, Tertullian says, *"Docuit etiam adversus diriora daemonia jejuniis praeliandum."* The fasting mentioned for catechumen by Justin Martyr (Apol. 2.93), Clement of Alexandria (Strom. 7.877), and Eusebius (Hist. *Eccl.* 5.24) move along the same ascetic-penitential axis. The *Shepherd of Hermas* (3.5) advises the one who fasts to give an equal amount of the food abstained from to the poor widow or orphan, a meritorious action; however, he regards it still as non-virtuous.

Asceticism has deep roots in Eastern and Hellenic religions, primarily because of their general leaning towards the negative (in respect to body and matter) pole of the religious pendulum. However, it does find its manifestation even in the Hebraic-biblical and African religious life. Biblical-Hebraic and certain African religious ideas incline toward the same negative point of the pendulum, in as much as Eastern and Hellenic thought also incline toward the positive pole. The Egyptian teaching against greed and the biblical "man does not live by bread alone" (Dt. 8.3) are rather commonsensical and rational maxims of life, but some interpret them as manifestations of ascetic tendencies. Better examples of ascetic ideas are found in later Egyptian religious developments: the practice of the priests of Isis who, as Plutarch described, did not eat fish and garlic because they are "unnecessary and luxurious articles of diet" (De Is. *et Os. M.).* Similarly, we learn from Apuleius, the Roman writer, in his moving description of the Mysteries of Isis, that abstinence from meat and wine and luxurious foods were part of the requirement for the initiates to mysteries *(Metam. 11).* Among the Jews, Samson (Jgs. 13.4,7) and John the Baptist (Mt. 3.4) appear to have led ascetic lives at least to some degree.

The distant origin of fasting may certainly be found in the negative attitude toward the world, the philosophy that the body should not be pampered by food and drink and that all desires should be chocked. Nevertheless, it is wrong to ascribe ascetic reasons only for fasting as it developed historically.

Biblical fasts (*som,* complete abstinence from food, *cn'a,* afflict one self; or *anah nefesh,* afflict one's soul), whether private or public, remain in fact non-ascetic. They are connected with mourning (seven day fast for the death of Saul and Jonathan, 1 Sm. 31.13; 2 Sm. 1.12), prayers for compassion (David fasting for Bathsheba's first child, 2 Sm. 12.16-23), wartime (I Sm. 14.24; Jgs. 20.16; 2 Chr. 20.3), or penitence (repentance for Ninevites, Lk. 11.32, of Israel, Jl. 2.12-13). We have also considered above the fasts for rain. There are also fasts associated with divine revelation (Moses receiving the law, Ex. 34.29; Saul meeting the soul of Samuel, 1 Sm. 28.30). The fixed public fasts are described as meritorious and pious disciplines, particularly such observances as Yom Kippur and the Monday and Thursday fasts of later times (*Ta'anit* 12a, Mt. *6.16ff.;* Lk. *8.12; Didache 8.1).* There are also commemorative fasts connected with great national tragedy, including the averted ones (Av 9; Adar 13; fast of Esther.

Est. *4.16.*) The non-ascetic character of Jewish fasts is explicitly asserted in the command that the four yearly fasts (or the fourth, fifth, seventh, and tenth months) should be "a season of joy, gladness, and cheerful feasts" (Zec. 8.19; Ta'anit 2.1).

Ethiopian church fasts, including Lent, should also be classified with the fasts of penitential, meritorious, disciplinary acts. The fasts of the *Didascalia*, like the fasts promulgated in the *Fïtha Nägäst* and incorporated into the Ethiopian church calendar, are directly related to the non-ascetic biblical, Jewish, and early church fasts in respect to their origin. Like the biblical, Jewish, and early church fasts, they are rooted in the desire for meritorious living, a position consistent with the ethical emphasis of the Hebrew Bible, rather than in the idea of true bodily mortification.

To be sure, various theological expositions and even some official church declarations present a rather ascetic rationale for fasting. One such exposition declares

> The Church, in her earliest days, recognized the necessity of her children to "chastise the body and bring it under subjection," St. Paul advises. The body is ever striving for mastery over the spirit; besides the external sources of temptation, "the world," we have always-another source with us, which is a pan of our nature. This is the mason for mortification. Self-denial in lawful things enables us to turn with great earnestness to spiritual things. It is on these grounds that the Ethiopian Church has strictly adhered to the injunctions of the *Didascalia* and enjoined on the faithful the longest and most austere fasts in the world.

Obviously, this is a simple statement of the ascetic position; and in some sense it does agree with certain ideas in the New Testament (I Thes. 5. 22; 1 Pt. 2.11).

Nevertheless, with the exception of the fasting habits of the hermitical *bahtawi* (loners) there is little, if any, ascetic feature to Ethiopian fasting. The *bahtawi* of Ethiopia are the true modern heirs of ancient Christian ascetics. As their name designates, they live alone in remote forests or deserts. They hardly eat the normal daily quantity of food, but occasionally feed on small amounts of wild herbs, nuts, and plants.

The Ethiopic *Didascalia (the Apostolic Constitution)*, the authority cited in the above quotation, does not, in fact, present the ascetic rationale of fasting. On the contrary, it explicitly teaches a penitential form of fasting with the assertion, "And let them examine the one who has sinned and if he would abandon his evil way and confess his sins and repent, let them bring him into the church and command him to fast in accordance to the degree of the sins that he had committed—two weeks, or three weeks, or five weeks, or seven weeks[5]." In the same work, little, if any, consideration is given to the fasts that have been ordained for Wednesday and Friday, the fourth and the sixth days of the week, the days Jesus was arrested and crucified respectively, as explained in the *Didascalia*. The only semblance of an ascetic rationale of fasting in the *Didascalia* is in the prohibition to fast on the Sabbaths, an implication that one should not retreat from bodily pleasure (feasting) to bodily mortification (fasting) on days of joy.

Ethiopian fasting varies in rigor from the most severe ones during Passion Week to the lighter Christmas fast. In either case, they are the most rigorous fasts known in any Christian church. Those who observe fasting must in all cases abstain from drinking milk, eating dairy products, eggs, meats, and all animal food; smoking is generally prohibited, but beer and wine may be consumed in moderation. All cereals, vegetables, fruits, and dry foods are allowed; fish, not known to be such a common food in Ethiopia, may also be eaten.

The rules of fasting in the Ethiopian church do not only involve abstinence from eating certain foods, but also total fasts during certain periods. Thus, no meal may be eaten, particularly by the clergy and the very pious, before the conclusion of church services on fasting days, that is, about three o'clock in the afternoon. Because it is a very long season (fifty-six days), Lent, one fast that is almost universally observed by Ethiopian Christians, allows those who fast to have breakfast on Saturdays and Sundays after nine o'clock in the morning, during the period following it, from Easter-Passover to Pentecost (fifty days), the Wednesday to Friday fasts are abrogated. It should also be noted that important Christian festivals such as Christmas, Timqat (Baptism-Epiphany), and the like supersede the Wednesday to Friday fasts if they happen to fall on those particular days. The strictness with which one keeps fasting varies of course from one individual to the other; whereas strictness and faithfulness are unequivocally expected from the clergy as their total duty and exemplary responsibility, these are left as matter of conscience and reputation for the laity.

The most staggering fact about Ethiopian fasting is the sheer number of days that are prescribed for it; about 250 days for the clergy (priests, deacons, and church officials, but particularly monks and nuns) and about 180 days for the laity, that is, all adults above the age of thirteen. In other words, there are more fast days than normal food consumption days during the year. The obligatory fast days do not still take into account the number of days of private penitential fasts (from seven to forty days, or even one year), the fasting of bishops at their installations, not to mention the perennial ascetic fasts of the *bahtawi*.

The question has been raised whether seasons of famine and the scarcity of food might have contributed to the rise and development of fasting. Histori-

---

5   *Didascalia*

cally, we find little evidence to substantiate such a contention. In the New Testament, Paul twice uses the *nesteuo*, *nesteia* (the common expression for fasting in the Septuagint and the New Testament) in the sense of hunger, perhaps implying possible fasting because of the lack of food (2 Cor. 6.5, 11.27). According to Genesis (41.46-57), in times of plenty, food should be set-aside for the periods of famine; but we do not know whether people had to fast to save food, or to abstain from eating certain foods for such purposes. Additionally, our records are silent about any relationship between fasting and obesity in the historic past.

The religious merits of fasting may include attaining a sense of humility from not eating filling foods such as dairies and meats; it could be a means of repenting for one's sins and sacrificing something of small significance; or possibly a way to gain an understanding of some degree of suffering (although incomparable to that experienced by Jesus Christ). Whatever personal reasons one may have for fasting, its disciplinary value in the present day should not be dismissed. Questions are being continually raised about what can be done regarding world food shortage. Moreover, the possible bio-psychological value of fasts for those who suffer from overeating and obesity should not be underestimated. Naturally, above everything, the importance of the health of the person who fasts is paramount. Yet it seems that recent scientific opinions are no longer so certain about the absolute value of eating fats and animal products as they used to be as recently as twenty years ago.

In Ethiopia, the eating habits of the people and their nutritional status are affected by the custom of fasting in a very decisive way. The studies available to us do not prove in any way that the health of the people is affected adversely by the bio-cultural phenomenon of fasting. It does appear that suckling infants may be getting less adequate calories and other nutrients that animal food provide, since their mothers do not have available to them a full diet, even though they themselves, like pregnant women, are not required to fast.

In general, Ethiopian fasting foods consisting of cereals, legumes, potatoes, kale, fenugreek, safflower, oilseeds, sunflower, flax, nug (niger), mustard, and other allowed foods and drinks like *täla* (beer) and *täj* seem to provide a broad and not unhealthy menu. Indeed some modern nutritional experts can possibly learn something from the Ethiopian experience, since as a rule the Ethiopians are not an obese people.

For Ethiopia itself, a country where famine was so recently ravaging the land and where agricultural methods are being slowly updated, fasting, if done under proper medical supervision, may turn out to be not only of religious but also of biological and economic benefit. It can be a means of controlling the excessive consumption of food. Already fasting does subconsciously serve as a type of check and balance in food consumption in a society in which people also engage in numerous weekly, monthly, and yearly festivals of feasts. Where such a large number of people abstain from the rarer foods for so many days of the year, the days of fasting outnumbering the days of indulgence, there are obviously other economic and biological benefits. Imagine the number of cattle, sheep, and goats (animals permitted for consumption), as well as chickens, which rest during the greater portion of the year, and can multiply to replenish the species instead of being slaughtered ceaselessly with adverse economic effect.

Chapter 7

The Ethiopian Liturgy and Calendar

At the heart of the Ethiopian Orthodox Church worship is the reading of sacred texts, the liturgy of the Word divided into two services: of the morning (*zä-nägïh*) but commonly known as Mahïlet (praise), and of Mass (*zä-qïddase*). The Wazema is also performed, as a vigil during the afternoon of the eve of an important feast.[1] The mass, *Qïddase*, is believed to have been instituted by Jesus himself the night he was arrested by the Romans (cf. John 18:3; I Cor 11: 23-25). This ties the *Qïddase* to the Passover meal as well as to the Sacrifice of the Mass, at which the sacrament of the Holy Communion is administered. The concept of sacrifice is therefore at the heart of the *Qïddase*, and that is why the Ethiopian Church, in agreement with the council of Nicaea, calls the Holy Communion the un-bloody sacrifice (cf. Also I Cor. 10:18-21; Heb. 13:10). The *Qïddase* (literally, "Hallowing") is celebrated daily in the Ethiopian Churches, following the morning office, occurring around 12 o'clock on fast days. *Qïddase* includes four lessons, read facing the four cardinal directions.[2]

Qïddase consists of two parts: the *anaphora* (lit. offering) and the *pre-anaphora*. The *pre-anaphora* (which is invariable) has several components: the entrance, incensing, preparation of the altar, blessing of the bread and the wine, prayers of thanksgiving, petitions, trisagion, the reading of the Epistle and the gospel, the dismissal of the Catechumens (if there are any), and the recitation of the Creed. The pre-*anaphora* corresponds to the *Mass of the Catechumens* of the Early Christian Church, and is a witness to the fact that the Ethiopian Church retains the practices and characteristics of the ancient Church more than any other Christian church today. In the ancient Christian church, a special early service, called the *Mass of the Catechumens* was conducted for those being

---

1 Fritsch, Emmanuel. *The Liturgical Year of the Ethiopian Church*. Ethiopian Review of Cultures, Special Issue, Volume IX-X, 2001 (29-30).

2 Fritsch, Emmanuel. *The Liturgical Year of the Ethiopian Church*. Ethiopian Review of Cultures, Special Issue, Volume IX-X, 2001 (31).

prepared as new Christian converts; after the completion of the reading of the Gospel and the sermon, the Catechumens would be dismissed and those baptized Christians would remain for the Communion Service. The *pre-anaphora* is still conducted in the Ethiopian Church even if there are not Catechumens in the congregation.

The Ethiopian *anaphora* corresponds to the Byzantine *hieratikon* (priestly-holy office) or *euchologion* or Canon of the Mass of the Western Churches. Whereas the Western Churches have one *anaphora*, the canon of the Mass with a preface, the Ethiopian Church Liturgy consists of fourteen *anaphoras*; in fact twenty, if one were to count the longer and shorter forms of some *anaphoras* separately. These are: Of the Apostles, Of our Lord Jesus Christ, Of our Lady Mary, Of St. John the Evangelist, Of St. Athanasius, Of St. Cyril, Of St. Dioscurus, Of the Three Hundred and Eighteen Orthodox Fathers, Of St. Basil, Of St. Gregory of Nazianzen, Of John Chrysostom, Of Gregory the Armenia, Of John Serug, Of St. Epiphanius. The *anaphoras* differ in several respects as well as in the words of the Institution. However, essentially all consist of two parts: The Synaxis (reading of Epistle and Gospel) and the *anaphora* (offering canon) proper. The most common *anaphora* in use is the Anaphora of the Apostles. The others are used generally at different feasts: Feast of Our Lord (*Of our Lord*); the Feast of Mount Tabor (*Of our Lord*); Feasts of our lady Mary, Gabriel, and Dacesius (*Of our Lady*); Feasts of St. John, St. Stephan, St. George, Christmas, the Martyrs (*Of St. John the Evangelist*); the Feasts of Passover Vigil, the Savior of the World, the Cross, John Chrysostom (*Of John Chrysostom*); Feast of the Christian Sabbath (*Of St. Athanasius*); Feasts of *Tïmqät* (Baptism-Epiphany), the Month of Rains (*Of St. Epiphanius*); the Feasts of Cana of Galilee, Ganna (*Christmas season*), the Twenty Four Heavenly Priests (*Of the* Three hundred and Eighteen); Feasts of Hosannah, Passion Week (Of Gregory of Nazianzen); Feast of Ascension, Pentecost (*Of St. Dioscorus*); Feasts of Patriarchs, and Bishops (*Of St. Basil*); Feasts of St. Cyril, the Prophets and Righteous (*Of St. Cyril*); Feasts of St. Michael, Gabriel, and Angels (*Of St. Serug*).

The veneration of the Holy Virgin Mary in the Ethiopian Täwahïdo Church is demonstrated in part by these *anaphoras*, as there are numerous feasts related to her life, honouring her name, and commemorating the miracle of her child's conception. There are five feasts celebrating the events in her life: The Falling-asleep *Erafta*, 21 Terr; The Covenant of Mercy *Kidanä mihïrät*, 16 *Yäkkatit*; The Nativity *Ledäta*, 1 Genbot; The Consecration of her church at Philippi, *Qïddase beta* 21 Sane; and The Assumption *Filsäta*, 15 Nahase.[3] Two feasts honour her name: Mountain of S'iyon, *Däbrä S'eyon*, on 21 *Hïdar*, and Covenant of Mercy, *Kidanä Mïhïrät*, 16 *Yäkkatit*. Three commemorate her

---

3   Fritsch, Emmanuel. *The Liturgical Year of the Ethiopian Church*. Ethiopian Review of Cultures, Special Issue, Volume IX-X, 2001 (62).

miracle: Saidnaya *Sedenya,* 10 *Mäskäräm*; Apparition to Ildefonse of Toledo *Ba'ala Daqseyos,* 22 Tahsas; and Apparition at *Däbrä Mät'maq,* 21 Genbot. There are also four feasts dedicated to Marian Sanctuaries: Debre Quesqam, on 6 *Hidar*; the source which her son caused to spring, Za-'anq'a Wäldä, on 8 *Säne*; the building up of the church bearing her name at Philippi (*Hensata betä krestiyan ba-sema*), 20 Sane; and the consecration of her church at Philippi (*Qiddase beta*), 21 Sane.[4] Through these holidays, as well as the consistent recitation of the Hail Mary[5], the Täwahïdo Church commemorates the mother of Jesus Christ.

Of the origin of these *anaphoras,* we know very little. The one *Of the Apostles* is basically similar to the rite used by the Coptic Orthodox Church (Egyptian Church) called the Liturgy of St. Mark, but it is more expanded and developed. The others, though ascribed and attributed to various well-known early Christian saints, and though scholars used to assume they were versions of liturgies of other Eastern Churches, have been adequately demonstrated to be original creations of the Ethiopian Orthodox Täwahïdo Church, consisting of sophisticated theological thinking and poetry. Even though they are thought to be of comparatively late date (post tenth century), there is really no evidence to support this view.

As previously stated, the standard *anaphora* of the Ethiopian Orthodox Täwahïdo Church is that one of "Of the Apostles." Its order is as follows:

INTROIT (chanted): Bread brought from Bethlehem--place where wine and bread are prepared--taken in procession thrice around the altar.

(Offertory prayers said as wine is poured into chalice.)

DOXOLOGY (chanted): Followed by Prayers of St. Basil, the Oblation, and the Veil.

ABSOLUTION (prayer): by bishop or priest and Deacon's Litany

(Prostration of people).

BLESSING: of the Censer and Offering of Incense

Invocation of St. Mary, Hymn or Song of Trinity.

---

4   Fritsch, Emmanuel. *The Liturgical Year of the Ethiopian Church.* Ethiopian Review of Cultures, Special Issue, Volume IX-X, 2001 (37).

5   The translation of the Hail Mary is as follows: O my Lady Mary, hail to thee by the salutation of the angel Gabriel. Thou art a virgin in mind and thou art a virgin in body. Mother of God Sabaoth, hail to thee! Blessed art thou amongst women and blessed is the fruit of thy womb. Rejoice, O full of grace, God is with thee! Pray and supplicate for mercy to they beloved Son Jesus Christ, that he may forgive us our sins. Amen. Source: Fritsch, Emmanuel. *The Liturgical Year of the Ethiopian Church.* Ethiopian Review of Cultures, Special Issue, Volume IX-X, 2001 (35).

EPISTLE: Prayer Before Reading and Three Lections.

GOSPEL: Trisagion, Procession of Gospel around altar,
(Litany of assistant priest, the Reading by bishop or priest),

PROCESSION: of Gospel and Kissing by the congregation.

MISSA FIDELIUM: Prayer for Peace by priest, Deacon's Litany
for All the faithful.

RECITATION: of the Creed by deacon

LAVABO: or washing of hands by priest, and Kiss of Peace.
(People bow to each other).

ANAPHORA: (proper): Sursum Corda, Preface (Thanksgiving
of Redemption), Commemoration of the saints and Intercession for all the faithful, Eucharistic Prayer and Sanctus,
Words of the Institution (see above), Anamnesis (invocation),
Epiclesis (invocation of Holy Spirit for consecration of the
elements).

The celebration of the Liturgy in the Ethiopian Orthodox Täwahïdo
Church requires at least three priests and two deacons. The celebratory language
is traditionally Ge'ez and continues to be so, but nowadays the readings can be
in Amharic (wholly or in part). The place of the celebration of the liturgy has
to be sacred, on the altar of a church, which has been consecrated with a *Tabot*
(the Ark) present in it. At the Festivals of *Mäsqäl* and *Tïmqät* it may take place
in the tent, of course with the *Tabot* present in them. The communion itself may
be administered to a sick person at home.

The altar must be clean and covered with a white cloth, bearing three
candles (made of beeswax), a cross, and other consecrated vessels: the chalice
(*säwwa*), paten (*sahel*), cross spoon, napkins for wrapping the Eucharistic bread
(*mahfadat*), ciborium (*mäsob*), the bread and the wine (*t'adiq* and *t'äbäl*). On
the right of the altar is placed a small table holding the wine and water flasks,
and a bowl and a towel for the washing of the hand. Other requisites are: the
censor, a processional cross, holy water (*tabal*), two crescent circles to be placed
over the Host (aster), sanctuary lamp (*andil*), and a small hand bell. Of course,
the *Mäs'hafä Qïddase* (the Missal), *Qeddus Mashaf* (the New Testament), are
indispensable; additionally, a list of the persons to be commemorated (whether
living or dead) called *Dibdikon* is also brought. The clergy wear elaborate vestments; the celebrant priest wears specially the alb (*qames*), stall (*motahet*), girdle
(*zennär*), chasuble (*Qabä lanqä*), and cuffs (*äkman*), referred to as the clothes of
the nobility (nay mekuwanint libsi).

Turning to the literature of the Ethiopian liturgy, we have already alluded to
the *Mäs'hafä Qïddase* (the Missal). The *Mäs'hafä Gessawwé* consists of the *anaphoras* with rubrics and notation for their proper chanting and recitation. Of all the

Eastern Orthodox liturgical bodies, the Ethiopic was the first to be published in the West, printed with the movable type in Rome in 1548.[6] The first modern printing of *Gessawê* was called *Mäs'hafä Aseleti*.[7] In recent years several other editions and/or translations of it have appeared: van Lantschoot (1945), containing seven *anaphoras*, J.M. Harden (1928), Marcus Daud (1959) trans. Arabic/Eng., rev. by Blatta Marsie Hazen, Ethiopian Orthodox Church (1964 E.C.) Ge'ez/Amharic edition, and Hammerschmidt (Berlin, 1961).[8]

Besides the *Mäs'hafä Gessawe* and its distinct purpose, there are several other books of ritual in the Ethiopian Church these are *Mäs'hafä Qandil* (Book of Lamp, or the service of extreme unction); *Dawit* (the Psalter, see below); *Weddase Amlak* (Praise of God, prayers for weekdays; *Mäs'hafä Sa'atat* (Horologium for the Canonical Hours); and other works for installations of bishop, ordination of priests, consecration of sacred vessels, blessings for food, drink, animals and buildings, and so on.

Mäs'hafä Sa'atat is the Breviary of the Ethiopian Church. It is believed to have been composed in the fifteenth century by Abba Giyorgis Gasacha, but that has not been proven. It is comprised of psalms, prayers, hymns, and discourses of the church fathers. It is primarily a form of public prayers (not necessarily said in public) recited during the seven canonical hours in monasteries (most regularly), churches, and other places. The seven canonical hours are: Night (mid-night); Prime (Dawn); Terce (third hour: 9AM); Sext (sixth hour, Noon); None (ninth hour, 3PM); Vespers (Evening); and Complin (last service before retirement). The clergy, particularly in the monasteries faithfully participate in the services of these canonical hours. Even young deacons are expected to rise at night to chant the Sa'atat; and certain *däbtäras* who live on church land are recruited to recite either the *Zama'alt* (Hours of the Day) or the *Zalelit* (Hours of the Night) in accordance with the prescribed arrangement. It is not obligatory for the ordinary people to attend the church for these canonical hours except for the Prime and the Vespers and especially on Saturdays and Sundays.

---

6   Fritsch, Emmanuel. *The Liturgical Year of the Ethiopian Church*. Ethiopian Review of Cultures, Special Issue, Volume IX-X, 2001 (38).

7   Also Mäs'hafä Qeddasse, Ge'ez-Amharic Text with extensive commentary by Ethiopian church scholars, Addis Ababa, 1918 (Eth. Cal.), Ethiopian Missal (Mäs'hafä-Qeddase) by the Sacred Congregation for the Oriental Churches, Rome 1938 (Eth. Cal.); The Liturgy of the Ethiopian Church, English translation of the Ethiopian Missal, by the Ethiopian Orthodox Church, Addis Ababa, 1954; J.M Harden, The Anaphoras of the Ethiopic Liturgy, London 1920; S.B. Mercer, The Ethiopic Liturgy, London, 1915; Abba Petros Hailu, Messa Ethiopica detta degli Apostoli, Rome, 1946; A. Teclemariam Semharay, la Messe Ethiopienne, Rome, 1937.

8   Abuna Maqarios (formely Abba Petros of Debre Bizen) affirms that they recite the sa'atat in some monastaries like Debre Bizen from 8PM on Saturday to 7 AM Sunday.

As said above, the proper execution of the ritual is very important. For this purpose, the deacons, the *däbtära*, and the priests attend many years of schooling in the numerous schools of Aquaquam and Zemare. As compared to the certain learned *däbtära* and highly well-read monks who specialize in study and writing, the deacons and priests need relatively simple education to be ordained and to perform the services. Usually there are professional teachers of the ritual: *Gebra Dequna* and *Gebra Qessina*, the functions of the deacon and the priest respectively, which mean primarily the carrying out of rituals of *Qeddase* and liturgy, reading, reciting, singing certain hymns, and administering the sacraments.

After the preliminary education is acquired, these priests and deacons are expected to perfect their art through experience and daily practice. In the past, the office of priesthood was rather attractive to landless young peasants who would be entitled to *samon* land as priests, and they would get their education usually by rendering certain services and manual labor for the monastery. Countless Ethiopian scholars, poets, philosophers, and musicians have emerged from the traditional schools of church education, demonstrating their efficacy at developing exceptional minds and talents. The next chapter will explain in further detail the different types of church education and their various purposes.

This review cannot be concluded without a reference to the Ethiopic Psalter, which has a special place in the hearts of every Ethiopian. For centuries, the Psalter has been used by all devoted and pious Ethiopians as the daily prayer manual *par excellence*. Besides the Psalms of David (151, following the LXX), it consists of the fifteen morning canticles of the Old and New Testament (Three Songs of Moses, etc.), the *Weddase Mariam* (Encomium of Mary) attributed to St. Ephrem of Syria, Angasa Berhan, the *Porch of Light*, another hymn to Mary, and *Song of Songs*. The inclusion of *the Song of Songs* is interesting in as much as this is also a Jewish liturgical book. The chanting of the Psalter as well as its *werdnebab* and *qumnebab*, and often its memorization is the most important stage in Ethiopian Church education.

Chapter 8
The Church and Education

The Abuna (Patriarch), the spiritual head of the Church in Addis Ababa, moving in accordance with the shift of the royal residence, has the authority and spiritual power to anoint and ordain the members of the clergy. He also has the authority to administer the sacraments. But by and large as a foreign Patriarch coming from the monastery of St. Anthony in Egypt, the Abuna was little more than symbolic, and played a small role in Ethiopian Church affairs until the present decade. Next to the Abuna, the clergy fall into the categories of archbishops, bishops, priests, archdeacons, and deacons. Bishops and priests have the authority and spiritual power to administer the sacraments except ordination, which is the function of bishops or their superiors. Each local church must have at least two priests and three deacons for a liturgical celebration.

Another very important personality included in the church order is the *Itchege* (Archabbot). The *Itchege* (term designating traditional title of the grand prior of the convent of Debre-Libanos in Shoa Province), is the administrative head of the Church and chief of all the monasteries. As the most esteemed member of the Ethiopian Church, the *Itchege* wielded more actual power than the Patriarch until 1950 when his Grace Abuna Basilios, an indigenous Abuna was installed. His deputies, called *Liqä kahnat* (chief priests), controlled the parish clergy in the provinces, presented candidates for ordination, and decided questions of protocol in respect to religious ceremonies.

As said elsewhere, Ethiopian national law is primarily derived from the Bible and the *Fetha Nagast* (a compilation of canon law as well as civil and penal legislation based on the Bible and canons of the early Councils)—consequently, the church hierarchy plays an important role in the traditional deliberations of justice. In this respect there exist four or five other supreme religious dignitaries of the Ethiopian Church hierarchy who used to enjoy preeminent status by virtue of their responsibilities at the imperial court. These are the *qes hatse* (the Imperial chaplain), the *'aqabe sa'at* [guardian of the (canonical) times], the *Liqä memmheran* (chief of the learned scholars), the *Liqä däbtära* (chief of the scribes and cantors), and occasionally the *Nebure id* (the title of the chief ecclesiastic of the sacred district of the ancient capital of Axum,[1] meaning the one who places, or, on whom is placed the hand). In a sense, it is accurate to say that it used to be these church dignitaries who were the chief Ethiopian Supreme Court judges.

A further interesting feature of the Ethiopian Church organization is the importance of the lay orders. Over each church is an *alaka*, a learned layman who commands the priests and the deacons. Then there are the *däbtära*, whose duty is teaching, copying manuscripts, and singing during church services. The choir leader is known as *mari geta*. The *gabaz* is a steward responsible for church property. He is a kind of justice of the peace, well versed in law. *Akabit* is a saintly widow who prepares the flour for the bread of the sacrament.

The monasteries also have their own orders, which are generally simpler than the ecclesiastical ones. Each monastery has an *abmnet* (abbot), *magabi* (steward), and *lika ardeit* (chief treasurer).

Until the introduction of modern secular education at the end of the 19th century, church schools were the only educational institutions in Ethiopia. Some writers have seen pre-Christian origins of such schools in the gatherings of learned men in the synagogues of Ethiopian Jews.[2] The primary purpose of these schools was to instruct children in Christian religion and literature and to recruit and prepare likely candidates for the priesthood. Generally, the most qualified students pursued their studies for twenty years or so, in the most famous centers of learning, the churches and monasteries of Northern Ethiopia. Their education continued until they became publicly recognized as Liqä *Liqa-wount* (scholars, most learned) or as *däbtära* (scribes), the well-known ecclesi-astical cantors, teachers, and copyists of sacred literature.[3] As well as being the institution through which religious continuity was maintained, the Ethiopian

---

1   Atse Menelik II built another church called Addis Alem Sion after Mariam Tsion in Axum. He also appointed the head of that church Nubura-ed, although not on the same level as that of Axum.

2   Douglas O'Hanlon, *Features of the Abyssinian Church*, London, 1946, p. 13.

3   Although the *däbtära* were occasionally members of the clergy or monks, they generally belonged to a lay order of the Church organization. The *däbtära* constitute a learned caste active in biblical scholarship and teaching of the Law, a group that takes an independent place alongside the priesthood. I have called the *däbtära* "scribes" because in some respects they are not a hereditary group like the Levites, but rather a class of highly learned men like the ancient Jewish *Sopherim,* who taught and transmitted the Law in early Judaism. The word *"däbtära"* (*Ge'ez*, Hebrew-Aramaic, perhaps originally Persian) means "a copybook, notebook, or writing material." A *däbtära* is one who writes on a *debtar*, hence, he is a scribe. Some Ethiopian scholars think that the use of the term to describe church singers corresponds to the duty of the Levites who ministered in the Tabernacle.

church school served as the main instrument for the development and propagation of a national culture, and for the creation of a national literature.[4]

Traditionally, every village had within the outer walls of its enclosure a church, which also served as the school. Or, the priests would gather groups of small boys[5] outside the village church and drill them in the rudiments of the Ge'ez syllabary.[6] There was no fixed place of learning; instruction might take place in the house of the priest or in the churchyard or under a tree. But in all cases, both students and teachers laboured under the most difficult conditions. Books and writing materials were very scarce, and seats and desks were for the most part non-existent. Yet the average teaching priest and pupil were earnest and painstaking. Sincere desire for knowledge was especially evident in the many who sacrificed home and comfort to attend school in a distant village or monastery. There they had virtually no means of substance, even when they worked as part-time servants for their teachers, or lived by "begging." What they achieved under these conditions was remarkable.

Lessons were largely oral, and the degree of memorization was the measure of ability and accomplishment. Generally, the students recited their daily lessons in unison to rhythmic tunes. The structure of education in the Ethiopian Church is sketched in more detail below.

There are roughly four levels of Church education. The traditional church school of writing and parchment books is known as *Nibabe*; the Institute of Singing and Moving (for Priests) is known as *Qene, Zema,* and *Woreb;* the Institute of Creative Writing (for Scribes) is called *Tsehof;* and the Institute of Literature (for Scholars) is called *Brana.*[7] It generally covers six or seven years

---

4   Ethiopia is the only country in Africa, which has its own extensive script. Most African countries use either Arabic or Latin characters. The Ethiopian syllabary is an indigenous development perhaps from Sabaean (South Arabic) scripts at least 2,500 years ago. (See Thomas O. Lambdin, "Alphabet" in *The Interpreters Dictionary of the Bible,* vol. 2, p. 89-96, New York, 1962).

5   Although small girls often learned the syllabary with the boys, and some families had their daughters tutored at home, women's education emphasized "home economics." Cooking well is regarded as an important skill in Ethiopian tradition and the expression *ba'ala-moyyá,* a term implying virtue and education, is ascribed to a woman who has achieved special skill in the art.

6   *Ge'ez* is the ancient language of Ethiopia, which probably gave rise to some of the modern Semitic languages of Ethiopia. Some scholars have wrongly termed it "Ethiopic." *Ge'ez* is still the official language of the Church; Amharic, the modern official language, is to *Ge'ez* what French is to Latin, while Tigrinya, another major Semitic language of Ethiopia, is to *Ge'ez* what Italian is to Latin. (See E. Ullendorff, *The Semitic Languages of Ethiopia,* Oxford, 1956.)

7   The alphabet has twenty-six basic characters in *Ge'ez* and thirty-three in Amharic, all of which are consonants. There are seven vowels indicated by vowel signs: vertical or horizontal dashes, rings, etc. These vowel signs which are attached to the basic letter-forms are

for pupils ranging in age from five to twelve. The first level of study in reading is the *fidel* syllabary.[8] After having learned the alphabets, the student passes on to the second level of study called *Fidel Hawaria* (the Apostles Syllabary), which includes reading and memorizing I John 1, 2. The third stage is the memorization of the Apostles' Creed and portions of the New Testament called *Gäbäta Hawaria*. The fourth, highly respected stage, called *Dawit*,[9] involves memorization of the Psalms as well as proper intonation in reciting. A feast celebrates graduation. A graduate of the School of Reading can read and recite fluently, but he is hardly at home in writing and is fit to serve as a good deacon in the church. Those who have the opportunity and the inclination for more than an elementary education will pass on to the higher schools.

The three other institutes are schools for highly advanced levels of study. The first of these is the School of Music (for Priests). It is traditionally known as the House of Melody (Chant) *(Zema Bet),* as it is the place where priests go to learn how to chant in church services. Nearly all Ethiopian religious poetry and prose are to be sung, and it is interesting to note that a student does not go to a theological seminary but to a music school to qualify for priesthood.

There are three departments of music each taking about three years to complete: *(1) Degguwa* - in Bethlehem, near Gondar; *(2) Zimare* and *Mewas'et* - in Zurumba, Bagameder; and *(3) Qiddase* and *Sa'atat* - in Serekula, Wallo Province, and Debre-Abbäi in Tegrai. The first, besides being the general name for church song, is a collection of hymns for singing throughout the year. Classified with this are the famous *Soma Digguwa* (Lenten hymns), *Me'eraf,* and other general hymns. The second are hymns sung after the liturgy *(Zemare)* and prayers for the dead *(Mewaset).* The third is, most appropriately, the section for priests who

---

combined with the consonants as to form 182 "syllables" in *Ge'ez* and 231 "syllables" in Amharic. Four letters, g, h, k, q, when accompanied by five dipthongs, are written individually to form 20 characters. Traditionally, students were required to master the whole table of syllables chanting to the sound of the seven vowels.

8   Special thanks to Liq Mamhera Demitrus for his assistance in translation.

9   The basic text of the Ethiopian Morning Service is the Book of Psalms (Dawit), supplemented generally by a collection of nine odeas all but one of which come from the Old Testament and other Hebrew sources. They are: (1) The Prayer of Moses (Exodus 15:1 ff., Deuteronomy 32:1 ff, Deuteronomy 32:22 ff.); (2) The Prayer of Hannah (I Samuel 2:1 ff.); (3) The Prayer of Hezekiah (Isaiah 38:10 ff.); (4) The Prayer of Prophet Minas; (5) The Prayer of Prophet Jonas (Jonas 3:3 ff.); (6) The Prayer of Prophet David (Daniel 9:4 ff.); (7) The Prayer of Three Holy Children (Hananiah, Azariah, and Mishael of the Book of Daniel). This song is contained in the LXX Daniel but not in the Hebrew Book of Daniel and is found in the Apocryphal English Bible. Verses 35 and 36 of this Song are known as "Benedicti Omnia Opera," used as a hymn in the Christian churches since ancient times; (8) The Prayer of Habakkuk (Habakkuk 3:2 ff.); (9) The Prayer of Isaiah (Isaiah 26:9 ff.); and The Prayer of Mary (Magnificat) (Luke 1:46 ff.). Benedictus (Luke 1:68-79), and Nunc Dimmittis (Luke 2:29-32) are usually added to these.

learn *Qïddase* (general liturgy) and the hours of night services *(Sa'atat)*. In close connection with each department of the School of Dancing, called *aqwaqwam* (literally, posture, manner of standing or balancing). This is the field of religious dance, where accompanying the music with rhythm and dancing is studied. The average priest is required to master the *Qïddase* and *Se'atat* and to have a general knowledge of the others. Students who have the aptitude for good scholarship often avoid the priesthood, as ordination will prevent them from studying or from assuming higher offices in the Church.

The Institute of Creative Writing (for Scribes) is known as the *Qïne Bet*, or House of Poetry. The *däbtära* are graduates of this level of learning. As in ancient Israel there are in Ethiopia two distinct religious orders: secular and ecclesiastical - priests and "Scribes" *(däbtära)*. The *däbtära* is a very interesting figure in the Ethiopian intellectual and religious hierarchy. He is at once a singer, dancer, poet, scribe, and sometimes, a diviner. Without him church singing and dancing are impossible, especially during the most important church festivals. Though religious literature is often copied by people whose standards are below those of the *däbtära* (by priests and deacons, some of whom have specialized in the art of writing), he is the writer *par excellence*. But not only is he a copyist, he is a poet and composer in his own right. As the name implies, the *däbtära* probably originally arose as a class of manuscript copyists or writers who eventually gained fame because of the massive knowledge they acquired, no doubt through the texts they were meticulously copying. Nonetheless, they represent today a class of comparatively enlightened and sophisticated, non-priestly, non-ordained teachers of religion. Neither *däbtära* nor priests earn their living by the professions they hold. Many of both classes may cultivate land or receive a share from the Church's revenues. But the *däbtära* have other possibilities of income, such as serving as court scribes, lawyers, or even as diviners.

The education required of a *däbtära* (beyond that minimal level necessary for priests) entails the study of philosophy and of a special genre of Ethiopian poetry known as *Qene*.[10] Thorough knowledge of *Ge'ez* language and grammar as well as a good knowledge of the Bible and the religious history of Ethiopia is a prerequisite for success in the School of Scribes. The student should have spent at least eight years in the School for Priests or the Schools for Chanting and Dancing. The best known Schools of Scribes are in Gondar and Wadala, and at Washara in Gojjam.[11]

---

10   Qene writing is believed to have been passed from one teacher to another from the time of Yared (6th century) until the present. A poet named Yohannes Balawi assured its continuity after a break in the tradition in the 13th century. (Cf. *Journal of Ethiopian Studies*, Vol. IV, No. 1, 1966.)

11   Other famous schools found in Tambyen, Chaq, out Qaqama. In Gonder they focus on chants and movements with s'enas'il; in Tambyen they focus on ...nmaship in which they excel.

In the School for Scribes, some aspects of Greek philosophy are studied. The main text used is the *Mäs'hafä Falasfa Tabiban - Book of Wise Philosophers, which* contains passages from Plato, Aristotle, Diogenes, and Cicero (and also David and Solomon!).[12]

More interesting is the study of the work of the 17th century Ethiopian philosopher Zär'a Ya'aqob and his pupil, Walda Heywat. Zär'a Ya'aqob was an enlightened man, far ahead of his time in his unbiased criticism of Christianity, Islam, and Judaism. The famous Ethiopist and scholar, Enno Litmann, says of him: "A man like Zär'a Ya'aqob gave utterance at the time of the Thirty Years' War to thoughts which first became current in Europe at the time of Rationalism in literature."[13] Zär'a Ya'aqob was born in Axum on August 31, 1599, a descendant of a line of priests although his parents were poor farmers. The sage attended traditional school, where he studied the Book of Psalms of David and Zema (singing). Lacking a good singing voice, he transferred to another school, where he spent a decade studying the Holy Scriptures. From that point on, he became a philosopher, whose ideas emphasized the importance of a matrimonial relationship of unity and equality between man and woman. He spoke out against monastic life, religious sectarianism, and the domination of men over women. Zär'a Ya'aqob spent his life preaching the existence of one God, the Creator; the need for people to set rules to live together in peace; and the importance of humans as thinking beings to not accept all ideas but to seek the truth for themselves.[14]

At the highest level of the Ethiopian educational system is the Institute of Literature (for scholars), called *Mäs'haf Bet,* or House of Books, which is a school of literature and history.[15] There are classes on oral exegesis of the Old and New Testaments, Church Fathers, monastic literature, ecclesiastical and civil law, Ethiopian and world history. *Awäled,* "imagination" (fiction) literature is also studied here. Although one need not be a monk to be a scholar, and indeed there are illiterate monks—besides the rank and file of unwed deacons, *däbtära,* and widowed priests; nevertheless, this higher school of study is centered at several monasteries and many famous Ethiopian scholars are monks.

---

12   See Harden, op. cit., p. 92 ff.

13   Conti Rossini denies the authenticity of this work and ascribes it to a 19th century religious cynic, Padre Giusto da urbino. This author concurs with E. Littmann (see *Corpus Scriptorum Christianorum Orientatium,* Vol. 31, London, 1904).

14   Giday, Belai. *Ethiopian Civilization.* Addis Ababa, December 1992 (161 - 162).

15   It should be noted that the life of the students is very rigorous. They live far away from home. So, they go around begging for their daily meals or helping farmers with farm work. Many scholars including Archbishop Marqorias have reported how they had to beg for food, even for their teachers.

Monks, especially hermits, have at times exerted great influence on Ethiopian society. Kings listen to their counsel, and they are esteemed as prophets. But other monks who have achieved a higher level of study can become advisers and high officials in the government. Whether it is a priest, a *däbtära,* or a monk who has reached this very high level of learning, all are regarded with esteem and referred to as *liq* (most exalted elder). The course takes about ten years, according to traditional pedagogy, and any graduate of the Scholar's Institute, by the schooling for at least thirty years, is as competent as any well-trained theologian in Europe or America in sophisticated philosophical and theological discourse.

It is interesting to observe how the different levels of learning fit into the social structure of the Ethiopian Church. The purpose and content of education are religious, but it must be noted that since in Ethiopia religion and life are intricately tied together, the learned man is not required to be a priest. Nor can the society function in the traditional sense without the enlightenment and guidance of the men of learning - all students of religion.

Within the confines of this educational system, very little change is taking place either in the aims and goals of education or in the structure and organization of the system. Nonetheless, the Ethiopian Church is intrinsically a more flexible institution than an outsider may think, especially as contrasted with Western Christendom. In this respect, it is not burdened with elaborate dogmatic and philosophical formulae that make flexibility impossible.[16] The hostility and suspicion that often seem to emanate from religious circles towards change are, however, unfortunate temporary reactions to many external forces that have been found dangerous through bitter historical experience. The confinement and isolation that resulted from the Christian-Moslem conflicts of the early era of Islam and the sixteenth-century Ottomans, the havoc and theological controversies that plagued the nation in the early decades of the seventeenth century as a result of Jesuit intrusion, and in modern times, the example of a leading Italian missionary who spied for the Fascists, have been the chief causes of the Church's tendency to doubt the sincerity of many things foreign, including imported educational ideas. In modern times, the alienation from the Church on the part of the many educated people has only reinforced the traditional concerns, and retarded its fuller participation in modern education.

Although past experiences have made the Church very cautious, there is some sign of hope that it will not be long before the Ethiopian Church will begin to realize the importance of adapting to new needs and times. It already appears that institutions are gradually becoming more receptive to modern education and is beginning to absorb some innovations. On the elementary level, these include teaching simple arithmetic. And since 1950, after it was urged by the government,

---

16   Cf. H. M. Hyatt, *The Church of Abyssinia,* London, 1937, pp. 85 ff, 281 ff.

more emphasis has been put on learning and teaching the art of writing in comparison to traditional oral practice. Many younger Church children who formerly would have entered Church services as deacons are now gradually seeking secretarial positions in village offices and courts. Besides, the Church no longer objects to modern rather than traditional schools.

Though many scribes and manuscript writers are still busy, the limited introduction of printing has robbed them of prestige and livelihood. Nonetheless, many priests and *däbtära* have found their way into government schools, especially as teachers of Amharic or of morals and religion, and the Ministry of Education has instituted special training for teachers of the latter. They also rank among modern authors of general literature, short stories, historical sketches, grammars, and small textbooks used especially on the elementary level. Despite the great contribution they are making to Ethiopian progress-consciousness, university-trained people to a certain extent lag behind the traditional scribes in producing substantial works of literature and scholarship. This is, in a way, understandable because the *däbtära* or other Church-trained people have first-hand acquaintance with Ethiopian languages, literature, history, and tradition compared to those educated abroad; and the traditional men of learning indeed deserve great credit for the initiative they have taken. Even among the educated, many who received Church education before going abroad and some who were, in fact, sent abroad to study theology are now leaders in Ethiopian studies and professors for the Addis Ababa University.

A major innovation in Ethiopian Church education was the establishment of a modern theological school in Addis Ababa. The Trinity Theological College was originally established in 1944 to enlighten churchmen in modern and secular learning. At that time, it looked to the Ministry of Education for its administration and to the Church for its guidance, but now the University provides administrators as well. The former departments of deacons' and priests' education have been re-organized under the new administration, and the theological school is now a college in its own right, with a small, modern library. The lecturers have theological training. Some received degrees from Union Theological Seminary in New York. Students have to qualify for college entrance exams, and after four years receive B. Th. degrees. There is also a new theological seminary in Axum.

One of the achievements of the former theological school, before it was incorporated into the University, was producing a group of advanced students who were sent to Orthodox seminaries abroad, to such places as Alexandria, Athens and Istanbul. Some of the returnees are now providing new leadership for the Church. Several, especially those who proceeded to study in Germany, have distinguished themselves as young scholars. Not only are these theological graduates providing leadership in administration, but also they are helping to bring some new reform into the Church. The growing tendency for Church services to be conducted in Amharic, the use of the radio as a medium of religious education, the providing of adequate translations of the Bible and other Church literature in Amharic, are results of the co-operation of former Church scholars with new theologians.

But, in the final analysis, even the Theological College with its emphasis on modern theological study, cannot be a substitute for traditional learning. By and large, the teaching of such subjects as *Qïne*, Ethiopian philosophy, and literature must either be taught in modernized institutions, or they must be absorbed into regular university curricula if the desire of the educated, who continue to be interested in traditional learning, is taken seriously. The introduction of the study of Ethiopian history and languages, even if at present only rudimentary, and the establishment of the Institute of Ethiopian Studies could lead in the latter direction. There is no question that the subjects taught in the third (writing) and fourth (literature) levels of traditional schools of learning fit properly into a university program. But although at the present time the study of *Digguwwa* (chanting - second level) seems restricted to traditional schools, its future is still uncertain due in part to the nature of the subject. To preserve Ethiopian chanting one need not introduce the difficult program of *Digguwwa* chanting into a university or secondary school curriculum, but perhaps establish for it a modern *Digguwwa* institute or incorporate it into a modern school of music.

The beginnings of modern Ethiopia date back to the reign of Emperor Tewodros (1855-1868). Emperor Tewodros was not of the Solomonic dynasty, but reunited Ethiopia after the regionalized Zämänä Mäsafint (Era of Princes). Recognizing the danger of impending attacks from foreign forces, Atse Tewodros began the process of modernization in Ethiopia. He sought combat equipment, technology, and weaponry by importing foreign arms and attempting to produce arms within the country. Despite Atse Tewodros' conviction that the fellow Christian monarchy of Britain would come to Ethiopia's aid against Muslim attacks, Queen Victoria ignored his diplomatic attempts of communication. The British Queen was more concerned with her imperial endeavors of trade and investment in Egypt than with any alliance in the name of Christ. Infuriated, Atse Tewodros imprisoned the British mission to Ethiopia, and Britain responded by sending Sir Robert Napier and a military force to Ethiopia. Tewodros released the prisoners and sent a peace offering (a herd of cattle), but the British forces continued to fight, looting the capital of Maqdala and taking the treasures to Britain, where they still remain today. On the battlefield, Emperor Tewodros committed suicide rather than be taken captive by the British Army. There ended the calamitous career of Emperor Tewodros and his program for training Ethiopians in modern skills.

The main ambitions of this far-sighted and vigorous ruler were to unify and consolidate the Ethiopian state, and to free Jerusalem and the Holy Land from the Turks by uniting all Christendom under one banner. He accomplished the first to a great extent and further initiated a program of educating Ethiopians in modern skills with the help of craftsmen whom he brought from Europe

The greatness and far-sightedness of Emperor Tewodros educational plan lay in its recognition of the importance of European technical skill and placing a priority on the development of an extensive technical education. Emperor Tewodros understood that Ethiopia's real need was not a new order of academic and humanities institutions, which remotely paralleled the already existing Ethiopian Church educational system. He is said to have thought that Ethiopian Church education, if totally reformed, expanded, and made available to all, could provide a basis for modern institutions that could compete in academic matters with any available in Europe. Therefore, he was anxious not to introduce the European system of academic education, but to press for men skilled in technology. Unfortunately, this plan for special emphasis on technical education faded out.

Under the influence of another innovative Ethiopian ruler, Emperor Menelik II, modern European-style elementary and secondary schools were finally established in Addis Ababa and Harar about 1908. As a result, mere decades ago, 96 percent of all Ethiopian school children received more or less classical academic education while only about 6 percent received the technical training that is so necessary and important in the modern world (yet the children of today's Ethiopia are not even given the same level of education and skills training offered during Menelik's time, a whole century ago). Around 1930, state education was finally constituted with the creation of a Ministry of Education. Before the Italian invasion in 1935, some thirty government and mission primary schools existed in Ethiopia, and some fifty Ethiopians were being educated abroad.

During their occupation of Ethiopia (1936-41), the Italians closed down most of the government and mission schools, except Italian Roman Catholic schools with a few centers where children got token education and learned to march and sing Fascist songs. Soon after the war ended in 1942 the Ministry of Education was reopened; the British educational system was made the basis of Ethiopian education, and Emperor Haile Sellassie himself took the portfolio of the Minister. In 1967 there were 378,750 elementary school students, 50,438 in secondary education, 2,619 in University education, 1,565 enrolled in foreign universities, and some 3,451 in technical education.[17]

---

17 "Patterns of Progress," Ministry of Information, Addis Ababa, 1967.

It is said that when modern education was introduced into Ethiopia, it was met by opposition. An American sociologist wrote of hardy youngsters in some regions of Ethiopia who, opposed by their parents, sought education on empty stomachs and attended school wearing rags. Missionaries give many examples of the Church's opposition to modern education. These incidents, however, cannot tell us what may have been the Church's real attitude towards modern education. Whatever opposition existed was partially due to occasional resistance by individual clergy, and to many parents' fears that their children were being converted to foreign ideas or religions. The reason for their concern is understandable when one considers the unhappy effects of foreign contact in the past, and the Fascist intrusion only confirmed the fears of many. Furthermore, one can readily understand the attitudes of families whose children formerly stayed at home and assisted in family chores. On the whole, while the Church has given no special impetus to modern education, neither has it undertaken a systematic and official programme of opposition, even when many of the Church's educated young people are turning their backs on it. Quite to the contrary, many priests and *däbtära* have found their way well into the modern public schools as writers and teachers.

Ethiopians have always regarded learning very highly, and Ethiopian children continue to crave knowledge today. But the incorporation of modern learning inevitably produces a certain amount of strain in a culture with deep historical roots. The Church's concern and sensitivity to this issue are, therefore, entirely natural. If, at the beginning, the Church had some hesitation about modern education, it is because the modern schools were structured like the missionary schools in which many members of the Ethiopian Church were proselytized. For it must be noted, after all, that the Ethiopian Church, which throughout the ages offered the only type of education, and which to this date still runs perhaps up to some four thousand institutions, cannot have an indifferent attitude.

Though modern academic or classical education with its certainly great potential has not yet really made a sufficient and significant impact on the development of Ethiopian society, it has nevertheless succeeded in inducing some change by creating a new element in the Ethiopian social structure: a highly educated class of young people who can become the leaven of progress. About ninety per cent of these educated people were formerly affiliated with the Ethiopian Church. An American sociologist claims "most Ethiopian students mention 'religion' more frequently than any other subject except success in school as the question on which they are most in accord with their parents."[18] Yet he, too, recognizes a constant decrease in conventional piety as the students move from secondary to college levels. Secularization turns a number of stu-

---

18   Donald Levine, *Wax and Gold,* 1965, p. 128.

dents from traditional religion. But, by and large, in a society in which religion has been and still is a national, not personal, institution, it is hard to determine the extent to which the Church is losing power when a few members drift away due to secularization.

The Ethiopian Church, the storehouse of learning and knowledge throughout the past centuries, can, if it chooses to be enlightened by its great past, facilitate the path to modern education and development. The Church's lack of fundamental dogmatism, its willingness to introduce new curricula even if on a minor scale and to play a part in modern schools, its readiness to use modern vehicles such as the radio, to make itself relevant to modern society, and especially its support of a new theological school are hopeful signs of the Church's readiness to participate in extensive educational reform. One must bear in mind that the Church had held no official, systematically imposed, position on the curriculum of the traditional schools. In one respect, one cannot really speak about an organized Church education, but rather of traditional—to be sure religious—teaching and learning which every village and every Church played a part in autonomously.

Chapter 9

Ethiopian Church Music

❖

The story of the composition of the Ethiopian church music is told in the *Gädlä Yared* and *Mäzgäbä Digguwa*. The composition of the most well-known books of church chants, the *Digguwa*, is attributed to the patron Saint Yared (501-576 CE). Saint Yared lived during the reign of Gebra Masqal, who was one of the famous Emperor Kaleb. Born in Axum from a line of priests, Yared was sent to church school but found mastering the alphabet difficult. He ran away to nature, giving up on his education. The story tells of a little ant who attempts to climb a tree, six times unsuccessfully but the seventh triumphantly, inspired Yared to persevere in his studies. Some ascribe to Yared a supernatural revelation, in which he was taken to heaven by angels to learn the plainsong of Paradise. In Ethiopian church paintings, the saint is usually depicted with singing doves of Paradise that sing divine music to him:

> O Yared Priest of the altar on high in the Heavenly Places, whither the glorious hand of the Father hath led thee, lead thou me also with thee that with thee I may chant together.

It is said that Yared was transported to heaven by three angels in the guise of three white birds. He was taken to the Garden of Eden, and inspiration for his music was born from the Garden's sights and sounds. Saint Yared founded a music academy at Beta Qetin in Axum. After selecting four of his pupils to teach and spread his musical system, Yared retreated into the Samen Mountains in the Gonder region and disappeared.

Through revelation, Yared learned the notation for writing Ethiopian music, which previously was transmitted orally from generation to generation. These notations (called *seraye*) consist of Ge'ez syllabic characters and numbers of curving and waving signs, lines, and points. They are small symbols, generally placed above the words to be sung and sometimes written in red, if it is ezel but black if rararay, indicating the melody and rhythm of the music. In effect, they are abbreviations that indicate musical phrases, groups of notes, or rhythmic values. Dynamics, modes and tempo are indicated by written signs (see illustration of a page from the *Digguwa*). The modes may be *Ge'ez* (*forte*), *E'zel* (*legato cantabile* and *piano*), *Arārāi* (*plaintive con motto*). The tempo may be *Marged* (*largo*), *Ne'us marged* (*andante*), '*Abiye Sefat* (*allegro*), and *Sefat* (*presto*). Anyone who has received church musical education is expected to know how to sing correctly using the traditional notation.

There are three modes or melody types in the music of the Ethiopian Church. These modes, called *Ge'ez* (major) daily, *'ezel* (minor) holidays, and *ara*ray (daily and holidays), are said according to the Synaxarion to have been directly revealed to the founder of Ethiopian Church music, St. Yared (see below). Musical scholars consider these modes to be melodic units with an initial syllabic section and concluding melismatic cadence. E. Wellesz and B. Velat have done extensive research to study these modes.

Velat gives the basic scale of the *'ezel* as chromatic, divided into two sections on the tenor range of a little less than two scales (g-f); the *Ge'ez* he takes to be built on the three basic notes of the major scale of about the same range from (g flat to e flat); and *ara*rai a pentatonic scale. These three zemas may be employed in the same hymn; and the chromatic intervals may also appear in any of the modes. Though Velat's analysis may be more accurate, I think we are still in need of a more thorough study and research into the meaning of these modes.

Some scholars compare the Ethiopian church modes to the Byzantine ones, and the melodic units with the *heirmoi* melodic units. According to Hannick, "whereas in Byzantine hymnody entire melodies are adopted to new texts, in the Ethiopian chant each small musical phrase is independently adopted."

Another interesting feature of Ethiopian church music is the notation used as mnemonic devices in chanting and singing. There are two types of these devices *melekets*, lit. sigla: the neumes and the letter signs. The signs are used to indicate the melodic phrase, emphasis, or manner of performance, not unlike what was used in the Middles Ages in Europe; they can indicate a tone or group of tones, rising, descending or steady tones. These signs of symbols consist of dot or dash-like signs, zigzagging and curving lines or the like. Their technical names: *cerat* (stroke), *darat* (chest), *fezz* (steady?), *anbar* (putting down), *defat* (press, push), *yezat* (pull), *rekrek* (trill), *qenat*, and the others give us a vague idea of what they stand for. There are generally about twelve of these signs. Wellesz gives about fifteen.

In their form, shapes, and function these neumes also have been compared to Byzantine *ekphonetikon* or *prosdicon*, Syriac *hagiopoli*, and Hebrew *Masoretic* accents (see Wellesz). Thus, though these signs have been attributed to Azaj Gerā and Ezra Rāguêl of the time of Emperor Galawedewos (1543-59) they are undoubtedly older. It is not unlikely that these two men rediscovered or reformed the use of these signs after the great cataclysmic period of Grān Mohammad, when it is said that many books of the Ethiopian church were burnt or destroyed. (Note: the neumes maybe used in conjunction with the abbreviations re, ti, res, ze, etc.).

Secondly, various Ethiopic alphabetic abbreviations consisting of one or more letters may be employed as musical notation, either alone or in conjunction with the above neumes. Of these types of musical symbols, varied numbers of them have been given, ranging from a few to over a thousand. Like the neumes, they are meant to indicate certain musical tones or group of tones, and they are based on abbreviations of one or more words called *serayu*. Essentially, mnemonic devices associated with the singing of certain phrases of some commonly used or well-known songs employing those words or phrases. As in the Byzantine tradition, if two such abbreviations are used together, they may indicate the beginning and end of a melodic line. Of course, certain songs, hymns or poems may (e.g. 'We shall overcome' or 'Silent night') be sang in more than one way or melody; in such cases, for example, two sets of signs, one red and one black, may be used to indicate the two respective melodies.

Another equally fascinating aspect of Ethiopian Church ritual or service is the custom of waving and moving the body and the use of certain musical instruments. In every respect the Ethiopian Church is deeply rooted in its African soil. If the African elements are not always evident in the syncretised religion, that cannot be said about this aspect of Ethiopian church practices. The use of bodily movements and sacred dancing is paralleled nowhere in Christendom but well known throughout Africa as part of various ritual services.

These body movements can be complex and require special training in the 'Aqwaqwam' School or "Movements School." There are however basically four types of *aqwaqwam* or dance; *qum* is simple movement with a *mäqwamya* or prayer stick (see below); *zïmare* is more elaborate with a *mäqwamya*; *marägäd* is movement together with drumming on percussion; *sef'at marägäd* occurs together with handclapping. Other traditional African musical expressions, such as dancing in a concentric circle with congregation participating, ululating, and even shouting of joy, humming, and the like are permitted in the Ethiopian church.

It is said that even purely instrumental performances of African music are generally verbally based. This is because music is regarded to be really a way of expressing one's deepest feelings and thoughts, and an effective expression of religious thought. So, the Ethiopian Church, like the rest of Africa employs various musical instruments regarded to be appropriate expressions to the function of the religious ritual. King David is depicted in many Ethiopian manuscripts either playing the lyre or dancing before the ark. Even though the lyre is now not used very much inside the church it is often used at Christian services outside the church. At some services, for instance at *Mäsqäl* or *Tïmqät*, trumpets, flutes, arched harps, shofars, lamellophones, stopped flute ensembles, and varieties of musical instruments known all over Ethiopia and Africa are brought by people for use during these occasions. What makes the *Mäsqäl* and *Tïmqät* festivals in fact so colorful and attractive to so many thousands of the Ethiopian people is the free employment of varieties of musical expressions found all over Ethiopia; and music generally associated with the secular world are freely used: for example--panting, bleating, buzzing, and various onomatopoéic sounds; unison signing of the Nuer, four part songs of Dorze, the fuk*ä*ra and martial songs of the warriors, the polyphonic songs (godelling) of the peoples of southern Ethiopia can be heard during these two seasons.

Instruments of Ethiopia have been compared to that of ancient Egypt (truncated egg-shaped drums, sistra), Sumeria (large-box harp), but most are the traditional ones of Africa (the kettledrums with long drum sticks and the lamellophone being the best examples). However, the three most important musical instruments used inside the church commonly are the *käbäro*, *sänas'ïl*, and *qac'ïl.*

The *käbäro* is a cylindrical or tapered kettledrum of varying sizes, some rather large and majestic in sound. The *sänas'ïl* has rightly been compared to the ancient Egyptian sistra (it was probably used at the festival of Isis): it consists of a fork-shaped lyre, small metal percussion discs strung on two to four horizontal metal wires; and it gives a percussion sound when jangled, and is helpful in setting the rhythm. The *qac'ïl* is a small hand bell used at communion service to summon the communicants and at church processions. To these three may be added the *mäqwamya*, a T-shaped prayer stick with a tang cross of silver or brass, and which is waved or banged on the floor at the time of body movements; at other times, it is a used to place one's chin against during times of contemplation.

The *Dïgguwa* is the general name of the church hymnody; however, there are about 22 types of classification. Specifically, it contains hymns used for all fasts and feasts with the exception of the Lenten season. The hymns for the latter, that is, the Lenten season are contained in *Soma Dïgguwa*, and are sung up to Palm Sunday. *Mäwaset* (response) is the antiphonary of the church; it is a special collection of hymns identified by the *incipits* and *finit* of the preceding Psalm and used for three offices of about 50 annual church festivals including funeral and matrimonial services. In some ways it corresponds to the congregational responses used in Western churches. Another collection of hymns and chants is the *Mï'ïrat*, containing the common of the Office, used without the drums for ordinary daily service. Finally, the *Zïmaré* consists of hymns and canticles used at the conclusion of the Eucharistic services singing of poetry (cf. Ps.). Thus the antiphonal chanting or singing called the *Digguwa* forms the basic body of the Ethiopian church music. These hymns may employ any of the three modes or *zemas*

Besides the *Digguwa* there are varieties of other collections of hymns. Among those, mention must be made of *Tïbäbä Täbiban* (used in monasteries) and *Mahbärä Mï'ïmänan*, sometimes used during the Eucharistic service at the communion moment. Certain types of Ethiopian hymns have become part of the popular genre of poetry called *Qene* (dirge, rhymed poems), which are often sung at specific occasions and fixed places during the office. They are generally short and extemporized and sung after certain verses of the Psalter. Related to these we have the interesting *salam* songs and *malks* chanted at the festivals of different saints. These poems (also rhymed) consist of numerous stanzas each greeting or praising a specific organ or part of the saint's body: hair, head, eyes, face, eyebrows, ears, cheeks, nose, lips, mouth, teeth, neck, chest all the way down to the soles of the feet.

Perhaps one of the most original features of the Ethiopian church is its music, unmatched elsewhere, having its own special modes as well as spectacular features such as body movements and hand clapping. The music goes in perfect harmony with the solemnity of the Ethiopian church and its feasts, expressing sorrow, joy, meditation, exultation, prayer, and thanksgiving. It is very rich and moving by any standard of musical evaluation.

Although tradition holds that the learned Saint Yared invented and coded Ethiopian church music, there are other ideas as well. One line of Ethiopian tradition holds that music was introduced to Ethiopia by the Levites, the musicians and choristers of Solomon's Temples in Jerusalem, who came to Ethiopia with the Queen of Sheba. The History of Kings, *Tarikä Nägäst,* ascribes to Geza and Raguel the invention of the notation in the time of Galawdewos (1540-1559). However, the church tradition attributes musical notation and creation to Saint Yared, with later revisions accredited to church fathers that followed.

Chapter 10
The Church and Its Institutions

Since church and society in Ethiopia form an inseparable entity, the leaders of the Ethiopian Church have come both from members of the ordained clergy and from learned laymen and churchmen. In some cases, the latter have had even more control over the Church than the former.

The chief executive of the Church has traditionally been the Emperor. Yet, at times when smaller kings and chiefs ruled the country, the Church organization has acted as a unifying force, overriding the limited power of one chief or monarch, and extending over the frontiers of smaller kingdoms.

In nominal rank, next to the Emperor comes the *Abuna ("Patriarch")*, who until 1950 was a Copt/ Egyptian appointed by the Patriarch of Alexandria from among the monks of the monastery of St. Anthony, near the Red Sea and different monasteries (estimated to be 110 Coptic Abunas; the last one is *Abuna* Qerlos). It is popularly believed that this tradition of bringing *Abunas* from Egypt was in accordance with the history and tradition of the Ethiopian Church. It is the accepted view that the first *Abuna (Patriarch)*, Frumentius, was ordained in 330 CE by the Egyptian Patriarch Athanasius (d. 375). To preserve this historic and friendly tradition, the government paid a large fee to the Moslem government of Egypt to send an Egyptian or Coptic *Abuna* to head the Ethiopian Orthodox Täwahïdo Church for many centuries. (It should be noted that Athanasius was not a Copt in the sense that we refer to the Egyptian Orthodox Church today, but in the grammatical sense he was a Copt meaning, Egyptian). (It should be noted that a Copt in the sense that we use the word today to designate the Orthodox Church of Egypt—that we use it today—in actual hierarchy, not only was the *Abuna* subordinate to the Emperor, but also, as far as actual power in state and church were concerned, very weak despite his nominal rank and the outward respect accorded to him. Furthermore, he was politically subordinate to native Church leaders as well. His main tasks were purely formal: he sat at the Emperor's right hand at all public occasions, he crowned the new Emperor; ordained priests and deacons; blessed the altar stones for churches; and upon the order of the Emperor or the Church, he could either issue blessings or excommunications; and finally he could liberate people from their oaths, generally for political reasons. Examples have been given elsewhere of how the *Abuna* released a whole army from allegiance to Emperor Susenyos (1605-1632), or how Tewodros, in 1854, intercepted and forced the *Abuna* to crown him instead of his rival Ras Wube of Tigre; in 1916, the *Abuna* released the Shoan leaders from their oath of allegiance to Lij Iyyasu, who was at the time suspected of favouring controversial political parties. But in all these cases, the *Abuna* always acted as agent of some powerful person or organization. He was never allowed to leave the country without permission. Church administration was, however, always relegated to the *Ichege*.

Though the Copts knew well how insignificant the position held by their envoy to the Ethiopian Church actually was, they still enjoyed seeing the Ethiopian Church as a subordinated daughter of their own. The 700-year relationship was only broken between 1500 and 1633; hence, the Copts made it difficult for the Ethiopian Church to install its own bishops and *Abunas*. Nonetheless, they understood that the Ethiopian Church was not a mere satellite of the Coptic Church, and that its ritual, doctrine, calendar, and practices proceeded along indigenous lines of development. For their part, the Ethiopians, who knew that the spirit of the nation had found intense expression in the national religion, never felt any dependence on the Coptic Church; therefore, they never considered it seriously necessary or important to break the old formal ties until new political developments in the nineteenth century necessitated such a course. Actually, it was neither a council nor a synod that decreed the appointment of Coptic metropolitans for Ethiopia. Frumentius, the first bishop, a Syrian Christian, not a Copt, was chosen by the Ethiopian Church itself and sent to Alexandria, where he was supposedly consecrated by Athanasius. Interestingly enough, however, Athanasius was neither a Copt (in respect to the later nomenclature of Egyptian Christians) nor a Miaphysite. From a historical point of view, it is still not clear what relationship, if any, the Ethiopian Church had with the Coptic Church before about 1270. At this time with the rise of a new political dynasty, there was adopted a forged Coptic canon enacting the appointment of Coptic *Abunas* and decreeing that no Ethiopian should be appointed metropolitan.[1] To guard this law, the Copts saw to it that the number of bishops in Ethiopia was limited. It was not until more than seven centuries later that Emperor

---

1   This is said to be the 42nd canon of the Pseudo Arabic Canons of the Council of Nicea. (Cf. H. M. Hyatt, *The Church of Abyssinia,* London, 1937, p.45.) It should be noted that the 20 official Nicean canons are different (associated with the work called Fitha Nagast 'Judgments of King').

Johannes (1872-1889) was able to obtain the concession of four bishops instead of the traditionally single one.

Emperor Johannes IV is also said to have taken the initiative in asking the Patriarch of Constantinople for Armenian bishops, but without the agreement of his Church. Around the beginning of the First World War, the Russian Church attempted unsuccessfully to replace the Coptic *Abuna* with a Russian.

The Ethiopian desire to replace the foreign primate who possessed supreme spiritual prestige, though an alien to the language, culture, and psychology of the Ethiopian people, developed more impetus during the Italian occupation of Ethiopia (1936-1941). More important than the fact that the Italians themselves encouraged the appointment of a native metropolitan – a political move on their part to appease the Ethiopian Church – was the behaviour of the Coptic Patriarch during the early days of the occupation, which sealed the fate of the Coptic *Abuna*.

The Italians, who quite correctly assessed the strength of the bond between Ethiopian nationalism and the Church, as well as the powerful influence of the Church on the people, proceeded very cautiously in matters pertaining to religion. Still they used the political ideology of "divide and rule" – divise et impera. On the one hand, they did all they could to win the favour of the Church; on the other, they decided to weaken and undermine its influence gradually rather than to arouse anger and resistance through open persecution. To accomplish the latter aim, the Italians used such methods as encouraging Islam and Catholic Christianity under the slogan of "absolute respect for (all) religions."[2] They claimed that their purpose was to free the Moslems and Catholics from domination and oppression, which they alleged to have existed. They also supported pilgrimages to Mecca and Rome; built mosques and Catholic churches (in some cases near their own headquarters); and encouraged the development of the province of Harar as a Moslem centre.[3] It is understandable, therefore, why many Ethiopian Muslims and Catholics supported the Italians, and why some even fought alongside Italian soldiers against the forces that fought to liberate Ethiopia in 1941. Finally, the Italians proclaimed that they had withdrawn the spiritual and traditional right of the Church to crown emperors, on the grounds that this was an offence to "three million Moslems."[4]

Another Italian method of exerting overt pressure was the encouragement of Italian Catholic missions. Not only were Protestant missionaries expelled and their property confiscated for use by Italian clerics, but also all non-Italian Roman Catholic societies, such as the respected French Catholics in Harar, were exiled from the country. Needless to say, Mussolini's government was not acting as an

---

2   M. Perham, *The Government of Ethiopia*, London, 1938, p. 123.

3   M. Perham

4   M. Perham,

agent of the Catholic Church, and many Fascist soldiers expressed open hatred for their Roman Catholic compatriots; nonetheless, the Italians made many efforts, even if non-coercive, to win over prominent persons to Roman Catholicism.

All these side pressures were occasionally accompanied by open persecution. In the early days of the occupation, many priests and monks who did not comply with the Italian authorities were mercilessly slaughtered. The *Itchege* (see below) had gone into exile with the Emperor; but of the four Ethiopian bishops in the country at the time of occupation, Bishop Petros was captured in 1936 and shot in the market-place in Addis Ababa, and Bishop Michael was put to death for helping the resistance movement. The worst incident took place in February, 1937, when after an attempt made on Governor Graziani's life, the Fascists exacted retribution by cold-bloodedly massacring about 12,000 citizens of Addis Ababa, as well as hundreds of monks in the monasteries of Debra-Libanos and Mount Zeqwala on the grounds that they had been collaborators and were hiding Ethiopia's fighting *arbagnoch* (patriots).[5]

By and large, however, the Italians realized that murder and persecution had but little effect on colonizing the country. It became more evident that they had to win the Church to their side to use its influence. The resultant behaviour of the Coptic *Abuna,* Qerlos, in this situation was destined to create further cause for Ethiopian criticism of the Copts. Qerlos is said to have preached submission; he suffered a wound at Graziani's side at a public occasion when the attempt on the latter's life was made. Cyril only parted company with the Italians when they pressured him on questions of the status of the Ethiopian Church, in relation to independence from Alexandria. The Italians, complying with the independence-minded national mood, pressed this issue as part of their attempt to win over the Church as well as perhaps to cut off any contacts with Ethiopian refugees in Egypt and Jerusalem. Therefore, the Italians, upon Cyril's return to Egypt, appointed the half-blind Ethiopian bishop Abraham as the first metropolitan. He submitted to the Italians and in turn ordained twelve bishops, one of whom, Johnness, succeeded him when he died. The fourth pre-Italian bishop, Isaac, was imprisoned until he, too, bowed to Italian policy. The Italians gave the Church a new constitution and divided Ethiopia into ten bishoprics based, ironically, upon laws from the *Fetha-Nagast,* but designed to result in dependence on the viceroy. However, a large number of clerics remained unsubdued and continued to oppose Fascist aggression. The Coptic Patriarch excommunicated the schismatic metropolitan, along with the twelve other bishops he ordained.

It was not until the Ethiopian liberation, then, that a nationally recognized Ethiopian metropolitan was installed and Ethio-Coptic relations were rede-

---

5   Trimingham, J. Spencer. *The Christian Church and Missions in Ethiopia.* WORLD DOMINION PRESS, London, 1950 (19).

fined. Upon the departure of the Church, authority remained in his hands, even though the old Coptic *Abuna* Cyril, who had returned to Ethiopia on his own initiative with an Alexandrian delegation sometime in the middle of 1942, was gradually and very reluctantly allowed by the government to resume, at best nominally, his old position. Tactfully, though not entirely happy, the government did not reject the excommunicated bishops. Instead, it focused on the criticism of Alexandria itself, which had been complacent in the moment of Ethiopia's travail. The nationalism, which had raised the question of the Church's relations with Alexandria even before the interference of the Italians, was now vigorously intensified.

It must be noted that Ethiopia's desire to part company with Alexandria was dictated by the new politics of the nineteenth and twentieth centuries; it was not a doctrinal rift that Ethiopia sought. As enunciated by a delegation in 1942, Ethiopia wanted its own native *Abuna,* who would also consecrate bishops and suffragans chosen by a wholly Ethiopian synod. After almost three years delay, the Coptic synod that met in 1945 flatly refused the Ethiopian request.[6] In November, 1945, leading government and Church officials deliberated extensively about the matter, and by a vote on November 26th 75 percent decided in favour of a proposal that Ethiopia choose her own bishop, defeating a second proposal to send another delegation to Egypt. This initiative caused the Coptic Church "to bow before the Ethiopian pressure for autonomy"[7] and the Coptic Holy Synod found itself in a position where it had no choice but to comply with the Ethiopian requests. Nevertheless, the election of an Ethiopian archbishop and the formation of an Ethiopian Holy Synod, which the Coptic Patriarch granted, did not define the exact power of the archbishop and his bishops. In this context, the Patriarch of Alexandria insisted in reserving the authority to consecrate bishops. The Ethiopian imperial-ecclesiastical council rejected this altogether. An appeal by the Egyptian government (which always indirectly enjoyed the Coptic tie with Ethiopia) on behalf of the Coptic Church was of no avail. The controversy, however, lasted for several more years until July 13, 1948, when an agreement was finally reached providing that the Patriarch of Alexandria, Yasob II, install five other bishops, and that afterwards, one of them should become the metropolitan, *Abuna* Bassilios, and could install other bishops. In 1950, upon the death of the last Coptic *Abuna* Cyril – who, as said above, had returned to Ethiopia uninvited after the expulsion of the Italians – Bishop Basileus, a former *Itchege* (see below) from Debre-Libanos, became the first

---

6 For details of these developments, see the *Ethiopian Herald* (November 26, December 3, 1945; February 2, July 1, 7, 15, 22, 29 (1946); the London: *Times* (February 2, 1946); *Misri, the Egyptian Gazette* (June, December, 1942; January, February, May, September, 1944); cf. M Perham, op. cit. p. 126 ff.

7 *Herald.* December 3, 1945.

nationally recognized Ethiopian *Abuna*. The 1948 agreement stipulated that the chief metropolitan would continue to be installed by the Coptic Patriarch. But in 1958, a further agreement was reached by which the Ethiopian Church was made conclusively independent, and authorized to choose and install her own Patriarch. Thus ended a 700-year-old relationship projected by the impetus of "the newer trend toward full national self-expression for the nations of the world."[8]

The rank and role of the *Abuna is* now significantly altered. Not only does being made a Patriarch raise his status, but also as said earlier, he is no longer a stranger. Furthermore, the late *Abuna* occupied the position of *Itchege* (see below) before assuming his present post, and seems to have incorporated and consolidated that duty. Not only will the *Abuna* now have the power to ordain priests and deacons, but also to appoint and consecrate bishops. In questions of dogma, morals, and discipline, he will be the head of the last court of appeal; the dispenser of vows; and the superintendent of theological education. No canon law or custom need deter him from promulgating doctrine without fear of opposition or national prejudice. Though he does not sit in the council of ministers (he was a member of the Crown Council – an honorary post), yet his religio-political authority can be extensive and his advice heeded in the councils of the government.

The singular autonomy that an Ethiopian Patriarch enjoys has not been fully incorporated by the late Primate; perhaps he was too advanced in old age to have been able to take full advantage of his powerful post. Who will succeed him was long an open question. The popular Archbishop of Harar, who was for all practical purposes the acting Patriarch of Ethiopia, was, as often been predicted, chosen. But, whether the ancient role of the *Itchege* will remain consolidated by the Patriarch or whether that office will be transferred to the *Liqä Seltanat* (see Page 38), who was a member of the Imperial Cabinet, or what the role of the monastery of Debre-Libanos will be, was not clear then.

The *Itchege* traditionally came next in rank to the *Abuna*, but surpassed him in actual power.[9] He was not an ordained ecclesiastic, but a monk who served as grand prior of the monastery of Debre-Libanos before being appointed by the emperor to his post. He is the direct successor of Tekle Haymanot, who was the founder and the father of both the monastery of Debre-Libanos and the office of the *Itchege*. Tekle Haymanot was also instrumental in bringing the Solomonic Dynasty to power, and in some respect, it can be said that the office of *Itchege*, who generally resided in Gondar, administered the Church, visited monasteries to correct abuses, and served as a check on the *Abuna* and the Coptic Church.

---

8   *Herald.* December 3, 1945.

9   The present patriarch has consolidated the office of both the *Abuna* and *Itchege*, a deed not approved by the majority.

His appointees, called the *Liqä Kahenat* (chief priests) served as his coadjutors, overseers of the monasteries and churches. With the *Abuna*, he supervised theological education, and he was in charge of all literature and manuscripts. His position as a government official and as head of a powerful order of monks always gave the *Itchege* tremendous influence. The last *Itchege* was made the first Ethiopian Patriarch, and as noted above, it appeared that the Patriarch had consolidated the former power wielded by the *Itchege,* however, it has been assumed by the chief priest of Trinity Church in Addis Ababa. He is called the *Liqä Seltanat* (chief of authorities) and was a member of the imperial cabinet. As has been suggested above, the changing roles of the *Itchege* and of the grand prior of Debre-Libanos must be taken into consideration before attempting to predict the direction that Church administration will take in the future.

The third most important ecclesiastic of the Ethiopian Church – the second in power traditionally – has always been the *Nebura'ed* of the sacred town and district of Axum. Although the provincial governor instead of the emperor sometimes appoints him, he is accorded a very high degree of respect and has the rare privilege of combining completely both secular and religious authority over the subjects of his district. In recent times another *Nebura'ed* has been appointed to reside in the small town of Addis Alam, near Addis Ababa, but the two differ greatly in historical importance.

Two other Church dignitaries enjoyed considerable political power through their activities at the imperial court. These were the *qeshatse* or the grand almoner, who acted as the King's father-confessor, and the *aqabe-sa'at* or the keeper of the seal or the watch (of canonical times), the chief ecclesiastic at the imperial court. The last *qeshatse* was killed in the 1960 coup and has not been replaced. Equal in rank to these two were also the *Liqä däbtära* (chief of the *däbtära*) and the *Liqä -mämhïran* (chief of the learned men), who together with them used to serve as the four supreme judges of the royal court. What significance these personages will have in the future is unpredictable.

To this list of dignitaries there have now been added at least fifteen bishops or archbishops who enjoy preeminent status by virtue of their ecclesiastical authority in each one of the governate-generals. Since 1958, all Ethiopian bishops, including the Patriarch, have been entitled "*Abuna*"; the Patriarch is referred to as *Liqä p'ap'asat wa patriarch,* chief of bishops and Patriarch, and each bishop of a governate-general is referred to as *Liqä -p'ap'as* or archbishop.[10] Since

---

10   In an attempt to keep the Ethiopian Church subordinate to the Coptic Church, the Pseudo-Arabic canons, falsely attributed to the Council of Nicea, could have limited to no more than seven the number of bishops Ethiopia could have. Later, the number was even reduced to two. Though originally the *Abuna* consecrated his own bishops, for several centuries the Patriarch deprived the *Abuna* of this privilege. Furthermore, whenever bishops were demanded, they were sent from the Coptic monasteries of Egypt and appointed and

1958, Ethiopia has had more than the number (twelve) of bishops required to consecrate the Patriarch, and the archbishops of each province enjoy much more power and prestige than the former bishops occasionally imported from Egyptian monasteries. The archbishops and bishops in the Church hierarchy, the most recent element in the Church's 1600-year history, will, it seems, be playing an increasingly significant role especially as a group.

Priest and deacons come after the archbishops and bishops in the clerical hierarchy. The duties of a priest *qes* (*cf. Aramaic qasis*) or *kahen* (*cf. Hebrew cohen*) include conducting daily services, baptizing, holding funeral services, visiting people and hearing confessions, occasionally solemnizing religious marriages, and performing extreme unction. Not only do they devote a great deal of time to people within their communities, of all classes and degrees of wealth, but they also often engage in agriculture (like the average Ethiopian peasant) and do business in local markets. Though a priest daily attends church and receives communion, he is not expected to burden the community with his own religious standards. On the contrary, he must not be a purist; according to a law promulgated in the fifteenth century, he must accept every penitent unquestioningly no matter how often he has sinned.[11] In turn, the priest is treated with respect and is given land to cultivate as well as a share of the revenues and gifts in kind. Church feasts, especially the memorial feasts for the dead or *tazkar* (see below, also cf. Hebrew zkr), provide occasion for merriment for the priests; in addition, they spend some time daily in the "gate of peace," a small house next to the church where the clergy assemble after services to chat and drink. The education of a priest, though modest, involves learning at least fourteen varieties of Church chants (see Chapter 1), and reciting and reading the liturgy and the Bible in *Ge'ez*, a language that only the most learned of them understand. The qualifications for the priesthood include also Eucharistic matrimony before ordination by the *Abuna* or archbishop. Priests are always distinguishable by the white turbans they wear and the crosses they carry to be blessed and kissed by the people they meet; in addition, they wear elaborate and highly colorful robes and carry multicolored umbrellas at religious functions.

Foreign travelers have often falsely accused Ethiopian priests of "ignorance" and heavy drinking. Though some of these criticisms may be well-founded in a few cases, the fundamental misconception is rooted in the observers' own

---

consecrated by the Patriarch of Alexandria, though they were of little importance. Unlike the *Abuna,* the other bishops could, if they wished, return to Egypt. Their chief duty was to say a prayer of admission for new monastic candidates, to bless the monks" skullcaps, and to purify and bless a church Tabot (Ark) if it was accidentally touched by a deacon or by a layman. But they had virtually no authority over the priests or the churches, according to the law in *Fetha-Nagast.*

11 Mäs'hafä Berhan, *Book of Light*, CSCO, Vol. 47, Louvain, 1964, p. 44.

"ignorance" lack of perspective: in Ethiopian society, priests are not necessarily required to be holier than ordinary people. Among the rank and file of priests there may be some culprits, but as a class they represent ritual sanctity and high moral standards. Offending priests are liable to punishment if convicted by an ecclesiastical court and "benefit of clergy" is abused.

In order to achieve progress in Ethiopia in the spheres of both education and community development, it is absolutely essential to understand the ways and the social position of the priests. In many respects, they are not a privileged group; on the contrary, they are part of the poorer masses. A sensible programme of development cannot afford to alienate them or to override them; the priests must be made sympathetic to programmes of modernization, and with the right approach, this can be accomplished. Recently, in one province of Ethiopia, priests sermonized in favour of reforestation after the regular services, and local cooperation with the programme was said to have become readily available.

Very closely associated with the priests are the deacons (*diyaqon*); they are pre-adolescent boys ordained by the *Abuna*, whose duties are to serve as acolytes and prompters, directing actions and responses of the congregation during the Mass, singing in high-tone chants that they have learned in the Church elementary school, carrying holy books, fetching holy water, and assisting in the preparation of Eucharistic bread and wine. The last is regarded as a secret privilege. At least three but often seven deacons are required at each communion service. Though ability to read is a prerequisite for the deaconate, some writers have spoken of babes in arms consecrated in the company of hundreds of aspirants.[12] On reaching adolescence, deacons who are feared to be at the age of puberty are generally dismissed to complete their study of reading and chanting, to get married, and consequently to be ordained for the priesthood. They often travel in search of teachers, wearing sheepskins for clothing and begging for their daily bread. A great deal of change and improvement must be expected in the training and office of the deacons if the office is to survive.

An interesting feature of the constitution of the Ethiopian Church is the importance of the lay orders. Much has been said above about the *Itchege* and their provincial deputies, the *Liqä Kahenat*; but important also are the *'aläqa*, the *däbtära*, and the *gäbäz*. On the local level, the *'aläqa* play a leading role, and one foreigner, noting their wealth and power, called their position "the most enviable."[13] An *'aläqa*, a learned *däbtära* or monk appointed by the civil authorities in some cases, is the lay head of the Church, who exercises authority over the priests and the deacons, looks after Church revenues, and acts as judge.

---

12   Alvarez, *Narrative of the Portuguese Embassy to Abyssinia* (translated by Lord Stanley of Alderley), Hakluyt Society, London, 1881, Bk. II, p. 354.

13   Plowden, *Travels in Abyssinia,* London, 1868, p. 88.

The *gäbäz* works with the *aläqa* as keeper of the accounts and property of the Church, as collectors of revenues, and as a sort of justice of the peace.

Though they have no formal position in the Church hierarchy, the *däbtära* (see Chapter 4) form a very important lay group in the Ethiopian Church, as intermediaries between clergy and laymen. Without them, services could not be held, since no one else can execute their chief duties of chanting and performing religious dances. To become a *däbtära,* a person must have completed a course of study that includes singing, body movement, writing *Qïne* (a literary form special to Ethiopian though some have compared the genre to the biblical book of Lamentations literary style), poetry, and philosophy. *Däbtäras* may earn a living by cultivating the land, by teaching, by copying manuscripts, by rendering esoteric magical services, or by serving as court scribes. In addition, they may receive Church revenues for their cantorial duties.

Another important force in the Ethiopian Church is the monastic system. Ethiopian monks comprise a composite group of unmarried deacons or priests, widowed priests or widowed or aged laymen coming from all walks of life, who have renounced worldly gains for a life of seclusion and asceticism. Once a man has taken the monastic vow, he is declared dead and a legal nonentity, free from tax obligations or debts. Though literacy is not a prerequisite for monasticism, many monks gather in famous centres of learning. Others become extreme ascetics and live as hermits, troglodytes, and anchorites, eating only leaves and wild plants. Among the latter group, a few occasionally emerge as wandering teachers who proselytize non-Christians, among the former, many who have lived close to society, have assumed very important posts in the Church hierarchy or serve as imperial advisers and governors. The counsel of monks is heeded, and they undoubtedly exert a great influence, perhaps even more than do the priests. An angry monk may be the only person who can openly and without fear criticize the government. The role monks have played in education and literature is noteworthy.

In Ethiopia, as in traditional Africa or the ancient near East, religious and civil functions have been inseparably combined in structure and administration. On the one hand, the state is supreme in the civic but also in the religious sphere; on the other, the Church requires the rulers and citizens of the state to participate in public worship. It also furnishes high officials for the state administration. Unlike both Eastern Orthodox and Western Christianity, Ethiopian Christianity has never experienced persecution by the state. Especially in its administration, the Ethiopian Church has been geared from the beginning to maintaining a religious attitude that permits both deep spiritual fervor and a sense of duty and obligation to the state.

This is not to say that the relationship between Church and state has not altered with changing social conditions; but adjustments were made in harmony with the times. The Church and its administrators continued to rest under the Emperor. To maintain the dignity of the Church administration, the emperors set the qualifications for ordination, supervised the churches and monasteries, and called Church councils. In turn, they used the skilled administrators and immense moral and educational power of the Church. This close co-operation between Church and state proved to be of inestimable value in times when either party was harassed by foreign political or religious powers.

Any understanding of the future of Church administration and the direction of change in Ethiopia should be evaluated against this background of the Church's constitution. Regardless of some developments in the medieval period, when there was only one Christian society, with the emperor superior in the East and the Pope superior in the West, the churches of Europe have from the beginning developed the theory of two societies, ecclesiastical and civil, each with its own rights and privileges. Such a heritage helped Western churches, especially in the United States, to adjust to a system where Church administration is totally autonomous. The philosophers of the Enlightenment offered a materialistic explanation for the origins of the universe and for the political and social order, maintaining that the state evolved from practical necessity and was dependent on popular will. Such ideas dissociated the church from civil power. It is such a background and such an experience that the Ethiopian Church lacks.

The administration of the Ethiopian Church had realized that reform was necessary if the Church was to adjust to the larger world. But no reforms would save the Church from difficulties unless Church administrators and officials were properly educated. In the last decade or two, more reform has taken place in the administration of the Ethiopian Church than during any other period of its history. Although it is too early to predict the effects of these changes, nevertheless, they represent the types of reforms that would enable the Church to move toward total independence from the civil government. The most important change is that the church since 1994 now has the complete autonomy to choose and to install its own national Patriarch. A native-born leader, who understands the language, culture, and psychology of his people, can wield the power and authority necessary to run the Church independently and give it a strong national administration. Such a momentous development can give a strong new structure to the Church. To be sure, if any one traditional institution in Ethiopia has an elaborate structure and organ, it is the Church. But the survival of this structure very much depends on the education and background of its leadership and the modernization of its offices.

The second important development in the Ethiopian Church since 1942 is the institution of new laws concerned with Church consolidation and incorporation. The new laws deal with centralizing the Church, and especially with rationalizing its finances. Church lands are to be taxed, and the revenues used for Church maintenance, education, and charity through the central Church treasury. The 'aläqa have been made responsible for collecting and paying into local church treasuries all the fees and offerings as well. The clerics are to be appointed in a fixed number to each church according to its needs; they will be assigned work on the basis of their qualification and paid for their services. An ecclesiastical council will make higher appointments. Another very significant provision of these decrees is that while the Church will have private jurisdiction over its congregation to inflict spiritual penalties through the confessional, it will give up its former temporal jurisdiction, which now will be in the hands of state judges. This reform is gradually becoming effective, especially since at the start, many Churchmen were elected as state officials to serve as local justices with government salaries, although in some areas the new laws exist only in theory. The large-scale reforms they are intended to achieve cannot be accomplished without more clearly-worded edicts supported by popular education.

Here arises the issue of participation by Ethiopia's educated young people. The indifference of the Church and the aloofness of the educated have resulted in a lack of dialogue between the two parties. It seems important that there must be those who can take the initiative to lead such a dialogue, perhaps from among the educated, who understand what progress means to the nation and who do appreciate the importance of eradicating poverty, disease, and illiteracy from the country. Such a mediating group gradually emerged in the Ethiopian Orthodox Students' Association, founded in 1958 by students representing all the nation's colleges and some secondary schools. The members of this organization have been concerned with achieving a better understanding of the Church and adapting its activities to contemporary needs. They have been active in the Church's reformist efforts to revise the liturgy and to translate it from Ge'ez into the modern language of Amharic.

The Association began to introduce many ideas and activities with which the traditional Church has not been particularly concerned. They now have weekly religious services, sponsor lectures by leading Ethiopian and foreign churchmen, and issue a monthly publication. Its annual conventions have been very well attended. It is significant that before the formation of this organization, nation-wide voluntary association was not officially encouraged or approved.

At a time when the secularization of life is overtaking the Church, and when young people are turning away from religion – if not in belief, at least in practice – the Church's educated men and progressive members of the faithful will have to make further readjustments. Many young Ethiopian Christians have found a solution in conversion, especially to Protestantism; others have attempted to formulate varieties of personal creeds, which are different from that of the Ethiopian Church. A progressive Orthodox Students Association is an important alternative that gives some chance to a renovation of the Ethiopian Church. But the barriers that exist between this organization and the religious tradition on the one hand and the members of the educated class on the other must first be removed. If this is achieved, its members may emerge as new leaders in promoting modernization of the Church.

A well-organized and progressive clergy with good administration and capable leaders can play a tremendously constructive role in the educational, social and moral development of a modernized Ethiopia. (Indeed, this holds true for the other religions and religious groups in Ethiopia). The clergy are as powerful as ever in Ethiopia, and their influence is considerable. Many foreigners, and perhaps some Ethiopians, are apt to misjudge the vulnerability of the clergy in the educated sector of Ethiopia and to assume that traditional piety and learning bear little relevance to the social and intellectual needs of the modern world, or that its position will wane in the process of modernization. But religion is as powerful as ever in Ethiopia, and its influence continues to be considerable. Nonetheless, in order to survive, the Church must prove its ability to modernize its administration, providing effective leadership in moving the traditional clergy to make the necessary adjustments. The creation of the Orthodox Students Association and the establishment of the Trinity Theological Seminary are some signs of awareness of change. But if the respected status of the Church is to continue, its future leaders must be thoroughly well-educated, not only in religious affairs but also in matters relevant to the progress of Ethiopia. Furthermore, the leaders must not only understand the need for development and change, but must positively take steps to support extensive education. Education and efficiency – these will determine the future course of the leadership and administration of the Ethiopian Church.

Chapter 11

The Church and Writing

❖

The ability to communicate verbally and in writing is one of the fundamental elements of progress. Nonetheless, whereas verbal communication is limited in scope, writing has revolutionized human history. As Alan Gardner points out in his *Egypt of the Pharaohs* (London 1961, p. 21) "Writing extended the range of [people's] communication in both space and time." In other words, writing not only increases the distance at which one can communicate with another but also extends memory, enabling one generation to inherit the cumulative experience and discovery and knowledge of another. In this way knowledge is preserved and expanded and civilization as we know it becomes possible.

Ethiopia is fortunate to be one of the few countries of the world where writing developed from time immemorial, and where literature was developed and preserved for over fifteen hundred years. Very few, outside the circle of scholars of ancient languages truly realize the importance of this extensive body of literature found in Ethiopia and written in *Ge'ez*. This literature represents an invaluable source of information not only for the understanding of Ethiopian history but also for the study of world history and the major religions of the world: Judaism, Christianity, Islam, and the Traditional African Religions.

Many scholars trace the origin of writing to the ancient Near East in general and to Mesopotamia, in particular, where they believe the first system of writing was invented by the Sumerians about 3500 years BCE. Others, however, consider Egypt the home of the first system of writing dating back to the end of prehistoric times, or roughly about the same time as in Mesopotamia. In my judgment, not only is the first theory unconvincing, but also without a strong base. On the other hand, evidence supports a continuous and systematic development and use of writing in the Northeastern regions of Africa, all along the Nile valley, for over five thousand years. It seems to me that it is in the prehistoric rock engravings and paintings of Africa that we may find invaluable insight into the ultimate origin of writing; for there is indeed good reason to believe that art and writing branched off the same human tendency tree of prehistoric ancient rock art. Prehistoric artworks provide us with extensive information concerning the daily life, customs, and outlook of those who created them; in other words, they are a form of social and personal record and not only the result of instinctive and innate artistic impulses or expressions. Scholars have not seriously begun to examine the link between prehistoric African art and ancient Egyptian hieroglyphic writing, so the ultimate origin of writing may remain a subject of heated debate for a long time.

Scholars do agree that ancient Egyptian and Sumerian writings developed from pictographic origins—that is, from pictures that told stories. The Egyptians may have been the first to reduce ancient pre-historic engravings and paintings to a systematic form of writing. This pictographic writing was eventually developed into ideogrammic writing, as in the hieroglyphs in which the pictures not only designated the objects depicted but also the ideas associated with them. The ideograms, also called logograms, and then evolved into homophonic phonetics (0=I) in which a word having the same sound was used to designate a homophone, and determinatives in which the grammatical elements were expressed by the use of signs. Then unilateral, bilateral, and trilateral phonetic symbols were all incorporated into the system. (For example, the symbol used for the letter "r" symbolized the word "Ra" or mouth when accompanied by a down stroke.)

Through this method, the Egyptians developed a whole series of unilateral symbols, in fact an entire alphabet of 24 characters. Their alphabet was, however, not quite complete; for instance, it had no symbol for the Egyptian sound "l." Moreover, the early use of phonetic writing (and the use of abbreviated and derivative forms known as the hieratic and demotic) did not result in a fully developed alphabetical writing; for the Egyptians officially chose not to give up their ideograms until Roman times. They used the hieroglyphic alphabet to designate pronouns, prepositions, particles, and similar grammatical expressions, as reminders when used with various consonantal groups. Nevertheless, inspired by the Egyptian system of writing, the alphabet was finally invented (perhaps unofficially) sometime during the early second millennium BCE.

The alphabet is a very ingenious device of symbols of the sounds that exist in human speech. Its invention, even more than that of the discovery of the wheel or the making of fire, has completely revolutionized knowledge and learning, and marks a watershed in all of human history. As Professor Cross says, "It democratized writing.... We may describe the alphabet as the sound computer, which enables people to write down all the words of any language in a simple and efficient manner by the use of the common elements of the language."[1]

---

1   F, M. Cross, "The Alphabet."

Writing may have developed spontaneously and slowly; but the alphabet must have been the result of an incredible process of invention. By whom and when the alphabetic system was invented is still a matter of conjecture, but the earliest known examples of it, the Proto-Sinaitic, have so far come from about twenty-five inscriptions in the Sinai peninsula, discovered in 1906 in Egyptian turquoise mines by the English archaeologist Flinders Petrie. Proto-Sinaitic is a linear script written in a consonantal alphabet and developed from hieroglyphs on the acrophonic (a specific object whose name began with a particular sound) principle. All (except Korean) known comparable methods of reducing a language to a written form are derivatives of it, and Ethiopic is a very good example of one of the early branches of Proto-Sinaitic.

Scholars had conjectured at different times since the seventeenth century the origin of the Ethiopic alphabet to be Samaritan (Ludolphus, Silvestre), Syriac (Kopp), or Sabaean (Glazer, Homel, Conti Rossini). But we now know that Ethiopic is a cursive form of monumental Sabaean, and hence the immediate Southern branch of Proto-Sinaitic or the first known alphabet, in other words, it is the sister alphabet of the Phoenician (Canaanite) script.

Sabaean (which can rightly be called Proto-Ethiopic) and Phoenician, from which the Hebrew characters are derived, are two of the oldest alphabetic forms of writing. As a direct descendant, Ethiopic's Ras preserved to this day many of the original forms and shapes of the original Proto-Sinaitic. The letters of the English language are derived from the Roman or Latin script, which in turn was derived from the Chalcidian (Western Greek) of Southern Italy, which ultimately was derived from the Phoenician through the Ionic Greek script. On a ladder of history or the tree of the alphabetic ancestry, Ethiopic thus becomes the uncle of Greek script, the great-uncle of the Roman script, the great grand-uncle of English.

Early Sabaean or Proto-Ethiopic writing, mostly votive inscriptions, is today found extensively in the surroundings of the northern Ethiopian and Eritrean (*Yäha*, Axum, Senafe, *Qohaito*, *Daqamahari*, Malazo, Taconda', etc.) as well as in Yemen, representing respectively the ancient kingdom of Axum, the city-states of ancient Southern Arabia (in particular, Saba', Main, Qatabān, and Hadramāwt.) A monograph incised on a shred in South Arabia has been dated to the 8th century BCE by the radiocarbon method, and in fact, Sabaean inscriptions of about this period have been found in Etzion Geber, a rather early development of Sabaean. Earlier inscriptions have been dated to the end of the second or early first millennium BCE on paleographic grounds. In northern Ethiopia, also, writings that can be dated as early as the eighth century BCE have been found. They primarily begin to abound in early Christian times. These inscriptions have been planned and executed symmetrically with great care, and famous scholars like Thomas Lambdin rightly say that Sabaean inscriptional writing is "not rivaled elsewhere in the Semitic world for its elegance." Ethiopians also designed decorative writings that may have given rise to Arabic.

From our epigraphic sources we learn that about the end of the fourth century BCE the Sabaean Proto-Ethiopic monumental script began to evolve in Ethiopia into a less symmetrical form. The Dutch scholar, A. J. Drewes, attaches great significance to this stage of the development of the Sabaean Proto-Ethiopic script, and considers it the origin of the *Ge'ez* (Ethiopic) alphabet, and the rise of Axum as the capital of Ethiopia. Many texts containing invaluable information about the political, economic, and religious history of the horn of Africa come to us in the inscription from about this period to about the middle of the 4th century of the Christian era. The most famous among these are of course the inscriptions of Emperor Ezana, which are rather detailed and offer invaluable information on the history of the *Ge'ez* script, the expansion of the Axumite Empire, and the introduction of Christianity to Ethiopia.

Whereas the earlier forms of these characters also remained simply consonantal, sometime around the 4th century, when the Bible began to be translated into the Ethiopic language, the Ethiopians modified and vocalized the script (possibly the work of an individual) for ease in manuscript writing and reading. To do so they transformed the alphabet into a kind of a syllabary, using innovative vocalic signs for ease in pronunciation. Ethiopic is not only unique among all the early Semitic writings to be so vocalized, but also the earliest among them to develop vocalic signs; Hebrew, for instance, did not use such signs until the 9th century.

The Proto-Ethiopic inscriptions were read much like Egyptian, from right to left or from top to bottom as well as boustrophedon. But due to Christian influence, the Ethiopians standardized the direction of reading and writing from left to right, as we still do today. The orders of the letters of the alphabet were originally probably like that of Phoenician, but gradually a new order was created for reasons not yet fully known.

The period from the time of Ezana, in the first half of the 4th century, to the time of Emperor Kaleb, in the 6th century is germane to our understanding of the roots of Ethiopian culture, art, architecture, literature, in general, and to Christianity, in particular. It was probably during this time that the ancient shrine of Axum was converted to the famous church of St. Mary of Zion, where Ethiopian Christians believe the original and complete Tablets of the Law given to Moses are still found. It was during this time that the nine famous monasteries of the Nine Saints were built, including that of the famous Debre Damo.

However, the most significant single development of this period is the rise of Ethiopian Christian literature. Thanks to the *Ge'ez* alphabet, Ethiopic became the repository of many ancient writings and the nurturer of an extensive body of literature and the medium for literary creativity. Equally significant is the fact that Ethiopic became the only script of the south Proto-Semitic, in which literature was produced and continues to be in use up to our own time.

No other known literary work has had such an impact upon world culture and literature, and the great religions Judaism, Islam, and Christianity as the book that we call the Bible. *Geʿez* (or classical Ethiopic, as western scholars call it) is one of about seven of the most important languages of the world in which the Bible and cognate works were first translated. Because of this, scholars of biblical textual study and criticism learn *Geʿez* (or classical Ethiopic) and adduce textual witnesses from the Ethiopic Bible to establish many variants and/or readings. Of all the European languages none shares such a high position with the exception of Greek and Latin. (Examples of writing in other European languages with the exception of the Ulfilas Bible appear much later: Old English, Seventh Century; Old High German, Eighth Century; Russian, Ninth Century; Old Norse and Old Dutch, Twelfth Century; Old Swedish and Danish, Thirteenth Century.

Even more important is that Ethiopic preserved many ancient writings that have been lost in the original languages. The most distinguished example of these is beyond a doubt the *Book of Enoch* and the *Book of Jubilees* called *Kufalle* in *Geʿez*. These works exist today in their entirety only in Ethiopic, and are still the subject of richly deserved worldwide scholarly attention. In fact, in the eighteenth century, when James Bruce first took some manuscripts of the *Book of Enoch* to Europe, the impact it had on the scholarly world was like the excitement generated by the discovery of the Dead Sea Scrolls in our own century. Like the scrolls, the *Book of Enoch* offers valuable insight into the religious and cultural milieu of the time of Jesus and his first followers.

The sacred scriptures of the Ethiopian Orthodox Church consist of 82 books - 39 books of the Hebrew Bible, the 27 canonical books of the New Testament, and numerous Apocryphal and Pseudepigraphic works. After a period of slackening since the Second World War, interest in the Apocryphal and Pseudepigraphic works is beginning to emerge again, as evidenced by the recent first American publication of the two-volume *Old Testament Pseudepigrapha* by the Doubleday Press. Any glance at this publication as well as other recent works on the religious and social ideas of the Second Temple period will reveal the high position *Geʿez* holds among ancient languages as an important repository and nurturer of many ancient literary works. Moreover, there are numerous other venerated works such as hagiographies, chronicles, and homilies, calendaric and theological works that offer insight into the history of early Christianity. For instance, a German Ethiopist in the late seventeenth century discovered the liturgical usage in Italy in the late second century after studying the first version of the Apostolic Church Order of Hippolytus of Rome (170-236 CE), in the Ethiopic version. Likewise, in his recent work on Ethiopian Astronomy and Calendar, the late, noted historian of mathematics Otto Neugebauer has shown that only in the Ethiopic work known as *Hasab* do we find preserved in detail the Judaeo-Hellenistic calendar which was the basis of early Christian calendar.

Furthermore, the examination of Ethiopic literature may shed light not only on the history of early Christianity, but also on other early Jewish literary works as well as on the history of Jewish communities in Ethiopia and Southern Arabia. In my own study of *Mäs'hafä Berhan*, a fifteenth century Sabbath homily, I have demonstrated the preservation of certain *halachic* gleanings in Ethiopic literature. I have also shown that the oldest manuscript of the *Book of Enoch*, microfilmed by a German team some twenty years ago reveals archaic readings that help us understand certain interpretations of this important work. Like the *Book of Enoch*, the calendaric work called the *Book of Jubilees* is another example of early Jewish books that throws light on early Jewish *Midrash*. The Ethiopian Jewish work known as *Tï'izazä Sänbät* gives us deep insight into the nature of the Jewish relationship with the personified Sabbath, perhaps more than any other work of comparable size that we know. Where else do we find Jewish Aramaic words such as *meswat* or *'arb* in such common language as in Ethiopic?

Finally, it is well-known that the Prophet Muhammad's earliest followers sought refuge in Ethiopia. The scholarly works of the last century, (Noldeke, Polotsky, *et al*) have in fact shown that numerous fundamental terminologies found in Islamic literature (*mashaf, menbar, tabot, fat'ara, ta'ot...*) are in their original classical Ethiopic expressions. It is indeed not unlikely that future investigations and studies of Ethiopic literature may throw new light on the Christian and Jewish components of early Islamic theology.

In short, the importance of the many unique ancient religious and historical works found in classical Ethiopic for an understanding of early Christianity, Judaism, and Islam cannot be exaggerated. Let me only mention briefly such works as the Physiologus, the Greek collection of study of animals and plants, the type of natural history popular in the Middle Ages; Qerlos, a collection of important Christological writings attributed to the Church Father Cyril; the monastic Rules of Pachomius all from the first period in Ethiopic literary development (4-6th cent.); the *Kebra Nagast*, the most detailed *haggadah* on the Queen of Sheba; *Fetha Nagast*; the Synaxarium; the Book of the Mystery of Heaven and Earth, from the second period (early 14), and the many works on miracle stories, songs and poetry, and so on.

The largest body of written material coming out of Ethiopia remains untapped for scholarly purposes. This is a sad state of affairs, for as said above, Ethiopic contains some important material, which will and could illuminate our knowledge of ancient learning. Only recently Professor O. Neugebauer has made a study of Ethiopian calendaric works and found out that the ancient

Alexandrian Jewish lunar calendaric system that was later adopted by the Christian churches has been preserved nowhere in Christian literature but in the Ethiopic. Moreover, he has demonstrated recently that at least one method of reckoning time in the European Middle Ages, called the Spanish Era or 38 BC, which has been enigmatic for scholars to explain, can only be explained on the basis of Ethiopic sources.

The existence of such a large body of written material coming from Ethiopia is of considerable significance for all of Africa. The denial of the existence of African history in the 19th century was based on the *a priori* assumption that only cultures that have writing have history. According to one 19th century thinker, it is the existence of writing that disqualified Ethiopia as an African country.[2] In the same vein, one can say much of northern Europe also had no indigenous writing culture until the Middle Ages; but one does not claim that they therefore have no history. Greece and Rome have been the fountainhead of ancient cultures of Europe, as is Ethiopia for Africa. Moreover, students of oral history today do not define history as only that which is written. Indeed, oral literature is the basis of a good deal of world history, in particular, the origins of ancient peoples and cultures throughout the world. Additionally, many ancient writings, Biblical or Hellenic, are known to have been based on earlier oral traditions that were later collected and recorded.

Though not much remains of the artistic works of this period, besides of course the great monumental building of Axum, Ethiopia is a land where ancient alphabets have been preserved and where ancient literature was nurtured.

---

2   F. Hegel, *The Philosophy of History* (1837 - E. Gans, ed.).

Chapter 12

Church and State

Nothing states more concisely and more definitively the former relationship between Church and state in Ethiopia than the chapter quoted above from the *Kebra Nagast*. The *Kebra Nagast* (literally, "The Glory of Kings") is a large compilation of legends and traditions, some historical and some mythical derived primarily from the Old Testament, Jewish *haggadah,* and other Semitic and Ethiopian sources. As noted by some scholars like Sir E. A. Wallis Budge, its English translator, it contains oral traditions, current in the Roman and Hellenistic world during the first four centuries of the Christian era. The oral traditions first came to be written down in Coptic about the sixth century; subsequently translated into Arabic, and finally into *Ge'ez* (Ethiopic) sometime in the thirteenth century, by a redactor who called himself *Nebura-ed* Isaac. The work purports to prove that: *(a)* the lawful kings of Ethiopia descend from King Solomon and the Queen of Sheba through their son named Menelik (I) (Son-of-King); *(b)* the original Tables of the Law that God gave to Moses were removed from Jerusalem by Azariah, the son of the Jewish High Priest, brought to Ethiopia with Menelik, and placed in the holy shrine at Axum (the ancient ecclesiastical and political capital of Ethiopia); (c) the world is divided into two empires -Rome and Ethiopia - and that Ethiopia is the legitimate successor to Israel, as the God of Israel has transferred his place of abode from Jerusalem to Axum; the kings of Ethiopia are, therefore, of divine origin:

> Now it is not a seemly thing to revile the king, for he is the anointed of God. It is neither seemly nor good. If he doeth that which is good, he will not suffer loss in three realms: FIRST, God shall overthrow for him his enemy, and the hand of his enemy shall not seize him. SECONDLY, God shall make him to sit on His right hand. THIRDLY, God shall make him to reign upon earth with glory and joy, and shall direct his kingdom for him, and shall bring down the

nations under his feet. And if he treats God lightly, and doth not do that which is good, and doth not himself walk in the path of uprightness, God shall work as He pleases against him; on earth He will make his days to be few, and in heaven (*sic*) his place of abode shall enjoy neither health nor gladness (and he shall live) in fear and terror, without peace and (*sic*) perturbation. "It is not a good thing for any of those who are under the dominion of a king to revile him, for retribution belongs to God. Now the priests are like the prophets, for the mysteries are given unto them, so that they may lay hold upon the sun of righteousness, whilst the Seraphim, who were created out of fire, are only able to lay hold upon the mysteries with tongs. As for the priests 'lamp' and also 'light of the world,' and also 'the sun that lightest the darkness,' CHRIST, the Sun of righteousness, being in their hearts. And a priest, who hath in him understanding, rebukes the king concerning the work that he hath seen; and that which he hath not seen God will enquire into, and there is none who can call Him to account. Moreover, the people must not revile the bishops and the priests, for they are the children of God and the men of His house, for which reason they must rebuke (men) for their sins and errors. And thou, O priest, if thou sees sin in a well-known man, do not hesitate to rebuke him; let neither sword nor exile make thee afraid. And hear how angry God was with ISAIAH because he did not rebuke King UZYAN (UZZIAH). And hearken also concerning SAMUEL the Prophet, how he rebuked SAUL the king, being in no way afraid of him, and how he rent his kingdom (from him) by his word; and (hearken also) how ELIJAH rebuked AHAB. Do thou then fear not, and rebuke and teach him that transgresses." "And ISRAEL from of old reviled their kings and provoked their prophets to wrath, and in later times they crucified their Saviour. But believing Christian folk dwell in peace, without sickness and suffering, without hatred and offence, with our king ... who loves God and who removes not from his heart the thing of righteousness, and faith in the Churches and in the believers. And his enemies shall be scattered by the might of the Cross of JESUS CHRIST."[1]

Although the *Kebra Nagast* cannot furnish historical proof for the existence of the Solomonic Dynasty before 1270, the powerful religio-political myths that it contains, as used by the churchman Tekle Haymanot (1215-1313)[2] in 1270, did prove very effective not only in overthrowing the existing *Zagwe* Dynasty

---

1   From *Kebra-Negest,* Chap. 44, translated into English by Sir E. A. Wallis Budge, "The Queen of Sheba and Her Only Son, Menelek I," London, 1932, 2nd edition, p. 64.

2   A saint by a Syrian name Takle Haymanot is believed to have in the 7th century and that his body has been found in Egypt.

of that time but also in giving rise to the supposedly Solomonic Dynasty under Yekuno- Amlak (1270-1312). The national saga has provided the cast in which an unbroken line of Ethiopian rulers has been molded for almost seven hundred years (since the thirteenth century until the dethroning of Emperor Haile Sellassie I in 1974). In the eyes of the people of today, the Solomonic tradition imparts to the existing dynasty much greater antiquity and sacredness.

Before the Revolution of 1974, constitutionally, Church and state were one. Moreover, the two were linked by historical associations and mutual interests. Therefore, it is extremely difficult to determine which of the two had ultimate power. In reality, as many observers have contended, the emperor had more actual power, political and military than the *Abuna* or Archbishop. Their conclusion is based partly on the obvious *de facto* authority of emperors exercised over the affairs of the Church, and partly on the historical evidence in respect of the *Abuna's* subordination to the emperor. But this conclusion reflects only a one-sided picture. For, on the other hand, according to the above passage from the *Kebra-Nagast,* the Church is superior to the emperor: "a priest, who hath in him understanding, rebukes the king concerning the work that he hath seen ... and there is none who can call him (the priest) into account." The *Abuna* also anoints the Emperor and the Emperor kisses his cross. Within the context of this tradition, the Church had more intrinsic power than the state; it is the high priest who anoints the emperor. As we shall see below, however, in actual practice there was more or less equilibrium between the spheres of influence of the Church and state.

A correct formulation of the power of the state over the Church may be that the authority of a believing Emperor rises above the powers of the *Abuna*.[3] In the early days of the Church, perhaps before the thirteenth century this was true without exception. This trend persisted to a certain extent until modern times.[4] James Bruce, the Scotsman who traveled in Ethiopia in the eighteenth century, when the prestige of the rulers was low, wrote: "all ecclesiastical persons are subject to the secular power in Abyssinia as much as they are in Britain or in any European Protestant state whatsoever."[5] As an example, Bruce, who often must not be taken literally because of his exaggerations, cited the case of a high church official who was executed because he had cooperated with the *Abuna* in excommunicating the emperor. Furthermore, Bruce related that the king reviled the ecclesiastic, saying, "The *Abuna* is a slave of the Turks, and has no king; you are born under a monarchy; why did you ... take upon you to advise him at all ...

---

3   In the Bible, king Solomon seems to have had spiritual power. He dedicated the Temple and removal the ....priest Abiathar (I Kings 8; I Kings 2:26-27).

4   De. L. O'Leary, *The Ethiopian Church*, London, 1936, p. 45.

5   James Bruce, Travels.

and abuse his ignorance in these matters?"[6] The primacy of the emperor over the *Abuna* was also conformed by Plowden and Rassam, two Englishmen who were in Ethiopia at the time of Tewodros. The former speaks of an exiled *Abuna*,[7] and the latter reports that Tewodros kept the *Abuna* as a slave.[8]

Other examples of the disposition, imprisonment, exile, and even the execution of *Abunas* can be found throughout Ethiopian history. But it would be wrong to judge that these isolated instances show the unconditional power of the emperors over their Church. In the first place, it must be noted that such cases come from a period of Ethiopian history during which stability in law and order was at stake. But more important, one must not identify the power of the Ethiopian Church with that of the *Abuna*. Until 1950, the *Abuna* always was a foreigner who knew very little of the customs, language, and history of the country. Furthermore, coming from a weak mother church - a point the Ethiopians had always seen as a virtue - he could play only a very small role in the actual affairs of the Church, let alone of the state. Indeed the *Abuna* had never been more than a symbol of the historic tie with the ancient church of St. Athanasius, the Patriarch who was popularly thought to have installed the first Ethiopian *Abuna* in 330. No wonder that few names of *Abunas* stand out at all in Ethiopian history, despite the fact that the entire development of Ethiopian national identity was so infused with religious life.

As alluded to above, it would be wrong to look for the power of the Church in the *Abuna*. In the past, the power of the Church was in the hands of high Ethiopian Church officials such as the *Itchege*. They in turn dictated the course of action to the *Abuna* and directed the affairs of not only the Church but, to a certain extent, even of the state. *Itchege* is the traditional title of the grand prior of the convent of Debre-Libanos in Shoa. In theory, the *Itchege* was second in rank to the *Abuna;* in actual practice, however, he wielded more power than the *Abuna* and was superior to him. He served as administrative head of the Church and had jurisdiction over all monasteries, chose candidates for ordination, and decided questions of protocol in connection with religious ceremonies. He has always been a native of Ethiopia, appointed by the emperor. His position as a government official and his duties as head of a powerful order of monks gave him tremendous influence in the political and national areas. His appointees were generally laymen whose functions were mainly secular. His coadjutors, called the *Liqä Kahïnat* or "chief priests," were in charge of monasteries in the provinces. The tasks of the *'aläqa* or "authorities" included caring for churches and Church property and revenue, as well as settling disputes among the clergy.

---

6   Bruce, James, *Travels to discover the source of the Nile,* Edinburgh, 1790, Vol. IV, p. 73.

7   J. C. Plowden, *Abyssinia and its People,* London, 1868, p. 162.

8   H. Rassam, *Narrative of the British Mission to Tewodros,* Vol. I, London, 1869, p. 249.

The latter are especially noted for their material wealth. Alvarez, a Catholic priest who visited Ethiopia in the beginning of the sixteenth century, described the *Itchege* as "the greatest prelate there is in these Kingdoms."[9] Bruce wrote that in a period of trouble, he was of much greater importance than the *Abuna*.[10]

It would not be inaccurate to say that the *Abuna* or the Patriarch of Ethiopia and the *Liqä Sültanat* (a prominent office in Emperor Haile Sellasse), a member of the Imperial Cabinet, used to jointly share the role of the *Itchege*. As said earlier, the *Abuna* appears to combine the ecclesiastical power of his office with more of the secular power of the *Itchege* in one. This is a new development in Ethiopian history, and what consequences will follow remain to be seen. So far, it seems to have resulted in the rise of the spiritual prestige of the *Abuna* on the one hand but in the decline of the secular power of a single ecclesiastic, on the other. At any rate, it would be premature to conclude that this may be the sign of the decline of the power of Church over state.

Although, as said above, some of the Church's power over the state was centered traditionally in the *Itchege,* a high native official, it would nonetheless be wrong to identify the power of the Church with a single personality. Even if some emperors had persecuted certain *Abunas* or even *Itchege,* no king had ever dared to mistreat or injure the Church as a body. The Church, as a corporate, spiritual body, transcends the State. This corporate religious organ diffused its force through a large and spiritually-united clergy to a pious peasantry, nobility, and leaders of the military. Some foreign observers, struck by the large number of Ethiopian priests, have been led to guess that one-quarter of Ethiopia's Christians were members of the clergy; others have suggested that one Ethiopian in five is a priest.[11] Though this figure may be too high, nonetheless, there is no doubt that the proportion must be large, especially in view of the fact that an estimated 20,000 churches and monasteries exist in the country. Bruce in the eighteenth century thought that no country in the world had so many churches as Ethiopia.[12] Though each church requires at least two priests and three deacons, churches that have up to five hundred clergymen are known to exist. Even though the greater concentration of churches is found in the North and Northwest, there is no area of Ethiopia, even where adherents of other religions predominate, where Ethiopian Christian priests and churches are not found. The priests as a group, though not rich, are bound together by the power of tradition; and, if not systematically or in an organized manner,

---

9   F. Alvarez, *Portuguese Embassy to Abyssinia,* translated by Lord Stanley of Alderley, the Hakluyt Society, London, 1881, p. 161.

10   Bruce, James, op. cit., Vol. III, p. 319.

11   C. Sandford, *The Lion of Judah Has Prevailed,* London, 1955, p. 98.

12   Bruce, James, op. cit., Vol. III, p. 313.

culturally and spiritually, they form a formidable force to reckon with. It is the priests, furthermore, as individual temporary landowners—not the Church as an organization (until recent times) -who used to hold most of the one-third of the land in Ethiopia, often regarded as Church property.

In the final analysis, it must be emphasized that it is neither a single powerful Church dignitary nor individual priests, nor even, as hinted above, the priests as a class who have power over the state, but the spirit of tradition - the Church as the embodiment of Ethiopian culture - that transcends both Church and politics.

As stated above, the believing head of state has power and authority over the ordained head of the Church. Consequently, emphasis must be put on "believing," for the ruler can exercise power over the Church only as its member and as its protector and head. All in all, the Church as the visible manifestation of Ethiopian tradition can be said to hold intrinsically, if not extrinsically, more power than the state. It is the Church that sanctioned the rise of the Solomonic Dynasty; it is the Church that has been the symbol, if not the patron, of law and order in Ethiopian history and tradition up until the end of Emperor Haile Sellassie I's reign. It was the church that removed Iyassu from power on the suspension that he is not a loyal Christian.

The Solomonic Dynasty that emerged in 1270 achieved success under the guardianship of the Church. Unfortunately, our knowledge of this development is still largely shrouded in mystery. But as far as we can tell, a monk named Tekle Haymanot is closely associated with the rise of the Solomonic Dynasty, as well as with the overthrow of the then ruling *Zagwe* Dynasty. Legend has it that Tekle Haymanot influenced the last king of the *Zagwe* Dynasty to abdicate voluntarily in favor of the Solomonic scion. The story may contain a grain of truth that becomes extremely fertile for the historian. We learn from the legend that the Church played a primary role in putting the Solomonic Dynasty under Yekuno-Amlak into power. This hypothesis is supplemented in two ways by other sources of Ethiopian tradition. In the first place, the last *Zagwe* king, whom legend tells us voluntarily abdicated, was killed in the church of St. Qirkos (in Lalibala) where he had gone to seek refuge and sanctuary; unfortunately, instead of finding protection, he was handed over to his assassins. In the second place, it is beyond question now that Tekle Haymanot or the Church promoted *Kebra Nagast* as the powerful religious propaganda that proved so effective in rallying the people behind the leader of the revolt, Yekuno-Amlak.

In return for his accomplishment, Tekle Haymanot was established as the leading monk, the first *Itchege* of Ethiopia, and was made both councilor and confessor to the new emperor. He is known to have made famous the monastery of Debre-Libanos, established six hundred years before by Abba Libanos (one of the nine saints). Furthermore, he insured that one-third of the land of Ethiopia would be given in perpetuity to the *Itchege* - the grand prior - and to his successors for the maintenance of his office and the support of the churches and monasteries. Today, Tekle Haymanot is remembered as the most pious saint of the country, the saint who never slept but diligently stood in prayer on one leg (the other leg eventually fell off) with spears pointing at him from all directions to awaken him should he fall asleep and interrupt his incessant prayers.

Not only did the Church give momentum to the rise of the Solomonic Dynasty, it also ordained and invested with charisma (power) each new monarch, and it ensured that the monarch remains faithful to the terms of his anointment. The ceremony of inaugurating a new ruler was purely religious and liturgical. It opens with the reading of Psalm 122. Then the Patriarch, in the presence of leading ecclesiastics, places the crown upon the monarch, seated on a throne, and says: "May God grant that this crown be a halo of holiness and glory. May you, by your prayers, preserve your faith unshaken and unconquerable! May you be pure in heart even as this gold is pure." To this blessing the emperor replies, "Amen." The *Abuna* presents the monarch as "(So and so) descended from the Dynasty of Menelik I, first-born son of Solomon and the Queen of Sheba, a Dynasty which has been perpetuated without interruption until our day." With his hand on the Bible, the ruler takes an oath, "to maintain the Orthodox religion, the laws of the Empire, the integrity of the territories of the country, and to support the founding of religious (and secular) schools and institutions." The emperor is given a sword known as the "Sword of Solomon," with the exhortation: "By this sword execute true justice, protect the Church, the widows, and the orphans, restore that which needs to be restored, chastise the wicked, render honor to the righteous; and with it serve our Savior Jesus Christ." After the chanting of Psalm 110, the emperor is given the royal scepter and orb. Then they place a ring on the emperor's right hand, saying, "Accept this as a symbol of your Imperial glory." The actual anointing of the sovereign with holy chrism takes place after the chief priest of the convent of Debre-Libanos says a long prayer. (The role this convent played in political power must here again be noted). The ceremony is concluded by the *Abuna* with the blessing "May it be the will of God that this be a crown of sanctity and glory." May you, by our prayers, preserve your faith unshakable and your heart pure, and inherit the crown of eternal life. Amen."

Sometimes during the ceremony the two persons closest to the emperor - the empress and the crown prince - are presented and blessed. Following the crowning of the emperor, the empress is given a ring by a bishop, who says: "Let your faith shine even as these jewels." Then the emperor, taking her crown from the Archbishop, says: "As I have been made to receive from your hands the Crown of the Empire which our God has given unto me, so it is my firm desire that my empress shall in my glory receive from me this crown which I ask your holiness to place upon her." The Archbishop then places the crown upon the empress. At the end of the ceremony, the crown prince, if present, professes his allegiance to his father. The emperor presents his right hand, saying: "May the Most High make you a worthy successor to my force, my power, my throne, and my crown." The crown prince replies, "Amen," and kisses the right hand of his father.

Finally, it was the Church that gave religious sanction to the legitimacy, authority, and power of the State. The emotional need to surrender to authority on the part of the people, beliefs that rationalize the value of submitting to authority, and in some instances, personal interests best served by compliance with authority, are based on it. Such religio-psychological motives underlie the attitude, which Weber would have described as those showing a disposition to conform to the demands of traditional authority figures.[13]

The ancient manuscript of *Ser'ata-Mangest* (Order of the Realm) describes the coronation ceremony as follows:

> The Emperor, on horseback, appears before the daughters of the city, who bar his way with a length of cord. Thrice the women, after which they allow him to cut the cord, challenge him and their proclamation rings out: "Verily, verily, thou art the King of Zion, son of David and of Solomon." Whereupon the sovereign is led to the ancient throne known as the Throne of David, where the crowning takes place, and then to the throne on which he is blessed.[14]

In both accounts of the coronation, the biblical legitimacy of the dynasty is emphasized, and the blessing of the priest is pivotal.

The Church interprets the Bible, stressing the importance of all earthy authorities. The sociologist, Donald Levine, claims that many of his Ethiopian Christian students gave as a reason for obeying the order of a superior "because the Bible says so."[15] The fifth article of the first chapter of the 1955 *Constitution of Ethiopia* explicitly upheld the teaching of the Church that "by virtue of his imperial blood, as well as by the anointing which he has received, the person of the emperor is sacred. His dignity is inviolable and his power indisputable ... He

---

13   Weber, Max. *The Theory of Economic and Social Organization*. Translated by A. M. Henderson and T. Parsons, New York, 1947.

14   Doresse, John. ETHIOPIA. Translated from the French by Elsa Coult. London, ELEK Books. 1959 (p. 14, 15).

15   Levine, Donald. "Legitimacy in Ethiopia." Lecture at 1963 Annual meeting of the American Political Science Association at the Unviersity of Chicago, September 9-12, 1964, unpublished manuscript, p. 4.

is consequently due to all the honors due to him in accordance with tradition." Only the Church, as we saw in the *Kebra Nagast,* can rebuke the ruler.

The Church did not only vest authority in the head of the state; it can also undermine the effectiveness of his legitimacy or divest him of power, if he does not remain faithful to the beliefs and practices of the Church. In the seventeenth century, two emperors, *Za-Dengel* (1606-1607) and *Susenyos* (1608-1632) were overthrown because they were disqualified by the Church for their predisposition toward Roman Catholicism. The clergy opposed these rulers and the *Abuna* released the army from allegiance and obedience to the sovereign. This was repeated in the twentieth century, when *Lij Iyyasu* (1913-1916), presumably suspected of favoring Islam was deposed with the help and blessing of the Church.

Regardless of the fact that the emperor has superior external powers over the State and the Church, in the final analysis his power and his autonomy are circumscribed and checked by the power of the tradition of the Ethiopian Church, which in the first place legitimizes his authority. The Church is the giver, the propagator, and the protector of the charisma that imparts the tremendous power of the ruler over his people.[16] First, there is the "family" or "hereditary" charisma - the common charisma of those who claim descent from Solomon and Sheba. All emperors since 1270, including Tewodros (Tewodros) (1855-1868), who was also anointed by the Church and was a great supporter of it, have legitimized their statuses by claiming to be descendants of Menelik I, son of Solomon and Queen of Sheba. Second, the Church reaches and stresses the ruler's special, historic role as repository of a sacred legacy, portraying the emperor as the legitimate successor to the kings of Israel, and hence, the sole legitimate bearer of Judeo-Christian faith. The transfer of religious priority from Israel to Ethiopia is represented in *Kebra Nagast* by a prophetic dream attributed to Solomon, in which God's favor, symbolized as the sun, moved from Israel to Ethiopia, and eventually by the actual transfer of the Ark of the Covenant *(Tābot)* from Jerusalem to Axum. Thirdly, the Church "imparts" the charisma of authority to the ruler by means of the rites of anointing and crowning. All these principles of charisma - the Solomonic genealogy, the historic role, and the anointing with oil - have been fused together to legitimize political authority.

What were the consequences of all this for 20th-century Ethiopia? Observers who had not looked at the relations of Church and state closely, or those who think that Ethiopia has passed into the 20th century, might not admit the continued effectiveness of the ancient sacred rites and the charisma they provide,

---

16 Levine, Donald. "Legitimacy in Ethiopia." Lecture at 1963 Annual meeting of the American Political Science Association at the Unviersity of Chicago, September 9-12, 1964, unpublished manuscript, p. 7.

or acknowledge that religion is any longer the basis of authority. Jean Baptiste Colbeaux, a Roman Catholic scholar, speaking of Church and State relations, linked it to a marriage, the Church appearing to the observer as a smiling wife or as "a single moral being, an amphibious personality" communicating movements to the national life as a motor.[17] The state owed the Church so much for its existence that especially in times of crisis, it turns first to it even for physical and military aid. During the Italian invasion of Ethiopia in 1935, not only did the State get spiritual guidance and courage from the Church, but also in the last minute, an elderly churchman in whom the state placed more confidence replaced the younger Minister of War. It would be premature to think that substantial changes had occurred in the effectiveness or content of the Church's function of providing a moral sanction in support of the established State or even in the Church's contribution to Ethiopian nationalism.

Until recently, the imperial office was never questioned; popular opposition was always related to charges discrediting legitimacy. Spokesmen for public liberties, for representative institutions, separation of Church and State, and the distinction between economic and administrative leadership—reforms, which would have been uncalled for under the traditional system—have begun to emerge since the 1950's. Young educated Ethiopians had begun to feel that the traditional monarchy cannot cope successfully with modernization: to promote social and economic reform which, as Samuel Huntington puts it succinctly, would involve changing traditional values and behavior, expansion of education and communications, broadening of loyalty from family and village to nation, secularization of public life, rationalization of authority structures, promotion of functionally specific organizations, substitution of achievement criteria for ascriptive ones, and furthering of a more equitable distribution of material and symbolic resources.[18] In the 1960s, both the Ethiopian Students Association in North America and the Union of Ethiopian Students in Europe concurred in their resolutions in this respect - that "the institution of absolute monarchy be replaced by a democratically instituted government . . . a democratically instituted Parliament be recognized as the sole and ultimate spokesman for the people of Ethiopia."[19] These organizations, furthermore, recognized that the Church "serves to propagate the myth of Divine Monarchy" and therefore resolved "State and Church be completely separated" and "to distinguish between faith in God and government of men."[20] One student who analyzed

---

17 J. B. Colbeaux, *Histoire politique at religieuse de l'Abyssinie,* vol. 1, Paris, 1929, p. 49.

18 S. P. Huntington, "The Political Modernization of Traditional Monarchies," unpublished manuscript of Stimson Lecture delivered at Yale.

19 "Challenge," *Journal of Ethiopian Students' Association in North America,* vol. VI, No. I, August, 1966, p. 23.

20 Ibid., p. 84.

the problem wrote that "the monarchy ... in large measure, owes its existence to the Church . . ."[21] After having recognized and analyzed the problems in the interplay of the power of the Church with that of the State, the two organizations emphasized in a resolution the need for the complete separation of Church and State. It is interesting to note that the progressive youth had been generally more outspoken in their criticism of the monarchy than of the Church.

The Church in the past has indeed been the light of Ethiopian culture and nationalism, and the fire of the sentiment of freedom and self-respect of the nation and the State. The connection between Church and State is based on the Church's belief that the State is a responsible guardian of justice and peace, as well as social welfare. The virtue of the Ethiopian Church is that though its institutions and its intellectual culture are rooted in old and even antiquated ideas, nonetheless, it is not extravagantly concerned with the next world or detached from the worldly affairs of society. Even in the midst of present day confusion and conflicts it can, with proper guidance, promote ideas that can cope with a new inner structure of the State. Moreover, it can create a strong, social influence in the development of a stable modern State.

The tie between Church and State is rooted more in ancient national customs than in any implicit or explicit teaching of the Church. It has persisted perhaps due to the need for expression of the authority of a community in search of a common ground of unity. The State and the Church, before 1270, though officially interdependent, in reality were essentially separate powers. This does not mean that there was originally a dualistic attitude towards "the world," as was the case with the early church in the West. As far as we know, the Ethiopian Church has never entertained the doctrine of dualism. On the other hand, its clergy and bishops have never known what it means to take over directly the functions of the State, as in Medieval Europe. The Church has always been a separate organization from the State, but an organization, which accepted the world and the State in accordance with the fundamental principles laid down in the Bible.

The absence of such a dualistic attitude on the part of the Church, which distinguishes it from Western Christianity, may make it difficult for it to adjust to a situation of total separation from the State. On the other hand, as hinted above, the Church's involvement in worldly affairs can make it a useful channel of social modernization, especially in the realm of education, if the Church chooses to become a force for progress. The course of action will be determined by the Church, subject to variations depending on the temperament and outlook of the modernizing State. If given freedom to exercise its faith, the Church can adapt to whatever relations it has with the modern State. Under educated leadership, the Ethiopian Church can benefit from the experiences of

21   Ibid., p. 49.

reason, and exude the wisdom necessary to adjust to changing situations even in difficult times.

The Ethiopian Church has every potential to be an active participant in education that can lead Ethiopia towards new times of favorable social situations. Its teaching that the world is a divine creation and that secular conditions of life are necessary as the basis and means for actual ethical and religious values, can aid it to be a positive catalyst for creative change.

An illustration from Abba Garima Gospel, the earliest known illuminated Gospel in the world

ABUNE TEKLE HAYMANOT

MOSES AND AHRON

MOSES, CHIEF OF ALL PROPHETS

ST. MARY PERFORMS MIRACLES

THE DESCENT FROM THE CROSS

ST. MARY AND CHILD RECEIVING FOLLOWERS, AND THE
DISTRIBUTION OF THE HOLY EUCHARIST

ST. MARY IN BOAT WITH FOLLOWERS

THE SCRIBE WHO WAS CONVERTED AT HIS DEATH BY
ST. MARY BECAUSE HE WROTE HER NAME IN GOLD

St. Mary with Baby Jesus flanked by archangels Michael and Gabriel

ST. MARY AND HER FAITHFUL FOLLOWERS

ZECHARIAS CROWNING THE VIRGIN MARY WITH ROSES
AND ADORING/VENERATING HER

CHURCH OF ST. GEORGE IN LALIBELA (TOP VIEW)

CHURCH OF MEDHANE ALEM IN LALIBELA

A CANNIBAL BECAMES CHRISTIAN AND IS SAVED
BY ST. MARY FROM HELL

BARUCH OF PHOENICIA GIVING FEAST
IN HONOR OF ST. MARY

TWO BROTHERS WRITING A BOOK OF ST. MARY'S
MIRACLES FALL INTO SIN. ONE OF THEM SEES A DREAM
IN WHICH ST. MARY SAVES HIM FROM HELL

DEACON HOLDING CROSS AT CHURCH CEREMONY

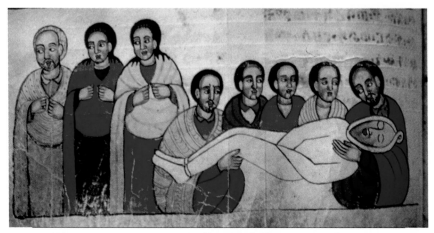

The preparation of Christ's Body for Burial

King David plays the harp

QUEEN OF SHEBA

ST. JACOB

ST. GEORGE KILLING THE DRAGON

ST. MARY WITH THE CHILD JESUS
FLANKED BY TWO CHERUBS

ST. SUSENYOS (POSSIBLY ARCHANGEL RUFAEL) SPEARING
THE DEMON WURZILYA WHO ATTACKS PREGNANT WOM-
EN AND CAUSES PREMATURE ABORTION

ABUNE GEBRE-MENFES KIDUS
A FAVORITE HERMIT SAINT IN ETHIOPIA WHO TAMED LIONS
AND MADE SERVANTS OF WILD BEASTS

Chapter 13

Church and Society

❖

A midst the social confusion of our day, with its clamor of conflicting voices, practices, and ideologies, the Ethiopian Church is slowly but surely making its voice heard. These social conflicts are not necessarily due to the industrial revolution — which is barely making an appearance in Ethiopia — or to any form of mass emancipation, as in the West in the last century. Rather, they are occasioned by the meeting of cultures—ancient and modern—resulting in a rise of conflicting social values. At the root of the whole matter is the desire of all parties to find what they respectively think to be a way to maximum happiness for the people and at the same time to create what they respectively think to be a stable society in which the standards are justice and peace. But the problem is complicated by the fact that on the one hand the Church — the bulwark of past history and culture — sometimes finds an easy solution to social stability in everything traditional perhaps due to lack of adequate training and education, whereas on the other hand many individuals among the leaders of change often tend to find a panacea in almost everything modern and, in everything modern, an antidote to poverty, disease, and illiteracy.

In the midst of care for stability, by one, and enthusiasm for change, by the other, very little time is found for a dialogue between the priests of tradition and the prophets of modernization—a dialogue that would assess both the positive and the negative aspects of the old and the new. Perhaps the initiative and leadership will be provided by the younger generation who are profiting and benefiting from the double privilege of being able to impart of modern knowledge as well as of the heritage of the past. They must understand that tradition is not necessarily complacent or spontaneously responsible to the society. Yet these problems as well as the confusion of cultural conflicts do not merely concern the educated politicians, political economists, and social reformers; they also concern the Ethiopian Church, whose root is intertwined with the cultural development and vital energy of its great historical past.

In a sense, the Ethiopian Church is attempting to use its considerable powers of organization to try to find solutions to some of these problems. But unfortunately, it also cannot help but be influenced to a great extent by various political interests. Moreover, for various reasons, it is gradually being more and more restricted to only exercising its influence within the religious domain. The modern situation has certainly brought the Church face to face with new and complicated problems in the ordering of social life; in spite of that, however, and in spite of many obstacles, it seems that the Church may not lack a potential both to survive the shock and even to support endeavors to understand and solve these questions.

To attempt to estimate how the Ethiopian Church is actually facing the shock and what it is doing and achieving in the realm of social reform is a broad task with which only a social scientist who has devoted all his energies to the investigation of these issues would be qualified to deal. In this brief chapter, one cannot do better than offer an assessment of the question of the churches' attitudes towards modernization and modern social problems, and a prediction of possible future attitudes. To understand the answers to these questions, one must also ask the question of what the basis of the Ethiopian Church teaching consists of without going into its theology.

Fundamental Ethiopian religious teaching is rooted in the Old Testament tradition no less than in the teachings of the early Christian Church. Hence, on the one hand it proclaims the coming of the great Day of Judgment when sin, suffering, and pain will be overcome; on the other, all emphasis is laid on a community that is, at least theoretically, busily occupied with the keeping of God's laws, justice and social responsibility in the here and now. I say theoretically since in practice the Ethiopian Church at times appears indifferent to high standards of justice and social responsibility. It has been accused of insensitivity, because it stands aside when acts of injustice are being committed to people and when there are merciless acts of exploitation committed against the rural people. Sadly, this may often be the case. Nevertheless, the actual moral theory of the Ethiopian Church maintains very lofty standards. Thus, as a matter of fundamental principle, the Ethiopian Church explicitly teaches that man is saved by his merits and good deeds, such as by keeping the Ten Commandments of the Old Testament and the Six of the New Testament ("feed the hungry, give water to the thirsty, invite the stranger to your house, clothe the naked, visit the sick, visit the prisoner" based on Is 58:6-7), by fasting, and by fulfilling his moral obligations, rather than by faith in Jesus alone as the principle of Pauline and Augustinian Christianity dominated in the West. The moral commandments are conceived from the viewpoint of ordinary practice and general human interest. They are to be obeyed with devotion and inner simplicity. All that is done takes place under the eye of God, which penetrates every disguise and tests human motives to the utmost. The will is to be given to God in absolute obedience so that it may fulfill all the demands of the moral law. There is no significant distinction between divine and state law; as pointed out elsewhere, the Bible and the *Fetha Nagast,* both containing religious laws, provide the basis for the Ethiopian legal tradition. One who is obedient to the Church attains eternal spiritual value in the sight of God, as well as happiness on earth.

The idea of the moral law, as well as the popular expectations of reward and punishment, have definite connections with Jewish ideas, but we need not go into that here[1]. The point is that the Ethiopian Church does put more emphasis on good works including almsgiving than on faith, though not to the extent Protestant and Catholic missionaries have thought. Obedience to the moral law is regarded to be of the utmost importance in the sight of God, a quality the Church itself can hardly achieve.

As far as character is concerned, sincerity, integrity, and conscientiousness are regarded as virtues. Humility is especially esteemed as a means of realizing one's smallness before God and great men. Sacrificing love of pleasure or comfort is not, however, deemed necessary. Self-denial and sacrifice are seen as virtues of special saints, and all Christians need not be called upon to exercise them. Although indifference to material happiness and money and sexual self-restraint are exalted as virtues, the rich, especially those who have land, are looked upon as having special blessings from God, and those who enjoy sex are looked upon as naturally virile and strong. Asceticism and/or the mortification of the body-for-its-own-sake are not required from the Christian, but they are prescribed for widows and widowers, and those who wish can choose the monastic life or the extreme *bahtawi*[2] customs.

Though some sociologists have occasionally erroneously accused the Ethiopian Church of the opposite qualities, it puts a prize on gentleness, readiness to forgive others, warmth of feeling in social and personal relations, and modesty. Overcoming hostility and seeking peace and love are all great virtues, but revenge may not always be regarded as sin. The claim for justice and equity is touched upon, but sometimes in a casual manner.

These ideas of religious ethics determine the sociological characteristics and basis of the Ethiopian Church. They have the potential to foster both respon-

---

1   E. Isaac, *The Book of Enoch*: A New Translation from the Oldest known Manuscript, with Introduction and Notes in *The Old Testament Pseudepigrapha* (J. Charlesworth, ed. Doubleday, 1983). See chapters 40ff.

2   *Bahtawi* are ascetic persons totally detached from the world, living in caves, woods, or deserts. Dressed in sheepskins, they can occasionally turn up in a town or a court or even the king's palace, to utter some angry or pungent social and prophetic message without political fears, and have always been regarded as very useful political critics. *Bahtawi* literally means "the loner."

sible independence and responsible interdependence. On the one hand, one may have to go to great lengths in obedience to religious demands based on assertions of personal responsibility to God, and by concentrating entirely upon differences in character among individuals. On the other hand, this ethic contains a strong idea of responsibility not only to oneself but to others; in the last analysis, indeed, the idea of obedience to the moral law is based on the concepts of urgent love, conquest of evil by good, and the union under one law of God, Church, and people participating in a national form of worship. Theoretically, therefore, there exists a real possibility indeed for a healthy and balanced attitude toward the creative individual and the co-operative community.

From this point of view, foreign sociologists who make of Ethiopian Christians either egotistic or conformist individuals do not do justice in their analysis. Indeed, sheer individualism is not regarded as a value. But, forced to fight in mountainous isolation and imbued with a sense of messianic purpose derived from their religious tradition and history, the people could only accept the virtues of the individual warrior—courage, leadership, and loyalty—as primary social values. However, it is precisely because of service to society and contribution to the persistence of the community at large that high value is placed upon personal courage, self-reliance, or self-assertiveness. Such individual heroes with special gifts are thought to be rare, and the conclusion that Ethiopian Christianity fosters the cult of the individual is unwarranted. Yet for all the adulation of the heroic individual, the non-conformist individual without a cause is less tolerated.

If anything in the Ethiopian social *weltanschauung is* to be criticized, it is not, therefore (as these sociologists maintain), the traditional religious ethic which fosters egotistic individuals, but rather the tendency not to cherish individual originality or creativity. The sociological characteristics of the egotistic individual from Western society are being applied to Ethiopian society. Donald Levine says, "The atomism of the Ethiopian intelligentsia is a conspicuous feature of their condition, sometimes manifested in basic distrust in their orientation towards one another as well as toward the rest of Ethiopian society."[3] But his conclusion that this reflects the attitudes and customs of the traditional culture is simply incorrect. The individualism, ineffectuality, and lack of orientation of modern educated elite in many developing countries is due to their abrupt severance from their respective traditions and unenlightened exposure to foreign ideas. Modern European education is capable of developing creative and genuine individualism; but outside its context, implanted in foreign cultures, the extent to which it exalts individual accomplishment apart from social responsibility, the emphasis it puts on knowledge for the sake of knowledge *(scientiae causa)* and its materialistic inclinations are more capable of creating

---

3   Levine, Donald. *Wax and Gold.* Chicago, 1965, p. 273-275.

egotistic individuals than the traditional Ethiopian Church ethic and spiritual moral teachings.

As alluded to above, the Ethiopian Church does not particularly exalt asceticism. There is no trace of contempt for life and pleasure, nor does the Church glorify poverty for its own sake. Food is necessary to life; fast, therefore, must be kept not because hunger has any ascetic value but because God has commanded them as one way of approaching God for favor in prayer, and because self-discipline, though not self-mortification, can in itself be a good thing.

Here it is important to comment on the well-known monastic traditions of Ethiopia. Monks still enjoy high esteem in the country and traditionally have exerted great influence in the preservation of *Ge'ez* literature and national philosophy. Also, their counsel, warnings and predictions have been influential in national politics. Their reserved behavior, exaltation of silence, and manner of speaking in a low voice and with a serious air, have been inherited by the modern educated generation, even if subconsciously. Nonetheless, contrary to traditional Western views of monasticism, it is really not their asceticism that is most admired by the people but their ethical heroism. Many men and women become monks and nuns after having fully participated in normal physical life, and the extreme mysticism and wholesale renunciation associated with monasticism[4] are alien to Ethiopian thinking.

The Ethiopian outlook on economic questions is like that of the gospel, and is very simple: all that men have to do is to live from day to day, trusting God to provide for each following day. Thus, there is no need for producing goods beyond that necessary for subsistence living. The gospel ethic emphasizes sharing what one has with those in need; thus, dependence on the generosity of relatives, friends, and benefactors becomes a way of life for those in distress. Besides the Ten Commandments of the Old Testament, the Church teaches that there are Six Commandments of the New Testament: to feed the hungry, to give water to the thirsty, to clothe the naked, to visit the sick, to entertain the stranger, and to visit the prisoner.[5] God has commanded everyone to earn his living by means of work; wealth is a gift of God, but it must be feared as a snare to the soul.

The basis of Ethiopian economic life is agriculture and animal husbandry. "Land is valued as the source of all sustenance and as an inheritance from one's ancestors, even though ownership may not go back more than a few generations. The structure of society, its institutions, the ways of tilling the soil and the way of building a house, are all precious and to be conserved as parts of a general

---

4   Harmack, A. *Das Mouchtum, seine Ideale und seine Geschichte.* Berlin, 1907, p. 9.

5   *Mäs'hafä Berhan (Book of Light)*, ed. Conti Rossini, CSCO, Vol. 47, Louvain, 1964, p. 23.

inheritance that goes back to the Deity."[6] This analysis, which reflects in part the Hebraic trait in Ethiopian Christianity, correctly assesses religious attitudes.

Farming, animal husbandry, fishing, hunting, food-cooking, and all other forms of occupations are regarded both as natural and as God-given responsibilities. But as many foreigners have noted, the majority of Christians "like Arabians, generally ignore or look down on many types of craftsmen, some of whom belong to despised classes or to ethnic minorities. In the Northwest, for example, iron smithing and pottery are done by the Jews, or *Falashas*; weaving is largely in the hands of Ethiopian Muslims and Jews."[7] It is thought that this attitude toward craftsmanship is based on the Biblical story that crafts were originally practiced by the descendants of Cain (Genesis 3), but it is really due to an ancient custom of looking down upon menial tasks, as was prevalent amongst the ancient Greeks.

It is a sad fact that occupational skills or manual work, which are so important for the development of any country, can become a cause of psychological burden. But surely the Church alone is not to be blamed for the perpetuation of such negative social values. Modern institutions are also at fault. To instill into the minds of younger Ethiopians the love of all types of productive work is the desire of many far-sighted Ethiopians. One can only hope that this goal can be accomplished through vigorous and creative educational programs, as it seems to be happening in more recent years and throughout the influence of returnees from the Ethiopian Diaspora.

There is nothing inherent in the teachings of the Church that hinders it from joining with educational institutions to lead men to the love of excellence in all handiworks and of that manual skill which God endowed to man alone. It is through these God-given abilities that man has been able to extend to society new economic possibilities through various forms of industry and new levels of spiritual progress. Not only in this respect, but also in all aspects of modern economic development, the Ethiopian Church with its zeal for keeping the law of God to do good for one's fellow man and to help those in distress, can potentially act as a catalyst to activate or inspire its adherents to accelerate the creation of a responsible and productive society. This can happen, perhaps, when members of the younger, educated generation, including those who choose not to practice religion, engage in dialogue with the Church.

The basic social unit of Ethiopian society is not the individual but the family, which forms a homogeneous community with its own characteristics. Much as in Biblical days, the *betäsäb* (house of man) is the community of common flesh and blood centered on the father of the house. Thus, the man is

---

6   *U.S. Army Handbook for Ethiopia*, p. 8.

7   Simmons, F. J. *Northwest Ethiopia: Peoples and Economy.* Madison, 1960, p. 174.

mentioned first, children are always called by their father's name, and kinship is reckoned through his ancestral line. After the man, his wife, who helps to maintain the family, is mentioned, and then the children.

Nevertheless, patriarchal dominion does not necessarily imply feminine inferiority. Even those who formerly had such a view now admit that women enjoy considerable marriage, property and inheritance rights.[8] Despite the claims of some foreign observers that women occupy the position of a depressed class, such women, for instance, as Empress Eleni, Empress Sabla-Wangel in the sixteenth century, Empress Mentwab in the eighteenth, Empress Taitu in the nineteenth, Empress Zewditu in the twentieth, and others, have immensely influenced the course of Ethiopian history. Certainly, women in Ethiopia work extremely hard; yet there have been times when they used to enjoy special legal rights such as men did not.

Donald Levine writes in *Wax and Gold* that "children are considered inferior because they are governed by ignorance and passion."[9] This statement is not based on an understanding of Ethiopian social attitudes. Children are loved and considered great gifts of God. Parents give children little or no freedom not because they look on them as inferior, but precisely because they love them. The attitude of the Ethiopian father is to bring children up in an orderly fashion, so that they do no harm to themselves physically when small, or psychologically when adults. As Ethiopian sages also hold: "As the twig is bent so the tree grows." Parents love their children and give utmost consideration to their welfare, but in turn likewise, expect love and respect from them; and they discipline them, bearing in mind the proverb, "Spare the rod and spoil the child." They consider discipline an exercise of ethical and religious responsibility in the care of children.

According to the Church's religious teachings, the monogamous family is the basis of society and of the state; in other words, the state is composed of congregated families. By and large, the Ethiopian Church has a liberal and natural attitude toward sex. It expects the few who are married in the Church to uphold an indissoluble union; yet because of this strictness, it gives freedom to, and even encourages, its members to have secular or civil marriage, which it blesses. It condemns adultery, but concubines are tolerated. It expects unwed girls (under fifteen) to be virgins, but divorce need not be difficult, and leverite marriage is practiced. The Church has no scripture against birth control, and probably will not oppose its introduction. The Ethiopian Church, having not developed an ascetic view of life, as said above, faces little or no special difficulties in coming to grips with the progressive sex ethics. Individual families may have rigid views of

---

8   Levine, Donald. Op. cit, p. 79, 259.

9   Levine, Donald. *Wax and Gold. P. 79.*

sex of their own choice, but the Church itself regards sex as a normal condition and a natural basis of life.

The *Fetha Nagast* contains laws regarding marriage, but by and large matrimonial problems are dealt with on the basis of customary Christian law. The Church respects virginity but it is not puritanical; it forbids polygamy, but it does not look down on divorce. Though it objects to promiscuity, relations between sexes which are sometimes free and unrestrained are not interfered with. What is most interesting is that the Ethiopian Church is not anxious to insist on marriage within the Church; in fact, it discourages it, for Church weddings are strictly indissoluble. In reality, only those few married long enough to feel sure that divorce can be ruled out enter into religious covenant, usually in the form of taking communion together. The Church, which considers marriage a sacrament encourages and blesses civil marriages, generally entered into by the parents of the prospective bride and groom with the blessings of local elders and family priests. Engagement takes place early, and marriage at puberty. Following the Biblical custom, the girl will have to prove her virginity, which is relayed to the public by the best men accompanying her in a form of dance displaying her stained nuptial veil. This important custom is now retained only in symbolic form, especially in larger urban areas like Addis Ababa. Of course the modern life style has brought with it later marriages, and the stiff requirement on virginity is being eased; yet the Church seems to tolerate even this development. Individual practice among the educated younger generation, however, may vary from loosely traditional to strictly European forms of marriage ceremony. At any rate, tradition continues to dominate in the majority of the communities, and young couples continue to be closely dependent on family and village. The young couple usually obtains a plot of land for their new home, near their families.

A very interesting form of a marriage contract in Ethiopian society is called a *demoz,* or salaried matrimony, whereby a woman agrees to live with a man at a specified remuneration for a specified time. It is somewhat like the "arrangements" that some of America's young college people have lately adopted. Though the Church does not necessarily look upon such arrangements with favor, it, nevertheless, tolerates them and considers them legitimate. The rights of inheritance of children born from such unions are regarded as equal to those of children born in lawful wedlock. Such contracts have become rather common in some circles of the educated class of Addis Ababa, who though often critical of tradition, find this to be a convenient arrangement. On the other hand, many of the young educated class often choose to be married in the Church. Without much opposition; traditionally church weddings were open only to those who solemnly vowed to enter marriage once only in their lifetime.

In discussing some of the several aspects of the influence and the role of the Ethiopian Church in the lives of ordinary people we must return to the principle which must always be kept in mind: the Ethiopian Church, as compared specially to the Western Churches, is highly flexible in its theological structure and rarely dictates dogmatic doctrines to the people. In reality, its teachings are enmeshed with the social customs of the country. Of course, the Church has laid down certain major practices, especially baptism, as prerequisites for entering the Christian fold. But beyond these, it has by and large adopted itself to control their lives. The Church has succeeded in doing this in two ways. First, it has reinforced the idea that religion and society are indivisible. Christianity is, in fact, regarded by an average man not as a religion but as a peoplehood, and it is not unusual to find references to Psalm 68:31 "Ethiopia shall soon stretch out her hands unto God," meaning "Christian Ethiopia." Secondly, the Church has propounded and practiced the belief that there is more than one level of sanctity. Thus, the Church welcomes believers who still feel that they are not worthy to enter the Church, and makes provisions for them to worship in the outer court and in the churchyard, according to the worshipper's own choice.[10] In a 15th-century religious work allegedly attributed to Emperor Zär'a Ya'acob (1434-1468), we find the teaching that "let alone Christians (inhabited by demons), even Jews and Gentiles and those who are even inhabited by demons should be welcomed by the Church to participate in Christian law if they so desire; but the priests should teach them the fear of God and sit them with 'minor' Christians until the time of the approach of their death when they will baptize them."

It is admirable that the Ethiopian Church has such a flexible theological structure to accept whatever society accepts as normal and natural. On the other hand, however, it can be envisioned that such tolerance can sometimes lead to too much licentiousness on the part of both the laymen and the clergy, some of whom do occasionally falter into the realm of inebriated state and hedonistic orgies or debauchery. Such matters can bring the Church's authority into disrepute. Therefore, it is important that the Church, while maintaining its flexibility, does not abdicate its spiritual responsibility but encourage and foster honest and proper education necessary for moral discipline and responsible citizenship.

In matters of birth and death ceremonies, the Church continues to play an active role, even in places like Addis Ababa. Many people who claim to be agnostics do still bring their children to baptism and have the priests give them religious names. At death, people prefer to be buried in churchyards. As the African and Semitic belief in the importance of one's name goes very deep, the educated Ethiopians—who prefer to wear European dress, to use European forms of greeting, to drink European alcoholic beverages, and eat European food—have resisted strongly the adoption of European names. A personal

---

10   *Mäs'hafä Berhan (Book of Light)*. Op. cit., p. 25.

name, like one's nationality, is regarded—consciously and unconsciously—as having great importance in one's life; and practically every Ethiopian name, sometimes even those used by non-Christians, has a religious connotation.

Some Ethiopian folkways reflect Biblical customs and traditions that are still quite common among Jews, such as circumcision. This is, of course, a general practice in many parts of the world, but in Ethiopia, it has an explicitly Biblical character. When in the 16th century, Jesuit missionaries denounced the Ethiopians for their non-Christian customs, the Emperor Claudius (1540-1556) wrote in reply that circumcision is on the contrary a Christian law "practiced as a respectful remembrance of a ceremony appointed by God to Abraham " (Genesis 17). The Church faces no serious problem in ensuring the continuation of this custom, even among modernized Ethiopians. Clitoridectomy (of young girls), also a common but not as a religious practice, is perhaps more in danger of disappearing among the younger generation.

The Church may have a problem with another set of customs consisting of food regulations, dietary laws, and fasting. Traditionally, the Ethiopians made a distinction between "clean" and "unclean" foods on the basis of the prescriptions of the Bible (Leviticus 11) regarding mammals and birds and concerning the forbidden sinew (Genesis 32:33). Educated young Ethiopians, however, care little whether they make such distinctions or even whether they keep the large number of fast days. The average village, however, sticks to tradition, by and large. As for a more developed community like Addis Ababa, a story was told that only a few decades ago, nonobservant young men used to go to restaurants and sit very shyly because they were afraid to be discovered eating forbidden food or meat on fast days or during Lent. Then, they would order *shifinfin* (literally, doubly folded over), a meat plate with a heavy layer of bread and vegetables on top! Presently, however, the course of events is said to have changed so fast that it is now the observant elderly person who goes to a restaurant and sits rather shyly. Having taken precautions that he is not seen to be observant, he would call the waiter to the corner and ask if by chance the restaurant serves *tsom wat* (a plate not defiled by meat). Thus, the modernistic society of Addis Ababa appears to have achieved a somewhat revolutionary attitude in regard to dietary laws, without much resistance from the Church.

Though drinking has always been a social custom in Ethiopia, the wiser men of the Ethiopian Church have always taught and practiced moderation. Except for *arake* (Ethiopian vodka), which does have a large content of alcohol, no strong drinks were used in the country until modern times. Both *tela* (Ethiopian beer) and *tej* (mead) contain very low percentages of alcohol (perhaps 5-10 percent). Along with everything so-called "modern" have come stronger and more harmful drinks, and Ethiopians, not to speak of foreign-trained people, have had generous recourse to imported liquor. When it first appeared in Ethiopia, eighty years ago, a leading Ethiopian churchman saw whisky as a vice. In a poem addressed to one of the Emperors, he wrote:

> There was a flower,
> A prize of the flora.
> The bee her friend, lost in caressing,
> Did not see when the wasp, the gnat, and the mosquito suddenly invaded.
> Woe, sweet smell of flower, thou hast become foul from flies!
> That flower of splendor which is Ethiopia,
> Is now bound hand and foot with the chain of alcohol,
> By Greeks and Armenians who bring it from abroad,
> "It is pure," they say, and snare the innocent,
> Cajoling him, flattering him, deceiving him by a ruse:
> "For myself and only for myself lately did I import-,
>
> But if now you -you! my friend art here, open and impart I must"
> Innocent youth! When they pour out and give you
> Liquid of wickedness, secret of madness,
> Suspectest thou not, understandest thou not,
> Quickly lap it down, alas for you,
> Thy health is sunk in phthisis and rheumatism,
> Woe, dear Ethiopia, Liquor has come against us![11]

Not many seem to have grasped the intent of such a reflection, and many young people today are incapacitated by liquor. The most unfortunate thing is that imported drinks have become customary in villages, where much-needed money and time are sometimes wasted in bars. Since the time of the churchman, author of the Amharic poem above, the Church has become rather indifferent as regards the people's drinking habits; at present it voices no special view on such matters.

Customs associated with holiday celebrations, some of which reflect Biblical influence, are continuing to enjoy widespread popularity, not only in the villages but also in a modernizing city like Addis Ababa. But the ancient strictness with which Ethiopians kept both Saturday and Sunday as days of rest has loosened. The Ethiopian Church's New Year on September 11, celebrated by performing ritual immersions in water, slaughtering of animals, and exchange of flowers, or the solemn holiday of *Fasika* (Passover- Easter) are the only religious holidays which have gained in popularity, even among the youth, and generally claim banner headlines and editorials in Ethiopian papers. Still, of great significance in the social life of modern Ethiopians are the two great festivals

---

11   Eadie, J. I. *An Amharic Reader,* Cambridge, 1924, p. 224. Translation by Ephraim Isaac.

of *Mäsqäl* (Feast of the Cross) and *Tïmgät* (torches of fire) all over the country, and the latter, accompanied by solemn processions, dancing, and singing and joyful bathing, draws the attention even of excited foreigners. These festivals will certainly continue in the years to come to be more and more part of the national—not only the religious—heritage of Ethiopia.

The Ethiopian Church appears to be losing its hold on the segment of society that is partially modernized. Modern educated persons are now exercising many of its ancient functions and many of its ancient practices seem to be in danger of dilution and even disappearance. The modern social problem is vast and complicated. Ethiopian awakening finds itself faced with a traditional economic philosophy—more or less feudally structured. The introduction of mechanical techniques, which produce goods at a fast speed, but treats men and labor like machines, is a new phenomenon in Ethiopian society. The growth of the new militaristic and bureaucratic state is also a puzzle. These are the results of the rise of a new elite in Ethiopian society.

Yet, despite all its shortcomings and in the face of vast, serious problems and radical ideals of social reform, the ecclesiastical organization seems to maintain itself by virtue of its historic weight. The Ethiopian Church has accommodated itself to the 20th century world. In this respect one can only say that the Ethiopian Church must be fortunate for not having dogmas which it would be embarrassed to abandon publicly; or for not being one that necessarily regards subjective holiness as a prerequisite for membership. On the contrary, regardless of its outward ceremoniousness, the Church has always upheld religious ethics as an integral part of Ethiopian social and legal custom. It must be understood that not only has the Church shaped the Ethiopian nation, but also that the mode of Ethiopian social life has shaped the religious community.

Many religious customs are gradually going to wane. If Ethiopia is to be economically productive, the people cannot afford to keep the Church's numerous festivals any longer. The simple rules of a balanced diet will affect the laws of fasting. Yet, when most festivals disappear, the important ones like New Year's, *Mäsqäl, Tïmgät* and *Fassika,* in particular, are going to be more thoroughly incorporated into Ethiopian national life. These festivals have shown to be a common possession of not only Christians but of all Ethiopians. The Church's life and character, however, will continue to pivot on them. Secondly, even if fasting will no longer be popular, the major Ethiopian dietary habits and laws will be continued by some if for no other reason because of the psychological inhibitions of not eating food one is not used to. Family life may change its external characteristics, but the historic influences with which the Church has shaped the basic attitudes toward sex, marriage, and man-woman relationships, are presently in no danger of major revision. Whatever happens, however, the Ethiopian Church appears to have the potential to adjust to all forms of social movements and changes. Educated Ethiopian priests and Ethiopian churches in Addis Ababa have proved that the Ethiopian Church does, in fact, welcome innovation. But, of course, until all the priests have been educated and the whole Church has undergone new experiences, one must not be overoptimistic about the total absence of clerical resistance.

Not only will the Church show ability to adjust to the changing ways of life, but it will undoubtedly affect the course and the pace of development in the future. In fact, without its co-operation and its influence, the educated leaders of Ethiopia will have a difficult time executing extensive and necessary reform programs within the existing system. Many reform programs can be undertaken only when the new generation of the educated becomes willing to enter into dialogue with the Church; whether the educated class will do so will depend to a great extent on its comprehension and appreciation of Ethiopia's past and present, on the one hand, and its critical assessment of the modern life on the other.

Understanding Ethiopia's past and present will mean not only better self-understanding for the educated elite, but it will also expose them to the negative and positive attributes of tradition; for surely as some tend to think today, not all aspects of Ethiopian tradition are diametrically opposed to progress. To look at the past and boast about its great historic moments, as some do, is not productive; to reject it altogether, as do others, is not responsible. To look at the past in order to interpret the course of the future, however, may not only be extremely valuable but necessary.

The attitude toward manual work; the attachment to land; Church involvement in politics; the strong reliance of individual members on party or family or on love that extends beyond the limits of generosity to dependence; the sense of temporality and progress outside the concept of the past and the eternal, and therefore, the relaxed attitude to movement, plan, and time; the low regard for inquisitiveness and for open and audible speech; an often unanalytical reliance on memory in learning; perhaps slight exaggeration of formalism and ceremoniousness, and love of festivities—all these may in one way or another furnish obstacles to technical progress and productivity. On the other hand, warmth of personality, a strong sense of mutual respect, the potential that the teachings of love, justice, and peace have in the assessment of social consequences, the psychological value of a limited, relaxed attitude toward time, and still other aspects of traditional culture can have positive results in the right *sitz im leben*. To appreciate critically every social phenomenon in its proper context can help to create a new approach that helps to assess it in the proper perspective and to guide one in choosing what to retain of the old and what to adopt of the new.

Still important is an understanding of what one may call "modernization" and its counterpart, which one may call "modernism," for lack of better terminologies. There is in "modernism" the ever-present danger of looking at everything "modern" as good and right no matter how relative these concepts may be. Just to walk with one's hands in one's pockets, to frequent such places as night clubs and movie theatres, to drink phenomenal amounts of whisky, to puff a cigarette, to wear a necktie or a mini-skirt, and, on a more sophisticated level, to disdain religion while siding with "absolute" science, are subconsciously regarded today by many "young intelligentsia," all over the world as manifested signs of modern progress. Each person surely has the right to conduct himself the way he chooses and to develop his own particular tastes. But when, in the name of progress, one imports *only* such forms of behavior, making much of them, without at the same time exemplifying the more productive aspects of progressive cultures, such as punctuality, planning, organizing, working hard, self-sacrifice, co-operation and responsibility—then those who look to the educated for guidance and leadership will be misled. To be educated and to be progressive would then be regarded as attaining a level of certain types of behavior and certain beliefs deserving respect and attention. Surely, if those who are educated do not produce more concrete and positive ideas and ideals that can be shown in action to be productive and useful for Ethiopian society, not only the Church, but society itself will gradually react. Modern man is basically Hellenic at heart; he is impressed by logic and form. The average Ethiopian Churchman is primarily impressed by social and moral responsibility, as well as by practical things, even if he does not possess all the efficient modern gadgets.

"Modernization—is not "modernism." "Modernism," as used above, refers to the superficial trappings and outer forms of what one may call "being modern." "Modernization," also for lack of a better term, is used here to describe the process of progress in line with present-day patterns of development and automation. I use it in the same sense that some modern sociologists, for instance, Marion J. Levy, Jr., do. By the modernized society, I mean one in which human efforts are multiplied by the use of tools. I mean, a society in which there is a very high rate of "mechanical advantage" to the extent that the productivity of man and the restructuring of society gain maximum efficiency, order, and speed. "Modernization" in this specific sense may be the process that might enable man to overcome poverty, disease, and illiteracy most efficiently; and if actualized, I assume, it may not only be regarded by the Church as positive, but indeed also as highly desirable.

It may be inevitable that the use of more tools and machines and multiplication of inanimate objects will increase man-object relationships or conversely, would decrease man-man relationships. The more time man spends relating himself to all the objects that have been created by "modernization," the less time he has to communicate with his fellow man. Though, religion may not necessarily conflict with positive "modernization" and could, in fact, assist in education, and bless the easing of man's burdens by mechanization, it can still come into indirect conflict with "modernization" when modernization produces dehumanizing practices. This will be a far more serious problem for the Church than a struggle with the superficiality and triviality of what I have called "modernism."

The really serious problem is, then, how can the traditional Church welcome "modernization" if "modernization" contains elements of dehumanization? The answer to this is as complicated as the answer to the question which psychologists and sociologists in "developed" societies ask today; how can man return to "humanization" in a "modernized" society? My contention is that it is not necessary to take for granted the theory that dehumanization is a logical consequence of "development," "modernization," or industrialization. The burdens and problems of the depressed and despairing modern man, the too well-known facts about modern society, and the results of the studies of modern sociology may perhaps contradict this assertion. I realize that, as I have said, the more machines occupy man's time, the fewer occasions there will be for self-reflection or for traditional human closeness such as that which the religious atmosphere attempts to engender. I would, however, still contend that the preoccupation in the minds of modern thinkers that "man," "spirit," and "machine" are incompatible is too often exaggerated.

The Church of Ethiopia cannot be prejudged as an obstacle to modernization. It must be called to a dialogue; it must be given a chance to speak for itself. For unless the Church is involved in the process of modernization, it will be difficult to bring any change in Ethiopia within the existing system. The Church presently cannot be said to be standing in the way of social change and amelioration; it is merely not involved, perhaps because it had not been called on, or perhaps because it has not had a chance to do so. If anything stands in the way of progress in Ethiopia today, it is "modernism" and the superficial manners and behavior of the present-day elite—even more than religious conservatism.

Many things will keep Ethiopian communities Church-centered. But there is no question that several formal aspects of religion will gradually disappear. The small monthly feasts that occur almost every two or three days or the arduous task of fasting almost two hundred days in a year have long been seen as draining the economy of the country and the health of the people. Today the Church, thanks to its flexibility, has begun to regard as sufficient the celebration of the major festivals, the special holy days of family patron saints, and fasting during the eight weeks of Lent. And even these are stringently practiced only by the most devout. Through its flexibility, the Church has caused little mass alienation; on the contrary, it has consolidated more popular interest in local fasts and feasts. If the Church continues to be liberal in social matters, it will have gone a long way in retaining its position of centrality.

Again to its credit, the Ethiopian Church has not involved the people in theological disputes and controversies. Its professed adherence to *Täwahïdo* involves subtleties that make very little difference to the people or the clergy. Some theological disputes have been encountered, especially through foreign missionaries. But these disputes have not resulted in conflicts, even when many foreigners, as well as Roman Catholic and Protestant missionaries have come with condescending attitudes, stereotyping the Ethiopian Church as "formalistic," "pagan," or "Jewish" and criticizing the priesthood as "ignorant" or "besotted." One wrote "Twelve thousand clerical drones ... fatten in idleness on the labor of the working classes."[12] Another spoke of "the almost daily spectacle of their drunkenness, excesses, and immorality."[13] On top of such criticism, some missionaries have tried to introduce theological debates which have caused friction both with foreigners and sometimes among Ethiopians.

That some priests have been superstitious or poorly educated may be true, but surely these extreme judgments are founded upon a lack of sympathetic understanding of Ethiopia and its life. For one thing, except for the fact that they have received some theological training, the priests are still part of the common folk who often work hard to earn their own living. Though the priests may own some Church lands, as a class, they are certainly not a "bourgeois" group. Furthermore, taking into account the isolation of Ethiopia for so many centuries, one could not have expected more accomplishment from them. Under these conditions, it is not surprising that the priests have retained the affection and respect of the people, and that they play an important part in village life.

Examining the relation of the church to the village can bring out a concrete relation between church and society. The village is different from the bustling lifestyle and dynamics of the countries largest city, Addis Ababa. Addis Ababa has been a growing and changing city. Since its foundation more than a century ago, it has developed from a small, almost rural village to a modern city. Practically all the changes, modernization, and development that are taking place in Ethiopia seem to be concentrated here. More than 50 percent of all Ethiopians who have received any form of modern schooling live here, and perhaps more than 90 percent of foreign-educated persons are employed in major government offices, business and trade firms, and educational institutions centered in Addis Ababa and the vicinity. But most of Ethiopia, its villages and small towns have seen very little change, and the social structure still remains largely traditional.

Traditional Ethiopian society and life in general have been described by scholars over and over again as well as within this book as predominantly biblical in character. One scholar described it as the living world of the Bible, and

---

12   Harris, W.C. *The Highlands of Ethiopia.* Vol. III, London, 1884, p. 131.

13   Hotten, J.C. *Abyssinia and its People.* London, 1868, p. 161.

another has called it "a haven of peace where the courtesies of the ancient Orient continue to live."[14]

Ethiopian society is much more homogeneous and unified than observers sometimes think, especially socially and culturally. There is a long history of interaction and sharing of common problems and events among Ethiopians. Despite the tribal warfare that has existed in Ethiopia since antiquity, the country as a whole always unified against foreign invasion. The diversity in languages and dialects or ethnic communities does not reflect the more profound feeling of unity among Ethiopians, just as the existence of the apparent ethnic units (English, Jewish, Irish, Italian, etc.) in Boston does not reflect the more profound unity of the American people. In other words the experience of Ethiopia definitely differs from the experience of countries in which there are tribal units that are exclusively separate bodies. In this respect, even sociologists and anthropologists who tend to overemphasize ethnic differences have had to admit that:

> the racial, linguistic and cultural characteristic of Ethiopia results ... from its geographic position ... from numerous invasions of the region by alien peoples, from the diffusion into the area of new culture traits and culture complexes, including Judaism, Christianity and Islam, and from extensive culture contact, acculturation and biological intermixing... Biologically, however, there was such extensive mixing that today the Semitic speaking groups are indistinguishable physically from the Cushitic-speaking groups ... many writers consider both the Cushitic-speaking and Semitic-speaking peoples of Ethiopia to belong to a common "Ethiopian" ... type.[15]

A 1965 study by a German anthropologist throws new light on the common heritage and deeper unity of the Ethiopian people:

> Any attempt to gain deeper insights into the course of cultural history of Africa through the methods of ethnology must give special consideration to the African kingdoms. Their traditions reflect an imminent feeling for that which is history, in contrast to the small tribes or kin-organization.... All the evidence seems to indicate that the peoples of southern Ethiopia and the original Cushitic speaking peoples of the Highland (northern Ethiopia) were once joined by a

---

14 Ullendorff, op. cit., London, 1964, 2nd edition. 206.

15 Simons, op. cit., p. 20.

common culture, prior to the Southern Arabian immigration and before the introduction of Christianity.[16]

This becomes evident when one looks more closely at the villages and towns of Ethiopia, which, since ancient times, have existed independently with an importance like the communities described in the Bible. Most of these villages and towns, often including districts around them, have internal coherence and unity though their inhabitants came from more than one area of the country, or from more than one linguistic group of the people. Town after town and village after village, each acted as a unit. As a rule, a single family dominated a village. Even if it did not have a common sanctuary or religion, the most well-known Ethiopian Church festivals such as New Years (September 11), *Mäsqäl* (September 27-28), and *Tïmqät* (January 17-18), were held in common. In the more traditional areas of Ethiopia, the ruling family was from a priestly line. As in Biblical times on, it descended from a national hero. Though no municipalities existed in the past, the unity of the villages or towns was so strong that responsibility was common to all. The idea that responsibility for bloodguilt and theft rests upon the whole of the village has been recognized in the practice of *afarsata* in many traditional areas of Ethiopia.

One example of a town that is between a large modernizing center—like Addis Ababa and wholly traditional communities in other words, a traditional community affected by some change — is Nazareth of the 1970s. Its population was made up of people originating in different regional and linguistic areas. Many changes have taken place in Nazareth: the 20 percent literacy rate of the town is at least 50 percent higher than that of traditional villages that have not seen any change. In contrast with the traditional way of life, only 10 per cent of the population is engaged in agricultural activities, while the majority are daily laborers employed mainly in public and private construction work and at the town's railway station. Many of the residents are in trade and crafts, and even work in the government and business offices. Fifty percent of the homes use electricity and about 16 percent have running water; 81 percent of the inhabitants live in only semi-traditional buildings, and about 70 percent pay rent. In Nazareth, there are hotels, bars and liquor stores besides the traditional *Tej* and *Tella* houses. There are also retail shops selling various modern goods and gadgets, government offices, railroads, bus stations, schools, the Anti-Malaria Training Institute, hospitals, a small airstrip, and other semi-modernized institutions. Regardless of many changes taking place in Nazareth, it is still very much a religion-oriented town, with about 90 percent of its population Christian and about 10 percent Moslem. According to local informants, it had five churches, with at least six priest-families per church, a few priest schools, and one mosque.

---

16   Haberland, Fike. *Untersuchungen zum Aithiopischer Konigtum.* Wiesbaden, 1965, p. 317-318.

Even if we had adequate or better sources of information, a full description of religious life, the social, psychological, economic and political consequences of changes that are taking place in a town or village like Nazareth is beyond the scope of this book. But brief reference can be made to main features of the life of the Church and the effects of change in Ethiopian communities. It must be emphasized that this is based on an assessment not of a largely modernizing society like that of Addis Ababa, or on largely traditional communities, but rather on an analysis of smaller communities that are beginning to absorb some change.

Change has brought about not so much differences in the content, as in the form of beliefs and religious attitudes. Priests and congregations still stand in very close relationship, and public and private events frequently involve clerical ministrations. The Church has never involved itself closely with questions of intimate personal practices or individual beliefs. The categorical confession of a tenet of faith is not formally demanded. Whoever is not an open opponent of the Church or whoever does not publicly profess another religion is regarded in Ethiopia as a Church member. Participation in sacraments, except for baptism, has never been a requirement and is left, to a large extent, to individual desires and decisions. This liberal-mindedness on the part of the Ethiopian Church makes it possible for the people of any community to adjust to change without sacrificing their religious loyalties. So long as the Ethiopian Church does not press the issue of "correct" or "true" belief, which it never did in the past, the community can remain Church-centered—or better, Church-conscious—and would want to retain its identity with the Ethiopian Church and its traditions.

As an example, we can look again at the Ethiopian code of sexual ethics which we have already considered above. The Ethiopian Church considers chastity a virtue and an ideal. Ethiopians have a high regard for monks; and they expect the clergy to be married only once and that before ordination. Furthermore, the Church teaches that monogamy is the Christian ideal and allows no divorce on any grounds. Nonetheless, so long as a person remains loyal to his confession, the Church does not oppose local customs of marriage that are less strict. A person can consider his life Church-centered without feeling embarrassed even if his sex ethics do not stand up to the high standards of the Church. Ironically, having Church weddings is more frequent among modernized Ethiopians than among the traditional. This is an aspect of the influence of European practice, and it does not mean that the younger generation is necessarily committed to a higher standard of matrimonial loyalty.

Some foreign observers think that the majority of Ethiopian Christians are technically excommunicated because they do not accept the restraints of Christian marriage; furthermore, they believe that this is why people generally attend the service of the Eucharist standing outside the church, as mere spectators.[17]

17   Perham, Margery. *The Government of Ethiopia*. London, 1947, p. 116.

However, it is actually better to say that the people are under a self-imposed excommunication. Whatever the case may be, the scarcity of Church weddings and the lack of mass participation in the Eucharist are not regarded as serious, either by the Church or by the people. Baptism and confirmation are administered at birth, penance appears, for the most part to be a mere formality, and extreme unction is practiced only by those who choose to undergo it. A religious funeral is allowed to all who profess to be Orthodox Christians, regardless of the form of ceremony and status or habit of their marriage and their past life. It is again this broad attitude of the Ethiopian Church that continues to give the priesthood a strong hold on the people.

Furthermore, the village continues to be Church-centered as the importance of the clergy and the sanctuary is brought out by the religious festivals, which are part of the national, cultural, and public heritage of all Ethiopians, regardless of religious adherence. The life of any Ethiopian community, for that matter even that of the capital, Addis Ababa, continues to revolve around such spectacular festivals as *Timqät* (Feast of Immersion) and *Mäsqäl* (Feast of the Cross), both of which have pre-Christian elements rooted in the homogeneous aspects of Ethiopian culture. Even Easter, a day of social festivities that is among the most important religious festivals of Ethiopia, as well as the less popular holy day of Christmas, accompanied by the favorite game of *Ganna,* have public sanction and attract general public attention.

Though ideas of modern law are gradually influencing Ethiopian society at large, by virtue of their sanction by the Church and the *Fetha Nagast,* customary regional laws continue to retain a measure of importance, especially in many local villages and village courts. Although on the national level the *Fetha Nagast* has been drastically altered, especially since the reign of Emperor Menelik II (1889-1913),[18] and the *muslins,* modern chiefs of villages and towns have replaced the *cheqa-shums,* traditional chiefs elected by the villages or nominated by district chiefs; traditional religious laws continue to play a significant role in local communities, even if not with apparent official sanction or official approval. In addition, the majority of appointed local *danyas* (judges) and law-makers to date are Church-trained men, in many instances, priests or *däbtära.*

The material that constitutes the juridical basis of customary law is generally not reduced to writing. At meetings of village elders and notables, general principles are established which are retained in public memory and guarded by the written laws of the Church. Ethiopians, despite their reservedness, when it comes to legal matters generally exhibit a great capacity for brilliant and eloquent exposition and self-expression, and prefer to conduct their own lawsuits themselves rather than through lawyers.

---

18   Marein, Nathan. *The Ethiopian Empire, Federation and Laws.* Rotterdam, 1954.

Ethiopian justice offers a fine example of Church (biblical) customs still preserved in the folkways of the people. The administration of local or village justice is the most important part of the traditional legal system. The impromptu court, which meets in the marketplace or in some other outdoor center, carries the same weight among the people of the community as it did in ancient Ethiopia or in Biblical days. Two men who have a dispute find an arbitrator, preferably a priest or a *däbtära,* to act as judge between them. No man may refuse to perform this duty. The judge, or *dannya* (a word related to the Biblical "din" or lawsuit), gathers witnesses, hears the case, and gives his judgment. There are also permanent local *dannya*, usually religiously educated elders of the community, who act as judges and advisers and give relevant interpretations of the existing laws in difficult cases. Although new legislation and new forms of administering justice are being extensively developed by Parliament, judgeship has become professional under the Ministry of Justice; and a law school has been established in Addis Ababa. Nonetheless, the voluntary and spontaneous forms of administering justice in the villages are still daily practice, and religious laws are an integral part of the public life of the masses as in biblical times.

The Ethiopian Church continues to play a conspicuous role in the life of village and rural communities, especially in bringing their children to the church for baptism, on the fortieth day if a boy and on the eightieth if a girl. Civil marriages are blessed by family priests *(yänäfs abbat*—soul father) who play an important role in the social life of the people. At death, ritual wailing and mourning as well as elaborate commemoration on feasts, *tezkar (cf.* Jewish customs of mourning and remembering the dead), held on the third, seventh, twelfth, fortieth (the most important), eightieth day, sixth month, first and seventh year, continue to absorb the attention of the society. Though fasting has somewhat subsided and perhaps only the clergy and devout members observe most of the regulations, in the local communities strong national consciousness still exists even among the educated. Regarding fasting customs as well as making some distinction between the flesh of clean and unclean animals, only few Ethiopians really enjoy eating pork or ham, and none of the indigenous restaurants of even modernized Addis Ababa serve traditionally prohibited meat. The large number of Church festivals which appear almost every two days are practiced with rigor in remote regions, though only the best-known Church festivals are greeted by the younger generation with great enthusiasm. Each person may have a favorite or patron saint or angel, for whom he makes a special service for its community on the angel or the saint for whom he makes a special feast in the presence of a family priest and close friends *(zikirt)*. Moreover, each village holds a special service for its community on the day of the angel or the saint for which its local church is named.

Religion is so deeply rooted in the national consciousness of the Ethiopian people that many modern customs cannot replace ancient ones. Ethiopian Christians have always believed that they are the "chosen people of God," and the only true Christians. Those who reject this idea subconsciously give assent to it. In this, converts to other forms of Christianity Protestantism or Catholicism—are generally regarded even by non-practicing educated persons, with some suspicion as representatives of alien and heretical creeds.

The lives and values of most people are still permeated with religious overtones. The average man in the village, for example, feels the personal presence of angels very profoundly. Saints are asked through prayers to intercede for support, succor, and rescue from enemies. The Devil is dreaded, and children are made to carry on their arms or necks a leather scroll called *lifafa s'idq* (scroll of righteousness) for protection against the Devil or the evil eye.[19] Though the Church officially condemns such beliefs, some people, especially among the learned priests, are thought to be able to communicate with angels, demons, or dead spirits. The Church also condemns the spirit cult called *Zar*, believed to exist both by Christians and non-Christians.

It is thought that there are respectively more churches in the Christianized districts of Ethiopia than in other regions of comparable sizes in the world, and some travelers have estimated that one man out of five is a member of the clergy or a cantor in the church.[20] Nevertheless, popular church attendance is not necessarily regarded as a measure of faith—if it appears occasionally a measure of piety; yet church attendance is indeed very high, though a small part of religious obligation.

In the remote villages all men still dismount when they pass the church, and devoted church people wash lepers and tend their sores. The courtesy and kindness of Ethiopian priests and the effects of religion upon the character of the Ethiopian people still continue.

---

19   Some church people are critical of Lifafe S'idq.

20   Simoons, op. cit., p. 29.

Chapter 14

The Ethiopian Church
and Other Religions

"Ethiopia is an island of Christianity in a sea of Muslims."
-Atse (Emperor) Menelik II[1]

Three of the large world religions are represented in Ethiopia: Judaism, Christianity, and Islam. In addition, nature religions are adhered to by about fifteen percent of the population. These nature religions are remnants of the ancient Ethiopian religions and cults associated with the worship of trees and water, a serpent-king, the sun and the moon, and a goddess called Astarte. Some of these ancient cults produced an unusually impressive type of art and architecture such as we have seen ancient temples and palaces and the outstanding monolithic stele of Axum.

The roots of Ethiopian Judaism go back to the ancient beginnings of the country, probably antedating Christianity. The faith has retained some of the original forms of the ancient biblical religion of Israel, as well as taken on many indigenous peculiarities. It is therefore substantially different from normative Judaism elsewhere. Its adherents, called *Falashas* (meaning "migrants"), are not at all distinguishable from other Ethiopians, except in their religious practices.

Islam is an important religion in Ethiopia, claiming about twenty-five to thirty percent of the population.[2] It took root in Ethiopia in the time of its founder (c. 570-632 CE), for it was in this country that many early disciples of prophet Mohammed, following his advice to go to the "land of righteousness," found religious toler-

---

1   Trimingham, J. Spencer. *The Christian Church and Missions in Ethiopia.* WORLD DOMINION PRESS, London, 1950 (7).

2   According to the latest Official Ethiopian Government census of 2008.

ance and refuge. Taking this fact into account, the prophet issued a special decree that there should be no holy war against the Ethiopians. Of the three major religions, Islam is most conformable to its counterpart outside of Ethiopia. In Ethiopia both Judaism and Christianity have developed numerous indigenous peculiarities.

Christianity is professed by an estimated fifty percent of the population; it is the most influential religion in the country. It is interesting to note that the three great monotheistic religions of the world, Judaism, Christianity and Islam, can be characterized as the national religions of three branches of the Semitic linguistic groups: Jews, Ethiopians, and Arabs respectively. The Ethiopians are the only people of Semitic speech who hold Christianity as their national religion. In this particular study emphasis will be placed upon the Christian religion, but it will necessarily include brief discussions of Judaism, Islam, and indigenous religions.

To my knowledge, the Ethiopian Church has rarely been charged of religious intolerance or of holding persecuting attitudes towards members of other religions. One thing about which some foreigners have voiced some complaints is what they consider an attitude of suspicion. More astute observers, however, agree with Levine that such an attitude is "an adaptive response to some very real dangers with which Ethiopia has chronically been confronted: the threat of conversion to Western forms of Christianity by European missionaries, the threat of European imperialism, and the threat of encirclement and occupation by a militant Islam." Furthermore, Levine correctly concludes that realization of these factors has "undoubtedly intensified the apprehensiveness of Ethiopia's leaders."[3]

In the first place, conflicts have, at times, arisen between individual priests or Church leaders and Christian missionaries. The accusation by mission institutions that the Church has sometimes persecuted them or their Ethiopian converts is often based on misunderstandings that developed between them and individual priests or Churchmen. The Ethiopian Church has never systematically organized its forces (and perhaps never needed to do so) to persecute another religious group.

In the second place, we know from history about several periods of warfare between the Christian and the non-Christian states of the Ethiopian Empire. Such wars between Christian and Moslem or Ethiopian Jewish, then known as *Falasha*, states were primarily political rather than religious. This is not to minimize the significance of the part played by the Church hierarchy in political matters, for in Ethiopian history one cannot so easily distinguish politics from religion. As far as one can judge, however, the actual hostilities rarely originated from basic issues of doctrine or faith as due to the refusal of the non-Christian states to pay homage to the central predominately-Christian-government. They often involved questions of "border" conflicts, trade transactions, and such

---

3   Levine, Donald. *Wax and Gold*. Chicago, 1965, p. 252.

matters. Generally, the Ethiopian clergy have been exempt from military service though often they accompany the fighting army.

Ethiopia is almost totally surrounded by Islamic sovereign states to the north, the cast and the west. In the country itself, the people who inhabit the Harar Province, as well as a large block of people living mainly in the Wollo, Arsi, and Kaffa provinces in the highlands, comprise a significant Moslem group. In general, the highland Moslems, referred to as *Jabarti*, are of the same racial stock as all Ethiopians, except for colonies of Yemenite Arabs who are socially independent, though not psychologically alien. Most of the Moslems of Ethiopia are traders and merchants, but there are many good artisans and peasants.

Because Arabia is near to the Horn, Islam arrived in Ethiopia in the lifetime of its founder. Some scholars believe that the development of Islam was influenced by this early contact with Ethiopia and Ethiopian Christianity. When the Quaraish in Mecca was persecuting his disciples, the prophet Mohammed instructed them: "If you go to Abysinnia, you will find a king under whom none are persecuted . . . It is a land of righteousness where God will give you relief from what you are suffering."[4] So in 615, the fifth year of prophet Mohammed's call, refugees crossed the Red Sea and made an emigration (known by Moslem writers as the first *hajira*) to Ethiopia.[5] Though the Quraish demanded their return, the King of Ethiopia, the *Najashi*, gave refuge to the exiled disciples, especially upon their demonstration of the proximity of their faith to Christianity. The noted Islamic scholar, Sir William Muir, says that, "If an Arab asylum had not at last offered itself at Medina, the prophet might haply himself have emigrated to Abyssinia, and Mohammedanism dwindled, like Montanism, into an ephemeral Christian heresy."[6] It is thought that the prophet Mohammed, who regarded Ethiopia with considerable respect, is said to have taught, "Leave the Abyssinians in peace so long as they do not take the offensive."[7] No *jihad* was directed against Ethiopia in the great days of the initial impulse when Islam spread over country after country.

Later developments, however, had different repercussions, and Islam spread into Ethiopia by *jihad* as well as through migration. The first reported military expedition against Ethiopia took place in 640, but the Arab fleet suffered so

---

4   Hisham, Ibn. *Sira*. Cairo, 1927, p. 343.

5   Trimingham thinks that prophet Mohammed himself was in contact with Ethiopian traders, artisans, and soldiers residing in Mecca, as evidenced by a number of Ethiopic words in Qur'an. (Ahrens, K. *Christians in Qoran*. Z.D. M. G., LXXXIV, 1930, (15-68, 148-190).

6   Muir, W. *The Life of Mohammed*. London, 1923, p. 70.

7   Trimingham, J. Spencer. *Islam in Ethiopia*. London, Frank Cass and Co., Ltd. 1965 (p. 46).

disastrously that they would not dare try another invasion.[8] But more than half a century later, the Arabs occupied the Dahlak archipelago, which lies opposite the now Eritrean port of Massawa and established "the first bridgehead which was to lead to the occupation of other coastal bases and the gradual penetration of Islam into East Africa."[9] As a result of general Arab conquests and the gradual rise of Islam on the coastal areas of Ethiopia as well as of the expansion of nomadic people called the Beja into the northern part of the country, the Christian Empire of Ethiopia fell into complete isolation. Edward Gibbon wrote: "Encompassed on all sides by the enemies of their religion, the Aethiopians (*sic*) slept near a thousand years forgetful of the world, by which they were forgotten."[10] Henceforth, Ethiopia's only contact with other Christians was with the Coptic Church in Egypt and to a limited degree with the Christian community of Jerusalem. Axum, the great city of Ethiopia, which thrived on its control of the Red Sea trade routes, entered a gradual decline both economically and culturally. The ruins of great temples and palaces points to the greatness of its past before 650 CE The history of Ethiopia from about 650 to about 1270 generally, but from c. 650 to c. 950 particularly, crucial for the understanding of Ethiopian history as well as of Christian-Islamic relations, is shrouded in obscurity due to lack of sources, either foreign or native. But every evidence points to the fact that during this period of internal reorganization Islam made considerable progress in Ethiopia (as in most of Coastal East Africa) in such regions as Ifat, Adal, Fatagar, Dawaro, Bali, and other areas in eastern and central Ethiopia. The subjects of these provinces often rebelled against the emperor. Islam also succeeded in making converts among the *Bejas* in the north and among the *Afar* and the Somali in the east.

The Christian government of Ethiopia remained tolerant as long as the Moslems paid taxes and as long as the surrounding states did not enter into open conflict with her. But with the rise of the Solomonic Dynasty in 1270, it soon developed a reaction against the first period of Moslem expansion; for at this time the expansion of Islam was becoming more menacing and the need to check this expansion especially that of the Sultanate of Ifat over the region of Shoa, was becoming more evident. Here begins the long struggle within the Christian Ethiopian Kingdom and the Moslem states.

As said earlier, and as some scholars have observed quite well, the battles that ensued did not constitute a "war of religion, but a struggle for political predominance."[11] To be sure, Christian missionary work was heightened,

---

8   Trimingham, J. Spencer. *Islam in Ethiopia*. London, Frank Cass and Co., Ltd. 1965 (p. 47).

9   Trimingham, J. Spencer. *Islam in Ethiopia*. London, Frank Cass and Co., Ltd. 1965 (p. 48).

10   Gibbon, E. *Decline and Fall*. London, 1936, Chapter XLVII.

11   Trimingham, J. Spencer. *Islam in Ethiopia*. London, Frank Cass and Co., Ltd. 1965 (p. 65).

particularly under the leadership of Tekla-Haymanot, and church reform also began to take place. It must be noted, however, that these missionary activities and reforms were part of the political reformation and reorientation of the New Dynasty, not a reaction against Islam. Among his first acts as ruler, Yekuno Amlak, the founder of the Solomonic Dynasty, took measures to check the South Arabian missionary expansion through Ifat into Shoa. The Alexandrian Patriarchate, which had been co-operating with the Moslem rulers of Egypt at the same time, refused to send an *Abuna* to Ethiopia.[12] But Ethiopian campaigns against the South Arabian Moslem traders continued and the Adal (Zeila) collaborators were successfully checked. Relations with Egypt were later restored under Yagbe'a Sion (1285-1294), and Arab merchants were allowed into Ethiopia in return for Egyptian permission to allow Ethiopia to re-acquire its rights in Jerusalem and to have a new *Abuna.*

In 1298, an Arab Moslem sheik, Mohammed Abu Abdallah, who was believed to be acting under angelic revelation, determined to conquer Ethiopia. His attempt failed as Ethiopian Moslems did not collaborate, and Ethiopia strengthened her hold on all her provinces. Finally, although South Arabian military ventures continued to fail, Ethiopia's steady tolerance left room for a sufficient advancement of Islam in the country. It can be said that, in general, Islamic religious expansion thrived more on Ethiopian non-reaction or toleration than on military initiative and success.

The campaign to counteract Islamic political expansion initiated by the Solomonic House was greatly intensified during the reign of Amde Tsion I (1314-1344). Amda-Sion successfully checked the expansion of Islam, subjugating the now rebelling, predominantly Moslem states of Ifat and Adal. He was so successful in his campaigns that he demanded, in 1321, that Egypt refrain from persecuting the Copts and restore their churches. If Egypt refused to heed his warning, Amda-Sion threatened to take reciprocal action against Arab merchants living in Ethiopia and, in addition, would divert the course of the Nile to starve the Egyptians. Egyptian indifference and continued uprisings in 1328 in Ifat and Fatagar induced Amda-Sion to overwhelm Moslem outposts in Eastern Ethiopia. He subsequently appointed Sultan Sabre-ad-Din, brother of the Sultan, who was the leader of the rebellion, as chief of the combined vassal state of Ifat and Fatagar.

But Sabre-ad-Din himself rebelled against the king after having gathered the support of the other predominantly Moslem provinces of Hadya and Dawaro. Furthermore, he sought to stir up the Agaos and turn the king's attention to them. Amda-Sion however, a great military man, intercepted Sabre-ad-Din and subjugated all the rebellious provinces. He then appointed Jamal ad-Din, another brother of Sabre-ad-Din, as governor of the combined provinces. Ifat

---

12   Trimingham, J. Spencer. *Islam in Ethiopia.* London, Frank Cass and Co., Ltd. 1965 (p. 64).

initially had Egyptian support, but her final appeal to the Sultan of Egypt accomplished little, resulting merely in a supplicatory letter to Amda-Sion from the Patriarch of Alexandria.

Not taking into account the experiences of his brothers and predecessors, Jamal ad-Din himself rebelled, this time relying on the help of Egyptian mercenaries and the forces of the two new provinces of Adat and Mora. But Amda-Sion continued to triumph, extending his power over all the Ethiopian states and consolidating Dawaro, Ifat, Bali, Hadya, and all of the other predominantly Muslim states under his rule.

Amda-Sion is glorified in song and prose as having accomplished all his deeds through the power of God. His victories earned a new prestige for the Ethiopian Church and established a new direction in Christian-Muslim relations in the Middle East. Ethiopia even assumed the role of the protectorship of the Patriarchate of Alexandria. Thus, in 1352, Sayfa Arad (1344-1372), Amda-Sion's successor, intervened strongly against the persecution of Egyptian Christians by Amir Shaikun and Sultan al-Malik as Salih.[13] Egypt then turned to the Coptic Patriarch in order to plead with the Ethiopian king to save the Egyptian merchants who were being persecuted.

Ethiopia's relaxation of control over Ifat brought another period of revolt in 1376. However, under Emperor Dawit (1382-1411) the hostilities, which had recommenced, were again suppressed. The last official leader of Ifat, Sa'ad ad Din II, was killed in 1415 by Emperor Yishaq on the island of Zaila, then occupied by Ethiopia. Henceforth Ifat was erased from history, and the struggle between the Christian and Moslem states of Ethiopia momentarily subsided until the Ottoman Turks succeeded in inciting the governors of Adal, who had by now gained new energy, bringing this time a brief Moslem triumph in Ethiopia.

At the close of the first period of hostilities, Ethiopia's relations with both Egypt and Turkey actually became friendlier. Under Emperor Zär'a Ya'aqob (1434-1468), Ethiopia continued a period of more or less peaceful reconstruction, a new era of art, literature and architecture. Zär'a Ya'aqob also expanded Dawit's policies of establishing relations with world Christianity and reforming the Ethiopian Church. During this relatively peaceful time, the second period of Moslem expansion in Ethiopia also began with the restrengthening of the eastern part of the province of Adal. The partial impetus given to the expansion of Islam in Ethiopia during the first period came primarily from Arabia, and then from Egypt. During the second period, it came first from Egypt, and then from the Ottoman Empire. It meant that Ethiopia had to contend eventually with the greatest military power in the world at that time—the United Islamic

---

13   Perruchon, J. op. cit. I, 1893, (p. 177-182). See also Trimingham, J. Spencer. *Islam in Ethiopia*. London, Frank Cass and Co., Ltd. 1965 (p. 73).

Empire under the Ottoman Turks, who controlled the Red Sea and the gateway to Ethiopia. Like the first, the second confrontation was also brought about not necessarily by the result of a program of expansion and consolidation of Ethiopian Islam and a Christian counteraction, but it was primarily a clash between an expansionist foreign power which happened to be Islamic and the Ethiopian government which happened to be Christian. Thus, it was similarly political in nature.

As has been indicated, the Christian rulers of Ethiopia, perhaps because of their self-confidence or perhaps for reasons of tolerance, left the Moslem provinces to govern themselves always, even after difficult conquests. Moreover, there were few pressures, if any, from evangelistic efforts, and the Church did not undertake a campaign of systematic conversion. Not only this, but according to reports by Portuguese travelers in Ethiopia during the days of the sixteenth and seventeenth centuries, the Moslems were allowed to live in their own villages even in the midst of Christian areas.[14] The Ottoman Turks took all these advantages to strengthen their position. Moreover, the proximity of Adal, a predominantly Islamic Ethiopian province, to the Red Sea and the Indian Ocean gave them some fair opportunities for contact with an Ethiopian province.

The Ottoman Turks gradually strengthened their position among the Afar (Dankali) and the Somali, but their stronghold was soon to become the Sultanate of Adal in the region of Harar. Here, momentum was gathered that was soon to develop into a real *jihad*. As Trimingham indicates, this was characterized in the titles of the two famous leaders of Adal whom the Turks specially befriended; Mahfuz and Ahamed ben Ibrahim, who were given the religious title *imam*, instead of the feudal title of *amir*. "The invisible meanings which lay behind . . . now struck a responsive spark in the hearts of the populace and kindled fire to emulate the swift conquests of early Islam."[15] With Ottoman encouragement, Adal first tested its power by significant victories over two military units sent in 1473 and 1474 by Emperor Baeda Mariam (1468-1478), whose only success was not against the Moslems, but against the *Beta Isreal*. Though this marked a turning point in Ethiopian military supremacy, it does not appear that Ethiopia took it seriously. One of Baeda Mariam's wives, Empress Eleni, the converted daughter of a Moslem ruler of Dawaro, Al Jarad Abun, was the only one who sensed the dangers that were coming to ahead. This is no contradiction, but a proof that Ethiopian Moslems, like their Christian compatriots, were equally alarmed at the growing world power of the Ottoman Turks, whom they considered dangerous for their sovereignty. When, however, at last her friends failed her, she had no choice but to turn to Europe and to make an alliance with

---

14   Alvarez. *Narrative of the Portuguese Embassy to Abyssinia*. Translated and edited by Lord Stanley of Alderley, Hakluyt Society, London, 1881, p. 95.

15   Trimingham, Islam in Ethiopia

Portugal.[16] During the reign of Emperor Naod (1494-1508), a sagacious and firm ruler who followed the cautious policy of the Empress Eleni, the leaders of Adal—who then had made alliance with the Turks—pursued peace with the Christian government of Ethiopia.

But Lebna Dengel (1508-1540) soon assumed the reins of government when the regent Empress Eleni retired. Though at first Lebna Dengel followed her advice, he soon began to follow a course of his own. In opposition to her plans, he turned down the Portuguese offer of general military alliance and occupation of Zeila on Ethiopia's behalf. His rule climaxed with the events of the Ethiopian Christian-Moslem struggle: the cataclysmic conquest that brought socio-political and ecclesiastical changes, and the virtual subjugation of Ethiopia to Moslem leadership.

Much has been written about this period of Ethiopia's control by the Moslem forces under the able leadership of Amir Ahmed ben Ibrahim, nicknamed Gran, the left-handed. It would be a mistake to attribute weakness to Lebna Dengel. In fact, it was Lebna Dengel who, in 1516, routed out the Ottoman forces under the famous Adalite ruler, Amir Mahfuz, governor of Zeila. When Mahfuz himself was slain and Zeila burned, Lebna Dengel got a hero's welcome, and the Christians of Ethiopia thought that Ottoman expansion in imperialism was forever stopped.

However, almost a decade later the Ottomans renewed their efforts by giving spiritual and material support to the militant and effective commander, Ahmad Ibn Ibrahim (1506-1543), who began to consolidate power by conquering the Afar and Somalis utilizing his strong position in Adal. Initially his limited objectives of raids and incursions brought success. In 1529, in Shimbra Kurie, he won a major victory over Lebna Dengel. Within a period of five years, infused with a spirit of a holy war, he overran Shoa and Dawaro first, and, eventually Bali, Hadya, Begemeder, and Lasta (Wollo), and reached Tigrai in 1534. Highland Ethiopia had never seen such misery, ruin, and devastation. Much precious literature was lost, and many famed churches praised by Portuguese writers of earlier days were burned.[17] For the next six years, the Emperor fled from one mountaintop to another, seeking refuge. At last, he gave up and as a matter of expediency turned his last hope to Europe to enlist Portuguese aid even if that meant allowing other foreigners who may also be a threat to Ethiopian sovereignty, into the country.

He, therefore, dispatched the Ethiopian envoy, Zagazab, and a certain Joao Bermudes, whom he had detained from an earlier Portuguese expedition, to summon help. But, for all practical purposes, it was too late; the country had

---

16 Besha, Girma, Merid Aregay, *Question of Churches in Luso-Ethiopian Relations.* Lisbon, 1964, p. 24.

17 Deressa, Yilma. *Ye-Ethiopia Hizb Tarik be'asera sidstegna Meto'amat.* Addis Ababa, 1966; German and Merid, op. cit., p. 37; Trimingham, op. cit. p. 84.

been overrun, one of his sons had been killed, one had been captured, and in 1540 before any help could come Lebna Dengel died at the age of forty-four. However, he did not die with despair, for he trusted his courageous wife, Queen Sabla-Wangel, and his eighteen-year-old son, Gelawedewos, whom he designated to succeed him.

Portuguese help at last arrived in 1541. From the first encounter with Ahmed Gran in 1542, the Portuguese artillery proved a strong adversary. The Portuguese were repulsed, however, by Turkish harquebuses: on August 28, 1542, the Portuguese were vanquished by a superior number of fire arms, but their valiant leader Dom Christavao da Gama, brother of Vasco da Gama, did Gelawedewos a great service by weakening Ahmed's army.

In November, 1543, the Emperor with 500 horsemen and 8,000 footmen had begun to win victories over several of Gran's military units. Consequently he joined forces with the Empress, who had a force of 120 Portuguese soldiers stationed in Southern Tigre. At last, on the decisive day, at a place called Waina Dega they met face to face with Gran's force of 1,300 cavalry, 14,000 infantry, and 200 Turks; and won a victorious, final battle. Gran himself was struck down by a shot from a Portuguese musket; of his entire army, only his wife Del Wambara and a few Turks managed to reach Adal; and his son Mohammed was taken prisoner. So ended the fifteen dramatic years of Ottoman-Moslem ascendancy in Ethiopia.

The effect of the Islamic conquest of Ethiopia was profound. Countless people were forced to convert to Islam; the bonds of allegiance to the monarchy were weakened; and many great treasures of the Church were lost forever. The effect on the Moslems was as important: Moslem states were totally impoverished and internally deteriorated.

The king and the Church, despite all their losses, never submitted to the conquerors, nor betrayed their religion, and, consequently, this factor contributed to the partial reconstruction of the country. To be sure, military movements somewhat occasionally revived in the East and the North under the successors of Gran and the Ottomans; but the Empire continued to hold onto its own until the time of Emperor Sarsa-Dengel (1563-1596), who ended the existence of the most powerful military state in the horn of Africa and eliminated the Ottoman threat in 1578. Sarsa-Dengel died in peace, but the devastation Ethiopia had experienced became a cause for new threats of internal disintegration and feudalism.

The third stage of Christian-Moslem relations in Ethiopia was not as militarily dominated as the first and second. It opened with the breaking of Ethio-Portuguese relations and the peaceful expansion of Islam during the rule of the Ethiopian Masafent (1769-1855), a period of internal disintegration and rule by regional chieftain kings. During the period of internal religious confusion, when the attention of the Ethiopian Church was focused on what it considered the Roman Catholic threat, Islamic religious mission took advantage of the opportunity afforded by the friendly Emperor Fasilides (1532-1567) and his program of Christian-Moslem alliance against the Portuguese. Most Ethiopians—Christian and Moslem alike—had been opposed to domination by a foreign Moslem power. They reacted similarly when a foreign Christian power attempted to do the same thing. However, Yohannes I (1667-1682), Fasilides' successor, became aware of the advances Islam was trying to make under this advantageous condition and made new laws to keep the Moslems in separate villages hoping to curb their progress.

When the central monarchy collapsed, and Ethiopia was controlled, during the period known as *Zämänä Mäsafint* (1769-1855), by feudal kings with regional sovereignty, Islam took advantage of the ebbing morale and morals of the Church and again began to expand in Ethiopia, particularly among the highland Christians. Though this expansion was first enhanced by commerce, it was equally furthered by the Egyptian activities and pressure on the borders of Ethiopia during the time of Muhammed Ali Pasha (1805-1848) who conquered the Sudan and most of the Red Sea literally and proceeded with his aggressive designs against Ethiopia. He would have brought a new era of devastation to Ethiopia, were it not for the fact that his imperialistic ambitions were neutralized by a competition with European imperialism.

Ethiopia was eventually reunited, in part because of continuing external threats, especially that of Egypt. A valiant soldier named Kassa proved a successful fighter in thwarting all attempted Egyptian raids, causing Egypt to abandon its plans. "The triumph of Kassa and his eventual anointing as Emperor Tewodros II (1855-1868) were part of a charismatic or messianic self-consciousness that an old prophecy had come true in him that a king of that name would appear to destroy Islam and re-conquer Jerusalem. His two chief goals were to unify Ethiopia and to convert the Moslems to Christianity. Tewodros opened a new era in Ethiopian history, and in his time Egyptian pressure temporarily ceased.

Egypt renewed its attempts to conquer Ethiopia in 1872, four years after Atse Tewodros' battlefield suicide. Egyptian expeditions in 1875 and 1876 as well as those of the Dervishes of the Sudan in 1887-88 in the reign of the valiant Emperor John (1872-1889), however, resulted in Egyptian defeat, which contributed significantly to her ouster from all the East Africa.

Johnnes IV, like Tewodros before him, was a religious militant who would have liked to see the conversion of all Moslems and Jews, African Monotheists and European Christians to the Ethiopian Orthodox faith; and he was specially anxious to re-Christianize the Wollo province where, to some extent, Moslems were ordered to be baptized and to build churches in their towns. It is thought that more than a million Moslems and African Monotheists became Christians although it is not known to whether a genuine conversion actually took place. It is significant that even John who had so much trouble with the neighboring Moslem States, remained within the sphere of the traditional Ethiopian norm of tolerance. About the latter, Munzinger wrote in 1867: "Abyssinia is generally a country of tolerance: Christians of all confessions, Moslems, Jews, pagans living very peacefully together and can also make proselytes as they wish."[18]

Emperor Menelik II (1889-1913) continued the reconsolidation of the work of Emperors Tewodros and John, and succeeded in re-unifying Ethiopia. Though not fully substantiated, according to tradition, his grandson and successor, Lij Iyasu (1913-1917), surprised the Church by embracing Islam altogether, the Church reacted by excommunicating him and replacing him with Menelik's daughter, Empress Zewditu (1916-1930).

The imperial government gave tacit recognition to Islam and in its revised constitution of 1955 stipulates freedom of confession for all religions. The conflicts between Ethiopia and Somalia and the unrest in Eritrea, which seem to have religious overtones, are basically political. This is expressed in an Ethiopian government publication containing the testimonies of Ethiopian Moslems: "Although religious tolerance is a recognized attitude in Ethiopia, certain alien interests have recently conducted false campaigns based on religion against Ethiopia for the purpose of advancing their covert political aims."[19] The Sixth Moslem World Congress, which met in Mogadishu in December 1964, and the Islamic Congress, which met in Mecca in March of 1965, have both claimed that religious intolerance exists in Ethiopia and that Moslems are denied social justice. At the same time these congresses passed resolutions supporting the "lawful rights of the Somalis" as well as other resolutions which seek "to give the Somali people and the 'occupied parts' the rights of self-determination." Ethiopia submitted a strong complaint that what was discussed at this religious congress was not a religious but a political issue. Ethiopia further contended that religious tolerance is part of its tradition, law, and constitution. According to almost daily reports in the *Ethiopian Herald* during late 1967, Ethiopia claimed to have uncovered sources that prove valid its accusation that certain Moslem countries, especially Syria, have expansionist intentions in Northern Ethiopia.[20]

As can be observed from the preceding brief history of Christian-Moslem relations in Ethiopia, it must be emphasized that religious persecution has had very little to do with the history and tradition of the Ethiopian Church. Ethiopia's internal conflicts involving its Moslem population have often been rooted

---

18 Quoted in French in Trimingham, op. cit. p. 123, translation mine.

19 *Religious Freedom in Ethiopia.* Foreign Language Press Department, Ministry of Information, Addis Ababa, 1965, p. 5.

20 *Ethiopian Herald.* October, November, December, 1967.

in foreign instigation: at first that of Arabia and Egypt, then of Turkey, and in recent times, by Sudan, Somalia, and Syria. Islamic expansion in Ethiopia by means of Arab traders and artisans proceeded peacefully for a long time until the revolt of Ifat was followed by conflict. That revolt, as Trimingham correctly analyzes, was not fundamentally religious (though religion was used to rally the forces) but political. After Ethiopia's proof of supremacy, the Moslems were allowed to live and grow freely. Then hostilities resumed with the ambitious conquests of the Ottoman Turks who won over Imam Ahmed Gran, who re-inflamed warfare in Ethiopia. Again, this was political rather than religious. As soon as attempts to conquer all Ethiopia by foreign Moslem powers failed, the native people of Islamic faith continued to live and proselytize in freedom. Islam in the last period of expansion beginning in the seventeenth century, thrived, in particular, on the slave trade.[21]

One cannot think of any other country with a state religion of Christianity besides Ethiopia in which a large Moslem minority has lived along with Christians. In this respect, Ethiopia offers an amazing opportunity for the study of religious tolerance in general and of Christian-Moslem relations in particular. Trimingham says that Islam in East Africa "would have no history without Abyssinia."[22]

What is amazing is of course that the Ethiopian Church survived altogether. "One of the social curiosities of a latter-day Great Society," Arnold Toynbee reflects, "(is) the survival of her (Ethiopia's) political independence in the midst of an Africa under European dominion; the survival of Miaphysite (sic) Christianity in the borderland between Islam and paganism."[23] Islam in Ethiopia will continue to flourish as long as foreign pressure and intrusion remains minimal. The Christians and Moslems of Ethiopia equally consider themselves citizens of Ethiopia first; they feel no allegiance to other nationals of their respective confessions. In other words, Ethiopian Moslems and Christians have that common feeling of national spirit that transcends race and religion. "The survival of Abysinnia was due to these two factors," says Trimingham, "the first of them, the national spirit based upon legendary foundation and the common faith, and the second, physical impregnability."[24] It would be a mistake to think, as perhaps does Trimingham himself, that "common faith" and "national spirit" are possessions of one or another group—they are the common possessions of all Ethiopians regardless of confessions. It seems that this factor will determine the future course of relations between Ethiopian Christians and Moslems.

---

21   Trimingham, op. cit., p. 139.

22   Trimingham, op. cit., p. 142.

23   Toynbee, A. J. *A Study of History*, II. London, 1945, p. 365.

24   Trimingham, op. cit. p. 143.

Just as the Ethiopian Church's reaction toward Islam involved political issues, such was the case which determined its attitude towards other Christian groups. In both cases it was a reaction against religious conversion and loss of national identity: in the first case conversion by foreign military forces; in the second, conversion by foreign missionary activity. Just as the impulse against Islam was based on the desire of the Ethiopians to defend themselves against domination by Middle Eastern Moslem nations, so that against other Christian groups was rooted in Ethiopia's determination to keep its independence against European Christian power encroaching on the whole of Africa.

The Ethiopian Church's attitude towards other Christian groups was in the initial stages very amicable. Ethiopia not only welcomed early Syrian Christian missionaries but even made some of them national saints. It not only established relations with the Coptic Church in Egypt but even allowed a foreigner and a Copt to be the country's chief spiritual leader throughout a long part of its history. At a time when Byzantine emperors were persecuting other Christian minorities of Miaphysite beliefs, they made an exception and made friendly relations with Ethiopia because Ethiopia reciprocated this friendship by cooperating with them in supporting the Christians of South Arabia.[25] Ethiopia took the initiative through its church in Jerusalem in establishing contact with Roman Catholicism in the fourteenth century, and it voluntarily sent observers to the Council of Florence. In more recent times, Ethiopia has cooperated with foreign mission organizations in the translation of religious scriptures.

But as alluded to above the history of the Ethiopian Church and its relations with other Christian groups was not without its bitter moments, due to the extravagance and self-confidence of the missionaries who wanted to convert the Ethiopians *en masse*. Such was the case of the sixteenth-century Jesuit missionaries, or of those who worked as intelligence agents for foreign domination, as the recent history of the missionary Abba Masias in Northern Ethiopia proved. In this light one can understand why many Ethiopians grew suspicious of foreigners. It was the cautious Emperor Tewodros who, in offering missionaries freedom of action in his Empire, nonetheless instructed them to proceed: "on the condition that my subjects do not say 'I am French because I am a Catholic' or 'I am British because I am a Protestant.'"[26] The conduct of the missionaries who did not heed his message proved his fears justified when he was finally forced to change his mind and brand foreigners perceptively as

---

25   Vasliev. *Byzantine Empire*. Vol. I. Madison, 1964, p. 131.

26   Quoted in Trimingham, *The Christian Church and Missions in Ethiopia*, London, 1950 (27).

"First the missionary, then the consul, then the soldier."[27] Trimingham quotes Emperor Haile Selassie, who wrote in 1936 to the League of Nations:

> Throughout their history, they (the Ethiopians) have seldom met with foreigners who do not desire to possess themselves of Abyssinian territory and to destroy their independence ... For this reason prudence is needed when we have to convince our people that foreigners ... are generally innocent of concealed political aim.

History attests to the accuracy of this statement both as seen above in the instance of foreign Moslem agents and, as we shall see below, in the case of foreign Christian missionaries.

We have alluded in several places to the Ethiopian Church's relations with the Coptic Church, the single foreign church with which it has been very closely associated. In general, the relationship has been a happy one, primarily because it was rooted on ancient sentiment and on the ordination of Abba Salama by Athanasius (329-330), as well as on close confessional ties. The insignificance of the power of the *Abuna,* who as said elsewhere, was a Copt, as well as the weakness of the Coptic Church itself, helped relax Ethiopia's fears of unprecedented foreign intrusion: once the *Abuna* entered Ethiopia, he was a captive and never left the country. (As pointed out elsewhere, Ethio-Coptic relations were defined by a forged decree of the Council of Nicea, according to which Ethiopia constituted a single bishopric of the Patriarchate of Alexandria).

But Ethiopian relations with the Copts were not without their hardships. Sometimes great inconvenience was created when the bishops sided with the Moslem state of Egypt. For example, Abba Sawiros (c. 1280) made agreements with the *wazir* of Egypt to encourage the propagation of Islam during his term in Ethiopia.[28] The Church checked him in time when he was caught building more mosques than churches. In recent times, *Abuna* Cyril was said to have cooperated[29] with the Italians in 1936 during their occupation of Ethiopia. But by and large, Ethiopia had had very little to fear from the Coptic *Abunas* whose power was controlled at all times.

Ethiopian Church relations with Eastern Orthodox Church groups have been minimal, and even in modern times there seems to be very little contact. In the nineteenth century the Russian Orthodox Church wanted to bridge Ethio-Russian relations, but Ethiopia's cautious attitude kept communica-

---

27   Quoted in Trimingham, *The Christian Church and Missions in Ethiopia*, London, 1950 (27).

28   Trimingham, *Islam in Ethiopia*, p. 63. Badir Al Jamali promised to build five mosques but did not succeed.

29   He also wanted to assume the authority of the *Ichege* but did not succeed.

tions at a low ebb. The Greek Orthodox Church, which considers Miaphysites heretical, had established friendly relations in modern times and trained in its seminaries, especially in Istanbul (Constantinople), many Ethiopian Orthodox Church students for the priesthood. Other Miaphysite churches like the Armenian (Georgian) Church and the Indian Malabar, have been seeking closer ties, especially in providing staff for the new Trinity Theological Seminary. The first Eastern Orthodox Church general council was held in Ethiopia in 1964. But the Ethiopian Church, more highly semitized than all the denominations of the Eastern Orthodox block and the other Miaphysite Churches, seems to keep aloof from significant influences of Orthodox groups. In the future, there may be more contacts between the Ethiopian Church and Eastern Orthodox churches but these contacts will remain more official and formal than any closer associations in the past.

It can be regarded that the history of Western Christian missions in Ethiopia began in the early fourteenth century. The coming of Catholic missionaries to Ethiopia was given impetus by two forces: the search for the legendary empire of Prester John, whom Europeans believed to have the power to rescue world Christianity in a messianic way from the threat of Islam, and the desire of the Ethiopian Church to establish contacts with world Christianity, especially through its church in Jerusalem and then through the Luso-Ethiopian alliance to fight the Turks.

It is one of the problems of history, however, that this mutual search for alliance and better relations between Ethiopia and Europe, which began to be realized in the fifteenth century, all crumbled in the seventeenth century due to the misguided ambitions of enthusiastic missionaries. A succinct historical outline of this period written by two Ethiopians opens:

> Religion brought together Portugal and Ethiopia. Europe hoped to eliminate Islam with the support of the Eastern Christian potentate, Prester John. Boundless enthusiasm and expectations, therefore, characterized the early relations between Portugal and Ethiopia ... Religion also introduced the first discord that led to the final rupture of the relations between the two countries ... When the Ethiopians discovered that Catholicism meant more than a revision of a few Orthodox doctrines, that it entailed a revolution from deeply embedded customs and ways of life, their reaction was quick and crushing.[30]

Sometime in the ninth century a certain Jewish writer called Eldad Hadani, alleging to be a member of the legendary ten lost tribes of Israel, propagated a

---

30   Germa and Merid, op. cit. (7).

story about the land where powerful Jewish kingdoms had existed. It is believed that a Christian reaction and a counterpart to his story gave rise in Europe to the legend of the land of Prester John, about the middle of the twelfth century. After a long search sometime in the beginning of the fifteenth century, Ethiopia was identified as that famed Christian land that held the hope of salvation for Europe. The search itself greatly inspired the Portuguese travelers and discoverers of the thirteenth, fourteenth and fifteenth centuries.

Ethiopia took no less initiative to establish contact with European Christians. In 1427, Emperor Yishaq (1414-1429), interested in European craftsmen, sent two emissaries to the court of Alfonso of Aragon, an indefatigable seeker of Prester John; but the messengers unfortunately perished on the way. Alfonso later tried to re-establish contact with Ethiopia in the time of Zär'a Ya'aqob (1434-1468).[31] The head of the Ethiopian monastery in Jerusalem took the initiative in sending delegates to the Council of Florence in 1439 to see if relations with Rome could be established. But despite the excitement they created, the Ethiopian delegates proved to be reserved and cautious in their dealings with Rome. Some of them who stayed in Europe contributed a great deal to the study of Semitic languages.[32]

Once contact between the Ethiopian Christian and Christian Portugal was firmly established, the course of their relationship was gradually intensified because of their common interest in checking the progress of the Ottoman Turks. An Ethiopian ambassador met the Portuguese in Goa in 1512;[33] the Portuguese welcomed this as an opening for military and commercial alliance. The contact was specifically furthered by the ingenious Empress Eleni, widow of Emperor Ba'eda Mariam (1468-1478), who was regent when young Lebna Dengel took the throne at the age of twelve in 1508. The Ethiopians, who for many centuries had felt that they had a messianic mission to liberate Jerusalem and to free the persecuted Christians of especially Arabia and Egypt (the sultan of Egypt charged an exorbitant tax for the *Abuna*), were quite well-disposed to cooperate with Catholic Portugal.[34]

The initiative later taken by Portugal to cooperate with Ethiopia has been described for us by Francisco Alvares, the chaplain accompanying the Portuguese Embassy to Ethiopia in 1520. At first, Portugal was more interested in military alliance, but Lebna Dengel was desirous of technical and cultural

---

31   Ponciere, Charles de la. *La Decouverte de l'Afrique en Moyen Age*. Cairo, 1925-27, Book III, p. 119.

32   Wijnman, H. F. *An Outline of the Development of Ethiopian Topography in Europe*.

33   Girma and Merid, op. cit., p. 23.

34   Alvares. *The Prester John of the Indies*. Edited and translated by Stanley Alderley and C.F. Beckingham, London, 1961, Book II, p. 503.

exchange. In his wish to further European technical skill in his country, he was following the interests of Emperor Yishaq, mentioned above. Alvares took advantage of Lebna Dengel's motivation to open communication between the Emperor and the Pope. Lebna Dengel wrote a letter to Pope Leo X[35] asking for friendship and possible diplomatic relations with the papacy. Alvares and the Ethiopian delegate, Zaga ZeAb, arrived in Lisbon late in 1526 with the mission. There was much initial enthusiasm in Rome and Portugal, generated by the wrong assumption that Ethiopia was volunteering to welcome Roman Church influence at the expense of Alexandria. Nevertheless, conditions in Europe at the time—the situation in Italy, overrun until 1529 by the contending armies of the Holy Roman Emperor Charles V and Francis I of France—prohibited immediate Roman response. Even in 1533, when at last Alvares reached Rome and met Pope Clement VII, who also was very interested in the matter, Portugal's involvement in negotiations on the Inquisition held up further progress. In the meantime, Alvares, who had been neglected in the later proceedings, died around 1536.

Two or three years after Alvares reached Europe, Emperor Lebna Dengel, who for the first time had experienced defeat at the hands of the valiant soldier Gragn Mohammed in 1529, was experiencing the ravaging of his country by the Ottoman Turks. Ethiopia could no longer wait for the return of Alvares and Zaga ZeAb. A certain John Bermudes, who had come to Ethiopia with Alvares had remained in the country. Lebna Dengel now urgently dispatched him to Europe asking for immediate Portuguese help against the Moslems. Unfortunately, instead of emphasizing the grave conditions in Ethiopia, Bermudes scandalously sought personal honors in Europe by trying to persuade Pope Paul III to recognize him as Patriarch of Ethiopia. Bermudes failed to fool either the Pope or the king of Portugal, John III, who had received more definite news of the difficulties in Ethiopia and eventually instructed his representatives in Goa to send military aid to the country. The part played by this Portuguese contingent in the Ethiopian wars with Gragn Mohammed has been discussed above. The heroic sacrifice of the Portuguese Catholics was fully appreciated by the Ethiopians.

Emperor *Gelawdewos* (1540-59), Lebna Dengel's son and successor, held in great esteem the 170 or so Portuguese survivors, and made them his trusted advisers and companions. But this amicable relationship between the Catholic soldiers and the Emperor found an obstacle in Bermudes, who had come back to Ethiopia. He pressured the Emperor to be converted to Catholicism and that he Bermudes, be appointed as head of the Ethiopian Church. To support

---

35   Alvares. *The Prester John of the Indies*. Edited and translated by Stanley Alderley and C.F. Beckingham, London, 1961, Book I. p. 60, Book II, p. 498; see also Girma and Merid, op. cit., p. 24.

this procedure, he further began to claim that already the king's father, Lebna Dengel, had submitted to Rome under the auspices of Alvares. Glawdewos who reacted angrily at first wanted to punish Bermudes, but he proceeded with caution in order not to offend the king of Portugal, and until he had ascertained whether Bermudes was an imposter or a real Patriarch. He wrote about the latter matter to the king of Portugal who, misunderstanding the nature of Glawdewos's letter, responded with a promise that he would send a real Patriarch for Ethiopia. Ethiopia was ready to welcome a Patriarch for the Portuguese Catholics in her territory, but she had no intention indeed to have a Catholic head for her own Church. Meanwhile, the Emperor brought an *Abuna* from Alexandria and exiled Bermudes. However, according to tradition most of the Portuguese settled in Ethiopia, took Ethiopian wives, and were converted to Ethiopian Christianity.

The exiled Bermudes escaped in 1554 to Goa where he met the Jesuit Joao Nunes Berreto and Andre de Oviedo, who had been appointed as the Patriarch and bishop of Ethiopia, respectively. He reported to them that neither the Emperor nor his people were ready to embrace Catholicism, and he convinced them that only force would make Ethiopia submit to Catholicism. The governor of Goa, however, was somewhat reluctant to use force, especially since he could not provide the 500 or 600 well-armed soldiers which Barreto, Oviedo, and the other Jesuit priests had requested.

At last it was decided that the Patriarch Barreto should remain in Goa until the authorization for an escort of 600 men of force was approved by Portugal, and that in the meantime Oviedo and five other Jesuit priests would go to Ethiopia and attempt to convert the Emperor. The latter group was very well received, but *Gelawdewos* wanted friendship, not conversion. Nonetheless, while remaining in the background himself, the Emperor approved of public debates that began to be held between the Jesuit and Ethiopian scholars. The impatient Oviedo, however, issued a manifesto condemning the Ethiopian Church and threatened to bring armed forces.[36] Oviedo's behavior recalled the misdeeds of Bermudes, offended the clergy and the nobility, and aroused the indignation of the Ethiopian Church.

Gelawdewos was succeeded by his brother, Minas (1559-1563). Though at first Minas was feared to have been won over to Islam during his days of captivity (Minas was captured as a child by Gragn Ahmed and sent to Zebid as a tribute to Suleiman the Magnificent, but was later freed in exchange for Ahmed's son, who had been captured by the Ethiopians), he proved to be an ardent supporter of the Ethiopian Orthodox faith and a reformer of the traditional system of government. With the cooperation of his mother, Queen

---

36   Pais, Pero. *Historica da Ethiopia*. 1717: Livraria Civilizacao, Lisbon, 1945-46, vol. III, p. 197.

Sable-Wangel, he welcomed Catholic friendship but staunchly opposed conversion. Continued self-assertion and imprudent reaction on the part of Oviedo only brought restrictions bordering on persecution; in fact, the privileges and freedom to worship as Catholics allowed to the Portuguese were prohibited to Ethiopians, including native wives of the Portuguese. However, Ethiopians who remembered the tolerant and liberal rule of Geladwedos began to react with uneasiness to the strictness of Minas. A revolt in northern Ethiopia, heartily supported by Oviedo and the Portuguese, ensued. The revolt was crushed, and the Portuguese movements were restricted. The situation became even more complicated for Oviedo and his priests, because the Turks had made communications between Ethiopia and Goa so difficult that the news that the king of Portugal did not want to use force against another Christian government never reached them. Moreover, the invitation extended to Ethiopia in 1561 to attend the Council of Trent never arrived. It was meanwhile assumed in Europe that Ethiopia's silence meant compliance with the Jesuit priests and bishops. Besides, Barreto, the Patriarch-designate, died in Goa before even reaching Ethiopia.

When Sarsa Dengel (1563-1596) succeeded Minas, the obstinate Oviedo continued to instigate revolt by organizing dissident members of the militia. Upon learning of his struggles, the Society of Jesus and the Papacy tried to obtain military aid for him, but the rulers of Portugal continued to resist the use of force. So, there was no alternative for the Portuguese Catholics in Ethiopia but to submit to the will of the Ethiopians and to be reconciled to the Church, and, finally Oviedo himself died in 1577 in despair.

The cause of Roman Catholicism did not, however, vanish with the death of Oviedo. In the person of Pero Pais, who came to Ethiopia in 1595 after almost seven years of detention by the Turks, it got a shrewder and more clever spokesman. The reform-minded king, Emperor Za-Dengel (1603-1605), Sarsa-Dengel's nephew, invited Pais to teach him about European law and government. Pais's humility and tact won him favor from the king and the nobility, and he was given permission to teach publicly. His approach was diametrically opposed to that of Oviedo. Thus, it was indeed against Pais's warning that Za-Dengel first issued a proclamation manifesting his Catholic sympathies by prohibiting the observance of Saturday as the Sabbath. Pais, who had become well-acquainted with public sentiment and was waiting for more Portuguese support before such a proclamation, tried to convince the Emperor to rescind the law, but in vain. His fears came true when the *Abuna* sided with the revolting nobles who defeated and killed the king. After two years of unrest Susenyos (1607-1632) gained control of Ethiopia. Though he was very cautious in his movements, Susenyos was inclined towards Catholicism from the start. Having first proved to be a strong ruler, he had no difficulty winning over the Jesuits. Girma and Merid think that one of the reasons why the emperor liked the Catholics was his ambition to centralize his power: "He came to learn that the Jesuits were in many ways the opposite of the Ethiopian clergy. The former stood for order and hierarchical organization. They were for absolutism in religion as well as in politics. The latter, on the other hand, had a distaste for a centralized authority and rigid subordination." These statements, incidentally, concur with this study's contention that the Ethiopian Church has always been relatively unburdened with dogma and, therefore, less resistant to change and innovation. At any rate, Susenyos gradually turned to the Jesuits for help and advice and secretly admired Pero Pais. He also encouraged dialogues and debates in open courts between Jesuits and Ethiopian *däbtära*, in which noblemen and learned Ethiopians participated.

Sela Christos, Susenyos' younger brother, outwitted Pais in logic, but was soon won over by the latter.[37] Sela Christos' conversion encouraged other prominent young persons to embrace Catholicism. The king himself secretly espoused Catholicism, and, in 1613, he decided to send an ambassador to Pope Paul V explaining the need for military support from Portugal before he would publicly confess his new faith and receive a Roman Patriarch for Ethiopia.[38] However, the ambassador was intercepted on the way by Ethiopian Church sympathizers.

Nevertheless, the Emperor, pressured by the new Catholic zealot, Sela Christos, finally decided to issue a proclamation condemning the Ethiopian Church doctrine of *Täwahïdo* (one nature both divine and human) and upheld it with the death penalty.[39] The *Abuna* retaliated by excommunicating all Catholics and believers in the doctrine of the two natures. Susenyos rescinded his strong decree and issued an edict of religious freedom. The *Abuna* took further steps to arouse the public against Pais and to intimidate the emperor. Although the emperor was momentarily tamed, he soon realized, as he had formerly thought, that only force could ensure the change of character of the Ethiopian Church.

Encouraged by initial success in 1617, when he successfully crushed the Ethiopian Church leader's revolt and killed the *Abuna*, Susenyos issued a proclamation in 1620 condemning the doctrine of the one nature of Christ and the observance of Saturday as Sabbath. He received the Roman Catholic sacrament from Pais in 1622 and pledged loyalty to the Pope and the Roman Catholic Church in spite of public dissent.[40] Ethiopia was made a Catholic country by law: besides prohibiting keeping the traditional Sabbath day, circumcision and

---

37   Chronica de Susenyos, *Rei de Ethiopia*. Translated and edited by Francisco Mabia Esteves Pereira, Lisbon, 1892-1900, (p. 126-150).

38   Girma and Merid, op. cit., p. 105.

39   Girma and Merid, op. cit., p. 105.

40   Girma and Merid, op. cit., p. 92.

levirate marriage were forbidden, eating unclean meat (Lev. 11) was proscribed, divorce made illegal, the Gregorian calendar introduced, religious books (especially *Haimanot Abaw,* Faith of the Fathers) revised, and the Ethiopic liturgy adjusted to the Catholic Mass. More missionaries were brought to Ethiopia after the death of Pais (1622) who was succeeded by the Patriarch Dom Alfonso Mendes, Bishop Dom Apollinar de Almeida, the priest Jeronymo Lobo, and others.

Susenyos had won over the nobility. It was the peasants and the common people who became the champions and defenders of the Ethiopian Church, especially since they were the ones who were being robbed of their customs and their land. Beginning in 1624, peasant uprisings and revolts started to break out, and it became impossible to establish central authority. The situation became even more complicated for Emperor Susenyos as the Portuguese refused to understand his predicament and to co-operate with him in making some concessions. Thus, contrary to his wish, they decided that no Ethiopian priests should officiate at services until more Catholic priests were ordained. After some fifteen years of total confusion in the country, the peasants' uprising eventually triumphed when in 1632, the council of the state under Fasilides, (1632-1667), son of Susenyos, who inwardly sympathized with his native church, forced the emperor to abdicate. Susenyos, stricken ill, withdrew in favor of Fasilides, retracted his Catholicism by proclaiming Orthodox *Täwahïdo* his true faith, and died a crushed man in 1632. The real architect of Catholic progress in Ethiopia, Sela Christos, was imprisoned, and the Catholic patriarch and all Jesuits were expelled from the country.

The history of the Jesuits in Ethiopia in the sixteenth and seventeenth centuries provides a very important background for the understanding of Christianity and society in Ethiopia and the attitude towards Western people. As noted many times elsewhere, the Ethiopian Church is dominated by a tolerant and liberal attitude. To this extent, Ethiopia took the initiative in establishing friendly relations with the Catholic Church. Unfortunately, Ethiopia's tolerance and friendliness were not received with the same degree of openness and acceptance. On the contrary, Ethiopia's tolerance was abused by over-enthusiastic missionaries laden with dogma alien to the Ethiopian disposition. The Jesuits, when they had the upper hand, displayed lack of wisdom and extreme intolerance in suppressing ancient customs and traditions, desecrating tombs and monasteries (such as those in Debre-Libanos and Abba Gerima), and making force the dictum of their religion. Even after their expulsion from Ethiopia, they did not succeed in getting sympathy in Europe; on the contrary, they were accused in their native Portugal (and by the papacy) of pride, cupidity, insolence, and introduction of tyranny and the Inquisition into Ethiopia.[41]

---

41   Pais, Pero. *Historia da Ethiopia.* Vol. I, p. 246.

Religion in Ethiopia goes beyond beliefs and tenets: it is rooted in customs and ways of life. The goal of the Catholics was to implant a doctrinal point; that of the Chalcedonian formula of the double nature of Christ. In order to accomplish this, they thought they had to uproot ancient Ethiopian practices such as those pertaining to food regulations, marriage customs, and keeping Saturday as the Sabbath. It was when Catholicism tampered with such deep-rooted customs that the populace unleashed its forces of resistance.

Above all, the Ethiopian respects and cherishes the practices of his ancestors, and he would not forsake them in exchange for alien logic. Furthermore, the traditional Ethiopian is convinced more by action than by words or theory. That is why Pero Pais had more success than all the other Jesuits. Pais was not only a man of words, although to be sure, he was a capable orator and logician. He was also a man of deeds whose modesty and skill impressed everyone. He, of all the Jesuits, helped introduce European skills in the arts, crafts, and building. The still extant palace he built in Gorgora on Lake Tana is a lasting monument to his untiring industry. Both his predecessor and his successor, Oviedo and Mendes, were men too deeply rooted in dogmatic belief and theory to be able to make any impression on Ethiopia.

When Ethiopia sought an alliance with Portugal, it did so on the assumption that Portugal was a friendly nation. Ethiopia did not expect its faith and tradition to be challenged or insulted by the Portuguese. Furthermore, Ethiopia wanted to forge this alliance to achieve two objectives: (1) to get European skills, and (2) to secure a strong stand against the neighboring Moslem Empires, which threatened the integrity of its borders and harassed its political freedom. Ethiopia was impressed not by European beliefs but by Europe's art and skill. It is interesting to note that some of the enlightened rulers of Ethiopia such as Yishaq, Zär'a Ya'aqob, Sarsa-Dengel, and Tewodros had complete faith in traditional Ethiopian religion as well as in its learning and literature. These emperors, however, were fascinated by European skill and, for that reason, sought European friendship. Pais, who brought that skill, lived and died in Ethiopia with great honor and success.

Threatened by the neighboring empires, Ethiopia furthermore wanted to establish relations with Europe to insure her political integrity and independence. But she had to learn from bitter experience that the Portuguese, whom she had thought to have a common basis of belief, were as dangerous to her political freedom as the Islamic Empires. Not only did the Jesuits try to impose their unwanted beliefs, but they also advocated both through the use of force— as did Oviedo in Ethiopia, Mendes in Goa, and Jeronymo Lobo in Europe, and the annexation of part of Ethiopia to Portugal. In the latter case, the Portuguese openly claimed land on the basis of a legend that *Gelawdewos* had made an agreement with the Portuguese not only to introduce Catholicism but also to give one-third of his empire to Portugal in return for their aid against Gragn Ahmed. In this, Pais was as much to blame as the other Jesuits.[42] This made it difficult for the Ethiopians to trust foreigners, and ironically, after the expulsion of the Portuguese in the time of Emperor Fasilides, to seek more alliances with her former contestants such as the Ottoman Turks. Ethiopian political integrity was part of the national tradition. The Ethiopian Orthodox Church did in principle oppose foreign evangelization, but more passionately it opposed the missionary who seemed to serve a foreign soldier or mercenary.

In modern times, it is little wonder that the Ethiopian Church, in the light of bitter, historical experiences, was not more opposed to the return of foreign missionaries to Ethiopia. Perhaps this again shows the extent of its patience and tolerance. Yet, unfortunately, the new missionaries who began to flock to Ethiopia during and after the reign of Emperor Tewodros (1855-1868), including Protestants this time, did not learn from the experiences of their predecessors. The Roman Catholic mission which steadily built itself up in Northern Ethiopia after 1860 produced men like Massaia (Abba Masias), who were more at the service of the Italian intelligence agency than of the Roman Church,[43] and who created more Ethiopian feeling of mistrust of foreigners. But Ethiopia's knowledge of Massaia's activities, as well as Italian Catholic activities in Ethiopia during the occupation (1936-1947), did not deter her from continuing her policy of tolerance after the liberation. In fact, since 1942, foreign missionaries, most of whom had been expelled by the Italians, began to return *en masse* to Ethiopia. To the credit of the Ethiopian Church, Catholics have not only regained full autonomy, but when in 1950 the administration of the first Ethiopian College fell into the hands of the Jesuits, very little opposition—and that from rival Protestants—was shown. In 1960, a British Catholic nun won national recognition after having won a prize for her humanitarian activities.

The history of modern missions in Ethiopia opens with the reign of Emperor Tewodros. Tewodros, due to his interest in European technology, had opened Ethiopia to Europeans, among whom missionaries were prominent. Since then, Ethiopia has seen the coming of Protestant denominations from many countries. The first and perhaps the most accomplished Protestant group is represented by the Egangeliska Fosteriands Stiftelsen of Sweden, which began work in Northern Ethiopia in 1866. One of their distinguished missionaries, Carl Sederquist, eventually succeeded in penetrating into the interior in 1905, opening stations in the western provinces, particularly in Wollega. The Evangeliska Fosterlands Stiftelsen (EFS) has been the most successful and, relatively, the most popular missionary organization in Ethiopia. During his visit to Sweden as a regent, His Imperial Majesty Haile Selassie I is quoted to have said:

---

42   Makuria, Takle-Tsadik. *Ethiopian History since Tewodros*. Addis Ababa, 1949.

43   Sandford, C. *Ethiopia under Haile Selassie*. London, 1946, p. 64.

The chief reason for my visit is my love for Sweden. Swedish missionaries have performed in my country a great and blessed work. They have founded schools and hospitals, they speak our language, and they, of all missionaries, have best known how to win the affection and trust of my people.[44]

Once the EFS had paved a smooth road for Protestant missions, others followed suit.

Such mission organizations include the Friends of the Bible, the United Presbyterian Church of America, the Sudan Interior Mission (also of America), the Missionsanstalt Hermannsburg of Germany, and the Bible Churchmen's Missionary Society of England entered Ethiopia in 1912, 1918, 1927, 1928 and 1934 respectively. Other missionary activities that were begun in Ethiopia before the Italian Occupation included those of the Seventh Day Adventists from the United States, and of the Bible Society from England. It is interesting to note that of all missionary organizations that were operating in Ethiopia when the Italians overran the country, the Italians decided to expel immediately only the EFS. All the others were temporarily allowed to remain, though under restrictions. But gradually most of the missionaries in the country, including the French Catholics (numbering 180) left of their own accord, or they too were eventually expelled. Their mission stations were occupied either by Italian forces or by Italian Catholic organizations. The Italians encouraged the expansion of Islam as a better weapon for dividing Ethiopian loyalty. If Italian Catholic missions collaborated with their government, it is perhaps not because they chose to do so, but because they had no choice.

After the Italian expulsion, missions that had operated in Ethiopia before the Occupation were given immediate permission to resume their work in Addis Ababa. Missions outside of Addis Ababa had to wait until 1944, when the government had defined its policies toward missions and published a proclamation of regulations. The proclamation provided regulations emphasizing that missions should concentrate their work in non-Christian areas and among non-Christians, but should do only educational and medical work in Ethiopian Church areas and give only religious instructions "common to all Christian Churches," without aims of proselytizing. The proclamation further outlined the creation of a Committee on Missions, under the presidency of the Minister of Education and including the Ministers of the Interior and of Foreign Affairs. This committee establishes regulations which define the areas as "Open Areas" and "Ethiopian Church Areas," the former being ones where missionaries may teach without restrictions. The wish of the Ethiopian Church and government

---

44   Quoted in full in Trimingham, *The Christian Church and Missions in Ethiopia*. London, 1950, Appendix B, p. 68.

is that the loyalty of the people not be divided by the multiplication of Christian denominations and that missions not be used as grounds for alien subversion. Outside of these restrictions, much freedom is left for missionary activities.

In spite of complaints by some proselytized Ethiopian Christians about occasional clashes with local leaders, the formulation of these regulations coupled with the general Ethiopian interest in religion has given many brilliant chapters to the work of Protestant missions in modern times. Trimingham correctly says: "The most important of all the results of the Italian Occupation and the withdrawal of foreign missionaries was that the new Christian communities which had emerged as the result of their work had in some cases achieved truer consciousness as churches in consequence of being left to stand alone. And not only that, they went out (i.e., they took the initiative) to draw others into their fellowship." The work begun by the Swedish mission established roots especially in Eritrea and the Wollega province.

After the restoration, the EFS which was allowed to return to Ethiopia has continued to distinguish itself. Many of those Ethiopians, educated by this mission before the war, who survived the Italian massacre for the "crime of being educated" emerged as prominent figures and leaders in the Ethiopian government. In recent times the EFS has succeeded in creating the autonomous Mekane Yesus Ethiopian Evangelical ("Lutheran") Church of Ethiopia, which has its own national secretariat. Next to the Ethiopian Church, this group forms the largest indigenous national Christian organization in the country, and is presently being led by educated and competent leaders. Their semi-modern seminary is making steady progress. Its example has been followed by the Bethel Evangelical Church of the American United Presbyterian initiation.

It was also due to Swedish work in Ethiopia that the Lutheran World Council decided in 1962 to establish in Ethiopia, with an initial grant of more than five million dollars, its largest global radio station (Radio Voice of the Gospel), primarily directed to African and Asian countries. The negotiations to establish this radio station had to be approved by the Ethiopian Church. The approval came with less opposition than some expected. Now the Ethiopian Church collaborates with the station, using daily about one hour of the program time (about half of the Amharic religious program time directed at Ethiopia). The radio had thus become one of the causes for the collaboration of the Ethiopian Church with the Ethiopian Protestant group.

Today new missions have multiplied in Ethiopia. With the freedom their organizations enjoy, Protestant Churches seem to be making steady progress all over the country, but particularly in the South and the West. The main problem of foreign Christian missions is not so much opposition from the national Church, as their own internal weakness, uninhibited enthusiasm not appreciated by Ethiopians, and lack of coordination and cooperation among various denominations. An intermission council formed in 1942 has not fully succeeded in bringing the often-varying mission groups together, and confusion often arises from rivalries, setting a bad example to Ethiopian adherents. There seems to be no question that the Ethiopian Church will continue to exhibit a detached but friendly attitude toward foreign missions.

The work of Catholic missions has not been discussed at great length in this section. Their work in recent times, especially that of the Capuchin missionaries in the mid nineteenth century, has been hampered mainly by the obstacles of Italo-Ethiopian relations of the last eighty years. But as this becomes gradually forgotten, they are gaining new status. Roman (Latin) Catholics, according to an estimate in the New Catholic Encyclopedia (1967), number some 63,000, mostly in the former Italian colony of Eritrea, a nation that was the mother of ancient Ethiopia, Catholics of the Ethiopian rite are said to number 60,000. According to the same encyclopedia, "the future of Catholicism in Ethiopia is in the formation of strong Catholics in the Ethiopian rite."[45] Seminaries have been established in Asmara and Adigrat in Tigre Province, primarily to develop this rite. In Rome, in what is known as the Collegio Etiopici in the restored Church of St. Stephen in the Vatican, Capuchin Catholics form diocesan priests of the Ethiopian rite Several Ethiopians have been trained in this college. In 1961, Addis Ababa was established as a metropolitan see, Asmara (with a titular bishop residing in Rome, where he ordains seminarians of Ethiopian rite) and Adigrat as Suffragan sees. The rest of Ethiopia has the juridical status of a mission divided into Apostolic Vicariates: Harrar, and Jimma. The Catholic policy is to assign the territory of the missions in the more densely non-Christian areas to the Latin rite; and in the more densely Ethiopian Church areas, the Ethiopian rite is followed. Several allusions have already been made to the question of the relation of the Ethiopian Church to foreign Christian missions and other Christian groups. Basically the attitude and disposition of the Ethiopian Church is friendly towards other groups, provided that these groups do not work against national unity and loyalty or Ethiopian political sovereignty and as long as they work outside the main strongholds of Orthodox Christianity. If foreign missions continue their work, avoiding the "holier than thou" attitude and refraining from purposely proselytizing Ethiopian Christians, they will win not only the understanding and sympathy of the people but also of the Church. The Ethiopian Church is gradually but surely moving in the direction of innovation, and as mature mission groups become more sympathetic, it is logical to assume that a closer association will be reached. Douglas O'Hanlon of England writes: "The opinion of the majority of missionaries prior to the Italian invasion was that the Church was too corrupt to merit any serious consideration. Rival churches were therefore formed ... The Abyssinian Church is not only too

---

45   New Catholic Encyclopedia, vol. II, Catholic University, Washington, D.C., 1967, p. 588.

powerful to be thus dismissed, but it does not deserve to be so treated. It has within it, especially among the *däbtära (sic)* or Cantors clan, men who are keen for reform and capable of promoting it. The missionary in his attitude of 'holier than thou' does more harm than he knows."[46] These remarks are still valid.

The Ethiopian Church is now also moving in the direction of ecumenism. Since ancient times it has been interested in cooperation with other Christian groups and nations. Perhaps there is not another church in history that, though totally independent, has had almost throughout its history a foreign patriarch more or less as an expression of cordiality to a church which ordained its first *Abuna*. Ethiopia was one of the first countries to welcome Christian missions from the Mediterranean World and to give them refuge in times of persecution. There is a story that Athanasius himself moved to Ethiopia when the Arian king, Constantius, was persecuting him. In the sixth century, Ethiopia collaborated with Byzantine Emperors to aid the Christians of South Arabia. In medieval times, it kept in touch with world Christianity through its church in Jerusalem. Later it took the initiative in opening relations with European Christianity. But its occasionally unfortunate experiences forced it to shut its doors to the world in the 17th century. After two centuries of isolation, Emperor Tewodros renewed contact with world Christianity by seeking friendship with England. Unfortunately, the British bureaucracy misjudged Tewodros's intentions and treated his offer of friendship with hostility. Today, the Ethiopian Church has become a member of the World Council of Churches (1954) and was represented by observers at the Second Vatican Council (1962-64). It has allowed many of its students to study in non-Miaphysite Greek Orthodox seminaries in Europe as well as in Episcopalian and Russian Orthodox seminaries in the United States. Some of the priest-students received direct financial assistance from the World Council of Churches. When the German Evangelical Lutheran Church donated some two million dollars for the establishment of hospitals under the auspices of the Haile Selassie Foundation, the Ethiopian Church, rather than the Ethiopian Lutheran Church, served as the chief channel. In recent times, foreigners of other faiths have been very welcome to visit Ethiopian churches, and have been given special privileges to watch services at close hand. At the famous monolithic Church centre in Lalibela, this writer witnessed several foreigners of other faiths being permitted to approach the priests carrying the *tabot* (the ark of Covenent), a matter strictly forbidden even to Ethiopian Christians. This writer also met a Swiss Protestant minister who was teaching Sunday school classes in the Holy Trinity Church, the largest Ethiopian Church in Addis Ababa. The young clergyman was the grandson of a famous missionary of the nineteenth century, Martin Flad, who was originally a missionary to the *Falasha* (Jews).

---

46   O'Hanlon, Douglas. *Features of the Abyssinia Church*. London, 1946, p. VII.

Throughout history the Ethiopian Church has continually sought to establish contact with other Christian groups. In recent times, however, the dogmas and politics of foreign missions have become obstacles to the furthering of this initiative. Again, today the Church is beginning to reopen its channels of communication with other Christian bodies, on an ecumenical level. Ecumenical dialogues are very likely to increase as more and more educated persons take the leadership of the Ethiopian Church. The interests in these dialogues are not superficial; they have deep historical roots. As in the past, the fruitfulness of these encounters will depend not on the attitude of the Ethiopian Church as much as on that of foreign missions, as the representatives of other Christian groups. In Trimingham's words:

> The policy which missions pursue in Ethiopia is of peculiar delicacy in view of the existence of an African State Church deeply rooted in the life of the land. The five years of Italian Occupation are burnt indelibly in the hearts of the people and those in authority are deeply sensitive to anything that affects their independence or hinders the task of building up a true national unity. Ethiopia is one of the few Christian countries where 'foreign missions' have established themselves and the sensitive attitude of the Christian Ethiopians needs to be fully sympathized with so that it may be taken into account and not lead to the creation of unnecessary obstacles. In the past this has often not been the case, and the failure of so much earnest but misguided endeavor in the nineteenth century has been due to that fact. The attitude of (Ethiopia)... has been reasonable, consistent, and encouraging ... The decree (of 1944) seeks to assure full cooperation between government and missions for the welfare of the people. It allows missions to establish and conduct medical and educational work with the so-called 'closed' or 'Ethiopian Church Areas,' in which the teaching of Christian principles is not prohibited, but encouraged. Only proselytization for a particular church amongst Christian Ethiopians is not allowed. Full freedom from restrictions in teaching and preaching was given in the rest of the country.[47]

Originally, most missions, with the exception of the Roman Catholics and the Seventh Day Adventists, did not come to proselytize, but rather to reform the Ethiopian Church. Subsequently, they changed their policy. As Trimingham says: "(They) felt as a result of their experiences that the possibility of spiritual renewal and internal reforms within the Ethiopian church was so remote that the Ethiopians should have an alternate community in which to seek new

---

47   Trimingham, J. Spencer. *The Christian Church and Missions in Ethiopia.* London, 1950, p. 46.

spiritual life."[48] If foreign Christian missions return to their original policy and follow the advice of Josiah Pratt, Secretary of the Church Missionary Society in 1829, that the Ethiopian Church possesses the internal potential for reform, if they abandon their relentless efforts to gain converts from among Ethiopian Church members, if they can minimize rivalry and quarrelling among their followers, if they learn to understand and appreciate the Ethiopian ethos and tradition, they can contribute significantly to the educational and medical needs of the country as well as to the ecumenism. Missionaries who have had the patience to understand the Ethiopian Church and who have shown a friendly and non-condescending attitude toward it and toward Ethiopian culture as a whole, have stimulated more interest among the clergy.

The policy of the Ethiopian Church towards adherents to traditional African beliefs has also been determined by her attitude of "live and let live." Though many monks do often travel to remote regions for the purpose of making converts, in general the Ethiopian Church attitude has never been militant or evangelization oriented. This lack of missionary zeal has contributed to better relations between the Ethiopian Church and her non-Christian fellow Ethiopians. She has often accepted converts who are coming of their own initiatives. According to Church statistics, no less than 200,000 converts came in Southern Ethiopia and were admitted to Church membership since 1942. Religion and nationality are bound together so inextricably that the practices of non-Christian Ethiopians are equally dominated by the many customs and traditions of the Ethiopian Church. This fact may facilitate conversion to Ethiopian Church for many non-Christians who do not in the least regard Christianity as an alien or white man's religion. But it may not be so easy to conclude, as Trimingham predicts, "that the majority of the pagans (*sic*) of Ethiopia will in time become nominal members of the national Church."[49]

There is more unity than is generally supposed by foreigners among Ethiopians of Christian and non-Christian convictions. Christians, Jews, Moslems, and "African monotheists" share many religious beliefs and practices of ancient Hamito-Semitic origin, which are fully integrated into the lives of the people: belief in God, religious festivals, and customs such as circumcision. Almost all Ethiopians recognize a supreme deity known by various names in various languages. In fact, without understanding the religious practices of the Jews, the Moslems, "traditionalists" and the Christians synoptically, not one of these groups can be fully comprehended.

---

48   Trimingham, J. Spencer. *The Christian Church and Missions in Ethiopia*. London, 1950, p. 46.

49   Trimingham, J. Spencer. *The Christian Church and Missions in Ethiopia*. London, 1950, p. 49.

A fine example of Ethiopia's religious harmony and intergroup tolerance can be seen in the degree to which the Jewish and Christian religions have mutually influenced each other. Not only do the Jews and Christians base much of their religion on the Old Testament, but they share many fundamental customs, to the extent that at times it becomes difficult to distinguish one from the other. This becomes clear as one looks at both the religious life of the Ethiopian Jews and at the Jewish practices of the Ethiopian Church itself.

The Jews of Ethiopia are known as Beta Israel or more popularly as *Falashas* ("migrants") and are thought to be of very ancient origin. The *Kebra Nagast* states that Jews came to Ethiopia in the time of Solomon. However, some believe that Jews came to Ethiopia after the destruction of the Temple in 70 CE Whichever of these explanations is true, some Jews probably did come to Ethiopia both before and after the Christian era. The historical course of events in the Middle East, the present linguistic situation of Ethiopia, and the existence of Jewish practices in the Ethiopian Church and culture cannot be explained otherwise.

Although the Beta Israel live in separate villages and some of their customs are more strictly Mosaic than those of Ethiopian Christians, they hold the laws of circumcision, "clean and unclean" food, the Sabbath, and many other customs exactly as Ethiopian Christians do. Their annual festivals and practices often correspond to those of the Ethiopian Church, but in general they have more affinity with those of "normative" Judaism. Their religious leaders, their language of prayer, their manner of religious dance, and many of their other practices also have counterparts in the Ethiopian Church. The major distinction between the Beta Israel and the Christians is that the former do not believe in the Trinity or recognize Jesus as the Messiah. We cannot go deeper into the beliefs, practices, and customs of the Beta Israel- Ethiopian Jews, but can only consider briefly the relations between Ethiopian Christians and the Beta Israel Ethiopian Jews, as well as the degree to which the Ethiopian Church itself has incorporated many Jewish customs.

As in the cases of all the other religions, the Ethiopian Church's attitude towards the Beta has been determined by political conditions rather than by religious questions. In other words, intolerance or persecution did not exist for religious reasons. The Moslem states of the early fourteenth and sixteenth centuries as well as the Jesuit missionaries of the sixteenth and seventeenth centuries sought to dominate Ethiopia by conversion to their respective confessions. Apart from the tenth century Jewish queen Yodit[50] who pillaged Ethiopia's land and churches, and sacked the holy city of Axum, the Beta Israel, unlike the other two religious groups, never precipitated a drive for the mass conversion

---

50   Ludelphus, Job. *Nouvelle Histoire d'Abyssinie ou d'Ethiopie*. Paris, 1963, p. 97; also Conti Rossini, *Storia d'Etiopia*. Bergamo, 1928, p. 286.

of Ethiopia to their particular religion; nor were the Christians preoccupied with a fear that this would occur. Hence, to an even greater extent than in the case of the two other religious groups, Christian-Jewish (*Falasha*) relations have been determined by those matters least involving religious issues, in particular, interstate border conflicts.

Although many support the hypothesis that Jewish settlements existed in Ethiopia in pre-Christian times, we unfortunately have no adequate historical sources to determine its veracity. On the basis of one legend, some scholars hold the view that before Christianity entered Ethiopia, half the people in the country were converted to Judaism. However, we cannot establish earlier Christian-Jewish relations in the country before the time of Emperor Kaleb whose campaign against Dhu Nawwas, the Jewish King of South Arabia, about 525 CE, has been referred to above.

Due to the loss of her coastal area to South Arabian invaders as well to internal weaknesses, the Ethiopian Empire began to decline about the middle of the seventh century (c. 650). Around 950, the country came under the rule of a strong queen, known in Ethiopian tradition as Yodit (or Gudit - Judith) or Isato ("fire"), believed to have been the daughter of Gideon, King of the Jews of Semien in Northwest Ethiopia. She was said to rule from a fortress called Ye'ayhud Amba (Jew's rock or fortress). Though the chronicles of Ethiopia and the records of the Alexandrian Patriarchate depict her as a cruel woman who burnt churches and devastated the country, nonetheless, we must assert that even these negative reports point to the fact that Yodit may have been the first strong ruler, after three hundred years of dormancy, to revive the country by creating a more centralized government further inland, relieving the weakened Axumite rule, and eventually giving rise to the brilliant *Zagwe* or Agaw Dynasty, most likely a Christianized branch of her line.[51] Perhaps the Solomonic Royal House was created as a reaction to these pro-Judaic rules. According to Ethiopian legend the *Zagwe*s (who probably originated the claim of Judean ties) descended also from King Solomon but through the line of the handmaid of the Queen of Sheba. Though we cannot now validate the historicity of this tradition, it would be difficult to explain many aspects of Ethiopian history, especially the development of the Ethiopic version of the story of Solomon and the Queen of Sheba without the rise of a strong Judaic influence in Ethiopia in this period.

As far as our available sources go, we have no mention of the expression Beta Israel, as others called them, by name before the early fourteenth century (in the Chronicles of Emperor Amda Sion). However, it is very likely that the Jews who were said to take control of Ethiopia in the tenth century, were the Beta Israel or their kin. As we have seen, Emperor Amda Sion was occupied in warfare with

---

51   Hess, Robert. L. *Toward a History of the Falashas.* Unpublished article.

Egypt and the Islamized states of Eastern Ethiopia. When Sabre-ad-Din, Governor of Fatigar, rebelled in the Southeast, the Beta Israel, who felt menaced by the Christians who had forced some of them to convert, turned their forces in the Northwest against Amda Sion, perhaps in willing alliance with the Moslem state of Fatigar. Amda Sion gave orders to Tsaga Kristos, the military governor of the province of Begemeder, to continue the fight in the East, but he himself eventually succeeded in pacifying the Beta Israel.

The Beta Israel states continued to keep their limited independence, even providing refuge to dissident Christians. One Christian, a monk called Qozmos (Cozmas), during the reign of Emperor Dawit (1382-1411) was said to have introduced Monasticism among the Beta Israel after having converted to Judaism. Qozmos was killed in a battle against the Christians. But the Beta Israel continued to be powerful, and Emperor Yeshaq (1412-29) also had to contend with them.

A distinguished convert to Judaism was Abba Tsega, the son of Emperor Zär'a Ya'aqob (1423-68). Abba Tsega collaborated with the Beta Israel, Abba Tsabra, to shape the foundations of Beta Israel monasticism. On the other hand, both the convert's father and brother, Emperor Baeda Mariam (1468-1478), campaigned against the Beta Israel, forcing them to convert and to rebuild the churches which they had destroyed.

Much attention has been given above to the events and the extent of the sixteenth-century war in Ethiopia. Ethiopian chronicles relate that the Beta Israel also suffered from the Ottoman onslaught until they gave up all resistance and, finding no alternative, submitted to the Ottoman demand to join forces with them. After the re-conquest of Ethiopia was accomplished, the Beta Israel were brought under Christian rule but retained their own leaders.

In the time of Emperor Minas (1559-1563) and his son, Sarsa Dengel (1563-1596), the Beta Israel under their brilliant and capable military leader named Radaii, successfully checked the Christian raiders. According to Ethiopian chronicles, a mysterious monk appeared and told Minas that it was not divinely ordained for him to conquer the Jews.[52] After a long battle with Sarsa Dengel, which proved fatal for many of the Beta Israel, Sarsa Dengel sought negotiations, and Radaii surrendered. Radaii's successor, Gweshan, committed suicide on the battlefield and his successor, Gideon, and his followers cut their own throats rather than surrender. It was not until 1594, two years before Sarsa Dengel's death, that the Beta Israel were subdued, though only momentarily.

The Beta Israel state came to an end with the militant reform program of the Catholic convert, Emperor Susenyos. The earlier Ethiopian emperors had contended with the Beta Israel primarily over political issues, and even if they

---

52   Bruce, James. *Travels*. Vol. VIII, p. 227.

at times forced the Beta Israel to conversion, nevertheless, they made no objection to Beta Israel practices. Due to the pressure of his Jesuit advisers, Susenyos refused to allow anyone, Christian or Beta Israel, to observe Saturday as the Sabbath, and suppressed everything that he felt to be a Jewish practice. In this respect, no other Ethiopian emperor can be said to have so zealously tried to root out the Beta Israel, even to the extent of extermination. At last, after a long series of valiant battles, the Beta Israel were completely defeated and those who refused to betray their religion either were killed or dispersed. Susenyos succeeded in confiscating the lands of the Beta Israel and redistributing them to his followers. Fortunately, however, for the Beta Israel, when he very soon fell out of favor with the Church, he was forced to abdicate his throne before carrying out his final program of destruction.

After the settling of religious conflicts in the middle of the seventeenth century, the Beta Israel regained new autonomy. They had become a dispersed people without land and political significance, but they emerged as a new economic factor in the state. As early as the seventeenth century they were the main weavers and smiths of Ethiopia and also gained reputation as good builders. James Bruce, who, for one reason or another, started with the impression that the Beta Israel were warrior-like, discovered instead that they were "wholly addicted to agriculture, hewers of wood and carriers of water and are the only potters and masons in Abyssinia."[53] In more recent times, Beta Israel workmen and masons were used by Empress Zewditu (1916-1930) to build other edifices.

In the last century, the Beta Israel held a great appeal to European Christian missionaries. In fact, the first Protestant mission organization in Ethiopia, the London Board of Missions to the Jews, began work among them in 1859. Martin Flad who has been alluded to above and his co-worker, a converted German Jew, Henry Aaron Stern, had the unrealistic goal of converting the Beta Israel in order to use them for "Christianizing" Ethiopia.[54] Their work cannot be called a success. Among the first Ethiopians to study in Europe in the nineteenth century were half a dozen Beta Israel converts.

The French orientalist, Professor Joseph Halevy, became the first Western Jew to reach the Beta Israel. Though he left some very useful records, his student, Dr. Jacques Faitlovitch, did the real work of establishing contact between Western Judaism and the Beta Israel. With the help of the American Pro-*Falasha* Committee, Faitlovitch first visited Ethiopia in 1904 and remained in close touch with the Beta Israel until his death. Convinced that they would carry the torch of modernization in Ethiopia, he opened village schools and a seminary in Addis Ababa, and trained several Ethiopians in Europe. Although

---

53   Bruce, James. *Travels.* Vol. VIV, p. 378.

54   Stern, H.A. *Wanderings among the Falashas.* London, 1862, p. 301, 309.

his prophecy did not come true, eight of his students were among the first Euro-pean-educated Ethiopians who achieved high positions in government service. The Italians persecuted the Beta Israel and closed their school in Addis Ababa in 1936.

The general attitude of uneducated Christians toward the Beta Israel is ambivalent. There are those who hold them with contempt because of their professions of craftsmanship, and with fear because of their supposed sorcery. However, there are others who treat them with awe and respect for their reputed wisdom and holiness. Perhaps nothing can express this double attitude more aptly than the word *tabib* often attributed to the Beta Israel. *Tabib* is, on the one hand, a derogatory term describing a clever and shrewd person such as a smith; on the other hand, it is a term applied to a "wise" man or a "sage."

As education spreads in Ethiopia, one can only predict that the positive attitude towards the Beta Israel will develop more. Ethiopia is aware of its need for smiths, potters, weavers, builders, and men skilled in every conceivable craft and industry. With this realization, many Christian youths are being trained to appreciate and to respect handiwork. As this trend takes root, the fear of the Beta Israel *tabib* will no doubt diminish and disappear. Furthermore, with their tradition of craftsmanship and with better training, these youths can continue to make a contribution to alleviating the shortage of skilled manpower in Ethiopia.

In 1954, the Jewish Agency Department of Torah Education and Culture in Diaspora reinforced the educational activities begun by Faitlovitch by estab-lishing a Rabbinic Seminary in Asmara and by sending two dozen students to Israel. Thirty-three village schools were eventually opened, and Christianized *Falashas* were encouraged to return to their original religion. Unfortunately, after two years, all schools except one closed down due to lack of funds. Though an English Jewish organization has given supplementary aid to the remaining classes, enough educational facilities for the Beta Israel do not exist. In the last year, a new group of American Jews—including some members of the Peace Corps—started collecting funds to support these educational efforts. Since the funds available for education in Ethiopia are so meager, the strengthening of such private endeavors will not only help the Beta Israel, but the total effort for Ethiopian educational progress.

Chapter 15

Ethiopianism – Significance for Africans and Afro-Americans

Ethiopia has long been a symbol of redemption for Africans and African-Americans. The Ethiopian Church evermore became their "spiritual homeland."

From this there developed the African-American intellectual ideology known as "Ethiopianism." Some historians wrongly believe that this idea solely derived from mystique of the word "Ethiopia" (Cush in Hebrew) that occurs in the Bible about fifty times, referring to individuals, places, and peoples. To be sure, the biblical mystique is definitely there, but the biblical passages unquestionably connected the African-American world to modern Ethiopia and the Ethiopian Church. A favorite of early African-American clergy was the use of Ps 68:31 "...Ethiopia shall stretch her hands unto the Lord...."—the ancient motto of the Ethiopian Church. Moreover, the use of the term "Abyssinian ... Church" is almost as early as the use of the name Ethiopia. Thus the biblical references were not used without its Ethiopian precedent.

Others have claimed that Ethiopianism is a movement founded in the 1880s by South African missionaries who formed independent African churches, like the Tembu Tribal Church (1884) and the Church of Africa (1889). They do rightly say that it started as religious movement that grew out of the yearning for religio-political freedom in the colonial period. Contrary to the claim that, ex-Wesleyan minister, Mangena Mokone, was the first to use the term when he founded the Ethiopian Church (1892), the term was used already in 1799 when the Ethiopian Baptist Church of Savannah, Georgia was established.

Similar developments occurred elsewhere and for similar reasons. In Nigeria the Native Baptist Church (1888), the formerly Anglican United Native African Church (1891) and its later divisions, and the United African

Methodist Church (1917) were important. Other Ethiopian-related move-ments were represented by the Cameroun Native Baptist Church (1887); the Native Baptist Church (1898), in Ghana; in Rhodesia, by a branch (1906) of the American Negro denomination, the African Methodist Episcopal Church and Nemapare's African Methodist Church (1947); and the Kenyan Church of Christ in Africa (1957), formerly Anglican.

Early Ethiopianism included tribalist, nationalist, and Pan-African dimen-sions, which were encouraged by association with independent U.S. black churches and radical leaders with "back to Africa" ideas and an Ethiopianist ideology. This ideology was explicit in the thought of such pioneers of African cultural, religious, and political independence as E. W. Blyden (1832-1912), and J. E. Casely-Hayford of Ghana (e.g., his "Ethiopia Unbound," 1911).

It is now known that Ethiopian movements played some part in the Zulu rebellion of 1906 and especially in the Nyasaland rising of 1915 led by John Chilembwe, founder of the independent Providence Industrial Mission. From about 1920, political activities were channelled into secular political parties and trades unions, and the use of the term Ethiopian then narrowed to one section of African independent religious movements (see Zionist church). These Ethio-pian-type churches originated by secession (and further sub-secessions) from a mission-connected church, which they resemble in beliefs, polity, and worship and from which they differ in certain cultural and ethnic practices. It appears that by the early 1970s, the term Ethiopianism was not in popular use outside southern Africa.

Others believe the primary mystique of the biblical references was rein-forced by the victories of the ancient independent Christian Empire of Ethiopia over the Italians at the battles of Dogali and Adwa in 1887 and 1896, respec-tively. The Battle of Adwa on March 1, 1896 under the leadership of Emperor Menelik II (1889-1913) and Empress Itege Taytu ranks as a watershed in modern world history. Armed with the Holy Ark of the Covenant, spears, and only moderate modern weaponry, the Ethiopians defeated the technologically advanced Italian army. An investigation of the history of African-Americans reveals not only the fundamental importance of the 1896 Adwa victory for all peoples of African descent, but a turning point in world affairs.

In an era of slavery, Jim Crow, and colonialism, the symbolism of biblical Ethiopia and the Adwa victory represents the dignity of Africans and the role of Ethiopia in a divine plan. Yet Ethiopianism has a long history preceding the Battle of Adwa that is not just based on the idea of biblical Ethiopia. At a time when Africans, the ancestors of African-American peoples, were denegrated as a cursed primitive animistic, fetishistic totemistic peoples, even incapable of superstition (Tyler, Muller, Frazer, Johnston...), who lacked history (Hegel) and the faculty of reasoning (Levy-Bruhl...) who could not even communicate with each other properly without facial gesticulations and gestures and therefore incapable to talk in the dark, or a peoples whose languages lacked proper grammar and syntax (Spencer, Calhoun...), and who live in a continent overrun by wild people and animals, the African-American slaves had to fight back with whatever historical and scientific information they could garner. Ethiopia provided that weapon and the Ethiopian Church the faith to withstand such assault on the dignity of the Black people.

The few educated Black slaves who were fortunate to delve into the study of world history and civilization forthrightly found in Ethiopia and the Church of Ethiopia the answer to their humiliation. Rightly or wrongly, they found their answer in the writings of Herodotus and Diodorus Siculas, and other Greek writers who depicted Ethiopia as the original home of mankind, and the Ethiopians as the first people to have belief in a supreme creator, belief in religion, system of civil government, and a people who were just, tolerant, and hospitable. They found their answer in the biblical passages that depicted Ethiopia as a land of great economic prosperity and the Ethiopians as valiant and just people highly respected that even Moses, the leader of the Israelites, married one of their women.

While the racialists argued that the Ethiopians were not their relatives, such learned men like William Wesley Brown countered in his writings in the middle of the ninteenth century that the Ethiopians were the true antecedents of the Black people pointing to modern Ethiopia.

When the first Black slaves were permitted to have their own congregation, they named the first one "Ethiopian." The word therefore represented Africa's dignity and place in the divine dispensation and provided a charter for free African churches and nations of the future. Independence begins with a clear sense of self-understanding, and the struggle for freedom from slavery and colonialism, for Africa and African-Americans led them to the quest for identity. W.E.B. du Bois, the great modern African-American leader of Pan-Africanism, rightly connected identity to "a careful knowledge of the past out of which the group as such has emerged." The slave and colonial masters tried to destroy the African identity. Science, religion, philosophy, and anthropology were used to denigrate Africans and African-Americans. The confused state of Black-American identity was an obstacle to freedom created by white power. Malcolm X described the distortion of black history and the resulting identity crisis as follows:

> You have to understand it. Until 1959, the image of the African continent was created by the enemies of Africa. Africa was a land dominated by outside powers. A land dominated by Europeans. And as these Europeans dominated the continent of Africa, it was

they who created the image of Africa that was projected abroad. And they projected Africa and the people of Africa in a negative image, a hateful image. They made us think that Africa was a land of jungles, a land of animals, a land of cannibals and savages. It was a hateful image...

And what was the result? They ended up with 22 million Black people here in America who hated everything about us that was African... We hated the African characteristics. We hated our hair... We hated our nose, the shape of our nose, and the shape of our lips, the color of our skin. Yes we did. And it was you who taught us to hate ourselves simply by shrewdly maneuvering us into hating the land of our forefathers and the people on that continent.

Our color became a chain, a psychological chain. Our blood -- African blood -- became a psychological chain, a prison, because we were ashamed of it. We believe -- they would tell it to your face, and say they weren't; they were! We felt trapped because our skin was black. We felt trapped because we had African blood in our veins.

This is how you imprisoned us. Not just bringing us over here and making us slaves. But the image that you created of our motherland and the image that you created of our people on that continent was a trap, was a prison, was a chain, was the worst form of slavery that has ever been invented by a so-called civilized race and a civilized nation since the beginning of the world.[1]

Ethiopia provided for African-Americans and Africans a crucial sense of identity, dignity, and the ultimate hope for freedom. "Ethiopianism" first served a symbolic role in African and Afro-American religious and cultural thought; Ethiopia became the spiritual motherland of African-Americans. Their earliest churches, songs and clubs were named after Ethiopia. "Ethiopianism" in the movement of the Abyssinian Baptist Church, the Universal Negro Improvement Association, Ras Tafarian Religion, the Black Jews and Muslims of America, the thinking of the Black leaders of the nineteenth and early twentieth century, and other aspects of African-American social and political history was of paramount importance.

In 1863, William Wells Brown, the first noted African-American poet, responded to those who tried to separate African-Americans from Ethiopia:

It is generally received opinion of the most eminent historian and ethnologists, that the Ethiopians were really Negroes, although in them the physical characteristics of the race were exhibited in a less

---

1   X, Malcolm. Malcolm X Speech on Anti-Africa Imagery. Pan-African Perspective. <http://www.panafricanperspective.com/mxatswp.html>.

marked manner than in those dwelling on the coast of Guinea, from whence the stock of American slaves has been chiefly desired. That, in the earliest periods of history, the Ethiopians attached a high degree of civilization there is even reason to believe; and that to the learning and science derived from them...[2]

Although the accuracy of his claim was challenged, his line of thinking became central in African-American intellectual thought and political ideology of independence. For example, St. Clare Drake, in his *The Redemption of Africa and Black Religion,* wrote:

Ethiopia came to symbolize all of *Africa*; and throughout the 19th century the redemption of Africa became one important forum of meaningful activity for leaders among New World Negroes... and Ethiopianism became an energizing myth in both the New World and in Africa itself.[3]

Until the Battle of Adwa, Ethiopianism was a spiritual idea, a focus of hope. That initial religious sentiment continues even to our time; religious establishments have been named for Ethiopia or African Zion. However, after the Battle of Adwa, Ethiopia, as the only free African state, came to be the symbol of African independence. Essien-Udom, in his Introduction to Hayfords' 1911 *Ethiopia Unbound,* writes: "The idea of Ethiopianism itself is *eclectic*, being a crystallization of *religious* and political notions, associated with Ethiopia, then the only truly independent island in the sea of colonial Africa." The fate of Ethiopia as the only independent country during the colonial era was sealed at Battle of Adwa.

More than any other event in modern African history, the Battle of Adwa reinforced the earlier religious conception with a new strong African political freedom component. Some of the first African-Americans in Ethiopia arrived in the country immediately after 1896: Daniel Robert Alexander, the businessman William Henry Ellis, Dr. Joseph Vitalien who became Emperor Menelik's personal physician, and Benito Sylvain, a Haitian poet who was one of the first to arrive.

However, it was probably Marcus Garvey, the founder of the Universal Negro Improvement Association (UNIA) who did more than anyone else to promote the significance of the Battle of Adwa among African-Americans. Garvey was nine years old in 1896, old enough to remember the story of the

2   Brown, William Wesley. The Black man: his antecedents, his genius, and his achievements. Boston, J. Redpath, 1963. New York, Kraus Reprint Co., 1969 (32).

3   Drake, St. Clair. *The Redemption of Africa and Black Religion.* Chicago: Third World Press, 1970.

Battle. His biographers do not emphasize enough the profound effect the Battle must have had on Garvey as a teenager. The UNIA national anthem is an example of how Garvey found the Battle of Adwa an answer to African people's search for pride and freedom:

> Ethiopia Thou Land of our fathers
> Thou land where the gods loved to be,
> As storm cloud at night suddenly gathers
> Our armies come rushing to thee.
> We must in the fight be victorious
> Where swords are thrust outward to gleam;
> For us will the vict'ry be glorious
> Where led by red, black and green
>
> Advance, advance to victory,
> Let Africa be free;
> Advance to meet the foe
> Where the might
> Of the red, the black, and the green

The echo of Adwa is heard in Garvey's call, "Let Africa be our guiding star... Wake up Ethiopia! Wake up Africa! Let us work towards the one glorious end of a free, redeemed and might nation. Let Africa be a bright star among the constellation of nations." Marcus Garvey prophesized a great king of Africa leading his people to freedom. When His Imperial Majesty Haile Selassie was crowned *Neguse Negest* (king of kings), he became a prominent leader of the anti-colonial struggle and the ruler of the only African nation to maintain 3000 years of sovereignty. Almost forty years after the battle of Adwa, the Italians attacked Ethiopia again, this time armed with more advanced weaponry including planes that illegally dropped poisonous gas (mustard gas and phosgene) on the land and people. During the five years that the Italian military occupied Ethiopia, the colonial forces were constantly under attack, as the Ethiopian people never capitulated or surrendered. Through King Selassie's diplomacy with the League of Nations, the British Empire eventually came to the Ethiopian patriots' aid and helped to exterminate the Italians from the country. Garvey's prophesy was actualized by Emperor Selassie I, who maintained the freedom of Ethiopia that symbolized the potential for a liberated Africa.

I would like to conclude this chapter with some personal reflection on the significance of the Battle of Adwa for Africans and African-American peoples. In 1954, when I was a first year student at the University College of Addis Ababa (now Addis Ababa University), I attended a meeting in Arusha, Tanzania. I met many young Africans from Kenya, Uganda, Zimbabwe, and South Africa. It was my first trip outside of Ethiopia and contact with other African students, many of who became future African freedom fighters. Through my meeting of the young fellow Africans, I first came to appreciate the fundamental importance of the 1896 Battle of Adwa for all Africans.

In 1954, not a single country in Africa except Ethiopia, Egypt, and Liberia were independent. When I introduced myself as an Ethiopian, a group of young South Africans exclaimed, "We are waiting for you to free us, free us from colonialism. We are waiting for you to fight for us, fight for our freedom. Your Emperor Menelik fought at Adwa and defeated the Italians; your Emperor Haile Sellassie followed his lead. Where are you Ethiopians? We are waiting for salvation from Ethiopia and Zion!"

Although I felt very proud to see such love and respect for Ethiopia, I must confess that I did not then fully appreciate the importance of the feeling of my fellow Africans. In those days, unfortunately, we were not taught a great deal about our own history at the University College. Moreover, I was a premedical student interested primarily in the study of science, not history. However, the enthusiasm of these fellow young Africans was contagious. Their regard for Ethiopia, its history of struggle against colonialism, their knowledge of the specific achievements of Emperor Menelik and the Ethiopian people at Adwa, and the Ethiopian struggle against Italian occupation in the thirties left such an indelible mark on my mind that it became the beginning of my own interest in the study of the history and culture of Ethiopia.

Then in the late fifties when I came to the States as a student, I discovered identical enthusiasm about Ethiopian victory at Adwa among African-Americans. Older African-Americans, Christian ministers, Jews, and Muslims, sought me out to tell me how much they loved Ethiopia and ask me for reading material. I remember meeting one person who was so proud to have been named Menelik himself. Then, in the summer of 1959, when I was President of the Ethiopian student association, we had our annual meeting at Howard University. We had among our speakers the late Prof. Leo Hansberry of the same University. He and every scholar of his generation that I met always spoke of the Battle of Adwa as their own victory.

It was only natural that my own love and respect for my country was reinforced by these experiences. It affected my interest in the study of ancient Ethiopian history and culture. Although earlier African-American religious and political leaders and some modern African-American historians have written extensively about the place of Ethiopia in African-American thought and intellectual history, not many Ethiopian scholars are fully aware of its significance.

As a scholar, my own field of specialty is ancient Semitic languages and civilizations within which I focus on ancient Ethiopia and Jewish studies. However, in 1969, I was fortunate to be appointed the first professor in the new Afro-American Studies Department. My area of teaching covered African religions, languages, and Ethiopian history. However, in my association with African-American scholars, I became interested in "Ethiopianism" and what the Battle of Adwa meant for African-Americans.

Indeed, although my being at Harvard in 1969 might have been an accident of history, my appointment to the Department was not an accident—it was related to "Ethiopianism." I finished my Ph.D. at Harvard in 1969 and was about to return home to Ethiopia. Some of my professors approached me to stay on at Harvard for at least one or two years as a professor in the new Department. The African-American students on campus were then strongly Pan-African oriented. They have read about Emperor Menelik and the Battle of Adwa, the Italian occupation of Ethiopia (1935-41) and its victorious struggles. Their reaction to my appointment was therefore more than enthusiastic.

My students and my colleagues, among them Prof. Ewart Guinier, Prof. Chirenge of Zimbabwe, Prof. C.L. R. James, the associate of Nkrumah - Prof. Nana Nketsia of Ghana, all enhanced my admiration for the achievement of Emperor Menelik, Empress Taytu, and the Ethiopian people at the Battle of Adwa—a legacy that continues to unite Black people of all nationalities.

Appendix
The Church & Development of Writing & Literature

The ability to communicate verbally and in writing is one of the fundamental elements of progress. Nonetheless, whereas verbal communication is limited in scope, writing has revolutionized human history. As Alan Gardner points out in his *Egypt of the Pharaohs* (London 1961, p.21) "Writing extended the range of [people's] communication in both space and time." In other words, writing not only increases the distance at which one can communicate with another but also extends memory, enabling one generation to inherit the cumulative experience and discovery and knowledge of another. In this way knowledge is preserved and expanded and civilization as we know it becomes possible.

Ethiopia is fortunate to be one of the few countries of the world where writing developed from time immemorial, even before the rise of Christianity, However, it was after the rise of Christianity that literature was developed and preserved for over fifteen hundred years. Very few, outside the circle of scholars of ancient languages truly realize the importance of this extensive body of literature found in Ethiopia and written in Ge'ez, This literature represents an invaluable source of information not only for the understanding Ethiopian history but also for the study of world history and the major religions of the world: Judaism, Christianity, Islam and the Traditional African Religions.

Many scholars trace the origin of writing to the ancient Near east in general and to Mesopotamia, in particular, where they believe the first system of writing was invented by the Sumerians about 3500 years BCE. Others, however, consider Egypt the home of the first system of writing dating back to the end of prehistoric times, or roughly about the same time as in Mesopotamia. In my judgment, not only is the first theory unconvincing, but also without a strong base. On the other hand, evidence supports a continuous and systematic development and use of writing in the Northeastern regions of Africa, all along the Nile valley, for over five thousand years. It seems to me that it is in the prehistoric rock engravings and paintings of Africa that we may find invaluable insight into the ultimate origin of writing; for there is indeed good reason to believe that art and writing branched off the same human tendency tree of prehistoric ancient rock art. Prehistoric artworks provide us with extensive information concerning the daily life, customs, and outlook of those who created them; in other words, they are a form of social and personal record and not only the result of instinctive and innate artistic impulses or expressions. Scholars have not seriously begun to examine the link between prehistoric African art and ancient Egyptian hieroglyphic writing. So I think the ultimate origin of writing will remain for a long time a subject of heated debate.

But scholars do agree that ancient Egyptian and Sumerian writings developed from pictographic origins—that is, from pictures that told stories. The Egyptians may have been the first to reduce ancient pre-historic engravings and paintings to a systematic form of writing. This pictographic writing was eventually developed into ideogrammic writing, as in the hieroglyphs in which the pictures not only designated the objects depicted but also the ideas associated with them: The ideograms, also called logograms, then evolved into homophonic phonetics (0=I) in which a word having the same sound was used to designate a homophone, and determinatives in which the grammatical elements were expressed by the use of signs. Then unilateral, bilateral, and trilateral phonetic symbols were all incorporated into the system. (For example, the symbol used for the letter "r" symbolized the word "Ra" or mouth when accompanied by a down stroke.)

Through this method the Egyptians developed a whole series of unilateral symbols, in fact an entire alphabet of 24 characters. Their alphabet was, however, not quite complete; for instance, it had no symbol for the Egyptian sound "l". Moreover, the early use of phonetic writing (and the use of abbreviated and derivative forms known as the hieratic and demotic) did not result in a fully developed alphabetical writing; for the Egyptians officially chose not to give up their ideograms until Roman times. They used the hieroglyphic alphabet to designate pronouns, prepositions, particles, and similar grammatical expressions, and as reminders when used with various consonantal groups. Nevertheless, inspired by the Egyptian system of writing, the alphabet was finally invented (perhaps unofficially) sometime during the early second millennium BCE.

The alphabet is a very ingenious device of symbols of the sounds that exist in human speech. Its invention, even more than that of the discovery of the wheel or the making of fire, has completely revolutionized knowledge and learning, and marks a watershed in all of human history. As Prof. Cross says, "It democratized writing". We may describe the alphabet as the sound computer, which enables people to write down all the words of any language in a simple and efficient manner by the use of the common elements of the language.

Writing may have developed spontaneously and slowly; but the alphabet must have been the result of an incredible process of invention. By whom and when the alphabetic system was invented is still a matter of conjecture, but the earliest known examples of it, the Proto-Sinaitic, have so far come from about twenty-five inscriptions in the Sinai peninsula, discovered in 1906 in Egyptian turquoise mines by the English archaeologist Flinders Petrie. Proto-Sinaitic is a linear script written in a consonantal alphabet and developed from hieroglyphs on the acrophonic (a specific object whose name began with a particular sound) principle. All (except Korean) known comparable methods of reducing a language to a written form are derivatives of it, and Ethiopic is a very good example of one of the early branches of Proto-Sinaitic.

Scholars had conjectured at different times since the seventeenth century the origin of the Ethiopic alphabet to be Samaritan (Ludolphus 1682, Silvestre de Sacy 1818), Syriac (Kopp 1819), or Sabaean (Glazer 1895, Homel 1898, Conti Rossini 1928.) But we now know that Ethiopic is a cursive form of monumental Sabaean, and hence the immediate Southern branch of Proto-Sinaitic or the first known alphabet, in other words, the sister alphabet of the Phoenician (Canaanite) script.

Sabaean (which can rightly be called Proto-Ethiopic) and Phoenician, from which the Hebrew characters are derived, are two of the oldest alphabetic forms of writing. As a direct descendant, Ethiopic's Ras preserved to this day many of the original forms and shapes of the original Proto-Sinaitic. The letters of the English language are derived from the Roman or Latin script, which in turn derives from the Chalcidian (Western Greek) of Southern Italy, which ultimately derives from the Phoenician through the Ionic Greek script. On a ladder of history or the tree of the alphabetic ancestry, Ethiopic thus becomes the uncle of Greek script, the greatuncle of the Roman script, the great granduncle of English.

Early Sabaean or Proto-Ethiopic writing, mostly votive inscriptions, is today found extensively in the surroundings of the northern Ethiopian and Eritrean (Yeha, Qohaito, Daqamahari, Malazo, etc.) as well as in Yemen, representing respectively the ancient kingdom of Axum, the city-states of ancient Southern Arabia (in particular, Saba', Main, Qataban, and Hadramawt.) A monograph incised on a shred in South Arabia has been dated to the 8th century BCE by radiocarbon method, and in fact, Sabaean inscriptions of about this period have been found in Etzion Geber, a rather early development of Sabaean. Earlier inscriptions have been dated to the end of the second or early first millennium BCE on paleographic grounds. In northern Ethiopia, also, writings that can be dated as early as the eighth century have been found. They primarily begin to abound in early Christian times. These inscriptions have been planned and executed symmetrically with great care, and famous scholars like Thomas Lambdin rightly say that Sabaean inscriptional writing is "not rivaled elsewhere in the Semitic world for its elegance." Ethiopians also designed decorative writings that may have given rise to Arabic.

From our epigraphic sources we learn that about the end of the fourth century BCE the Sabaean Proto-Ethiopic monumental script began to evolve in Ethiopia into a less symmetrical form. The Dutch scholar, A. J. Drewes, attaches great significance to this stage of the development of the Sabaean Proto-Ethiopic script, and considers it the origin of the Ge'ez (Ethiopic) alphabet, and the rise of Axum as the capital of Ethiopia. Many texts containing invaluable information about the political, economic, and religious history of the horn of Africa come to us in the inscription from about this period to about the middle of the 4th century of the Christian era. The most famous among these are of course the inscriptions of Emperor Ezana, which are rather detailed and offer invaluable information on the history of the Ge'ez script, the expansion of the Axumite Empire, and the introduction of Christianity to Ethiopia.

Whereas the earlier forms of these characters also remained simply consonantal, sometime around the 4th century, when the Bible began to be translated into the Ethiopic language, the Ethiopians modified and vocalized the script (possibly the work of an individual) for ease in manuscript writing and reading. To do so they transformed the alphabet into a kind of a syllabary, using innovative vocalic signs for ease in pronunciation. Ethiopic is not only unique among all the early Semitic writings to be so vocalized, but also the earliest among them to develop vocalic signs; Hebrew, for instance, did not use such signs until the Ninth Century. According to Munro-Hay (1991) some inscriptions might contain early rudimentary experiments with vocalization.

The Proto-Ethiopic inscriptions were read much like Egyptian, from right to left or from top to bottom as well as boustrophedon (as the ox plows back and forth.) But due to Christian influence, the Ethiopians standardized the direction of reading and writing from left to right, as we still do today. The orders of the letters of the alphabet were originally probably like that of Phoenician, but gradually a new order was created for reasons not yet fully known. A similar alphabetic order in part has been found in first century Sabaean or South Arabic inscriptions. The oldest Sabaean inscriptions are found in ancient Ethiopia – Eritrea and Yemen.

The period from the time of Ezana, in the first half of the Fourth Century, to the time of Emperor Kaleb, in the Sixth Century is germane to our understanding of the roots of Ethiopian culture, art, architecture, literature, in general, and to Christianity, in particular. It was probably during this time that the ancient shrine of Axum was converted to the famous church of St. Mary of Zion, where

Ethiopian Christians believe the original and complete Tablets of the Law given to Moses are still found. It was during this time that the nine famous monasteries of the Nine Saints were built, including that of the famous Dabra Damo.

However, the most significant single development of this period is the rise of Ethiopian Christian literature. Thanks to the Ge'ez alphabet, Ethiopic became the repository of many ancient writings and the nurturer of an extensive body of literature and the medium for literary creativity. Equally significant is the fact that Ethiopic became the only script of the south Proto-Semitic, in which literature was produced and continues to be in use up to our own time.

As we all know, no other known literary work has had such an impact upon world culture and literature, and the great religions Judaism, Islam, and Christianity as the book which we call the Bible; and Ge'ez (or classical Ethiopic, as western scholars call it) is one of about seven of the most important languages of the world in which the Bible and cognate works were first translated. Because of this, scholars of biblical textual study and criticism learn Ge'ez (or classical Ethiopic) and adduce textual witnesses from the Ethiopic Bible to establish many variants or/and readings. Of all the European languages none shares such a high position with the exception of Greek and Latin. (Examples of writing in other European languages with the exception of the Ulfilas Bible appear much later: Old English, Seventh Century; Old High German Eighth Century; Russian, Ninth Century ; Old Norse and Old Dutch, Twelfth Century; Old Swedish and Danish, Thirteenth Century.)

Even more important is that Ethiopic preserved many ancient writings that have been lost in the original languages. The most distinguished example of these is beyond a doubt the *Book of Enoch* and the *Book of Jubilees*. These works exist today in their entirety only in Ethiopic, and are still the subject of richly deserved worldwide scholarly attention. In fact, in the Eighteenth Century, when James Bruce first brought some manuscripts of the *Book of Enoch*, to Europe, the impact it had on the scholarly world was like the excitement generated by the discovery of the Dead Sea Scrolls in our own century. Like the scrolls, the *Book of Enoch* offers valuable insight into the religious and cultural milieu of the time of Jesus and his first followers.

The sacred scriptures of the Ethiopian Orthodox Church consist of 81 books; 39 books of the Hebrew Bible, the 27 canonical books of the New Testament, and numerous Apocryphal and Pseudepigraphic works. After a period of slackening since the Second World War, interest in the Apocryphal and Pseudoepigraphic works is beginning to emerge again, as evidenced by the recent first American publication of the two-volume *Old Testament Pseudoepigrapha* by the Doubleday Press. Any glance at this publication as well as other recent works on the religious and social ideas of the Second Temple period will reveal the high position Ge'ez holds among ancient languages as an important repository and nurturer of many ancient literary works. Moreover, there are numerous other venerated works such as hagiographies, chronicles, homilies, calendaric and theological works that offer insight into the history of early Christianity. For instance, a German Ethiopist in the late Seventeenth Century discovered the liturgical usage in Italy in the late Second Century after studying the first version of the Apostolic Church Order of Hippolytus of Rome, in the Ethiopic version. Likewise, in his recent work on Ethiopian Astronomy and Calendar, the late, noted historian of mathematics Otto Neugebauer has shown that only in the Ethiopic work known as Hasab do we find preserved in detail the Judaeo-Hellenistic calendar which was the basis of early Christian calendar.

Furthermore, the examination of Ethiopic literature may shed light not only on the history of early Christianity, but also on other early Jewish literary works as well as on the history of Jewish communities in Ethiopia and Southern Arabia. In my own study of MB, a fifteenth century Sabbath homily, I have demonstrated the preservation of certain halachic gleanings in Ethiopic literature; elsewhere, I have shown that the oldest manuscript of the *Book of Enoch*, microfilmed by a German team some twenty years ago reveals archaic readings that help us understand certain interpretations of this important work. Like the Book of Enoch, the calendaric work called the Book of Jubilees is another example of early Jewish books that throws light on early Jewish Midrash. The Ethiopian Jewish work known as Te'ezaza Sanbat gives us a deep insight into the nature of the Jewish relationship with the personified Sabbath, perhaps more than any other work of comparable size that we know. Where else do we find Jewish Aramaic words such as meswat or arb in such common language as in Ethiopic?

Finally, it is well-known that Muhamad's earliest followers sought refuge in Ethiopia. The scholarly works of the last century have in fact shown that numerous fundamental terminologies found in Islamic literature (mashaf, menbar, tabot, taot...) are in their original classical Ethiopic expressions. It is indeed not unlikely that future investigations and studies of Ethiopic literature may throw new light on the Christian and Jewish components of early Islamic theology.

In short, the importance of the many unique ancient religious and historical works found in classical Ethiopic for an understanding of early Christianity, Judaism, and Islam cannot be exaggerated.

Let me conclude that it is of course not possible to speak in any more detail about the many varied and rich literary works of classical Ethiopic literature in one short chapter, and I shall not attempt to do so. Let me only mention briefly such works as the Physiologus, the Greek collection of study of animals and plants, the type of natural history popular in the Middle Ages, Qerlos, a collection of important Christological writings attributed to the Church Father Cyril; the monastic Rules of Pachomius all from the first period in Ethiopic literary development (4-6ᵗʰ cent.); the Kebra Nagast, the most detailed haggadah on the Queen of Sheba, Fetha Nagast, the Synaxarium, the Book of the Mystery of Heaven and Earth, from the second period (early 14), and the many works on miracle stories, songs and poetry, and so on.

The largest body of written material coming out of Ethiopia remains untapped for scholarly purposes. This is a sad state of affairs, for as said above, Ethiopic contains some important material, which will and could illuminate our knowledge of ancient learning. Only recently Prof. O. Neugebauer [Ethiopic Astronomy and Computus, Vienna, 1979] has made a study of Ethiopian calendaric works and found out that the ancient Alexandrian Jewish lunar calendaric system that was later adopted by the Christian churches has been preserved nowhere in Christian literature but in the Ethiopic. Moreover, he has demonstrated recently that at least one method of reckoning time in the European Middle Ages, called the Spanish Era or 38 BC, which has been enigmatic for scholars to explain, can only be explained on the basis of Ethiopic sources.

The existence of such a large body of written material coming from Ethiopia is of considerable significance for all of Africa. As you all know, the denial of the existence of African history in the 19th century was based on a priori assumption that only cultures that have writing and literature have history. According to the famous 19th century philosopher Hegel, it is the existence of writing that disqualified Ethiopia as an African country (G.F. Hegel, *A Philosophy of History*). I say, of course, in the same way that Greece and Rome have been the fountainhead of ancient cultures of Europe, so is Ethiopia for Africa.

As said earlier, Ethiopia is a land where ancient alphabets have been preserved and where ancient literature was nurtured. These literature is so extensive going back at least fifteen-hundred year that it deserves a special monographic work to cover it. Many years ago, I started working on such a monograph. Unfortunately, due to the limitations of my other obligations to Ethiopia, especially my peace work, I have put this work on a back burner. But this book on the Ethiopian Christian Orthodox Täwahïdo Church cannot be complete without a short survey of Christian literature. One of the few attempts in this area has been Enrico Cerulli's *La Letteratura Etiopica; con un saggio sull'Oriente Cristiano*. [Ethiopic Literature; with an essay on the Christian East, the third enlarged edition published in 1968.] Hence in order to fill this vacuum, I have used Cerullis' work, and so the remaining part of this chapter on Ethiopia Church literature is largely a translated and paraphrased summary of his work with my own occasional commentary or additions. I haste to add that although I follow Cerulli closely, our knowledge of Ethipic literature is more extensive than the summary in his work.

Axum is the first unified state which developed its own literature based on local lore cross-fertilized and transmitted with the knowledge of the ancient peoples whose cultural, religious (pagan) and political traditions, they incorporated into an original Ethiopia body of literature. In particular, the Hebrews, they incorporated, as well as Greco-Roman navigation and the chain of ports of call on the sea route from Egypt to India brought Greek cultural influence.

The predominance of Mediterranean and Asiatic contributions to the cultural history of Ethiopia is even more evident in her literary history. For centuries, Ethiopic literature was the literature of the Court (or closely connected with court life) or religious literature. Even religious literature was connected, via the Ethiopian Orthodox Täwahïdo Church, with the sovereign Power, which in Ethiopia traditionally controlled jurisdiction in Church matters. Sensitivity of Ethiopic literature and its assimilatory reactions were faced with elevated cultural contacts. This explains why the interests of the literati and of artists coincided with religious subject matters that the sovereign and leaders of the nation were involved and the problems which they faced.

Cerulli speaks of two apparently contradictory aspects of Ethiopic literature. First, the Ethiopians were actively receptive, easily acquiring inspiration and doctrines from Hebraic, Greek, Aramiac-Syriac, Arab-Christian, and western sources. This receptiveness is never passive or literal. It is typically Ethiopian to gather and transform, immediately or progressively, elements of foreign cultural and literary experiences. This occurs to such an extent that the translations into Ethiopic are never simple, but often have supplements, additions, or even sometimes misrepresentations or insertion of original facts in such numbers as to veil the data transferred in the literal translation. Ethiopic receptiveness is affected by intense reaction of local tradition. Typical examples of this attitude are seen in all periods of Ethiopic literature: compare the *Rule of Pacomius* in the Aksumite period to the *Book of Miracles of Mary* in the 15th century to the *Fetha Nagast* 'Laws of the Kings' in the 17th century, etc.

The easy acceptance and assimilation of foreign literature is tempered by adaptation. Yet, Ethiopic literature is not infrequently inclined to freeze or harden newly accepted inspirations and expressions when they are not renewed with successive elements. The result is rigid canons that regulate artistic expression along pre-established models. They become absolutely obligatory, slowing down and stopping the initial impulse. The "literary genre", once constituted and recognized as such within the limits of its arbitrary norms leaves only a literary transmission which arises no longer from esthetics but from cultural history.

Pre-Christian inscriptions

The oldest pre-Christian religious inscriptions so far found in Ethiopia are in Sabaean script (that I prefer to call Proto-Ethiopic) and date to about 5th century

B.C.[1] One such inscription is a fragment found in Yeha, an altar dedication to the goddesses Astar and Naurau. Some of the subsequent inscriptions are those that clearly bear the name and dates of an Ethiopian ruler, a second or third century inscription in Greek that bears the name of "King of Kings of the Aksumites, the great Sembrouthes." The inscription dates to the 24th year of his reign.

Another important inscription of Aksum is trilingual: Ethiopic, Sabaean, and Greek. It contains the name of King Ezana, who ruled in the first half of the 4th century A.D. who subsequently became Christian (Chapter II: The Aksumite Period). The first of his major inscription concerns a military expedition against the Begia peoples whom he brings to submission and relocates from their original homes to a new territory. The inscription is very detailed, always one of the distinctive traits of Ethiopic chronicle tradition, and emphasizes a King who, instead of destroying the Begia rebels, transfers them with good treatment into a more easily controlled area.

The subsequent inscription attributed to Emperor Ezana is a Christian inscription and is of even greater historic and cultural importance. Without explicitly declaring his recent conversion to Christianity, he relates his victories over the Noba to the One God, substituting clearly the invocation to this G-d from the Pre-Christian divinities in his first inscriptions.

In this long narrative inscription several very clear characteristics emerge as well. His taste for detail (arithmetic precision) is apparent, as is his moral preoccupation with having fought a just war and of having dealt justly with the people, by which he explains divine aid and victory. More important is the almost (p. 18) ambiguous caution with which the very great event of the adoption of Christianity is inserted in the narrative of Ezana. He avoids expressly naming the God of Christians, called either "Lord of Heaven" or "Lord of Earth" (this latter has remained till today in Ethiopic languages to designate God). The sovereign was anxious to avoid giving too great a shock to his realm with his conversion. Here is also ancient indication of that pondered prudence of expression and of the studied use of complicated possibilities that for centuries has been typical of the Ethiopic language and the political literature of the land.

Cerulli believes in the notable continuity in literature. But one must keep in mind the great distance in time that separates the major part of Aksumite inscriptions and the literature of the period of the Salomonid kings, and the limitations of the epigraphic style. Certainly the authors of the inscriptions were not artists, yet they effectively expressed, despite the rigid tradition imposed on them, how they saw and felt those events in their country or life that they wanted remembered.

---

1 Since Cerulli's days, many more ancient inscriptions have been found and published in *Annales d'Ethiopie* and *Journal of Ethiopia Studies*. We now have inscriptions that can be dated as early as the eighth century.

The "Inscription of Ham" of 7th-8th century A.D. shows another aspect of religious and cultural Ethiopic history. This text is explicitly Christian, foreshadowing the intense use of biblical citations in later Ethiopic literature.

The three "Inscriptions of King Daniel", the last of the Aksumite period, survive from the 10th or 11th century. The form is Christian, although the narration is in the traditional style we've seen. Cerulli cites the narration about the expedition against the Wolqayt, written at the close of the Aksumite phase of Ethiopic literature. At the initial invocation (now, after six or seven centuries of Christianity, openly different), we have a narration that has varied little in its expressions.

The Dawn of Ethiopian Orthodox Christian Literature

Beginning in the fourth century through the seventh, we have a period of active literary work, notably the translation of Biblical works into Ethiopic from Greek and possibly Aramaic and Syriac. The Ethiopic versions reflect the influence of both Jewish Aramaic, Christian Aramaic or Syriac, and Koine Greek. They preserve texts that are generally even older than the Greek manuscripts we have today at our disposal.

The Hebrew Bible or the Old Testament was translated into Ethiopic from the Septuagint, the first Greek version of the Hebrew Bible. The translation work was not all completed at one time or within the same period. They seem to have been done at successive stages. Nor were they done by the same translators. (Please see the chapter on Biblical translation in this work.) Along with the development of the translation works, Christianity expanded into the high plains and occurred progressively. Since, the adherence to the new religion did not involve an immediate knowledge or use of the complete text of the Holy Books, a continued memory of the ancient names of the gods persisted, as can be seen in the _Book of Sirach_ or _Ecclesiasticus_.

The New Testament translation was based in what we call _textus receptus_ or the received text of the Patriarchate of Antioch, traced to the Western Syrian town of St. Lucian. It is very likely that the persecuted Syrian Christians, who in the fifth and sixth centuries sought refuge in Ethiopia, contributed to this translation work as well as to the further diffusion of Christianity and the propagation of the faith in the Axumite Empire.

In subsequent centuries, the version of the Hebrew Bible/Old and New Testament, after the first translation, were subjected to many revisions, especially centuries later using Arab-Christian texts, after the contact and relations with Patriarchate of Alexandria from the 14th century on.

Besides canonical books (as pointed out elsewhere in this work, the Ethiopic canon does not coincide with the tridentine one), other biblical books were translated which in Ethiopia are included in the canon itself and accepted as authentic. The Ethiopic translations of these books often have preserved the most complete texts, whereas in the other early versions, including the Greek, only fragments of these works have survived). This especially trues for the most famous *Book of Enoch* and the *Book of Jubilees* called Kufale in Ethiopic. The same is true for the *Shepherd of Hermas*, the *Apocalypse of Esdras, the Ascension of Isaiah* (which in Europe was adopted and diffused in the Middle Ages by confessions tied with Manicheism, like the Bulgar Bogomili, and later still, the Catari (Albigenses) of Languedoc) and *the Paralipomena of Jeremiah* of the second or third century, entitled in Ethiopic, *The Rest of the Words of Baruch*.[2]

Early Works on Monasticism

In the early Christian period, three works fundamental for Christian monasticism were also translated into Ethiopic from the Greek. These are *The Life of St. Paul the Hermit, The Life of St. Anthony* (by Athanasius, according to Cerulli's initial conclusion); and *The Rule (Guidebook) of St. Pacomius* (founder of cenobitism.) Cerulli believes that an original Ethiopic appendix, considered to be later than the translation, was added as a supplement. This appendix contain an account of "The vision of the ten rows of good and bad monks," sincere and humble faith expressed in simple ways and schematic order. This passage was successively imitated in later Ethiopic literature.

St. Cyril of Alexandria; the "Physiologist"

Similar to the above works (biblical texts, texts for monachism), the translation and preservation of another Ethiopic compilation borrowed from the Christian Greek is due to the teaching needs of the religious schools. This is Qirillos, the oldest patristic manual in Ethiopia for doctrinal teaching. It contains translations of some of the writings of St. Cyril of Alexandria: (p. 27) De recta fide ad Theodosium imperatorem; Prosphoneticus ad Reginas; Quod Christus sit; and a collection of homilies and extracts of various Greek Fathers of the Church, including Theodotus of Ancyra, Severus of Sinnada and Juvenal of Jerusalem. These writings of St. Cyril (and of other Fathers) in polemics against the Nestorians, after the Council of Ephesus in 431, vigorously insist

---

2   This work that contained the account of "The Sleep of Abimelek Who Slept 66 years" is translated in Cerulli. Many medieval and modern literatures derived inspiration from it (e.g. Rip Van Winkle) (p. 21).

on the divine and human unity of Christ incarnate. They have been adapted for the teaching of the Miaphysite doctrine of the Ethiopic Church, which has as its base the rigidly interpreted aphorism of St. Cyril: "one nature of God the Word, incarnate."

The translation from Greek of the "Physiologist" was perhaps also performed for the purpose of edification. The "Physiologist" is a noted collection of often legendary observations of animals, plants and minerals, each of which concludes with a spiritual moral. The "Physiologist", written in Syria in the third or fourth century, was widely known in the Middle Ages and was translated from the Greek into many eastern and western languages, including Ethiopic.

Regarding the Anti-Christ by Hippolitus

Another work translated directly from Greek is the little book (or pamphlet) by St. Hippolitus entitled *Regarding the Antichrist*. It was written about 202 to comfort Christians during persecutions by showing them the destruction of the Antichrist. It implies that any ruler including the Ethiopian Emperors who persecute Christian face the same fate.

Rapport has long existed between the Ethiopic Orthodox Täwahïdo Church and the Coptic Patriarchate Church of Alexandria, a relationship that some trace to the time of St. Athanasius (4th century) when Abba Salama, the first head of the Ethiopian Church was installed, although some scholars dispute any formal times between the two before 1270. In fact, the earliest Ethiopic literary works had already flourished when Coptic literature, that subsequently came to be supplanted by Arabic, begun to develop in Egypt in later part of the first Christian Millenium. Many of these later works in Coptic and Arabic, such as the liturgical books of the Egyptian Church, came to be translated into Ethiopic in post 13th century.

Abgar of Edessa

Ironically our knowledge of continued literary activity in Ethiopia during this period is still very scanty or non-existent, although the tradition of Abgar of Edessa might be traced to period of the Zagwe dynasty. At the dawn of the fourteenth century, the age of Amda Sion (1314-1344), the long silence in Ethiopic literary activity ends abruptly and literary activity in Ethiopia revives. Cerulli believes that the silence of the centuries (from the inscriptions of King Daniel to the works of the early 14th century) is due to a gap in the transmission of new manuscripts. In the new historic period, in the 14th century, from the reign of Amda Sion to Saifa Arad (1344-1371), literary and artistic expressions again came into full bloom.

Gadla Lalibala

The capital of Ethiopia during the reign of Zagwe was the city known today as Lalibela. It was named after the most famous of the Zagwe dynasty, the venerated King Lalibela whose great deeds were handed down in a regional literature, known as *Gadla Lalibala.*

The city of Lalibala was earlier known as Roha, the Syriac name of Edessa, perhaps because of the diffusion in Ethiopia of the legend of Abgar, King of Edessa, and of his correspondence with Jesus Christ. We have today the *Ethiopic Legend of Abgar* in recent manuscripts of the 17th century (Aqaryos negusa Roha). That correspondence was an apocryphal text, long and widely venerated in the Christian East. It attests to a rapport between Ethiopia and the Syriac Orthodox Church.

Zena Amda Sion

The first historic work of the period of the earliest Salomonids is *Zena Amda Sion* or the *Chronicle of the Wars of Amda Sion.* This chronicle seems to be contemporaneous, composed after the ascent to the throne by the Sultan of Ifat, Sabr-ad-din (ca.1330-1331) and before the death of Amda Sion I in 1344. The events are represented with the vivacity we expect only from a contemporaneous writer, one who had witnessed the wars of the victorious Amda Sion I against the Sultan and the other Moslem princes. The narrative is written in a simple but smooth (p. 32) style, full of vivid, artistically composed episodes that hold the interest of the reader. Cerulli rightly argues that the style is quite different from the usual dry form of chronicles and stands as a rare example in the historical literature of Ethiopia. The author attributes to his heroes various discourses that he includes in his text, often enhancing the dramatic effect of the account, inspired by tender family sentiments, which help to assuage the violence of war.

The culture of our chronicler is solidly based on the Bible, yet the citations from Scriptures are not so cumbersome as they become in later writings. This is a work of a churchman who lived at the court of Amda Sion I, probably one of the chaplains who officiated at the tent chapels of royal camp and on military expeditions. Because of his position he was especially close to the king, and thus disliked at times by the established hierarchy of the Ethiopic Church. Cerulli cites two distinctive passages. In the first, entitled "the leave-taking of the queens," Amda Sion is said to be sick in bed in his tent. Despite his grave illness he rises to go to battle with the Moslems. The younger queen begs the elder one to keep him home, but she declines, and much praying and weeping ensue. The second passage, "the submission of Sultan Sabr ad-din," recounts the great wrath of Amda Sion and his ultimate clemency in not killing the Sultan.

Poetry: Warrior Songs

Ethiopic poetry of the 14th century is represented by some songs in honor of Amda Sion I, composed by minstrels or by soldiers of the king related in Amharic, not literary Ethiopic, Amharic (of which we do not have evidence before the 17th century) (p. 50).

These songs are uneven but effective, inspired by sincere warrior sentiment. Though heavy with their lists of conquered enemies, they pave the way for the best lyric flowering that will follow. Cerulli gives a brief song on the victories of Amda Sion against the Moslems of the southern lands, Wag', Hadiya and Bali. In another song Amda Sion's prowess in battle is further praised.

The first traces of Sacred Poetry, of notable artistic value, but so far unpublished, belong to the 14th century. Heroic deeds of the martyrs are evoked through dialogues. Even in its archaic garb, this first hymnal is not yet grown sterile with the formal conventions of successive periods, revealing a profound faith that gives authentic poetic warmth that animates the verses. Cerulli gives the following hymns: a) *For St. Mercurius the Martyr* _ one of four military saints venerated in Ethiopia. According to this hymn, which differs from the version later inserted into the Ethiopian Synaxarium, St. Michael descended from heaven to put out the fire around the stake on which Mercurius had been burned to death. His body was then stolen away and buried; b) *For the martyrs of Nagran* _ in 523 A.D., during the reign of Justin I, Emperor of Eastern Roman Empire, a Yemenite prince, pagan or Jewish king attacked the Christian community of Nageran in northeast Yemen and massacred its inhabitants. This martyrdom is historically associated with the Ethiopian expedition for the conquest of Yemen in the time of Emperor Caleb who is celebrated in this hymn; c) *For the Crucifixion* – a dramatic poem.

The Kebra Nagast

A few years before the *Chronicle of Amda Sion*, but during his reign, another very important work entitled *Kebra Nagast* ("The Glory of the Kings") appeared. The *Kebra Nagast* narrates the origin of the ruling Ethiopian Salomonid Dynasty, going back to the Queen of Sheba and King Solomon. The first part of the work recounts the meeting of the Queen of Sheba and King Solomon and the birth of their son Ibn al-Hakim (Son of the Wise One, who later came to be called Menilek.) In the meeting of the Queen of Sheba and King Solomon" her humble adoration of and admiration for Solomon (illustrated at great length) is shown, as is Solomon's modesty and humility. He points to a passing worker to show that he, Solomon, is no better than, and is in some respects inferior to the poor worker.

The second part recounts the journey of Menilek and the secret importing of the Ark from Jerusalem to Aksum and the coronation of Menilek as King of Ethiopia. These two parts, taking up almost half the book, are notably the most interesting, but not emotionally as vivid as the *Chronicle of Amda Sion*. However, we do find the same oratorical style. The intent of the work is to celebrate the national glory of kings and regional glory of Aksum in a rich narrative.

Another part of the work is a series of stories and explanations to prove that the chief sovereigns of the world are descendants of the race of Israel. The stories are short, schematic novellas, in which we find a few motifs more prevalent in other oriental literatures. The premise of the book is the exaltation of the Ethiopian sovereign, who, as a descendant of Solomon and David, is nobler than other kings who come from a line inferior to that of Jesse, David's father.

The fourth main part of the work is a group of biblical passages foretelling the Redemption. They are followed first by explanations of the symbolic language used by the Prophets (in the scholastic style of the Terguame, i.e. "interpretations", which are frequent in Ethiopian manuscripts), and secondly by apocalyptic predictions of the final victory of the King of Ethiopia. The patriotic emotion of the author affirms the steadfast faith vigorously maintained in the difficult centuries during the struggles against the Islamic powers.

The author of the work said to be an Axumite clerc by the name of Yeshaq (Isaac) supposedly wrote the *Kebra Nagast* (Glory of Kings) between 1314 and 1322, in the early years of the reign of Emperor Amda Sion I. It is more likely that, Yeshaq elaborated upon, embellished, and unified traditions, with commentaries from the prophetic teaching of the Bible and late apocryphal literature current among the Christians of the East in honor of the Solomonic dynasty which had ascended the Ethiopian throne in 1270 (about 40 years earlier). It is possible that the narrative of the first section of the work, that of the meeting of King Solomon and the Queen of Sheba had already been circulating in Ethiopia in earlier centuries in different versions (Arabic according to Cerruli, but could be Aramaic/Syriac) before being rendered into Ethiopic.

An interesting passage in the work regards "The Pearl" which is the symbol of Virgin Mary, a symbol of man's salvation. The Pearl was transmitted from Adam's body down through the generations, via all the righteous and pure firstborn sons, up to the womb of Anna Mary's mother, finally passsing to the Virgin Mary: ("Those of you who have carried the Pearl in your belly will be saved, together with your wives, and none of you shall perish . . . because the Pearl will be carried by men who will be just, and the women who have carried it . . . shall be purified by that Pearl").[3]

Mashafa Mestra Samay wa-Meder:
The Book of Mysteries of Heaven and Earth

This symbol of the Pearl, identified in Ethiopia with the Virgin Mary and the Redemption of the Soul, is important in religious history of this period. The symbol of the Pearl is again found in another original work, the *Book of Mysteries of Heaven and Earth* from about the end of 14th century. The author is said to be a monk called Yeshaq (Isaac), a disciple of the abbot Ba-salota Michael, the saint of the monastery of Dabra Gol in Amhara during the reign of Amda Sion I. It contains "revelations" which were made via an Angel sent to (p. 43) Ba-Haile Michael, Yeshaq's's teacher. They are esoteric and very secret, i.e. this mystery should not be revealed to anyone, except learned and intelligent ones (persons of mystery.) These "revelations" of the mystery are related to those already in the "secret books" of the Scriptures -- passages which have remained secrets in 49 of the canonical books -- 21 in the Old Testament and 28 in the New Testament.

The *Book of Mysteries* is composed of four parts. The first part deals with the secrets of the creation and the rebellion of the angels. The second is an esoteric interpretation of the *Book of Revelations* or *Apocalypse of St. John*. The third consists of an interpretation of the Mystery of the Divinity and of the symbols therein. The fourth is a qabbalistic or, so to say, Pythagorean explanation of computations and numbers found in the Scriptures.

An example of one of the mystical passages reads, "an extraordinary white bird gives birth to the Pearl," supposedly impregnated by the sun. So, while she gives birth to her normal offspring (birds) from her left flank, from her right flank she delivers prodigious jewels that are the precious pearls. Last of all, she delivers one single, a very beautiful pearl, "the Pearl" whose name is Karbe Dinel. (p. 44.)

The Life of St. Ann

In *The Life of St. Ann*, the symbol of the Pearl appears again, also associate with a white bird. Cerulli refers to a single manuscript of the 15th century, and

---

3   In eastern Christian writings, influenced by gnostic ideas, the Pearl symbolizes (a) the Redeemer, a symbol which develops from Clement of Alexandria to St. Ephrem, the Syrian. In Ethiopian thought it is found in the translation of the *Physiologist* and *Weddasse Maryam*, The Anaphora of Mary, and in the Harp of Mary; (b) the redeemed human soul which returns to its heavenly dwelling.

claims that while the introduction has literary characteristics of that century, it is likely that we also find ideas and expressions from the earlier 14th century. In a section on "St. Ann and the full moon of the Pearl", in answer to St. Ann's and Joachim's prayer lamenting her sterility, God appears at night in the guise of a white bird (the Spirit of Life) descending from heaven. The white bird lands on Ann's head and the Pearl grows in her womb and becomes the body of the Virgin Mary.

According to Cerulli, at end of this period of literary history in which the personality of Amda Sion I dominates, begins a very active translation from Arabic under the patronage of Metropolitan Abuna Salama (c.1350-1390). (p. 55) Cerulli claim that he promoted this literary movement to encourage closer contacts between the Ethiopian Church and the Patriarchate of Alexandria, not so much to instruct Ethiopian clergy as to ward off the threat of dissident ideas which infiltrated the monasteries. Besides others are the major literary importance are the translations from Arabic of works of hagiography.

Zena Eskender:
The Christian Romance of Alexander the Great

The Zena Eskender was composed probably in the 14th century, apparently an original Ethiopic work, but inspired more likely by the well known Story of Alexander of the pseudo-Callisthenes that according to Cerulli, was translated into Ethiopic from Arabic, rather than from the Greek. The work contains many traces of Gnostic ideas and dualistic concepts of the Manichaeans. The style with many long discourses gives the book an oratorical tone. Alexander the Great is exalted already in the introduction, characterized as a model for chastity and purity. Thus he receives from the Spirit of the Omnipotent the revelation of the Incarnation of the Word, "because of the purity of your body and because of your prayer . . . to me".

In the story, Alexander crosses the Land of Darkness, carried by griffins, also called eagles, and reaches the Land of the Living. There he meets Enoch and Elias and finds the Water of Life, in which live prodigious fish no one can ever kill. He is trapped by a deceitful fisherman, but he can be kept in chains by Alexander. The former then becomes a hermit and finally dies, after having discussed at length the problem of the Resurrection. Cerulli relates the story as follows: "The griffins carry the soldiers of Alexander the Great from the Land of Darkness to the Land of the Living".

This Ethiopic *Romance of Alexander* is, according to Ceruili, evidence of a new current of thought which appears in the 14th century in the remote Christian land of Ethiopia, and which has a great importance not only for the literary history but also for the religious and cultural history of Ethiopia in the middle ages.

The Life of St. Alexis

The Life of St. Alexis is of uncertain date, but was a well-known legend in Ethiopia prior to the 15th century. It is cited in an inventory of the library of the Ethiopian community of Jerusalem in 1425 (now in a manuscript of Leningrad). The Ethiopic version of the legend, in which the setting is Constantinople rather than Rome, differs from those popular in western Europe. The work is particularly important because it has preserved a version almost certainly from Byzantine literature, but that is not extant in anther source. A passage from this work is found in Cerulli's own critical edition of the text: "the lament of the family at the death of St. Alexis, man of God".

Legend of Prophet Habakkuk

According to Cerulli, the first Ethiopic translations from Arabic are from the13th century, the oldest dated translation being the *Legend of Prophet Habakkuk* in c. 1293.

Senodos

Another, and much more important translation, probably from the end of 13th or the beginning of 14th, is a juridical and religious, rather than literary work, called the *Senodos*. The *Senodos* is a collection of canons of the Coptic Church, adopted in the Ethiopian Orthodox Täwahïdo Church. These canons are cited in the *Zena Amda Sion*.

Zena Ayhud

Zena Ayhud, a history of the Jews attributed to Gurion is also from the beginning of the 14th century. Cerulli and others claim the translation to be from the Arabic of the History of the Jews by Gorionides and that of the Universal History by al-Maken (George ibn al-Amid), which apparently was finished in 1293-1295. He also claims that these Ethiopic translations show an affinity to a variety of cultural and literary elements of Arabic Christianity.

Synaxarium

The Ethiopic Synaxarium is a large work about Christian saints and their lives for reading on each day of the whole Ethiopian thirteen months of the year. Cerulli claims the Synaxarium to be a translation from the Arabic made at the end of the 14th century. But the work also contains local Ethiopian additions and Axumite literary characteristics.

The Synaxarium was not transmitted literally as it was translated by Simeon. It was elaborated on with the addition of Ethiopian holidays and the lives of the Ethiopian saints, so that today the work has primary interest for the religious and civil history of Ethiopia. This reworking was done at various periods and by various copyists, scribes in Ethiopian monasteries who, while copying the manuscripts of the Synaxarium would add passages concerning regional and national holidays, along with traditions of famous saints, especially founders or heads of the various monasteries and convents.

Acts of the Apostles *(an apocryphal work)*

From the end of the 14th century comes a translation of the apocryphal *Acts of the Apostles*, a collection of traditions and legends on the preaching and martyrdom of the apostles (e.g., the voyage of St. Matthias in the land of the cannibals and the preaching of St. Thomas in India.) The stories have been expanded by successive Ethiopian modifications traditions.

Acts of the Martyrs

From about the same period there comes a translation of a collection of the *Acts of the Martyrs*, especially of the saints venerated in the Coptic and Eastern Christianity. The *Acts of Martyr St. Basilides* is dated 1397. The translator was an Egyptian monk named Simeon, of the convent of St. Anthony. This same monk translated the major work of the *Synaxarium*, a collection of brief narrations and lives of the saints, intended to be read each day of the year and on the occasion of a particular feast day of the Ethiopian thirteen months of year, substituting the Ethiopian names of months for the Coptic ones.

In short, according to Cerulli, the spread of Arab-Christian hagiographic writings of the second half of the 14th century profoundly influenced Ethiopian literature. He claims it provoked a rich flowering of Ethiopian hagiographic writings intended to exalt, or at least make known, the main persons venerated in Ethiopia, and to preserve their example and memory. It should be noted, however, that scholars like Cerullis often tend to exaggerate the magnitude of such outside influence.

The Writing of the 15th Century:
The Age of Zär'a Ya'aqob (1434-68)

Beginning in the 15th century, a new literary period begins and extends through the first decades of the 16th century. This period is named after the major Ethiopian sovereign of that time, Emperor Zara Ya'aqob (1434-68).

From the 15th century we have the hagiographic legends, the cycle of the "Acts" of the dauntless holy monks who were fearlessly challenged the royal authority. These works include the 15th century life history of very courageous antagonists of Emperor Amda Sion. In these writings, we find not the young, brave warrior Amda Sion, struggling in mortal combat for his Christian faith, as in the *Zena or Chronicle of Wars of Amda Sion*, but rather the autocrat who, adulated by the complacent clergy of his court, resists and attacks repressively the holy monks who defend the firm principles of their spiritual independence. The holy monks openly accuse the Emperor of marital misconduct. We see Emperor Amda Sion, and later his son and successor, Saifa Arad, who were involved in a serious disagreement with the powerful Abbots of the monasteries. Through their spiritual, cultural, and political influence, they impose their views, inspired by a greater observance of religious precepts. One such example of the cause of conflict between the religious leaders and the Emperor, although based on a custom already existing in southern Ethiopia, violently offended the Christian sentiments of monks and exacerbated their antagonism. The discord was based on the differences in outlook between the monastic holy monks and the clergy, including court clergy, who were closely allied with the Egyptian Metropolitan head of the Church. The latter were necessarily more accommodating to the wishes of the sovereign, and were therefore more favored by the political powers, whereas the former were ruled by their spiritual mandate.

This state of affairs came to be recorded in a cycle of *gadls*, *Acts* or stories of "great deeds" of individual saints and the monks who were the main hero or central character of the conflict. The writings are full of polemic vigor, typically representative of the austere and uncompromising attitude of the monks, described in clear, sharp, and simple prose. In the subsequent successive transmissions of the *Acts* occur a phenomenon already familiar in hagiographic writings. That is, here and there, other episodes are added, intensifying and amplifying the marvelous aspects of the stories, linking the life of one of these saints with that of others of the same cycle, and emphasizing the greater importance of the former's actions and powers. Thus analogous or identical episodes are attributed to one or the other of the central character of the various acts, sometimes making it difficult to see to which of these persons the episodes were attributed earliest.

Other motives characterized in the narrative of the *Acts* are the simony of the Metropolitan friend of Amda Sion, the calumnies of the clergy of the Court against the saintly monks, the accusation of polygamy in the successive conflict against Emperor Saifa Arad who took three wives, the taking of the veil by the daughter of the Emperor without his consent, the date of the celebration of Christmas. The description of these motives is followed by analogous scenes that, with variations, represent the dialogue between the Emperor and the holy monk, and the sufferings of the holy monk at the hands of the sovereign.

Five Gadles or Great Deeds/ Acts of Holy Monks

There are five *gadles* or "stories of great deeds" in the cycle, made up of the following five works so far found in the various collections of manuscripts in European libraries. 1. *Gadla Philippos* or *Acts of Philip*, the third abbot of the monastery of Dabra Libanos of Shoa, was written in the first years of the 15th century (one manuscript is dated 1424-1425). In this work, some parallels are made between the famed deeds of Philip and those of St. Takla Haimanot, founder of the monastery. 2. *Gadla Ba-salota Mikael* or *Acts of Ba-salota Michael*, abbot of Dabra Gol in Amara, who lived in the second half of the 13th and first half of the 14th century, is attributed to the authorship of a 15th century monk from the same monastery. 3. *Gadla Samuel Za-Dabra Wagag* or *Acts of Samuel*, abbot of Dabra Wagag in southeast Shoa, was written several years after Philip's. Abba Samuel was a contemporary of King Dawit I (1382-1411), but the author himself, or a later scribe inserted an episode of a conflict with Emperor Amda Sion I (1314-1344) in the first part of the *Acts*. 4. *Gadla Honorios* or *Acts of Honorius*, abbot of the Shoan monastery of Segajia, who died in 1374. The *Acts* was composed by Cyril, abbot of the same monastery, in 1478. 5. The *Acts of Aaron Taumaturg*, abbot of Dabra Daret in Baghemeder, who lived in second half of 14th century seems to be the most recent of the group.

Cerulli gives three passages characteristic of the literary themes of these works: the dramatically moving style of a story from the *Acts of Philip*, the scandal regarding Emperor Amda Sion, who had married his father's wife. Abba Philippos criticizes the Emperor for this scandal to his face, and stands firm in the face of his public chastisement. Likewise, Abba Ba-salota Michael criticizes the Emperor and his supporter, the Metropolitan, to their face; he is then put in chains and exiled. Finally the simple and ingenious narrative "Samuel meets King Dawit I," in which Samuel, favored by the king, is declared to be the saintliest of all.

The Za'gue Tradition

The acts or great deeds of the kings of the Zagwe Dynasty of Lasta (c.950-1270), is another group of writings about the lives of the kings who are venerated as saints. They come to us from the 15th century, nearly two hundred years after the Zagwe had lost the throne. Their capital city of Roha that later came to be known as Lalibala is today famed for its famous monolithic rock churches, the important complex of buildings and monuments of Ethiopia, now rightly classified among the great wonders of the world.

The most well-known of these acts of the kings and of a queen of the Za'gwe Dynasty are the *Acts of Lalibala, Acts of Na'akueto La-Ab, Acts of Yemerhanna Krestos, and Acts of Maskal Kebra,* (Maskal Kebra is Lalibala's wife.) We find a replication of episodes among these biographies. For example, both Lalibala and Na'akueto La-Ab threatened to divert the course of the Nile to protect the Copts, the Christians of Egypt. Also, it is repeated in three of the acts that the heir to the throne is not the son of the ruling king, but of the king's brother, or that it is prophesied he would not be the direct descendant. This often resulted in persecution by the sovereign of his nephew, as it happened to Lalibela, Na'akueto La-Ab and Yemerhanna Krestos. At the end of the account, in all three cases, the king voluntarily renounces the throne in favor of the nephew.

Other similar themes include the sovereign's visit to Heaven, guided by an Angel (Acts of Lalibela and Na'akueto La-Ab) and the choice of a wife made directly by the Lord, who has it announced by an Angel (Acts of Maskal Kebra). Such replications create a certain degree of uniformity or monotony, describing events and people of a distant time in less colorful and emotional ways than reports of contemporary events. Cerulli gives examples from the Acts of the Zagwe cycle: "King Lalibela bids farewell to his wife and departs for a pilgrimage to Jerusalem" ; "The Angel brings to Lalibela the divine order to marry Maskal Chebra"; and "The prophecy of the reign of Yemerhanna Krestos and the persecution by the King his uncle".

The Cycle of Monastic Founders: Acts of Iyasus Moa *and* Acts of Takla Haymanot

In the *Acts of Philip of Dabra Libanos*, while enhancing the fame of that abbot, risked obscuring the fame of the founder, Takla Haimanot. Thus, at the initiative of the monks of Dabra Libanos, we have the *Acts of Takla Haymanot*, written in two versions. The better-known is the version of 1515, when Abuna Petros was abbot; the second, called "Waldebbagna" after the monasteries of the Waldebba region in northwest Ethiopia, where it was compiled, seems to have been written after the reign of Yeshak (1414-1429) or possibly in the 16ᵗʰ century.

According to Cerulli, a confluence of two situations exists in these two Acts. Several events became common to the *Acts of Philip* and *Acts of Takla Haymanot*, including the nomination to the bishopric for both of them and the election of twelve disciples, later abbots of many monasteries united with that of Dabra Libanos which came to supercede that of Hayq. But even greater was the assimilation with respect to the acts of the founder of the rival monastery of St. Stephen of Haik, that is, the abbot Iyesus Moa. The greatest glory of Ethiopian monachism in relation to the State is the tradition that the restoration of the Salomonid dynasty in 1270 was effected essentially because of decisive intervention of a holy abbot. In *Acts of Iyasus Moa*, this abbot is himself, but in Takla Haymanot's, the abbot is he, and the events in the two accounts are analogous. In the *Acts of Iyasus Moa*, he meets and becomes a disciple of abbot Yohannes of the monastery of Dabra Damo in the Tigre; later Takla Haymanot attributes the same encounter to himself and illustrates the supremacy first of the monastery of St. Stephen and later that of Dabra Libanos over the convents of the Tigrai.

The *Acts of Iyasus Moa* (in the present form) is of the second half of the 15th century, a little earlier than that of Takla Haymanot. The *Acts of Iyasus Moa* has the usual introduction in rhymed prose, but also includes passages in candid, simple monastic prose. Cerulli gives an example of this: "Iyasus Moa, dying, blesses the monks of St. Stephen" (p. 74). A new good translation of the *Acts of Iyasus Moa* into the Amharic languages has recently been published by His Grace Abuna Atenatewos, Archbishop of the Wollo region where Lake Haik is found. The translation also includes the *Acts of Abba Bula* and *Abba Brtenewos*.

According to Cerulli, parallel to the movement of the exaltation of the founders of the powerful monasteries of the south there developed in northern Ethiopia a literary activity celebrating the glories of the convents of the Tigrai region and the lives of the founding saints (p. 75). He claims that acts of most of these *Tes'atu Qeddusan* or the Nine Saints, monks who came to Ethiopia in the sixth century from Syria of the then Byzantine Empire, were composed about the same period. However, we know that a strong tradition already existed in the north, where the Nine Saints were active and had been venerated. Whether the tradition about these saints existed only in oral tradition until the 15ᵗʰ century, as Cerulli implies, cannot be proven. He thinks so because he claims there are in these hagiographies episodes of pure fantasy or work of imagination, with only a vague recollection of a remote event, because nine centuries had elapsed from the actual period of their lifetime and activities till the date of the composition of their *Lives*. It is difficult to agree with Cerulli on this and to believe that some written but lost versions of the lives of the Nine Saints did not exist from the earlier active literary period.

The most important works of the cycle of the nine saints and their contemporaries, and the most diffuse, are the following: the *Acts of Za-Michael -Abba Aragawi* (with introduction in rhymed prose), founder of the convent of Dabra Damo; *Acts of Abba Libanos* (also called Mata); the *Acts of Abba Garima* and those of *Acts of Abba Pantaleone*. Regarding the latter, Cerulli claims without proof that the authors must be the Egyptian Metropolitan Yeshaq and the Bishop Yahannes, who had come to Ethiopia in the last decades of the fifteenth century. He basis this on what he claims to be a tradition that these foreign prelates compiled, or directed the compilation of, a first version of the *Lives* that were later rendered in good style by writers of local monasteries.

There also exist briefer versions of the *Acts of Abba Afse*, and of the *Life of Os of Cuezara*, a fragment found in a Paris manuscript of the *Book of Miracles of Mary*. Cerulli gives an example from this cycle: "The vision of hell and paradise in the *Acts of Os of Cuezara*."

The Acts of the Saints of the South: Acts of Gabra Manfas Keddus and John of the East

The hagiographic literature, which in the cycle of the nine saints was strongly given to imagination, corresponds to analogous biographic works of saints of southern Ethiopia. An example of these hagiographies are the *Life of St. Gabra Manfas Keddus*, founder of the mountain monastery of Zukuala in Shoa, long a bastion of Christianity against (p. 78) Islam in southern Ethiopia. The legend of the holy hermit, who lives among lions and leopards in the Egyptian desert and then arrives in Ethiopia carried by a celestial flying vehicle along with his lions and leopards, a rather colorful portrayal of imagination. To this same group belong the Acts of *Yohannes Mesrakawi*, John of the East, an apostle of Manz, northern Shoa, who is also known as John of Sagaro (Sagarus?) after the monastery founded by him. His *Acts* also concern a foreign monk who emigrated to Ethiopia, but less fanciful in their narration of legends. Cerulli gives as an example an authentic fable of animals concerning the fight of St. John of the East with the dragon.

The *Acts of Krestos Samra*, the mother of peace, comes from the last years of the fifteenth century. It is a very important work not only for the local history of the region of Lake Tana, Saint Krestos Samra, founder of the Convent in Guangut, island in that lake, lived, but also for the information it has about the extremely severe ascetic practices of those nuns, including being buried alive intentionally for several days. It is equally an important reflection on the severe religio-political conflicts of the period. The hagiography is characteristic of both the literature and religious psychology of the time. Most of the narration concerns the visions of a holy nun and emphasizes the almost physical relations she has with the supernatural world.

The Miracles of Mary *or* Ta'amra Maryam

This work is one of the most important and among the most typical works of Ethiopic literature. According to Cerulli, its origins and development are concrete proof of the adoption of Western Christian elements in Ethiopian culture and of their gradual, eventually total assimilation. More specifically, we find examples for the general history of medieval culture and for the rapport between East and West, that of the Latin Middle Ages.

According to Cerulli, this type of hagiography of miracles began to develop in France, toward mid-12th century, in reaction to the terrible epidemic that devastated the French provinces in 1128-1129. There were several collections of narrations of the *Miracles of Mary,* especially those associated with the Marian sanctuaries and pilgrimages of Laon, Soissons, Coutances, and Rocamadour. They became diffuse throughout France and in the Anglo-Norman realm. Soon anthologies were composed comprising of the most popular stories that soon spread throughout Europe, from Iceland to Germany,

Spain to Hungary, transmitted in Latin or in the other languages, in prose or verse. Many new stories, referring to miracles in other lands, especially Italy, were added with substitutions and adaptations that were made. Thus from the 12th to the 14th century, a vast tradition of stories, legends, and traditions developed in the compilation of miracle stories. Later on, some of greatest poets and artists derived inspiration and subject matter from them.

According to Cerulli, one of these collections, probably in French, was translated into Arabic in the Latin East between 1237 and 1289. The oldest Arabic manuscript so far identified is from 1289. The Arabic translation then passed from Palestine to the Coptic Church in Egypt. In the East (Syria, Palestine, Egypt), as in western Europe, local stories in honor of various sanctuaries were added and inserted in the large collection, which became an ever-richer combination of western and eastern traditions.

Cerulli argues that at end of the 14th century, in the reign of Dawit I (1382-1411), such a compilation of miracle stories, *Ta'amra Maryam,* was translated from Arabic to Ethiopic. Just like in the East, in Ethiopia it was enlarged with other accounts from local history and traditions. Thus, *Ta'amra Maryam* preserves for us a very important evidence of events, especially of the 15th century, including passages of Ethiopian works that have not survived directly in their original form. Moreover, Cerulli argues the stories translated from Arabic, especially the European ones, were altered in later editions (p. 83) becoming more and more "Ethiopicized", sometimes with the addition of new persons and details. These stories often acquired greater literary value when accompanied by intense fervor of devotion and constant inspiration, especially when contrasted with the first and oldest version (the straight translation from Arabic), with its generally more rigid style.

The various collections of miracle stories are numerous. The actual number varies in the different manuscripts because the choice of stories has varied among all the writers, copyists, and editors. A small number of these manuscripts (in the British Museum, Florence, Leningrad, etc.) have been studied or published in their entirety by a few scholars. The tendency to uniformity is greater in Ethiopia. Already during the reign of Zär'a Ya'aqob (1434-1468) readings from works of miracle stories were prescribed in church during ceremonies in honor of Mary. This custom was adhered to even more strictly than in Egypt. Only later, toward the mid-17th century, did a canonical series of stories appear in Ethiopia, numbering 33 in all. But, whereas in Egypt only the approved collection is represented from then on in the Arab manuscripts, in Ethiopia (because of great autonomy of widely scattered monasteries and strong regional sentiment) the canonical series of 33 is copied along with many other stories as well (p. 85). In fact, perhaps for the first time, miniaturists began to illustrate the 33 stories in Gondar (then capital of Ethiopia). It then became customary in the capital and in provincial monasteries to decorate the works of miracle stories in the Gondarine style with miniatures of the 33 stories that constantly appear at the beginning of manuscripts.

The Stories of the European Cycles: Spain, Italy, and France

In Spain, at least three groups of *Miracles* exist—those of Toledo, Oviedo, and Santiago of Compostella. The Toledo group mainly exalts St. Ildefonse, famed as the defender of Mary and for his role in a miracle with her. This latter was included in the European *Miracles* as well as in works of art from medieval miniaturists till Velasquez, Nurillo and Luca Giordano (p. 86). It is in fact the first in a series of stories in many medieval manuscripts. The Ethiopian canonic collection opens with the story of St. Ildefonse.

The largest group of Italian stories concerns Rome and the prodigies in the various churches of medieval Rome. It is a new and convincing example of the diffusion of medieval Roman traditions in the Christian East. Here we can also trace the successive assimilations in Ethiopia. The first components of *Miracles* were the French collections concerning the sanctuaries of Laon, Soissons, Rocamadour, and the abbey of Mont-Saint-Michel. These collections were also adapted into Ethiopian tradition.

The Eastern Additions to Miracle Story Books:
Syria, Palestine, Egypt and Ethiopia

To the above stories were added, in the Ethiopian woks, other narrations of wonders from the Latin East to eastern Africa, successively entered various countries.

In Syria there existed chiefly the stories concerning the sanctuary of St. Mary of Saidnaia near Damascus. This group had already passed from Syria to Europe via the Crusaders. Various stories of the Ethiopian *Miracles* occur in Palestine as well, mostly in Jerusalem or Bethlehem (p. 88). From Egypt come the most numerous of the eastern stories in the Ethiopian *Miracles*. There are many groups, but the richest one with the most artistically vivacious stories refers to the convent of St. Samuel of Kalamon in Fayyum. As usual, at end of a story about a certain angel, a long digression has been added in the Ethiopic *Miracles*, discussing the nature of angels.

In Ethiopia, the narrations of Saidnaia were so popular that in the 15th century the feast of that sanctuary was celebrated annually. Also, at least three different versions of the wonders of Saidnaia are in the Book of Miracles. In Ethiopia, the stories refer solely to the reigns of Dawit I and his son Zär'a Ya'aqob. After 1468, the date of Zär'a Ya'aqob's death, no other Ethiopian event has been recorded in the *Miracles of Mary* (p. 89), establishing precisely the chronology of the composition. These stories are doubly valuable to us because first, they mention historic facts not otherwise known, and secondly, they reflect artistically the immediate impressions of the writer because they were often written close to the time of the actual event discussed.

Cerulli gives several passages from this fundamental work, including the story of the "missed inheritance" in Cesarius of Heisterbach (Latin). As told in simple Latin by Cesarius of Heisterbach in Germany circa 1237, it serves as a first useful example of this type of composition (p. 90). In comparison, the Ethiopian version (in the Shoan tradition of the monastery of Dabra Libanos) was enlarged and altered for more lively contrast among the characters. The event itself was also made more complex. The story includes a money-hungry priest and his eventual punishment and a pious deacon who gives communion to a dying woman and is rewarded with a great vision of the Virgin Mary.

Literary transmission of these narrations was not inert and mechanical. Rather, the translation becomes the point of departure for successive proficiencies and at times artistic imaginations of the elaborators. In all these transformations, a vibrant faith gives the Ethiopian *Miracles* a singular power of suggestion. Another comparison can be drawn between the simple prose of Cesarius and the strophes in troubadour style and courtly manner in which (a few decades after Cesarius) King Alfonse the Wise of Castile rendered in Galician [Cerulli:

"gallego"] the scene of a deacon coming to a dying woman and seeing the Virgin Mary at her bedside. The initial theme recurs variously in the East as in the West, leading to the sometimes great artistic inspiration of major poets who transmitted this large medieval repertoire.

The story of the "One Mass", regarding the very pious priest of Mary who is accused but miraculously saved by Mary when he doesn't know how to celebrate any Mass but hers is very diffuse. This story is very popular in western collections, even in the legend of St. Thomas Becket of Canterbury. Transmitted into Arabic and then into Ethiopic, it had still other alterations in the East; and its motif of the "only Mass" was combined with other motifs for greater interest.

Cerulli gives the oldest Ethiopian text we have (beginning of the 15th century) and the story from the Italian book of *Miracles* (of the 14th century). The first part of these two texts survives according to Cerulli in its oldest state in the form in which it was introduced in Ethiopia as soon as it was translated, and as it was preserved in the simple form of 14th-century Italy. The first part of the story, limited to the essentials in the two simple texts, becomes complex in two embellished versions: the more recent Ethiopian one and the one in verses of the *Recueil Lyonnais* of the second half of the 13th century in langue d'oil influenced by Franco-Provencal dialect.

The Story of the Ethiopian Prince Confined on a Mountain

To the above stories from medieval Latin, in the Ethiopia *Miracles*, some narratives of the history of the land were added (information that otherwise we would have lost). The stories reproduce effectively the atmosphere in which known historic events unfolded, giving a novel impression of the Ethiopian environment of the early 15th century. It was an Ethiopian custom of the Middle Ages that the young princes of the reigning dynasty (at least those closest in line of succession) be held on an *amba* or steep mountain top, under the command of an official trusted by the sovereign. This stern measure, aimed at avoiding palace conspiracies and internal disorders is the motif of the story, showing how between the guard and the guarded agreements and assurances could be made which temporarily sweetened the daily life on the mountain of the confined.

In Ethiopian narration of this type, which refers to a contemporary sovereign and exposes possibly unpleasant facts, the names of the sovereign, his predecessor, and the princes are omitted. But according to Cerulli, it is likely that in the story the oldest prince who advises and guides the two frightened young princes is the one who later becomes the ruler Zär'a Ya'aqob, and who then (according to the story) keeps his promises to the kindly guard or governor of the mountain (p. 98). Another interesting story in the Ethiopian *Miracles* is one about "the thirsty dog and the Virgin Mary" that shows the spirit of the kindest pity. (Cerulli quotes the Shoan version of Dabra Libanos.)

Emperor Zär'a Ya'aqob and Works Attributed to Him

The extensive literature that Cerulli and others attribute to Emperor Zär'a Ya'aqob (1434-68) relates more to the difficult events and activities of his life and reign. He ascended the throne in 1434, after long confinement on the mountain. As Emperor, he had to confront the terrible problem of restoring political stability and religious unity of the State, in particular the schism caused by the Stephanites and the Michaelites as well as the Moslem uprisings in the south.

Whether he personally wrote them, or whether they were compiled under his direction, the works attributed to him give the impression of ambiance and his personal reactions. Of these writing, we have *Mashafa Berhan*, the *Book of Light*, and *Mashafa Milad*, the Book of the Nativity, which are vast theological compilations containing some repetitions and duplications. The works deal with exhortations to the people against practices hostile to the throne; rules against local customs considered by the king to be contrary to Christian Ethiopian law; strict laws against magical practices and non-Christian cults. They focus on long confutations of supposed heresies of the Stephanites and Michaelites.

These two books and two minor works, the *Book of Essence* and the *Custody of the Sacrament*, are inspired by a tradition in which the Ethiopian sovereign decides on all matters of the Ethiopian Church and its doctrines. For instance, in the *Custody of the Sacrament*, the king establishes the number of lashes he must inflict on himself in case of negligence in the custody of the Eucharist in royal chapels. The tone of the discourses is often oratorical, the style sometimes complicated. They reflect the rigorous, meticulous, detailed character of the works. According to Cerulli, in these books as well as in his chronicle, *Zena Zär'a Ya'aqob*, (written after his death by a priest who lived at his court), we see how the frequency of plots (for instance, Patriarch John, a palace plot and excommunication) described in *Mashafa Berhan*) and oppositions against him made Zär'a Ya'aqob a distrustful and suspicious person. His distrust was reflected in his very strict measures, especially against the princes of his family and dignitaries of his court.

In the preface to *Mashafa Milad, Book of the Nativity*, Zär'a Ya'aqob himself seems to describe the punishments he inflicted on traitors who were plotting to burn some volumes of *Mashafa Milād* and the *Mashafa Berhan*. The respective punishments of two men, one who had caused many people to be killed, the other who had committed various evils, including adultery, are detailed in "the plots of two dignitaries of the court" found in the Zena Zär'a Ya'aqob.

In 1439, an Ethiopian delegation attended the historic the Council of Florence (1439-1441). This is described in the "The letter of Abbot Nicodemus to Pope Eugene IV" and concerns the Ethiopian mission which was sent to the Council by Nicodemus, Prior of the Ethiopian community of Jerusalem. The letter is characteristic of the life and writings of this period of Ethiopian history. Nicodemus complies with the decision to establish contact with the European Catholic Church; at the same time, he had to leave every important and concrete decision to his sovereign, whom he eulogizes and compliments, and to the Church authorities in Ethiopia, with promises to send to Ethiopia the same mission when it returns from Florence. He also refers to the danger of the journey to Ethiopia through what he sees as hostile Moslem Egypt, but exalts the hard-hitting power of the Zär'a Ya'aqob for protection.

Chapter VII: The 15th century: age of Zär'a Ya'aqob: Poetry

During this period, poetry also develops in a manner analogous to what we have seen in the 14th century, and reflects upon traditional, technical ability of expression.

The martial "chant in honor of King Yishaq" (1414-1429) is, according to Cerulli, one of the most beautiful of Ethiopian poems. It is the unrefined and simple poetry of soldiers, lacking conventional schemes but re-echoing ancient poetic motifs expressing sincere feelings. This poem or song moves through successive images that overlap without confusion or repetition, because each is incisively concrete. The terror which the king inspires in his enemies returns like a refrain with variations to unite the various parts of the song. The mention of the king's terrifying face, an obsessively repeated motif, animates the sense of fearful exaltation which the poem reflects.

Religious poetry: "God has reigned" (Egzi'abher Nagsa) Collection

Perhaps less impressive than the war poetry is the religious poetry, the principal example of which is the collection of hymns supposedly composed by Za'ra Ya'acob's order. According to Cerulli, these hymns no longer have the vivacity and dramatic sense of the hymns of the preceding century. They are written in a stylistically correct form, giving a rather cold impression, whether because of the quality of the artist, the necessity for caution in treating religious matters, or the large number of citations and paraphrases of biblical passages. (Cerulli gives the beginning of "Hymn for Christmas", and "Hymn for the Presentation of the Virgin", as well as "Hymn for the Martyrs of Najiran".

The *Arganona Maryam* or *Harp of Mary* is a collection of religious praises and beatitudes. The work is believed to be composed by George the Armenian by Za'ra Ya'cob's order. The praises imitate the Bible in form, verse, as well as content. The *Harp* is a precursor of other later works, in which paraphrases of passages of Scripture constitute the main, if not the only, content of the work".

In the 15th century we also see the first kind of Ethiopian poetry that later became diffuse, with the kind of ancient language that is still cultivated today. It is now called *qene* which, in particular, was strictly enclosed in schemes that had become traditional, constituting an authentic hermetic poetry, the aim of which is reserved for the understanding of a few initiates. A proverbial saying states: "The *qene* to its author, the creature to his Creator".

These first examples of *qene* are not yet very elaborate. The language and doctrine are based on the use of simple biblical citations. The two oldest *qene* so far identified are from the reign of Negus Eskender (1478-1494). The first refers to the punishment to which the king had condemned several Stephanite heretics, and the second, to the threatened punishment of a rebel who had tried to seize the throne during the restless reign of Eskender. Despite their limitations, the poetry of this period preserves a tradition of strong language that we have seen _ apart from the court poetry _ in the martial poems of this same period.

The Literary Tradition of the Post-Ahmad Gran Invasion of the 16th Century

The 16th century conflict or *jihad* in Ethiopia led by Imam Ahmad bin Ibrahim al-Ghazi, popularly known as Ahmad Gran or the Left handed had lasting consequences in the history and literary tradition of Ethiopia, because of the destruction and impoverishment caused by the conflict. But a large volume of the works composed during the first period of the Salomonids survived. The Ethiopian national literary tradition of creativity was not interrupted, even in the dangerous decades of the 16th century, and even if the historic crisis directly influenced literary and artistic expressions. In a sense, the sufferings even contributed to creativity. Both Moslem and Christian Ethiopia were affected by the suffering. Still, both used Ethiopian languages in their writings, and even when, in the south, Arabic was also used, the writer was still an Ethiopian, tied to the tradition of his region. In the description of the invasion, the patriotic sentiments of the writers are now exalted. Even the humble chronicler with his meager, cold notes can change from a rhetorical tone to sincere, fervid, vibrant emotion.

Numerous foreign writings of the sixteenth, seventeenth, and early eighteenth centuries such as Jeronimo Lobo's, *A Voyage to Abyssinia*, Pedro Paez's, *Historia da Ethiopia*, Baltazar Téllez's, *The Travels of the Jesuits in Ethiopia*, contribute to our understanding of Ethiopian history and culture. One of the most interesting is *Futuh al-Habasa, The History of the Conquests of Abyssinia,* written by the chronicler Sihab ad-Din Ahmad bin 'Abd al-Qader b. Salim b. Uthman, known as Arab Faqih. This is an important dramatic eyewitness account of several of the tragic battles of the early sixteenth century.

There is little echo in Ethiopian literature of Portugese military exploits, except for a passage in the *Zena Galawdewos* or *Chronicle of King Claudius,* a celebration of the military valor of the Portuguese within the limits imposed on the chronicler by his work, primarily written to exalt his own king who died in a war against the Moslems. According to Cerulli, the Portuguese undertaking under da Gama facilitated rapport with the west and the Holy See, prepared the mission of the Jesuits, and contributed to Ethiopian cultural history, one the one hand, and on the other, the Moslems of the south intensified their rapport with Arab lands like Yemen and Turkey, and in general with the Moslem world.

Zena Galawedewos *or The Chronicle of Claudius in Ethiopic*

This chronicle is written either by a churchman or another member of the court. According to Cerulli it strongly influenced by Arab language and culture, because his Ethiopic has frequent "arabisms" but with numerous biblical references. It is a little panegyric where a less conventional account might have been expected (as in the heroic death of the Emperor). This is probably because of the necessity for a royal chronicler to adhere to certain rules and tastes of the official sources that commissioned his work. Cerulli gives one major passage from each of the above works, (in the same order): "The Emir Omar is killed by surprise (caught off guard)"; the Killing of Emir Addole" (by ambush); "King Claudius courageously faces sad prophecies" (of his death in battle). This last is one of the best passages from the Zena.

Anqasa Amin, *The Gate of Faith*

This interesting work is by a certain Enbaqom, an Arab author who had emigrated to Ethiopia and converted to Christianity and took the name Enbaqom. After his conversion, he became a monk and was subsequently appointed Abbot of Dabra Libanos, and head of Ethiopian monasticism. His work is a Christian apologetic text in relation to Islam. The frequent respective victory and defeat of Christians and Moslems also led to respective conversions as described in the respective Chronicles: for example, the Christian point of view is represented in the *Chronicle of Gelawdewos,* the Moslem in the *History of Conquests of Abyssinia.* This reciprocal situation made necessary works on the defense of Christianity. One such work is Mashafa Kedar, the *Book of Impurity,* which dictates the rituals of penitence for apostates who turn from Islam to Christianity. In apologetics, one of the most interesting works of Ethiopic literature is *Anqasa Amin* or the *Gate of Faith*. The work was originally composed in Arabic but translated into Ethiopic. It is written as a lively apology for Christianity against Islam, with a method then common in similar works, using predominantly passages from the Qur'an to demonstrate the truth of the Christian faith. For example, the motif of the antithesis of the Gospel's message and of the comparative teachings of the Muslim Prophet shows Enbaqom's genuine blind faith and conversion to Christianity, although his polemic ability causes him to distort some passages of the Qur'an. His defense of the cult of images is done with clarity and force. More rambling is an apology of the dogma of the Trinity; the comparisons used to explain it and to refute the accusation of polytheism well-argued, if sometimes simple or inspired by tradition than by reason.

Gadla Takla Alfa - Acts of Takla Alfa

The *Acts of Takla Alfa* by a contemporary Ethiopian writer describes the devastation of Christian Ethiopia during the invasion and the misery of life in Christian Ethiopia during these decades of war. The author was an abbot of the monastery of Dabra Dima in Gojjam, during the years of the invasion. His autobiography and the anecdotes collected in his miracles depict in a candid, ingenious, and effective manner the troubles of the Ethiopian religious communities forced to flee here and there during those years. Cerulli describes how monastic discipline suffered in his "Flights, Refuges, and Tribulations of Monks" during the invasion".

The Book of Duties on the Truths of Islam

During and immediately after the Gran invasion, literature in ancient Harari, and Ethipian Semitic language, written for the first time in Arabic characters appear along such literature as the *History of Conquests of Abyssinia*. One such work, a small book called the *Book of Duties* written in ancient Harari, a Semitic Ethiopian language, describes the truths of Islam. The truths of the Muslim faith are described in a large part using moral maxims and popular proverbs, the type that are still current among Somali and Oromo peoples, using "Proverbs in three", bound three by three in mnemonic formulas, aphorisms that are sometimes humorous. Also in this Book, we find in Ethiopia the other popular method of questions and answers in the manner of catechism. Cerulli thinks that this Book is a good example of the methods by which Moslem Ethiopian literature tried to reach the less educated.

Another ancient Harari work, called, *Song of the Four Caliphs* (*za-harat khalifat kasada*) is a long poem of almost 5000 verses divided into "monorhymed" quatrains, according to the strophic scheme, also inspired by popular poetry. In the song are alternating strophes praising the four orthodox Caliphs of Sunni Islam (with the rule that each of the four verses of the quatrain celebrates one of the Califs, and strophes exalting the Prophet and doctrines of Islam).

History of the Kings or History of the Combatant

Written by the chronicler, Abu Bakr ibn Mohammed Shanbal Ba Alwi, in the second half of the 16th century, it describes the terrible effect the war had on the Muslims as well as their post-war misery. This work and related compilations that have been found can help us to trace the history of Muslim Ethiopia from the 13th to the 17th century. In "Famine and raids in Moslem Ethiopia", Cerulli describes the sad condition of Muslim Ethiopia after the great struggle with the Christian State.

Zenahu za-Galla *or* History of the Galla

According to Cerulli, the motif of this small but interesting book or pamphlet, attributed to a monk of the court of Emperor Malak Sagad, Abba Bahrey, who wrote in the second half of the 16th century, is a document concerning the history and ethnic structure of the Oromo, called Galla in the pamphlet and Cerulli. Although Cerulli says it concerns the period of the Gran invasion, he also claims the work shows an uncommon, even unique, curiosity for the history of this people and for their political institutions: Bahrey discusses the ten classes of the Ethiopian population, of which only the tenth actually goes to war, and contrasts this system to the "Galla", among whom everyone, young and old, is trained for war.

Cerulli claims that although Bahrey's "history" is simple in form, it overcomes the usual limitations of chronicles, that is, 'the author is not afraid to confront the problem of the motive for those successes, and does so not in the usual fatalistic way of chroniclers, but by discussing the institutions of the two peoples, Ethiopic and "Galla"'. The passage Cerulli cites "Why the Galla are successful" is inspired by the historical partition into bands of good and bad monks in the Ethiopian Rule of Pacomius, but within the old formal and jealously guarded tradition the Ethiopian writer has instilled, with caution, attention to detail and a certain gentle and sly irony, his own ideas. This method renders his own ideas more acceptable, and is a typical phenomenon of this literature.

The importance of this so called *History of the Galla* by Abba Bahrey has been exaggerated by Cerulli and others. For one thing, it is not a history book but a pseudo-anthropological pamphlet. It is not about the history and culture of the Oromo peoples, a vast and wide spread ancient population that form the backbone of the Horn of Africa and the Ethiopian nation, but the monk's limited observation about a local branch of the peoples. It is a work that is being regarded now by the Oromo as a superficial and controversial work.

Fifteen and Sixteenth Centuries

During both the expansion and internal reform of the Ethiopic State in the 15th century, and in the troubled period of the Gran invasion, translating other Christian literary works to Ethiopic continued. Here too, whatever the ultimate original language, the common Ethiopic source was the Arabic Christian literary version and it inspired new methods in literary art. For the influence they had on the formation of the writers of this and successive periods (inasmuch as literary activity continued to be centered mainly in monasteries), Cerulli notes the *Masahefta Manakuosat* or the Books of the Monks. Among these, three books still considered fundamental for the religious education of monks are by Syrian writers. The first, the ascetic writings of John Saba collected in Ethiopia as The Spiritual Old Man, the second, Isaac of Niniveh's treatise, The Blessed Isaac or *Mar Yeshak* are both by writers are or the 6th century A.D. The third book is a questionnaire on monastic life, written shortly before John Saba by Philoxenus of Mabbogh, a new version of a work already translated into Ethiopic at the end of the 14th century.

Cerulli also includes among these the two Epistles of Timothy Elurus (the Cat), anti-Chalcedonian Patriarch of Alexandria (457-477 A.D.), not because of any real literary value, but because it's a new literary element in the religious history of Ethiopia. The Epistles contain a selection of passages from various Greek and Latin Fathers, which entered Ethiopia in this form as well as with the adaptations that Timothy Elurus and his successive translators brought to them. This brief collection of passages of the Fathers of Church (explained in a way favorable to the "Miaphysite" doctrine) was followed in the 16th century by a larger anthology in Arabic, entitled Confession of the Fathers, and in Ethiopic Faith of the Fathers-*Haymanota Abaw*. They include an ample selection of passages of homilies, pastoral letters, and various writings on the mysteries of the Trinity and of the Incarnation as support for the doctrine professed by the Coptic Church of Egypt. From the 16th century to the present, this book has been an important source of knowledge of patristic and post-patristic literature in Ethiopic schools, not only together with the ancient translation of St. Cyril, but in fact even more commonly than that earlier book, and because it figured in the theological disputes of the 16th and 17th centuries.

Barlaam & Yosaphat

Scholars believe that this is a Christianized story of one of the legends of the Buddha. It is said that many Indians were converted to Christianity by the Apostle St. Thomas in early Christian times. In the 3rd century, astrologers prophesied that the king Abener's son, Yosaphat, would one day convert to Christianity. In spite of his father's confinement to protect him from conversion, Yosaphat met a hermit called Barlaam and converted to Christianity. Later the king himself became a Christian and then even a hermit. Yosaphat became king, but he too later abandoned the throne and went into the desert, found his former teacher Barlaam with whom he spent the rest of his life as a holy ascetic.

The *Book of Barlaam and Josaphat* was diffuse in the western and eastern literatures in the Middle Ages, spreading from India through Georgia to the European West. The work is believed to have been translated into Ethiopic from the Arabic by the abbot of Dabra Libanos around 1553. Cerulli sees this work as one that shows Ethiopian – Christian Georgian contact or relations.

Cerulli considers the romance of Barlaam and Josaphat which Enbaqom (see above) translated to be most interesting. But there is enormous diffusion of this legend of Indian Buddhist origin in various literatures of the East and West. Barlaam and Josaphat found their way into the Roman and Greek calendar of saints, and the legend into Syriac, Arabic, Ethiopic, Armenian, and Hebrew. The Ethiopic derives from the Arab-Kan version (from before the 13th century). At the end of the Ethiopic work, Enbaqom says he finished the translation in (the year corresponding to) 1553.

Gadla Giyorghis, *Acts of St. George*

Gadla Giyorghis or <u>The Acts and Miracles of St. George</u> consists of the juxtaposition of two small works of Greek Christian literary origin. The author of the <u>Miracles of St. George</u> is Theodosius, Bishop of Jerusalem, and the Encomium of St. George is attributed to Theodotus, Bishop of Ancyra. Cerulli contends that the Ethiopic is a translation from an Arabic version of the Greek text. To the twelve stories of the Miracles by Theodosius were added, first in Arabic, several stories concerning the convents and churches of Egypt, and then some stories of local interest in Ethiopia to Ethiopic about 1487-1488. Most versions have been preserved instead only the twelve "canonic" Miracles of the Greek text. Cerulli thinks that the Egyptian additions did not arrive together with the first Arab translation, but were translated consecutively into Ethiopic. These added stories are notably interesting because of information on various aspects of monastic life in medieval Egypt; they seem close to the Arabic text. Less numerous are the Ethiopic stories referring to the reign of Zär'a Ya'aqob, and especially to his victory in December 1445 against the Moslems.

Miracles of Julis of Aqfahs

According to Cerulli this work about the life of the martyr Julius Aqfahs is analogous to the preceding and is of the same period. A devout Christian saint, and a compiler of Christian biographies, Julius of Aqfahs was tortured and martyred in the time of Emperor Diocletian (284-305) by Arkanius, governor of Samanoud.

Acts of St. Sebastian

According to Cerulli, in the 15th century, for the first time, Ethiopia began to enter into direct relations with European literatures. According to him, the first direct literary interaction of Ethiopia with Europe is evinced in the Acts of St. Sebastian, from about 1424. The Ethiopic Acts of St. Sebastian derives from the Life of St. Sebastian, attributed erroneously to St. Ambrose before the 9th century. According to Cerulli, the translation from Latin to Ethiopic had to be in the 15th century or early 16th century, and claims that like the Athanasian Creed by George of Sagla (c. 15th) to have been brought by Messer Zan of Italy.

As we saw earlier, Cerulli, and before him Conti Rossini (1928), claimed that the *Book of Mystery of Heaven and Earth*, a voluminous treatise against heresies and of great importance for the doctrinal history of the Ethiopic church, known to have been written by the Ethiopian George of Sagla, was composed after discussions with a European (Considered Italian by Conti Rossini.) It is possible that some Ethiopian works had European influence or based on works brought from Europe. However, we have to be careful with many such unproved claims by western scholars and writers who often rush to credit Ethiopic or African contributions to European authors or influence (pp. 144-45).

From the Time of Emperor Susenyos (1608-1632) to Emperor Theodros (1855-1868)

The arrival of the Society of Jesus (Jesuit) in Ethiopia was of fundamental importance to history of the country. The royal court and the monasteries came were exposed to the Jesuit missionaries and their world view (1556-1632.)

The church scholars of Ethiopia, who were always anxious to study and learn, were curious to discover and understand this new world view. The interaction with the Jesuits and theological disputes with them resulted in a movement of cultural renovation. There was a treatise of apology produced by one of the adherents of that movement on the occasion of discussions between the Jesuits and the Ethiopic clergy. In one of the treatise Dliichaelite doctrine the principal motif is the fundamental belief that the human intellect cannot know God, and that only the elect can gradually approach that superior knowledge. The treatise shows deep, bitter pessimism, the author persisting above all in maintaining that the dogma of "man made in the image and likeness of God" is false. This is somewhat like the teaching of the famous Jewish Rabbi Akiba of the early second century that the Hebrew of Genesis means that man was created like an image/picture, not in the image of God.

This doctrine, not known in Ethiopic theology, and already contested, is explained with caution. Many parts of the work, especially at the beginning, are written in an obscure *qine* style with double entendre, ambiguity, rhetorical style. However, Cerulli admits that the work, often with enthusiasm and a full liberty of expression, rises to poetic heights, even while remaining painfully bitter. For Cerulli it is one of the most beautiful works of Ethiopic literature, especially the original parts of the book, the parts explaining the Dliichaelite doctrine. As for the brief section on the unique nature of Christ, it is written in the normal style of Ethiopic theological discussions, and without particular distinction.

The Treasure of the Faith

The *Treasure of the Faith* is a work also occasioned by discussion with Catholic missionaries. The work gives an abbreviated story of the four early church Councils in the 4th and 5th centuries and a summary of a debate on several questions of Christology held in the presence of King Glawdewos. It is important as an historic document, full of subtle arguments founded on biblical citations. Cerulli rightly says the arguments in the work is objective, pure and simple exchange of ideas and expressions, devoid of personal attacks, uncommon in theological debates in other countries and in other historic circumstances.

Early Development of Amharic Literature

It seems that during this period literary Amharic begins to develop. Amharic, then spoken in central and southern Ethiopia, was employed in the disputes. This made it possible for the Ethiopic Church not to limit its discussion to the court and clergy who were the only ones who could understand Ge'ez. According to Cerulli, the work of making literature intelligible to all led to a profound cultural reawakening, preparing the way for the evolution of modern Ethiopia, beyond the literature of the court, limited in diffusion and comprehension. The Ethiopic Church and church writers were likewise induced to adopt in the form of questions and answers (catechism) to explain theological dogmas in Amharic. In addition to the, "To him who asks about faith, the answer of faith is this", there followed more development in Amharic religious literature and commentaries. These included a Commentary on the Psalms and the treatise, *Senna Fetrat* or "The Beauty of Creation". However, Ethiopic remained in use for other branches of literature, especially historical works such as the Royal Chronicles.

As was the case with Ethiopic poetry the court poetry written in Amharic in the 19th century gradually became limited to a particular rhetorical artifice. Amharic is especially rich in homophones and thus well suited to become the essential ornament of Amharic poetry, as the "Wax and Gold" did for poetry in Ethiopic. Cerulli argues that esthetically the result is the same, and the abundance of word games attests to the poet's knowledge of his language. Cerulli cites the distich on the death of the Shoan prince Saifa Michael and the verses for the marriage of Empress Zaweditu as exmples.

Zena Malak Sagad

The *Zena Malak Sagad* or Chronicle of King Malak Sagad (1563-1597) is a long work, and according to Cerulli, unusual for its minimalist style, and dignified tone. The writer occasionally tries to investigate the motives of various historical persons, offering some sharply observant psychological insights. According to Cerulli, this Chronicle is still one of the best works of Ethiopic historiography, after the artistically more lively *Zena Amda Sion*, written two hundred years earlier. Often clear and calm, the *Chronicle of Malak Sagad* is at times a bit detached and lacking in dramatic style. This can best be seen in two passages which Cerulli translates, such as the war against the "Falasha", Beta Israel, the mutual distrust and hostility described in detail with the resulting repression. The second, "the plots and submissions of Hamalmal", the Chronicle describes and contrasts Hamalmal's fickle and flight character and rebellion against the king to the utter loyalty of the prudent conduct of the Princess Amata Ghiorghis, the sovereign's aunt.

Zena Susenyos

According to Cerulli, the importance of the *Zena Susenyos,* the Chronicle of King Susenyos (1607-1632) derives from its historical merit that he describes as first rate rather than its artistic achievement that he describes as monotonous. It is a work written in the style of chronicle notes, similar to the additional parts of the shorter chronicles, but with more details.

Cerulli refers to the story of unusual religious movement in Ethiopia that occurred at two intervals in the early 17th century, that is, "The movement of the false Messiah and its repression" by King Za-Denghel (1603-1604) and by his succesor Susenyos.

Gadla Walatta Petros

Gadla Walatta Petros, "*The Acts of Walatta Petros*" is another important hagiography of one of the most remarkable women of this period in Ethiopian history. The *Acts* were written in 1673-1674 by a monk from the Afar-Faras community founded by Wolatta Petros, (she died in 1644.) Walatta Petros showed tremendous energy and passionate zeal in her fight against the Catholic movement which had gained dominance during the reign of Susenyos. During the subsequent reign of Fasiladas, after the restoration of Orthodoxy, she continued to oppose with equal passion any belief, or any deviation from what she considered true Christian discipline. Cerulli rightly considers the *Gadl* one of the best hagiographies, although more recent, because of the author's skill in depicting the saint's prideful character, a person scornful of compromises.

The Deggua

According to the Ethiopic tradition, the first sacred poetry and hymns go back to the Aksumite period to St. Jared. But other religious hymns were written probably in the 14th and late 15th century. Such normative religious poetry and hymns continued to develop even more in the traditional schools, so that collections of hymns came to be formed with permanently fixed forms that left lasting significance in artistic and literary history.

There were several collections of religious hymns, with various names, since at least the 15th century. The name *Deggua* was given to collections of the antiphons of the offices for the whole year "from St. John to St. John." According to Cerulli, a general revision of the common Deggua for use in the churches was made by order of Emperor Malak Sagad (1563-1597). In the last decades of the 17th century, the abbot of Dabra Libanos completed a new revision of the Deggua, especially with regard to the modes of singing.

Cerulli rightly claimed that preliminary study of the *Deggua* would be very important for knowledge of the hymnography and the knowledge of Ethiopian music, since the manuscripts of the Deggu have musical notations necessary for chanting. Such study did not exist in Cerulli's time but available now especially with the works of Bernard Velat and others. (Cerulli gives a few characteristic passages from this work: "To Jesus who is light"; "The beatitude in celestial Jerusalem; "For Palm Sunday".)

Qene

The Qene in Ethiopic is a form of hymnic poetry, so to say, differentiated according to the rules of Ethiopic liturgical music. It has its own metric law that cannot be solidly determined (according to Cerulli) until Ethiopic music and its notations are thoroughly studied. Various types of strophes of Ge'ez *qene* run from a minimum of two verses to a maximum of eleven verses, thus existing as very brief poems with a necessarily limited expression of ideas.

This artistic expression is governed by ever more exclusive rules. Dominant is the rhetorical figure of *samenna warq* "Wax and Gold" (referring to a goldsmith's technique), i.e. a parallel between two ideas or two narrations (referring to Scriptures) which develop along identical lines, an external one (the wax) covering the internal one (the gold). These two images are in juxtaposition with one another, or better, one image exists inside the other. At other times, instead of the "Wax and Gold" with its complications, we find - in less popular *qenes* simple parallels between two images that follow one another in the two semi-stanzas (hemistrophes), bound only by a metaphorical call in the second strophe to the first one. Along with the laws of "Wax and Gold", the rhetoric of the *qene* is enriched by the use of subtle word play, whereby the poet seeks to amaze and astonish.

Another ornament of the *qene*, according to the rules of the genre, is the use by the poet of games of concepts instead of words. He pretends to enunciate a principle or maxim contrary to the Law and Faith, and then, in the following verses, he explains, on the contrary, their edifying and highly moral value. Hymns with similar ornaments are called "hymns of fiction" and were particularly cultivated in this historical period.

Beyond the rigorous rules of rhetoric, we find the so-called "simple hymns", where poetry is not bound by figures of speech and word games. This type of *qene* seems to be more appreciated by non-Ethiopians, but less esteemed in Ethiopic schools. They sometimes express a moving sadness (inspired by the *Book of Job/Eyyob*.) Cerulli refers to another "simple" *qene* form that expresses melancholy about the decadence of Gondar at the end of the 18th century.

Another genre of poetry of this period is the *malk* (physiognomic hymn) a poetic conclusion of the hagiography of the acts of a saint and celebrates the praises of the saint in an undetermined number of stanzas. Each stanza sings the praises of one part of his or her body, beginning with the head and ending with the soles of the feet. This singular composition was so successful in the 17th and 18th centuries that we have several collections of manuscripts of this artful poetry. Cerulli cites several stanzas from "physiognomic hymns" of various persons (which sometimes contain more than one hundred verses, giving a lively impression of this curious genre).

Minor Works of History

Among the minor historic works we find the Story of Dejach Hailu, the Chronicles of King John I, Iyyasu I, and Bakaffa (at the end of the 17th century and the beginning of the 18th), and similar chronicles. All these chronicles are in Ethiopic. According to Cerulli they are of less literary value, coming fro the time that we call *Era of the Princes* but Cerulli calls it "a period of decadence" that ended with the ascendancy of Emperor Theodore II (1855-1868).

However, no chronicle or literature can be described as of less value. We find great exuberance in the minor historic works that illustrate the life of a single person, or describe a single important event. The Story of *Narga Sellasie* (18th) tells the lively story of how Queen mother of King Iyyasu II founded a sanctuary dedicated to Trinity on the inland of Narga on Lake Tana. The story of Dejach Hailu narrates the life of that military chief (called "feudal chief" by Cerulli) to whom we owe the interesting collection and preservation of the royal chronicles since ancient times. These stories reflect some imitation of the hagiographies of the saints. As usual, they are replete with many biblical citations.

Other Translated Works from Arabic

The translating of the Arab Christian works into Ethiopic was also frequent in these two centuries, but particularly within the second half of the 17th century. But cultural contacts became more rare because of internal strife during the Era of the Princes. It was a time of not only political turmoil but also of religious controversies. A long bitter theological polemics of the period involved the Qebat concept, "Unction and of the Union", based on diverging interpretations of a passage of the *Acts of the Apostles*. The controversies divided the land in two and even three adversarial factions.

Chronicle of the Bishop of Nikiu

We have in Ethiopic the important work *Chronicle of John, Bishop of Nikiu* (in Egypt.) The *Chronicle* starts with an account of the creation of world and ends with the account of the Arab conquest of Egypt during which time the Bishop seems to have lived. Some scholars think it was composed in Greek, translated into Arabic, which is not extant now, and into Ethiopic in 1602. Zotenberg published its text with translation (*Chronique de Jean, Évêque de Nikiou, Texte éthiopien publié et traduit,* Paris, 1883). The work is especially interesting to those who study Byzantine period and said to be of great importance for the study of the history of the Islamic conquest of Egypt. According to Butler, "It is the acquisition of John's manuscript by the British Abyssinian expedition which has made it possible to write a history of the Arab conquest of Egypt."

Angara Falasfa, *Dicta Philosophorum,* Mashafa Falasfa Tabiban, *Wise Philosophers*

Angara Falasfa or Dicta Philosophorum is a type of collection of anecdotes very common in the East and West in the Middle Ages. Another one of related genre is *Mashafa Falasfa Tabiban* or Book of the Wise Philosophers. Another work translated from Greek into Arabic and then Ethioic is the Story of Secundus, a philosopher from the time of Roman Emperor Hadrian. In this category of works translated from Arabic, according to Cerulli, is *Fawes Manfasawi*, Spiritual Healing (1680), a penitential manual by Michael, Bishop of Atrib, Egypt.

Fetha Nagast *or The Laws of the Kings*

The *Fetha Nagast* or The Laws of the Kings is a legal code of Ethiopia that centuries, along the Bible, a supreme national legal constitutional authority. The laws are derived from the Bible, the laws of the Torah with some commentary, the writings of early Church fathers including St. Basil and St. Hippolytus. The work has also been related to eighth and ninth century Byzantine law codes. The *Fetha Nagast* contributed to the strong Ethiopian tradition of respect for the rule of the law. It was the fundamental book for teaching the national law in Ethiopian schools and remained in force as the national legal constitution until the time of Empror Haile Selassie who for the first time introduced a modern constitution.

There is a claim that the *Fetha Nagast* was rendered into Ge'ez in the time of Empror Zär'a Ya'aqob (143-1468.) The first part of this work dealing with ecclesiastical laws already existed in Ethiopia earlier as part of the *Senodos.* The first part of Fetha Nagast describes the structure of the Church hierarchy, the sacramental laws and contains the canons of Nicea and Antioch. Certainly the Biblical laws were known for centuries.

However, Cerulli and other western scholars place the *Fetha Nagast* at a later date. According to Cerulli and others, it is a translation from Arabic of the *Nomocanon* composed by the learned Egyptian al-Asad ibn al-Assall in the first half of the 13th century for use in the Coptic Church of Egypt. The *Nomocanon* is derived from various sources, among them, Procheiros Nomos of the Byzantine Emperor Basil (870 – 878).

Hatata Zär'a Ya'aqob, *The Philosophy of Zär'a Ya'aqob*

Following Cerulli's I have placed this work at the end. However, I do not agree with his conclusions about the date and content of this work that he attributes to an Italian called Father Justus of Urbino on very insubstantial basis. Ceriulli claims that this work is composed by the Italia priest in Emperor Theodor's time. He refers to what he says "a very curious literary phenomenon of the so-called "Abyssinian Philosophers", i.e. two little works entitled "The Research of Zara Jakob" and "The Research of Wolda Maryam". He then concludes that both of these works are inspired by profound skepticism and a philosophy of doubt, which Cerulli says is not part of Ethiopian tradition(!) He concludes that these two works were written by a missionary Father Justus of Urbino, who, in isolation in his Ethiopian residence succumbed to doubt and disclosed his spiritual crisis in the two Researches (written in Ethiopic), attributing them to Ethiopic writers. By his unfounded claim, Cerulli reveals his Euro-Centric bias and prejudice so common in nineteenth and early twentieth centuries during which time westerners naively claimed that nothing good comes out of Africa. So they attributed all African inventions, writings, and cultural contributions to some westerners. Recent studies have by Claude Sumner (1986, 1998) and Teodros Kiros (2005) have studied the original Ethiopian context of Zär'a Ya'aqob.

POSTLOGUE ON LITERATURE:
Ethiopia and the Christian East

At the conclusion of his work, Cerulli tries to show that offering a new result of his research many questions of Ethiopic medieval cultural history cannot be answered except within the context of the Christian East as a whole.

In this regard, he points briefly to the literary overlap of some Ethiopic works with especially Armenian and Georgian. Ethiopian Armenian relations go back to the very beginning of Christianity. Indeed, some Russian scholars like D.A. Olderegge 1972) have tried to prove that Saint Mesrop Mashtotz, the inventor of the Armenian alphabet around 405, had met Ethiopian monks in Jerusalem in early fifth century and adopted the shapes (but not the sounds) of the Ethiopic/Ge'ez alphabet. Jerusalem has certainly been a meeting center of Eastern Christians and the Ethiopian and Armenian monks must have interacted in the Holy City. I have myself published an article describing Ethiopic manuscript folios that were apparently were used for binding Armenian Christian manuscripts now found in the library of the Armenian Patriarchate of Jerusalem. The interesting work *Gadla Ewestatewos* describes the travels of Ethiopian monks in Armenia.

According to the Gospels, the ministry of Jesus took place during the reign of the Roman Emperor Tiberius who appointed Pontius Pilate to be the Procurator of Judea. It is claimed by some early Church leaders as suggested by Tertullian and reported by Eusebius that Tiberius sympathized with the early Christians. Some legends have even called him a "Christian Emperor!" Cerulli refers to various narrations of the legend of Tiberius and of Pontius Pilate found in Ethiopic literature related to the Syriac, Coptic, Arabic, Armenian, and Georgian which are also related to those in Greek and Latin. The influence of the legend was such that even in the Ethiopic Orthodox Täwahïdo Church, Pilate is recognized as a saint based on Acts of Pilate and his wife Claudia Procula, as found in the Synaxarium under the date of Sane 25th. Cerulli also claims that the Ethiopic cycle of Tiberius legend has ties in Syriac with that the Syrian legend of Abgar, King of Edessa, and Jesus the healer. We have versions of the former legend in Syriac, Armenian and Ethiopic, and the letters Abgar was said to have exchanged with Jesus, in various versions, among them at least one (maybe more) in Ethiopic.

We have in Ethiopic, the Legend of Tiridates, King of Armenia in the time of Diocletian, and martyr Saint Ripsime, although from Cappadocia came to be known as an Armeian saint. King Tridates struck by the beauty of Ripsime ordered to torture her after she declined her proposition. Her body together with other nuns was fed to wild animals. Tridates then fell seriously sick but was healed by St. Gregory the Illuminato. Ingratitude, the kind adopted Christianity and ordered to build temples on the execution places. The impressive Temple of St. Ripsime was constructed in 618 and is said to be one of the masterpiece of early Christian architecture. Under the altar there is a crypt where according to the legend Ripsime was buried. The Legend of Tiridates was transmitted in abbreviated form from Armenia to Ethiopia, but already existed in one of the oldest Ethiopic manuscripts from the 14th century. Cerulli translated the antiphons in honor of the holy St. Ripsima translated by Cerulli.

Georgia and Ethiopia

Cerulli refers to a Georgian hagiographic document (translated from Greek to Arabic and Georgian) with the story of the investiture by the Patriarch of Alexandria shortly after 479 A. D. of a Georgian of Jerusalem as the Metropolitan of Ethiopia. He also refers to the legend of the "Stratagem of the Virgin" and an episode from Orlando Furioso (by Ariosto) that represent another concurrence between Georgian and Ethiopian literatures. We have in the "Stratagem" (in the Ethiopic collection of the Miracles of St. Julius of Aqfahs) an example of the vastness of the diffusion of the legend in the Christian East, from Georgia to Ethiopia and to Armenia, and from the Syria of the Crusades to Albania. The Syriac legend of the perfumed oil of the Magdalene is mirrored by the episode of the acquisition of Mary Magdalene in Arabic and Ethiopic in the apocrypha already known by the title Miracles of Jesus, now called the Apocryphal Gospel of St. John. In conclusion, for cultural history it is important to see how cycles of legends were constituted, some to celebrate places of pilgrimage and others for historic motives.

From the Time of Theodorus II (1855-1868) to the Present

Beginning from the time of Emperor Theodors, most of the literature, including his chronicles, the chronicle of Emperor Yohannes, and works by such modern Ethiopian writers like Afework, Aleqa Taye, Blaten Geta Heruy are not part of church literature. So I have omitted them in this analysis of Cerullis, *La Literatura Ethiopica*.

Oromo, Tigrigna, and Agau Languages

Important religious literature relevant for this topic began to be composed in the late ninetieth century. Among these are numerous translations of the Bible in Tigrigna, Oromifa, and other languages. Mention should be made of the great Onesimos Nasib who published a translation of the whole Bible into Oromifa and wrote Farsa or church songs.

Those wishing to go further into the history of the translation of the Bible into Ethiopian languages should consult my article in the Cambridge University *Dictionary of the Bible* (2012).

General Bibliography

A.S. Atiya, ed., 1991 *The Coptic Encyclopedia*, vol. 3: 975-979. New York: Macmillan International.

Abdassayid, A.S.1985 *The Egyptian Church and the Ethiopian Church, 1855-1909*. Cairo [in Arabic].

Abélès, M., 1980 Religions, traditional beliefs: interaction and changes in a Southern Ethiopian society: Ochollo, D.L. Donham & W. James, eds., *Working Papers on Society and History in Imperial Ethiopia: the Southern Periphery from the 1880s to 1974*, pp. 185-195, Cambridge: African Studies Center.

Agostino Tedla, Abba, 1969 A proposito di alcuni passi oscuri negle scritti teologici etiopici dei secoli XVIXVII, pubblicati da E. Cerulli, *Proceedings of the Third International Conference of Ethiopian Studies, Addis Ababa 1966*, vol.2, pp. 217-242, Addis Ababa: Institute of Ethiopian Studies, Haile Selassie I University.

Alemayehu Moges, 1971 *The Traditional Ethiopian Church Education*, Addis Ababa: Haile Sellassie I University, Theological College (M.A. thesis).

Alemayehu Moges, 1973 Language, teaching and curriculum in traditional education of the EOC, *Ethiopian Journal of Education* 6(1): 87-114.

Aleme Eshete, 1971 *La Mission Catholique Lazariste en Éthiopie*, Aix-en-Provence: Faculté des Lettres et Sciences Humaines-Institut d'Histoire des Pays d'Outre Mer.

Alvarado, S., 1998 Paralelismos entre la literatura etíope clásica y las antiguas literaturas eslavas, *Boletín de la Asociación Española de Orientalistas* 34: 313-30 [in Spanish].

Amdemariam Tesfamicael 1982-83 La chiesa 'Tewahedo' d'Etiopia. *Quaderni di Studi Etiopici* 3-4: 106-121.

Amsalu Tefera, 2000 *Worship in the Ethiopian Orthodox Tewahido Church focusing on prayer*, Addis Ababa: Holy Trinity Theological College (Senior essay).

Armenian Patriarchate of Jerusalem., *Le Muséon* 89(1-2): 179-194;

Armenian Patriarchate of Jerusalem.1981-83, *Calalogue of Ethiopian Manuscripts in the Princeon University Collections*, vol I, codices, vol. II, scrolls, Princeton University Rare Books & Manuscripts Department, Princeton, NJ.

Armenian Patriarchate of Jerusalem.1984-86, Shelf list of Ethiopian manuscripts in the monasteries of the Ethiopian patriarchate of Jerusalem, *Rassegna di Studi Etiopici* 30: 53-80.

Armenian Patriarchate of Jerusalem.1985, *Catalogue of Ethiopian Manuscripts in American Library and Private Collections,* American Philosophical Society, Philadelphia, Pa.

Arras, V., 1960 La collection éthiopienne des Miracles de Saint Georges, *Atti del Convegno Internazionale di Studi Etiopici (Roma, 2-4 Aprile 1959),* pp., 273-284. Roma: Accademia Nazionale dei Lincei.

Asfawossen Asrat, 2002 The rock-hewn churches of Tigray: why there? A geological perspective, Baye Yimam, *et al.,* eds., *Ethiopian Studies at the End of the Second Millennium, Proceedings of the XIVth International Conference of Ethiopian Studies, Addis Ababa November 6-11, 2000,* vol. 1: 1-12. Addis Ababa: Institute of Ethiopian Studies.

Ashenafi Kebede, 1980 The sacred chant of Ethiopian monotheistic churches: music in black Jewish and Christian communities, *Black Perspectives in Music* 8: 20-34.

Asnaqe Siraq, 1994 Das Kloster Zuraba. *Kirche und Schule* (Tabor Society, Heidelberg) 46: 17-21.

Ayalew, M., 1970 Problems of religion in Ethiopia, *Challenge* (Addis Ababa): 10(1): 36-45.

Ayele Tekle Haymanot, Abba (Mario di Abiy-Addì), 1956 *La Dottrina della Chiesa Etiopica Dissidente sull'Unione Ipostatica,* Rome: Pontificum Institutem Studiorum Orientalium (Orientalia Christiana, Analecta 147).

Ayele Tekle Haymanot, Abba 1958 *The Ethiopian Church.*Asmara [in Amharic, 1951 EC].

Ayele Tekle Haymanot, Abba 1966 I dogmi mariani nella Chiesa etiopica.*Continenti* 12(4): 27-29.

Ayele Tekle Haymanot, Abba 1981a Un faro di luce cristiano brilla da secoli sull'Ogaden. *Quaderni di Studi Etiopici* 2: 56-64.

Ayele Tekle Haymanot, Abba 1981b *The Ethiopian Orthodox Church and it Christological Doctrine,* Addis Ababa: n.p.

Ayele Tekle Haymanot, Abba 1988 The Egyptian metropolitan of the Ethiopian Church. *Orientalia Christiana Periodica* 54: 175-222.

Ayele Tekle Haymanot, Abba 1990 *Il Cardinal Guglielmo Massaja oggi, a cent'anni dalla sua scomparsa, Guglielmo Massaja, Vicario Apostolico dei Galla. Proceedings of the Symposium on Card. G. Massaja held in the Antonianum of Rome, February 24,1990.* Rome.

Ayele Tekle Haymanot, Abba 1994 Two fragments of Ethiopian church history. In: C. Lepage, *et al.,* eds., *Études Éthiopiennes. Actes de la Xe Conférence Internationale des Études Éthiopiennes, Paris, 24-28 août 1988*, vol.1, pp. 377-381. Paris: Société Française des Études Éthiopiennes.

Ayele Tekle Haymanot, Abba 1998 The struggle for the 'ethiopianisation' of the Roman Catholic tradition. Getatchew Haile, A. Lande & S. Rubenson, eds., *The Missionary Factor in Ethiopia*, pp. 135-154. Frankfurt/M.: Peter Lang.

Ayele Tekle-Haymanot, 1983 L'apostolato francescano in Etiopia., *Studi Francescani* 80-1-2): 221-240.

Aymro Wondmagegnehu & J. Motovu, 1970 *The Ethiopian Church*. Addis Ababa: Ethiopian Orthodox Mission.

Ayyalew Tamru, *Liqä Täbäbt*, 1970 The Ethiopian Church. In: *Proceedings of the Third International Conference of Ethiopian Studies, Addis Ababa 1966*, vol.2, pp. 197-212. Addis Ababa: Institute of Ethiopian Studies, Haile Selassie I University [in Amharic].

Baars, W. & R. Zuurmond, 1964 The project for a new edition of the Ethiopic Book of Jubilees, C.F. Beckingham & E. Ullendorff, eds., *Ethiopian Studies. Papers read at the Second Conference of Ethiopian Studies, Journal of Semitic Studies* 9(1): 67-74.

Bairu Tafla 1967 The establishment of the Ethiopian church. *Tarikh* 2(1): 28-42.

Bairu Tafla, 1986 Titles, ranks and offices in the Ethiopian Orthodox Tawahdo Church: a preliminary survey. *Internationale Kirchliche Zeitschrift* 76: 293-304.

Balicka-Witakowska, E., 1974 Illuminations of an Ethiopian magic scroll reported on the first expedition of Polish student to Africa, *Africana Bulletin* 21: 59-65.

Balicka-Witakowska, E.,1983 Le psautier éthiopien illustré de Belen Sägäd, *Imagines Médiévales. Acta Universitatis Uppsaliensis*. Ars Suetica 7.

Balicka-Witakowska, E.,1984-86 Un psautier éthiopien illustré inconnu, *Orientalia Suecana* 33-35: 17-48.

Balicka-Witakowska, E.,1989 The iconography of deposition in Ethiopian painting, *Proceedings of theFirst International Conference on the History of Ethiopian Art*, pp. 15-22. London: Pindar Press.

Bandrés, J.L., 1986 The Ethiopian *Anaphora of the Apostles*: historical considerations. *Proche-Orient Chrétien* 36(1-2): 6-13.

Bartnicki, A. & J. Mantel-Niecko 1969-70 The role and significance of the religious conflicts and people's movements in the political life of Ethiopia in the XVIIth and XVIIIth centuries. *Rassegna di Studi Etiopici* 24: 5-39.

Bausi, A., 1990a Alcune considerazioni sul "Senodos" etiopico, *Rassegna di Studi Etiopici* 34: 5-73.

Bausi, A., 1992c Il *Qalementos etiopico. La rivelazione di Pietro a Clemente. I libri 3-7. Traduzione e introduzione di A. B.* Napoli: IUO, Dipartimento di Studi e Ricerche su Africa ePaesi Arabi (Studi Africanistici. Serie Etiopica 2).

Bausi, A.,1990b Presenze clementine nella letteratura etiopica, *Studi Classici e Orientali* (Pisa) 40: 289-316.

Bausi, A.,1992a *Il Senodos Etiopico: Edizione Critica e Traduzione dei Testi Pseudoapostolici, Inediti,* Napoli: Istituto Universitario Orientale, 678 p. (Doctoral thesis).

Bausi, A.,1992b Heritage and originality in the Ethiopian Sinodos, *Journal of Ethiopian Studies* 25: 15-33.

Bausi, A.,1994 The critical edition of the Ethiopic Senodos, Some preliminary remarks, C. Lepage, *et al.,* eds., *Études Éthiopiennes. Actes de la Xe Conférence Internationale des Études Éthiopiennes, Paris, 24-28 août 1988,* vol.1, pp. 346-351, Paris: Société Française des Études Éthiopiennes.

Bausi, A.,2002 *La Versione Etiopica degli* Acta Phileae *nel* Gadla Sama'tat (Supplemento n. 92 agli Annali dell'Istituto Orientale di Napoli), Napoli: IUO, ix-64.

Bausi, A.,2003 *La "Vita" e i "Miracoli" di* Libanos (ed. and transl.), Louvain: Peeters (Corpus Scriptorum Christianorum Orientalium, vol. 595-596).

Beckingham, C.F., 1974 Church and state in Ethiopia: a review article. *Journal of African History* 15: 137-140.

Berhanou Abbebe, 1977 Les églises peintes du Lac Tana: dernière étape de la route historique en Éthiopie., *Communications UNESCO* 30: 13-17.

Berry, L.B. & R. Smith, 1979 Churches and monasteries of Lake Tana, Ethiopia, 1972. *Africa* (Roma) 34(1-2): 1-34.

Beylot, R. & M. Rodinson, 1995 *Répertoire des Bibliothèques et Catalogues de Manuscrits Éthiopiens,* Paris.

Beylot, R., 1980 Sur deux textes apocalyptiques éthiopiens, *Semitica* 30: 89-92.

Beylot, R., 1982 Une tradition éthiopienne sur la chûte des anges, *Semitica* 32: 121-125.

Beylot, R., 1983-84 Sermon éthiopique anonyme sur l'Eucharistie. Abbay 12: 79-116.

Beylot, R., 1993 Langue et littérature éthiopiennes, M. Albert, *et al.,* *Christianismes Orientaux: Introduction a l'etude des langues et des literatures,* pp. 221-260. Paris: Éditions du Cerf.

Beylot, R., ed., 1984 *Testamentum Domini Éthiopien. Edition et Traduction,* Louvain: Peeters (Corpus Scriptorum Christianorum Orientalium).

Beylot, R.,1962 Une épisode de l'histoire ecclésiastique de l'Éthiopie, le mouvement Stéphanite, *Annales d'Éthiopie* 8: 103-116.

Beylot, R.,1971-72 Le millénarisme, article de foi dans l'église éthiopienne au XVme siècle, *Rassegna di Studi Etiopici* 25: 31-43.

Bianchi-Barriviera, L., 1962-63 Le chiese in roccia di Lalibela e di altri luoghi del Lasta. *Rassegna di Studi Etiopici* 18: 5-76 and 19: 5-118.

Bianchi-Barriviera, L.,1966 Ristauri alle chiese di Lalibela. *Rassegna di Studi Etiopici* 22: 135-146.

Bidder, I., 1959 *Lalibela: Monolithische Kirchen in Äthiopien*, Köln: M. Dumont Schauberg, 137 p. [English translation: *Lalibela: the Monolithic Churches of Ethiopia*. New York: Praeger, 1960]

Bird, H., 1971 Primitivism in Ethiopian Christianity, *Reformed Bulletin of Missions* 6: 1-11.

Black, M. & J.C. Vanderkam, 1985 *The Book of Enoch or I Enoch. A New English Edition with Commentary and Textual Notes*, Leiden: Brill.

Bolay, A., Musique et pouvoir royal en Éthiopie, le chant des azmari (XIXe-début Xxe siècle), *Cahiers du CRA* 9: 7-37.

Bonacci, G., 2002 Ethiopia 1974-1991: religious policy of the state and its consequences on the Orthodox Church. In: Baye Yimam, *et al.*, eds., *Ethiopian Studies at the End of the Second Millennium, Proceedings of the XIVth International Conference of Ethiopian Studies, Addis Ababa November 6-11, 2000*, vol. 1: 593-605. Addis Ababa: Institute of Ethiopian Studies.

Borusso, P., 1989 Le missione cattoliche italiane nella politica imperiale del fascismo (1936-1940), *Africa* (Roma): 44(1): 50-78.

Bosc-Tiessé, C. & A. Wion, 1998 Inventaire des peintures datées du XVIIe au début du XIXe siècles: questions sur l'art gondarien (Éthiopie), *Cahiers du CRA* 9: 215-242.

Bosc-Tiessé, C., 2001 *Église et Royauté en Éthiopie au 17e et 18e Siècles: Écriture de l'Histoire et 'Fabrique' des Images dans les Églises du Lac Tana*. Paris: Université de Paris I (Thèse UFR d'histoire de l'art).

Boswell, W.P., 1989 Notes on the Ethiopian storypainting about the visit of the Queen of Sheba to King Solomon of Judea, *Proceedings of the First International Conference on the History of Ethiopian Art*. London: Pindar Press.

Brake, D.T., 1977 *An Historical Investigation of Monophysitism in the Ethiopian Orthodox Church*. Dallas: Dallas Theological Seminary (Ph.D. thesis).

Brown, C.F. 1972 *The Conversion Experience in Axum during the Fourth and Fifth Centuries*, Washington: Howard University, Department of History.

Brown, J., 1981 Religion and revolution in Ethiopia. *Religion in Communist Countries* 9(1-2): 50-55.

Bruce, F.F. 1989 Philip and the Ethiopian: the expansion of Hellenistic Christianity, *Journal of Semitic Studies* 34(2): 377-386.

Bruce, J. 1967 The Ethiopian Church. In: J. Forman, ed., *Christianity in the Non-Western World*, pp. 2-7. Englewood Cliffs, NJ: Prentice Hall.

Budge, E.A.W., 1976 *The Book of the Saints of the Ethiopian Church*. 4 volumes, Hildesheim - New York: Georg Olms Verlag [Reprint of the 1928 edition].

Bushell, W., Baidemariam Desta & K. Bushell, 1994 From hagiography to ethnography via psychophysiology: towards an understanding of advanced Ethiopian Christian ascetics. In: Bahru Zewde, R. Pankhurst & Taddese Beyene, eds., *Proceedings of the XIth International Conference of Ethiopian Studies, Addis Ababa 1991*, vol.2, pp. 41-60. Addis Ababa: Institute of Ethiopian Studies.

Campbell, I., 1994 The church of St. Täklä Haymanot at Däbrä Libanos. Sociology Ethnology Bulletin 1(3): 4-11. Merawi Entchale Belay; 2000 *A Brief History of Mahibere Selassie Monastery*. Addis Ababa: Holy Trinity Theological College (Senior essay).

Campbell, I., 2002 Byzantine iconography at the court of Zär'a Ya'ikob: an analysis of the sacred geometry of 15th-century Ethiopia, Baye Yimam, *et al.*, eds., *Ethiopian Studies at the End of the Second Millennium, Proceedings of the XIVth International Conference of Ethiopian Studies, Addis Ababa November 6-11, 2000*, vol. 1: 84-141. Addis Ababa: Institute of Ethiopian Studies.

Caquot, A., 1957 Un texte éthiopien sur les enseignes du camp d'Israël., *Annales d'Éthiopie* 2: 246-247.

Caraman, P.J., 1985 *The Lost Empire. The Story of the Jesuits in Ethiopia 1555-1634*. London: Sidgwick & Jackson.

Carlson, D., 1968 A contemporary Christian view of history: comparison with five-years plans of developing countries, *History Journal* (Addis Ababa) 2(2): 14-17.

Caulk, R.A., 1971 Religious coercion and political authority in nineteenth century Ethiopia, In: *Papers of the Annual Conference 1973, Historical Society of Ethiopia* (Addis Ababa), pp. 2-14.

Caulk, R.A., 1972 Religion and state in nineteenth century Ethiopia. *Journal of Ethiopian Studies* 10(1): 23-42.

Caulk, R.H. 1981 Islam and Christianity in Northeast Africa until 1500. In: *Cambridge Encyclopaedia of Africa*, pp. 117-124.

Cerulli, E. 1956 La dea mater ed il suo culto presso la gente dell'Etiopia meridionale. *Rivista di Antropologia* 43: 3-12.

Cerulli, E., 1956 *Atti di Krestos Samra*, Louvain: Imprimerie Orientaliste L. Durbecq (Corpus Scriptorum Christianorum Orientalium, vol. 163-164).

Cerulli, E., 1957 La festa etiopica del Patto di Misericorda e le sue fonti nel greco "Liber de transitu" e nel racconto latino dei Cinque Dolori di Maria, *Silloge Bizantina in Onore di Silvio Mercati*, pp. 53-71. Roma: Studi Bizantini e Neoellenici 9.

Cerulli, E., 1958 Il monachismo in Etiopia. In: *Il Monachismo Orientale* , pp. 259-278. Rome: Ponticificum Institutem Orientalium Studiorum (Orientalia Christiana Analecta, 153).

Cerulli, E., 1958-60 *Scritti Teologici Etiopici dei Secoli XVI-XVII*, (Vol. I, Tre Opuscoli dei Mikaeliti, 198 p., Vol. II, La Storia dei Quattro Concili ed altri Opuscoli Monofisiti, 204 p.), Città del Vaticano: Bibliotheca Apostolic a Vaticana.

Cerulli, E., 1959 Tre nuovi documenti sugli Etiopi in Palestina nel secolo XV, 48 *Studia Biblica et Orientalia* 3: 33-47.

Cerulli, E., 1964a The "Kalilah wa-Dimnah" and the Ethiopic "Book of Barlaam and Josaphat", (British Museum MS.Or. 534), C.F. Beckingham & E. Ullendorff, eds., *Ethiopian Studies. Papers read at the Second Conference of Ethiopian Studies, Journal of Semitic Studies* 9(1): 75-99.

Cerulli, E., 1965b I manoscritti della Chester Beatty Library in Dublino, *Rendi-Conti dell'Accademia dei Lincei, Classe di Scienze Morale, Storiche e Filologiche*, ser. 8, 11 (6): 277-324;

Cerulli, E.,1959 *Atti di Giulio di Aqfahs*, Louvain: Peeters (Corpus Scriptorum Christianorum Orientalium, vol.190-191), 2 volumes.

Cerulli, E.,1962 Gli atti di Zena Marqos, monaco etiopico del secolo XIV, *Studi e Testi* 219-220: 191-212.

Cerulli, E.,1964b De resurrectione mortum. Opuscola della Chiesa etiopica del secolo XIV, *Mélanges offerts à Eugène Tisserant*, pp. 1-27. Città del Vaticano: Bibliotheca Apostolica Vaticana.

Cerulli, E.,1965a Il codice di Leningrado del libro etiopico dei miracoli di Maria, *Rendi-Conti dell'Accademia dei Lincei, Classe di Scienze Morale, Storiche et Filologiche* ser. 8, 20 (1-2): 3-19.

Cerulli, E.,1967 Two Ethiopian tales on the Christians of Cyprus, *Journal of Ethiopian Studies* 5(1): 1-8.

Cerulli, E.,1969 «Il suicido de lla peccatrice» nelle versioni araba ed etiopica del Libro dei Miracoli di Maria, *Annali dell'Istituto Universitario Orientale* 29(2): 147-178.

Cerulli, E.,1969 *Les Vies éthiopiennes de Saint Alexis l'Homme de Dieu*, Louvain: Peeters (Corpus Scriptorum Christianor um Orientalium, vol. 298-299).

Cerulli, E.,1973 Tiberius and Pontius Pilate in Ethiopian tradition and poetry, *Proceedings of the British Academy* 59: 1-20;

Cerulli, E.,1975-76 *Un hymne éthiopien à Pilate sanctifié*. Beyrouth: Imprimerie Catholique ("Mélanges de l'Université St. Joseph", XLIX).

Chaillot, C. 2002 *The Ethiopian Orthodox Tewahedo Church Tradition*. Paris: Inter-Orthodox Dialogue.

Chaine, M., ed., 1962 *Apocrypha de B. Maria Virgine*, Louvain: Peeters (Corpus Scriptorum Christianorum Orientalium, vol. 22.)

Chapple, D., 1986 Protestant missionary attitudes in Ethiopia: Gobat, Isenberg, Krapf, *Proceedings of the Third Annual Seminar of the Department of History*, pp. 25-45. Addis Ababa: Department of History, Addis Ababa University.

Chernetsov, S. 1988 The role of Catholicism in the history of Ethiopia in the first half of the 17thcentury. In: Taddese Beyene, ed., *Proceedings of the VIIIth International Conference of Ethiopian Studies, Addis Ababa 1984*, vol.1, pp. 205-212. Huntingdon, U.K.: ELM Publications.

Chernetsov, S.B., 1981 Myth, painting and the historiography of medieval Ethiopia, *Sbornik Muzeja Antropologii i Etnografii* 37: 114-123 [in Russian].

Chernetsov, S.B.,1997 Ethiopian traditional painting with special reference to the Kunstkammer collection of Ethiopian paintings, *St Petersburg Journal of African Studies* 6: 128-55. [Also in: K. Fukui, E. Kurimoto & M. Shigeta, eds., *Ethiopia in Broader Perspective. Proceedings of the XIIIth International Conference of Ethiopian Studies, Kyoto, 12-17 December,1997*, vol.3, pp. 3-32. Kyoto: Shokado.]

Cohen, L. 2002 The Portuguese context of the *Confessio Fidei* of king Claudius. In: Baye Yimam, *et al.*, eds., *Ethiopian Studies at the End of the Second Millennium, Proceedings of the XIVth International Conference of Ethiopian Studies, Addis Ababa November 6 11, 2000*, vol. 1: 152-168. Addis Ababa: Institute of Ethiopian Studies.

Conti Rossini, C. & L. Ricci, transl. and ed., 1964-65 *Il Libro della Luce del Negus Zär'a Ya'kob*, Louvain: Peeters (Corpus Scriptorum Chirstia norum Orientalium, vol. 47-48).

Conti Rossini, C. and C. Jaeger, eds., 1962 *Acta S. Walatta Petros; Miracula S. Zär'a-buruk*, Louvain: Peeters (Corpus Scriptorum Christianorum Orientalium, vol. 68-69, reprint of 1912 edition).

Conti Rossini, C., ed., 1961a *Acta Yared et Pantalewon*, Louvain: Peeters (Corpus Scriptorum Christianorum Orientalium, vol. 26).

Conti Rossini, C.,1961b *Acta S. Basalota Mika'el et S. Anorewos*, Louvain: Peeters (Corpus Scriptorum Christianorum Orientalium, vol. 28-29,reprint of 1905 edition).

Conti Rossini, C.,1962a *Acta Marqorewos*, Louvain: Peeters (Corpus Scriptorum Christianorum Orientalium, vol. 33-24, reprint of 1904 edition).

Conti Rossini, C.,1962b *Acta Sancti Abakerazun; Acta Sancti Takla Hawaryat*, Louvain: Peeters (Corpus Scriptorum Christianorum Orientalium, vol. 56-57).

Coquin, R.-G., 1984 Le synaxaire éthiopien: note codicologique sur le Ms. Paris B.N.\ D'Abbadie 66-66bis, *Analecta Bollandiana* 102(3-4): 49-59.

Cornuau, R., 1994 *Moines et Monastères du Godjam et du Lac Tana en Éthiopie aux 14e et 15e Siècles. Évangélisation et Intégration dans l'Empire Salomonide*. Paris: Université de Paris I, Centre de Recherche Africaine (Mémoire de maîtrise).

Costa Tribe, T., 1997 The word in the desert: the wall-paintings of Debra Maryam Korkor (Ger'alta, Tigray), K. Fukui, E. Kurimoto & M. Shigeta, eds., *Ethiopia in Broader Perspective, Proceedings of the XIIIth International Conference of Ethiopian Studies, Kyoto, 12-17 December 1997*, vol.3, pp. 35-61. Kyoto: Shokado.

Cowley, R., 1973 An Ethiopian list of the Nicene Fathers, Abba *Salama* 4: 40-57.

Cowley, R., 1982 The Ethiopic manuscripts, M.R. Falivene & A.F. Jesson, eds., *Historical Catalogue of the Manuscripts of Bible House Library*, pp. 66-121. London: The British and Foreign Bible Society.

Cowley, R.W., 1970 The Ethiopian Church and the Council of Chalcedon.*Sobornost* 6(1): 33-38. Daoud, M., Rev.

Cowley, R.W., 1974 The Biblical Canon of the Ethiopian Orthodox Church today. *Ostkirchliche Studien* 23(4): 318-323.

Cowley, R.W.,1959 *The Liturgy of the Ethiopian Church* (English & Arabic). Revised by *Blatta* Mersie Hazen. Cairo: Egyptian Book Press (First edition: Addis Ababa 1954).

Cowley, R.W.,1987 A Ge'ez document reporting controversy concerning the Bible commentaries of Ibn at-Tayib, *Rassegna di Studi Etiopici* 30: 5-13.

Cowley, R.W.,1989 Zekre and Pawli - Ethiopic Bible translators or interpreters? *Journal of Semitic Studies* 34(2): 387-398.

Crummey, D. 1978 Orthodoxy and imperial reconstruction in Ethiopia, 1854-1878. *Journal of Theological Studies* 19(2): 427-442.

Crummey, D., 1972 Shaikh Zäkaryas: an Ethiopian prophet, *Journal of Ethiopian Studies* 10(1): 55-66.

Crummey, D.,1974 Doctrine and authority: *Abuna* Sälama, 1841-1854, *Atti del IV. Congresso Internazionale di Studi Etiopici (Roma, 10-15 Aprile 1972)*, vol. I, pp. 567-578. Roma: Accademia Nazionale dei Linceii.

Crummey, D.C., 1965 Foreign missions in Ethiopia, 1829-1868, *Bulletin of the Society for African Church History* 2(1): 15-36.

Crummey, D.C.,1968 The 'church-state ideal' in Ethiopia (part 2): the Apologica and Constantium and Ethiopia's conversion. *Ibadan* 24: 31-36.

Crummey, D.C.,1972a *Priests and Politicians, Protestant and Catholic Missions in Orthodox Ethiopia 1830-1868*, Oxford: Clarendon Press.

Crummey, D.C.,1998 The politics of modernization: Protestant and Catholic missionaries in moder Ethiopia, Getatchew Haile, A. Lande & S. Rubenson, eds., *The Missionary Factor in Ethiopia*, pp. 85-100. Frankfurt/M.: Peter Lang.

Crummey, D.E.,1993 Church and state in Ethiopia: the sixteenth to the eighteenth century. In: R. Grierson, M.E. Heldman, & S. Munro-Hay, eds., *African Zion: the Sacred Art of Ethiopia*, pp. 43-46. New Haven - London: Yale University Press.

Davis, A.J., 1965 The 'church-state ideal' in Ethiopia (part 1): a synopsis. *Ibadan* 21: 47-52.

Davis, A.J., 1967 The orthodoxy of the Ethiopian Church. *Tarikh* 2(1): 63-69; 1969 Pope Julius' Bull of 1554: its political significance in Ethiopia, *Ibadan* 26: 63-68. Ethiopian Orthodox Church (Sergew Hable Selassie, ed.).

Davis, A.J.,1970 *The Church of Ethiopia: a Panorama of History and Spiritual Life*, Addis Ababa: Ethiopian Orthodox Church, 97 p. Ethiopian Orthodox *Täwah?do* Church Holy Synod, ed.

Davis, A.J.,1982-83 *A Short History, Faith and Order of the Ethiopian Orthodox Tewahedo Church*. Addis Ababa: Ethiopian Orthodox *Täwah?do* Church [in Amharic].

Davis, A.J.,1996 *The Ethiopian Orthodox Tewahedo Church: Faith, Order of Worship and Ecumenical Relations*. Addis Ababa: Ethiopian Orthodox *Täwah?do* Church [in Amharic].

Davis, R.J., 1966 *Fire on the Mountains: the Story of a Miracle - the Church in Ethiopia*, Grand Rapids: Zondervan.

Davis, R.J.,1984 *The Winds of God*. Summer Hill, NSW/Cedar Grove, N.J.: SIM International Publications.

Dejene Aredo, 1990 How holy are holidays in Ethiopia? An enquiry into the extent to which Saints' days are observed in among followers of the Orthodox Christian Church, In: R. Pankhurst, Ahmed Zekaria, Taddese Beyene, eds., *Proceedings of the First National Conference of Ethiopian Studies, Addis Ababa, April 11-12, 1990*, pp. 165-176. Addis Ababa: Institute of Ethiopian Studies.

Delcor, M., ed., 1973 *Le Testament d'Abraham*, Leiden: Brill.

Derat, M.-L. & H. Pennec, 1997 Les églises et monastères royaux d'Éthiopie (Xve-XVIe et XVIIe siècles): permanences et ruptures d'une stratégie royale. In: K. Fukui, E. Kurimoto & M. Shigeta, eds., *Ethiopia in Broader Perspective. Proceedings of the XIIIth International Conference of Ethiopian Studies, Kyoto, 12-17 December 1997*, vol. 1: 17-34. Kyoto: Shokado.

Derat, M.-L., 1993 *Les 'Enfants' de Takla Haymanot: Naissance et Développement d'un Réseau Monastique au Šäwa du XIIIe au XVe Siè cles*. Paris: Université de Paris I, Centre de Recherches Africaines (Mémoire de maîtrise).

Derat, M.-L., 1998 *La Formation d'un Domaine Royal Éthiopien sous les Dynasties Salomonides: Espace, Pouvoir, Monachisme*. Paris: Sorbonne (Thèse de doctorat).

Derat, M.L., 1998 Une nouvelle étape de l'élaboration de la légende hagiographique de Takla Haymanot, *Autres Sources, Nouveaux Regards sur l'Histoire Africaine. Cahiers du CRA* 9: 71-90. Paris: Centre de Recherche Africaine.

Derat, M.-L., 2001 Gäbrä-'Endreyas de Däbrä Qozät et les généalogies monastiques du XVe au XIXe siècle: réécritures et réemplois. *Annales d'Éthiopie* 17: 229-256.

Derat, M.-L., 2003 *Le Domaine des Rois Éthiopiens (1270-1527). Espace, Pouvoir et Monachisme*. Paris: Publications de la Sorbonnne.

Derat, M.L.,1994 "Recherche sur la biographie de l'Abba Giyorgis de Gasecca (ca. 1365-1425)", Paper for the XIIth International Confence on Ethiopian Studies, Michigan State University, East Lansing 5-10 September 1994.

Devos, P., 1960 Les miracles de Saint Menas en éthiopien, *Atti del Convegno Internazionale di Studi Etiopici (Roma, 2-4 Aprile 1959)*, pp., 335-343. Roma: Accademia Nazionale dei Lincei.

Dombrowski, B.W.W. & F.A. Dombrowski 1984 Frumentius/Abba Salama: zu den Nachrichten über die Anfänge des Christentums in Äthiopien. *Oriens Christianus* 68: 114-169.

Doresse, J., 1963 Tsega-Krestos selon les archives franciscanes, *L'Éthiopie Aujourd'hui* 8: 9-12.

Doresse, J., 1969 Survivances d'écrits gnostiques dans la littérature Guèze, *Proceedings of the Third International Conference of Ethiopian Studies, Addis Ababa.*

Doresse, J., 1972 *La Vie Quotidienne des Éthiopiens Chrétiens (aux XVII et XVIII siècles)*, Paris: Hachette.

Embaqom Qaläwäld, 1969 Sïla qené tïmhïrtïnna sïla tïqïmu, In: *Proceedings of the Third International Conference of Ethiopian Studies, Addis Ababa 1966*, vol.2, pp. 117-132. Addis Ababa: Institute of Ethiopian Studies [in Amharic].

Embaqom Qaläwäld, 1970 *Traditional Ethiopian Church Education*, New York: Columbia University, Center for Education in Africa.

Encyclopaedia Aethiopica (Wiesbaden 2003), vol. 1, pp. 574-578.

Endalkachew Mekonnen 1970 Religion of our forefathers: is Christianity irrelevant to our modern way of life? Abba *Salama* 1: 191-199.

Ephraim Isaac 1967 *The Ethiopian Church*. Boston: H.N. Sawyer & Co., 60 p.;1971 Social structure of the Ethiopian Church. *Ethiopia Observer* 14(4):240-288.

Ephraim Isaac 1972 An obscure component in Ethiopian church history: an examination of various theories pertaining to the problem of the origin and nature of Ethiopian Christianity. *Le Muséon* 85(1-2): 225-258.

Ephraim Isaac, 1974 *A New Text-Critical Introduction to the Mäshafä Birhan. With a translation of Book 1.*, Leiden: E.J. Brill; 1983 New light upon the Book of Enoc from newly found Ethiopic Mss, *Journal of the American Oriental Society* 103(2): 399-411.

Ephraim Isaac, 1976, "Catalogue of Ethiopic (Ge'ez) MSS in the Manuscript Library of the Armenian Patriarchate of Jerusalem," Le Muséon, LXXIX (1-2), 1976, 179-194.

Ephraim Isaac, 1984-86, "Ethiopian Manuscripts in the Monasteries of Ethiopian Patriarchate, Jerusalem, Rassegna di Studi Etiopici, XXX (Rome), 53-80.

Every, G., 1963 Ethiopian anaphoras, *Studia Liturgica* 2(2): 156-160.

Eyayu Lulseged, 1990 Why do the Orthodox Christians in Ethiopia identify their faith with their nation? In: R. Pankhurst, Ahmed Zekaria, Taddese Beyene, eds., *Proceedings of the First National Conference of Ethiopian Studies, Addis Ababa, April 11-12, 1990*, pp. 3-12, Addis Ababa: Institute of Ethiopian Studies, 35

Ezra Gebremedhin, 1957 Lent in Ethiopia, *Ethnological Society Bulletin* (University College Addis Ababa) 7: 7-16.

Ezra Gebremedhin, 1998 *Aleqa* Taye: the missionary factor in his scholarly work, Getatchew Haile, A. Lande & S. Rubenson, eds., *The Missionary Factor in Ethiopia*, pp. 101-120. Frankfurt/M.: Peter Lang.

Ferenc, A., 1985 Writing and literature in classical Ethiopic (Giiz), B.W. Andrzejewski, ed., *Literatures in African Languages: Theoretical Essays and Sample Surveys*, pp. 255-300. Cambridge: Cambridge University Press.

Fikre-Selassie Gabre-Emmanuel, 1976 *Church and Missions in Ethiopia in Relation to the Italian War and Occupation and the Second World War*, Aberdeen: University of Aberdeen (Ph.D. thesis).

Filipos, Abba, Archbishop of Jerusalem, ed., 1960 *The Rights of the Abyssinian Church in the Holy Places. Documentary Authorities*, Asmara: Kokebe Tsebah Printing Press.

Filippini, L., 2002 The role of the missions (Protestants and Catholics) in 20th-century Ethiopia (1920-1975), Baye Yimam, *et al.*, eds., *Ethiopian Studies at the End of the Second Millennium, Proceedings of the XIVth International Conference of Ethiopian Studies, Addis Ababa November 6-11, 2000*, vol. 1: 606-633. Addis Ababa, Institute of Ethiopian Studies.

Forslund, E., 1993 *The Word of God in Ethiopian Tongues: Rethorical Features in the Preaching of the Ethiopian Evangelical Church Mekane Yesus*, Uppsala: International Tryk AB.

Fritsch, E., 2001 *The Liturgical Year of the Ethiopian Church. The Temporal: Seasons and Sundays*. Addis Ababa: St. Francis Major Seminary.

Fukui, E. Kurimoto & M. Shigeta, eds., 1991 *Ethiopia in Broader Perspective, Proceedings of the XIIIth International Conference of Ethiopian Studies, Kyoto, 12-17 December 1997*, vol.3, pp. 219-227. Kyoto: Shokado.

Gäbrä-Mäsqäl Täsfaye, 2000 *Extracts from the Gädl of St. Lalibäla*, Addis Ababa: Artistic Printers [in Amharic].

Gaguine, M., 1965 *The Falasha Version of the Testaments of Abraham, Isaac and Jacob*, Manchester: Manchester University (Ph.D. thesis).

Gascon, A. & B. Hirsch, 1992 Les espaces sacrés comme lieux de confluence religieuse en Éthiopie, *Cahiers d'Etudes Africaines* XXXII(4), 128: 689-704.

Gebre Yesus Gebre Mikael. The Basis of the Ge'ez Bible Translation, Unpublished Doctoral thesis (in Hebrew), Hebrew University of Jerusalem, 1978.

Gebre-Yessus Wolde-Mikael, 1977 *Investigation into the Religious and Cultic Vocabulary of the Ethiopic (Ge'ez) Bible Version*. Jerusalem: Hebrew University (Ph.D. Thesis).

Gerster, G., 1968 *L'Art Éthiopien: Églises Rupestres*, St. Léger-Vauban: Zodiaque.

Gerster, G., 1969 *Ethiopian Art*, Boston: Newbury Books.

Gerster, G.,1970a *Churches in Rock: Early Christian Art in Ethiopia*, London: Phaidon Press (English edition of 1968).

Gerster, G.,1970b Searching out medieval churches in Ethiopia's wilds, *National Geographic Magazine* 138(6): 856-884.

Gervers, M., 1988 The Mediterranean context for the medieval rock-cut churches of Ethiopia, Taddese Beyene, ed., *Proceedings of the VIIIth International Conference of Ethiopian Studies, Addis Ababa 1984*, vol.2, pp. 171-184. Huntingdon, U.K.: ELM Publications.

Getachew Haile, 1991 Ethiopian saints, A.S. Atiya, ed., *The Coptic Encyclopedia*, vol. 4: 1044-1056. New York, Macmillan International.

Getachew Haile, 1981a The letter of Archbishop Mika'el and Gäbrä'el concerning the observance of Saturday. *Journal of Semitic Studies* 27(1): 73-78.

Getachew Haile, 1982-83 The monastic genealogy of the line of Täklä Haymanot of Shoa, *Rassegna di Studi Etiopici* 29: 7-38.

Getachew Haile, 1983 On the identity of Silondis and the composition of the anaphora of Mary ascribed to Hereyaqos of Behnesa, *Orientalia Christiana Periodica* 49: 366-389.

Getachew Haile, 1988 A text on the saints of kädih, Taddese Beyene, ed., *Proceedings of the VIIIth International Conference of Ethiopian Studies, Addis Ababa 1984*, vol.1, pp. 653-664. Huntingdon, U.K., ELM Publications.

Getachew Haile, 1989 The legend of Abgar in Ethiopic tradition; *Orientalia Christiana Periodica* 55: 375-410.

Getachew Haile, 1990 The translation of the relics of Abunä Fileppos of Däbrä Libanos of Shoa, *Rassegna di Studi Etiopici* 34: 75-113.

Getachew Haile, 1993 Ethiopic literature, R. Grierson, M.E. Heldman, & S. Munro-Hay, eds., *African Zion: the Sacred Art of Ethiopia* , pp. 47-56. New Haven - London: Yale University Press.

Getachew Haile,1981b Religious controversies and the growth of Ethiopic literature in the fourteenth and fifteenth centuries. *Oriens Christianus* 65 (4th series): 102-136.

Getachew Haile,1983 The case of the Estifanosites: a fundamentalist sect in the Church of Ethiopia. *Paideuma* 29: 93-119.

Getachew Haile,1988 The forty-nine hour Sabbath of the Ethiopian church. *Journal of Semitic Studies* 33(2): 233-254.

Getatchew Haile, 1980 A note on writing history from forgotten documents, *Northeast African Studies* 2(1): 71-77.

Getatchew Haile, 1989 Empress Tayitu and the Ethiopian property in Jerusalem, *Paideuma* 35: 67-81.

Getatchew Haile, 1993 *The Mariology of Emperor Zära Ya'qob of Ethiopia: Texts and Translations*, Rome: Pontificium Institutum Studiorum Orientalium.

Getatchew Haile, 1998 The missionary's dream: an Ethiopian perspective on western missions in Ethiopia., Getatchew Haile, A. Lande & S. Rubenson, eds., 1998 *The Missionary Factor in Ethiopia*, Frankfurt/M.: Peter Lang.

Getie Gelaye, 1991 My impression of Dagala: a ceremony on Mount Zeqwala, *Sociology-Ethnology Bulletin* (Addis Ababa) 1(1): 11-12.

Ghali, M. Boutros,1999 Ethiopian Church autocephaly. A.S. Atiya, ed., *The Coptic Encyclopedia*, vol. 3: 980-984. New York: Macmillan International.

Giacomo, A. d', 1961 *"Historia" della Missione francescana in Alto Egitto-Fungi-Etiopia* (Ed. by G. Giamberardini), Cairo: Edizioni del Centro Francescano di Studi Orientali Cristiani.

Gigar Tesfaye & J. Pirenne, 1984 Inscriptions sur bois de trois églises de Lalibäla, *Journal of Ethiopian Studies* 17: 107-126.

Gigar Tesfaye, 1974 Reconnaissance de trois églises antérieures à 1314, *Journal of Ethiopian Studies* 12(2): 57-75.

Girma Amare, 1975 Aims and purposes of church education in Ethiopia, In: *Education in Eastern Africa* (Nairobi) 5(1): 43-56.

Girma Beshah & Merid Wolde Aregay, 1964 *The Question of the Union of the Churches in Luso-Ethiopian Relations, 1500-1632*. Lisbon: Junta do Investigaçoes do Ultramar - Centro de Estudos Historicos Ultramarinos.

Girma Elias, 1977 The monastery of Abrentänt in Wäldibba. Abbay 8: 93-118.

Girma Elias, 1997 *Aleqa* Estezia's church paintings and the sources of their captions in sacred books, *Bulletin de la Maison des Études Éthiopiennes* 11: 85-96.

Girma Elias, C. Lepage & J. Mercier, 2001 Peintures murales du XIIe siècle découvertes dans l'église Yemrehana Krestos en Ethiopie, *Comptes-Rendus de l'Académie des Inscriptions et Belles-Lettres* 2002, pp. 311-334.

Girma Fisseha, 1996 Architectuur en schatten van de Ethiopische kerk, 75-X. van der Stappen, ed., *Aethiopia. Volkeren van Ethiopië*, pp. 181-193.

Girma Fisseha, 1996 Het leven van een Christen in de hooglanden, In: X. van der Stappen, ed., *Aethiopia. Volkeren van Ethiopië*, pp. 194-201. Tervuren: Koninklijk Museum voor Midden-Afrika/ Berlin: Gordon & Breach Arts Interfnational [in Dutch].

Girma Fisseha, 2002 Depictions of St. Mary in Ethiopian painting from the 15th century to the present day, Baye Yimam, *et al.*, eds., *Ethiopian Studies at the End of the Second Millennium, Proceedings of the XIVth International Conference of Ethiopian Studies, Addis Ababa November 6-11, 2000*, vol. 1: 169-189. Addis Ababa: Institute of Ethiopian Studies.

Glaser, E. 1895. *Die Abessinier in Arabien und Afrika*. Munich: Franz.

Gnerre, M., 1991 Sacred volcano lakes: reflections comparing Zeqwala and Nemi. *Sociology-Ethnology Bulletin* (Addis Ababa) 1(1): 17-18.

Godet, E., 1976 L'église et les habitations rupestres du vallée de Kistana, *Annales d'Éthiopie* 10: 145-156.

Godet, E., 1983-84 La métrique du *qene* guèze, Abbay 12: 117-203.

Godet, E., 1997 Peut-on parler d'icones en Ethiopie? *Bulletin de la Maison des Études Éthiopiennes* 11: 1-12.

Gorgorios, Abba, 1994 Social ministry of the Ethiopian Orthodox Church in the past and the present.In: C. Lepage, *et al.*, eds., *Études Éthiopiennes. Actes de la Xe ConférenceInternationale des Études Éthiopiennes, Paris, 24-28 août 1988*, vol.1, pp. 391-396. Paris: Société Française des Études Éthiopiennes.

Gori, A., 1991 La "Silloge" de Shäh Zäkkareyas (analisi preliminare). Contributo allo studio della polemica cristiana contro l'Islam in Etiopia, *Rassegna di Studi Etiopici* 35: 73-134.

Göricke, F. & F. Heyer, 1976 The Orthodox Church in Ethiopia as a social institution. *International Yearbook of the Sociology of Knowledge and Religion* 10: 181-241.

Göricke, F.V., 1974 *Die äthiopische Orthodoxe Kirche als soziale Institution*, Heidelberg - Bielefeld: Deutsche Forschungsgemeinschaft.

Gragg, G.B., 1975 A magic prayer of Henoch from a manuscript of the Goodspeed Collection of the University of Chicago, H.G. Marcus, ed., *Proceedings of the First United States Conference of Ethiopian Studies, Michigan State University, 2-5 May 1973*, pp. 61-72. East Lansing: African Studies Center, Michigan State University

Gray, R., 1998 The missionary factor: an African perspective, Getatchew Haile, A. Lande & S. Rubenson, eds., *The Missionary Factor in Ethiopia*, pp. 9-16. Frankfurt/M.: Peter Lang.

Griaule, M., 1980 *Äthiopische Grafitti*, Frankfurt/Main - Paris: Qumran.

Grierson, R. & S. Munro-Hay,1999 *The Ark of the Covenant*. London: Weidenfeld and Nicholson.

Grierson, R., M.E. Heldman, & S. Munro-Hay, eds, 1993 *African Zion: the Sacred Art of Ethiopia*, New Haven - London: Yale University Press.

Gstrein, H. 1971 Äthiopische Kirche unter neue Fuhrung. *Wort und Wahrheit* 26(5): 456-459.

Gstrein, H., 1971 Anschluss (der äthiopischen Kirche) an der Weltorthodoxie.*Wort in der Welt* 51: 16-18.

Gstrein, H.1974 Kirche und soziale Unrast in Äthiopien. *Herder-Korrespondenz* 28(6): 297-300.

Gstrein, H.1976 Volkspatriarch in Addis Abeba. Die äthiopische Kirche nach der Revolution. *Evangelische Kommentare* 9(7): 428-429.

Haberland, E., 1964 The influence of the Christian Ethiopian empire on Southern Ethiopia, *Journal of Semitic Studies* 9(1): 235-238; 1976 *Altes Christentum in Süd-Äthiopien: eine vergessene Missionsepoche*, Wiesbaden: Steiner.

Haberland, E., 1973 Feste im Kirchenjahr des Christlichen Äthiopiens. *Zeitschrift für Kulturaustausch* (Special issue on Ethiopia): 56-58.

Haberland, E., 1979a The Ethiopian Orthodox Church. A national church in Africa. In: *Christian and Islamic Contributions towards Establishing Independent States in Africa South of the Sahara,* pp. 158-168. Stuttgart: Institut fur Auslandbeziehungen.

Haberland, E.,1979b Die äthiopisch-orthodoxe Kirche - eine afrikanische Volkskirche. *Zeitschrift für Kulturaustausch* 19(4): 441-447.

Habtä-Maryam Wärqenäh, *Liqä Seltänat,* 1976 *The Ancient Ethiopian Order of Teaching.* Addis Ababa [in Amharic].

Habte-Maryam Wärqnäh, *Liqä Seltänat,* 1969 A historical account of the Ethiopian Orthodox Monophysite Church creed. In: *Proceedings of the Third International Conference of Ethiopian Studies, Addis* 12 *Ababa 1966,* vol.2, pp. 266-271. Addis Ababa: Institute of Ethiopian Studies.

Habtemichael Kidane, 1996 Il Deggwa – libro liturgico della Chiesa d'Etiopia. *Orientalia Christiana Analecta* 251: 353-388.

Habtemichael Kidane,1997 La celebrazione della Settimana Santa nella Chiesa etiopica. In: A.G. Kollamparampil, ed., *Hebdomadae Sanctae Celebratio. Conspectus Historicus Comparativus.* Special issue of *Ephemeridas Liturgicae 111* (Subsidia 94).

*Habtemichael Kidane,*1998 *L'Ufficio Divino della Chiesa Etiopica. Studio Storico-Critico Particolare, Referimento alle Ore Cattedrali.* Rome: Pontificum Institutem Orientalium Studiorum (Orientalia Christiana Analecta, 257).

Haile Gabriel Dagne, 1987 Oral information on the establishment of churches in Addis Ababa, *Symposium on the Centennary of Addis Ababa 1986, November 24-25, 1986,* pp. 57-78. Addis Ababa: Addis Ababa University Press.

Haile Mariam Larebo, 1986 The Orthodox Church and the state in the Ethiopian revolution 1974-1984, *Religion in Communist Countries* 14(2): 148-159.

Haile Mariam Larebo,1987 The Ethiopian Orthodox Church and politics in the twentieth century, part I. *Northeast African Studies* 9(3): 1-17.

Haile Mariam Larebo,1988a The Ethiopian Orthodox Church and politics in the twentieth century, part II, *Northeast African Studies* 10(1): 1-23.

Haile Mariam Larebo,1988b The Ethiopian Orthodox Church. In: P. Ramet, ed., *Eastern Christianity and Politics in the Twentieth Century,* pp., 375-399, 450-452. Durham: Duke University Press.

Haile-Gabriel Dagne, 1970 The Ethiopian Orthodox Church school system, In: Sergew Hable Selassie, ed., *The Church of Ethiopia: a Panorama of History and Spiritual Life,* pp. 81-97. Addis Ababa: Ethiopian Orthodox Church.

Haile-Gabriel Dagne, 1972 The Gebzenna Charter 1894, *Journal of Ethiopian Studies* 10(1): 67-80.

Hailu Pietros,1978 *Breve Storia della Liturgia Etiopica.* 21 Rome.

Hamer, J.H. 2002 The religious conversion process among the Sidama of North-East Africa. *Africa* 72(4): 598-627.

Hammerschmidt, E., 1962a *Kultsymbolik der koptischen und äthiopischen Kirche.* Saarbrücken: Universität Saarbrücken, iii + 78 p. [Also published as: Kultsymbolik der koptischen und der äthiopischen Kirche. In: *Symbolik der Religionen*, Band 10, pp. 167-233. Stuttgart: Hiersemann].

Hammerschmidt, E., 1965 Jewish elements in the cult of the Ethiopian Church. *Journal of Ethiopian Studies* 3(2): 1-12.

Hammerschmidt, E., 1973 Die äthiopische Kirche und die klassische äthiopische Literatur, *Zeitschrift für Kulturaustausch* (Special issue on Ethiopia), pp. 50-55.

Hammerschmidt, E.,1962b *Stellung und Bedeutung des Sabbats in Äthiopien.* Saarbrücken: Universität Saarbrücken, iii + 75 p. (Also published by: Kohlhammer, Stuttgart, 1963, xvi + 84 p.); 1964 Zur Christologie der äthiopischen Kirche. *Ostkirchliche Studien* 13: 203-207.

Hammerschmidt, E.,1967 *Äthiopien. Christliches Reich zwischen Gestern und Morgen,* Wiesbaden: Harrassowitz.

Hammerschmidt, E.,1969 The liturgical vestments of the Ethiopian Church: a tentative survey. In: *Proceedings of the Third International Conference of Ethiopian Studies, Addis Ababa 1966.* Addis Ababa: Institute of Ethiopian Studies, Haile Selassie I University, vol.2, 151-156.

Hammerschmidt, E.,1987 *Studies in the Ethiopian Anaphoras.* Second, revised edition, Wiesbaden: Steiner, 181 p. (Äthiopistische Forschungen, 25). [First published 1961 by Akademie Verlag in Berlin, 182 p.]

Hannick, C., 1980 Music of the Ethiopian rite, *New Grove Dictionary of Music* 6: 272-275.

Hanson, H.M. & D. Hanson, 1958 *For God and Emperor,* Mountain View: Pacific Press.

Hecht, E.-D., B. Benzing & Girma Kidane, 1990 *Hand Crosses of the I.E.S. Collection,* Addis Ababa: Institute of Ethiopian Studies, Pankhurst, R. & R. Pankhurst; 1979 Ethiopian ear-picks, Abbay 10: 101-110.

Heidt, A.M., 1973 L'église éthiopienne orthodoxe d'aujourd'hui: interview avec l'*Abuna* Théophilos, patriarche d'Éthiopie, et l'*Abuna* Samuel. *Irénikon* 46(4): 489-496.

Hein, E. & B. Kleidt, eds., 1999 *Äthiopien – Christliches Afrika: Kunst, Kirchen und Kultur / Ethiopia – Christian Afric a: Art, Churches and Culture,* Ratingen: Melina Verlag.

Heldman, M., 1992 *The Marian Icons of the Painter Fere Seyon. Studies in Fifteenth century Ethiopian Art, Patronage and Spirituality,* Glückstadt: Orientalia Biblica et Christiana.

Henze, P.B., 1989 The illuminated manuscripts of Lake Zway, *Proceedings of the First International Conference on the History of Ethiopian Art.* London: Pindar Press.

Henze, P.B., ed., 1993 *Aspects of Ethiopian Art, from Ancient Axum to the 20th Century.* London: Jed Press.

Heyer, F., 1971 Die äthiopisch orthodoxe Christenheit als unser ökumenischer Partner. *Ökumenischer Rundschau* 20(1): 1-11.

Heyer, F., 1971 Die Tiere in der frommen Vorstellung des orthodoxen Äthiopien, *Ostkirchliche Studien* 20(2-3): 97-114.

Heyer, F., 1998 *Die Heiligen der äthiopischen Erde,* Erlangen: Lehrstuhl für Geschichte und Theologie des Christlichen Ostens, (Oikoumonia 37).

Hilprecht, Herman V. (ed.). 1898. *Recent Research in Bible Lands: its progress and results.* Philadephia: J.D. Wattles & Co.

Hoffmann, J., 1969 *Die Äthiopische Johannesapocalypse Kritisch Untersucht,* Louvain: Peeters (Corpus Scriptorium Christianorum Orientalium, vol. 297)

Hofmann, J. & S. Uhlig, 1993 *Novum Testamentum Aethiopice: die Katholischen Briefe,* Stuttgart: Steiner.

Hofmann, J., 1959 Der arabische Einfluß in der äthiopischen Übersetzung der Johannes Apokalypse, *Oriens Christianus* 43: 24-53.

Hofmann, J., 1977 The Ethiopic version, B. Metzger, ed., *The Early Versions of the New Testament,* pp. 215-256, Oxford: Clarendon Press.

Hofmann, J., 1983 Einige Gedanken zur äthiopischen Philosophie des XVII. Jahrhunderts, *Deutsche Zeitschrift für Philosophie* 31(4): 488-491.

Hommel, F. 1893. Süd-arabische Chrestomathie. Munich: Franz.

Horn, L.W., 1961 *Hearth and Home in Ethiopia,* London: Sudan Interior Mission.

Horner, N.A., 1974 *Rediscovering Christianity Where it Began: a Survey of Contemporary Churches in the Middle East and Ethiopia.* Beirut: The Near East Council of Churches.

Huntingford, G.W.B., 1966 The lives of Saint Täklä Haymanot, *Journal of Ethiopian Studies* 4(2): 35-40; 1979 The saints of media eval Ethiopia, Abba *Salama* 10: 257-341.

Hyatt, H.M., 1928 *The Church of Abyssinia.* London: Luzac and Co.

Jäger, O., 1957 *Äthiopische Miniaturen,* Berlin: Gebrüder Mann, 1960 Ethiopian manuscript paintings, *Ethiopia Observer* 4(11): 354-391 (Special issue); 1961 Some notes on illuminations of mss. in Ethiopia, *Rassegna di Studi Etiopici* 17: 45-60.

Jäger, O.,1966 Äthiopische Zauberrollen und ihre Bilder *Baessler Archiv* 14(1): 139-180.

Jeffery, P., 1993 The liturgical year in the Ethiopian Deggwa (Chantbook), *Studia Anselmiana* (Analecta Liturgica 17) 110: 199-234.

Jésman, C., 1969 La situazion religiosa in Etiopia durante il regni di Teodoro. *Africa* (Roma) 24(2-3): 157-181.

Jonsson, E., 1998 The missionary factor in the institutionalisation of the Ethiopian Evangelical Church Mekane Yesus, Getatchew Haile, A. Lande & S. Rubenson, eds., *The Missionary Factor in Ethiopia*, pp. 169-184. Frankfurt/M.: Peter Lang.

Juel-Jensen, B., 1977 The ground hornbill artist of the 17th-century Ethiopic manuscript, *The Book Collector*, Spring 1977, pp. 61-74.

Juel-Jensen, B., 1989 An Aksumite survival in late medieval Ethiopian miniatures, *Proceedings of the First International Conference on the History of Ethiopian Art*, pp. 41 43. London: Pindar Press.

Kane, T.L., 1981 An Amharic version of the origin of the Cross, *Bulletin of the School of Oriental and African Studies* 44(2): 273-289.

Kaplan, S., 1985 On the Ethiopian Judeo-Christian context of the history of the Beta Israel, *Pe'amim* 22: 17-31 [in Hebrew]; 1986 Histoire et tradition: les chefs des communautés Beta Israel et leur évolution. *Les Temps Modernes* 41(47): 80-100.

Kaplan, S., 1985 The Ethiopian holy man as outsider and angel. *Religion* 15(3): 235-249.

Kaplan, S., 1986 Court and periphery in Ethiopian Christianity, *Asian and African Studies* (Haifa) 20(1): 141-152.

Kaplan, S., 1988 Christianity and ther early state in Ethiopia. In: S.N. Eisenstadt, ed., *The Early State in African Perspective*, pp. 148-167. Leiden: E.J. Brill.

Kaplan, S., 1986 The Ethiopian cult of the saints: a preliminary investigation, *Paideuma* 32: 1-13.

Kaplan, S., 1959 The monastery of Däbrä Damo, Ethiopia. *Archaeologia* 97: 1-58.

Kaplan, S., 1986 The rise of the monastic holy man in the early Solomonic period. In: G. Goldenberg & B. Podolsky, eds., *Ethiopian Studies. Proceedings of the Sixth International Conference, Tel Aviv 1980*, pp. 343-358. Rotterdam: A.A. Balkema. Matthews, D.H. & A. Mordini.

Kaplan, S., 1987 On the origins of the Beta Israel: five methodological cautions. *Pe'amim* 33: 33-49 [in Hebrew].

Kaplan, S., 1992 Indigenous categories and the study of world religions in Ethiopia: the case of the Beta Israel (*Falasha*). *Journal of Religion in Africa* 22(3): 208-221.

Kaplan, S.,1993 The invention of the Ethiopian Jews: three models. *Cahiers d'Études Africaines* 33(132): 645-658.

Karpozilos, A.D.1970 Anglican and Orthodox relations to 1930, Abba *Salama I*, 206-217.

Kefeyalew Merahi, *Kessis*, 1997 *The Covenant of Holy Mary Zion with Ethiopia*.Addis Ababa: Commercial Printing Press; 2001 *Saints and Monasteries in Ethiopia*. Addis Ababa: Commercial Printing Press.

Kefeyalew Merahi, *Kessis,* 2003 *Saints and Monasteries in Ethiopia, II.* Addis Ababa: Commercial Printing Press.

Kinfä-Gabriel Altayyä, 1999 *The Order of the Church.* Addis Ababa: Ethiopian Orthodox *Täwahedo* Church [in Amharic].

Kiros, Teodros. 2005. *Zara Yacob: Rationality of the Human Heart.* Trenton: Red Sea Press.

Knibb, M.A., 1978 *The Ethiopic Book of Henoch,* Oxford: Clarendon Press.

Kopp, U. F. 1819. *Bilder und Schriften der Vorzeit.* Manheim.

Kropp, M., 1986 Arabisch-äthiopische Übersetzungstechnik am Beispiel der Zena Ayhud (Yosippon) und des Tarikä Wäldä-'Amid, *Zeitschrift der Deutschen Morgenländischen Gesellschaft* 136(2): 314-346.

Kropp, M., 1988 Armenische Osterfestberechnung in Äthiopien zur Zeit von Kaiser Lebna Dengel oder: Russica non leguntur. *Oriens Christianus* 72: 203-207.

Kunst [in Dutch], 2003 *Monks and Communist Cadres in the Land of Prester John: a Phenomenological Study of Modern Ethiopian Monasticism and its Encounter with Communism.* London: School of Oriental and African Studies (Ph.D. dissertation).

Kur, S., 1994 Les Stéphanites à la lumière des *Actes de Gunda-Gunde.* In: C. Lepage, *et al.,* eds., *Études Éthiopiennes. Actes de la Xe Conférence Internationale des Études Éthiopiennes, Paris, 24-28 août 1988,* vol.1, pp. 359-361. Paris: Société Française des Études Éthiopiennes.

Lambert, O., 1979 Ecumenism in Ethiopia, *African Ecclesiastical Review* 21: 172-179.

Langmuir, E.C., 1978 *Ethiopia: the Christian Art of an African Civilization,* Salem: Peabody Museum.

Lantschoot, A. van, 1960 Abba Salama, métropolite d'Éthiopie (1348-1388) et son rôle de traducteur, *Atti del Convegno Internazionale di Studi Etiopici (Roma, 2-4 Aprile 1959),* Roma: Accademia Nazionale dei Lincei, pp. 397-401.

Lash, Chr., 1972 "Gates of Light": an Ethiopian hymn to the Blessed Virgin, *Eastern Churches Review* 4(1): 36-46.

Launhardt, J., 1982 *Uns Erschrecken die Trommeln nicht mehr,* Erlangen: Verlag der Evangelisch-Lutherischen Mission.

Lawson, M.P., 1987 The "maqwadasha": a propitiation sacrifice among the Amhara. *Chicago Anthropological Exchanges* 16: 87-95.

Lazzarini, V., 1981 P. Giuseppe Sapeto e la ripresa cattolica in Abessinia, *Quaderni di Studi Etiopici* 2: 65-80.

Leiris, M., 1974 Mazmur le clerc, *L'Ethnographie* 68: 39-58.

Leroy, J., S. Wright & O.A. Jäger, 1961 *Éthiopie, Manuscrits à Peinture,* Paris: UNESCO.

Leslau, W., 1964 A monophysite epistle, "The consolation of the soul", *Orientalia Christiana Periodica* 30: 447-484.

Lintingre, P., 1965 Le concept judéo-chrétien de la monarchie éthiopienne.*Afrique Documents* 78: 31-44.

Littmann, E., 1961-62 *Philosophi Abessini,* Louvain: Peeters (Corpus Scriptorium Christianorum Orientalium, vol. 18-19, reprint of 1904 edition).

Lockot, H.W. *Bibliographia Aethiopica II: The Horn of Africa in English Literature* (Wiesbaden: Harrassowitz, 1998), pp. 377-380.

Lössl, J., 1993 One as the same. Elements of an Ethiopian Christology. *Ostkirchliche Studien* 42: 288-302.

Ludolf, Hiob. 1681. *Historia Aethiopica sive brevis et succincta descriptio regni Habessino- rum.* Frankfurt.

Ludolf, Hiob. 1691. *Commentarius ad suam Historiam Aethiopicam.* Frankfurt: Zunnerus.

Ludolphus, Job. [Hiob Ludolf], 1682. *A New History of Ethiopia. Being a Full and Accurate Description of the Kingdom of Abessinia, Vulgarly, though Erroneously called the Empire of Prester John.* London.

Lundgren, E., 1963 The Lutheran Church in Ethiopia, *Den Evangeliske Missionen* 17(6): 170-176 [in Norwegian].

Macomber, W.F., 1991 Ethiopian liturgy. In: A.S. Atiya, ed., *The Coptic Encyclopedia,* vol. 3: 987-990. New York: Macmillan International.

Maehlum, H. & S. Uhlig, 1992 *Die äthiopische Version der Gefangenschaftsbriefe des Paulus,* Stuttgart: F. Steiner Verlag.

Mandefro, L., 1976 *Order and Canon Law of Marriage of the Ethiopian Tewahedo Church.* Kingston.

Mara, Y., 1972 *The Church of Ethiopia: the National Church in the Making,* Asmara: Il Poligrafico.

Marcus, C., 2002 In praise of women: the veneration of the Virgin Mary in the Ethiopian Orthodox Church, *Journal of Ethiopian Studies* 35(1): 9-26.

Marcus, C., 2002. Imperial nostalgia: Christian restoration and civic decay in Gondar. In: W. James, *et al.,* eds., *Remapping Ethiopia: Socialism and After,* pp. Oxford: James Currey.

Mario di Addi Fedde, *Padre,* 1967 I Copti dell'Etiopia e il problema dell'unita. *Continenti* 13(1): 24-26.

Marrassini, P., 1990 Some considerations of the problem of 'Syriac influences' on Aksumite Ethiopia, *Journal of Ethiopian Studies* 23: 35-46; 1999 Ancora sul problema degli influssi siriaci in èta aksumita in Biblica et Semitica, L. Gagni, ed., *Studi in Onore di Francesco Vattioni,* pp. 325-337. Napoli, Istituto Universitario Orientale.

Marrassini, P., 1993 *Lo Scettro et la Croce. La Campagna di 'Amda Seyon contro l'Ifat (1332)*, Napoli: Istituto Universitario Orientale (Studi Africanistici, Serie Etiopia 4).

Marrassini, P., ed., 2003 *"Vita", Omelia", "Miracoli" del santo Gabra Manfas Queddus*. Louvain: Peeters (Corpus Scriptorum Christianorum Orientalium, no. 597-598).

Marwedel, W., 1978 *Äthiopien Zuerst. 50 Jahre missionärischer Dienst, Revolution und Eigenständigkeit*, Erlangen: Evangelisch-Lutheranische Missionsverlag.

Massari, C., 1962 Sulle origine dell'arte religiosa etiopica, *Archivio per l'Antropologia e l'Etnologia* 92: 385-390.

Matthew, A.F., 1959 The Church of Ethiopia, *Ghana Bulletin of Theology* 1(7): 11-17.

McClure, B., 1972 Religion and nationalism in Southern Ethiopia, *Current Bibliography on African Affairs* 5(5-6): 497-508

Meinardus, O., 1965 The Ethiopians in Jerusalem, *Zeitschrift fur Kirchengeschichte* 76: 112-47, 217-32.

Meinardus, O.F., 1962 The Ethiopian monks in Egypt. *Publications de l'Institut d'Études Orientales* 11: 61-70.

Meinardus, O.F., 1964 Some observations of Ethiopian rituals by mediaeval pilgrims. *Publications de l'Institut d'Études Orientales* 13: 129-136.

Meinardus, O.F., 1976 Some Ethiopian traditions of St. Luke as a painter, Abba *Salama* 7: 243-252.

Meinardus, O.F.; 1962 A brief history of the Abunate of Ethiopia.*Wiener Zeitschrift für die Kunde des Morgenlandes* 58: 39-65 [published in 1964].

Meinardus, O.F.1964 The Zequala, the holy mountain of Ethiopia. *Orientalia Suecana* 13: 34-47.

Meinardus, O.F.1965 Ecclesiastica Aethiopica in Aegypto. *Journal of Ethiopian Studies* 3(1): 23-35.

Meinardus, O.F.1965 Notizen über das Eustatische Kloster Debra Bizen. *Annales d'Éthiopie* 6: 285-291.

Meinardus, O.F.1967 The Church of Ethiopia in the light of philatelic motives, *Bulletin de la Société d'Archéologie Copte* 18: 147-174.

Meinardus, O.F.1970 Ethiopian monks in Egypt. In: *Christian Faith and Life in Egypt*, pp. 427-435. Cairo.

Mälkä Tsedeq, Archbishop; 1992 *Christian Teaching*, 2 volumes. Addis Ababa: Ethiopian Orthodox, *Täwahïdo* Church [in Amharic].

Mekonnen Desta, 1969 *Traditional Ethiopian Church Education and its System at Present*, Addis Ababa: Haile Sellassie I University, Theological College (MA thesis).

Mercer, S.B., 1970 *The Ethiopic Liturgy: its Sources, Development, and Present Form*, New York: AMS Press, xvi + 487 p. [Reprint of 1915 ed.]

Mercier, J., 1994 *Trésors de l'Art Chrétien Éthiopien/Christian Art Treasures of Ethiopia*, Thessaloniki: Institut Français, ca.

Merid Wolde Aregay, 1997 Japanese and Ethiopian reactions to Jesuit missionary activities in the sixteenth and seventeenth centuries, K. Fukui, E. Kurimoto & M. Shigeta, eds., *Ethiopia in Broader Perspective, Proceedings of the XIIIth International Conference of Ethiopian Studies, Kyoto, 12-17 December 1997*, vol. 1, pp. 676-698.

Merid Wolde Aregay, 1998 The legacy of Jesuit missionary activities in Ethiopia, Getatchew Haile, A. Lande & S. Rubenson, eds., *The Missionary Factor in Ethiopia*, pp. 31-56. Frankfurt/M.: Peter Lang.

Methodios of Aksum, Metropolitan, 1971 A letter of Emperor Yohannes to Patriarch Sofronios, Abba *Salama* 2: 105-107.

Methodios of Aksum, Metropolitan, 1973 The dialogue between the Orthodox and Oriental Churches, Abba *Salama* 4: 11-35.

Methodios of Aksum, Metropolitan, 1976 Epiclesis, Abba *Salama* 7: 231-236.

Mikre-Sellassie, G.A., 1993 The Bible and its canon in the Ethiopian Orthodox Church. *The Bible Translator: Technical Papers* 44(1): 111-123.

Molnar, E.C.S., 1969 *The Ethiopian Orthodox Church: a Contribution to the Ecumenical Study of Less Known Eastern Churches*, Pasadena: Bloy House Theological School.

Munro-Hay, S., 2001 A sixth-century *Kebra Nagast*? *Annales d'Éthiopie* 17: 43-58.

Musie Ghebreghiorghis, 1984 Franciscan missionaries to Ethiopia during the early Renaissance, *Quaderni di Studi Etiopici* 3-4: 34-62.

Nazarova, N., 1982 Ethiopian churches. *Aziia I Afrika Segodnia* 1982/7: 56-59 [in Russian].

Olderogge, D.A. 1974. l'Armenie et l'Ethiopie au IVe siècle: a propos des sources de l'alphabet armenien. *IVe Congresso internazionale di studi etiopici*. Roma, Academia nazionale dei lincei.

Pankhurst, E.S., 1960a The monolithic churches of Lalibela, *Ethiopia Observer* 4(7): 214-224.

Pankhurst, E.S., 1960b Imraha Krestos, *Ethiopia Observer* 4(7): 225-228.

Pankhurst, E.S., 1960c Mrs. Bidder on the trail [Book review], *Ethiopia Observer* 4(7): 229-234.

Pankhurst, E.S., 1974a The rock church of Tulu Leman near Adadi, south of the Awash, *Ethiopia Observer* 16(4): 226-227.

Pankhurst, E.S., 1974b The rock-hewn church of Gufti Gabriel, south of Tulu Bolo, *Ethiopia Observer* 1 6(4): 222-225.

Pankhurst, E.S.,1998 Ethiopia: the book and the cross. In: *Cultures of the Indian Ocean,* pp. 138-50. Lisbon: Comissão Nacional para as Comemoracões do Descobrimentos Portugueses.

Pankhurst, R., 1962 Traditional Ethiopian art, *Ethiopia Observer* 5(4): 291-301.

Pankhurst, R., 1973 A cave church at Kistana, south of the river Awash, *Ethiopia Observer* 16(3): 216-219.

Pankhurst, R., 1986 Fear God, honor the king: the use of biblical allusion in Ethiopian literature, *Northeast African Studies* 8(1): 11-30 (part I) and 9(1): 25-88 (part II).

Pankhurst, R., 1987-88 Some brief notes on the Ethiopian Tabot and Mänbärä Tabot. *Quaderni di Studi Etiopici* 8-9: 28-32.

Pankhurst, R.J., 1966 Mikael Aragawi: Ethiopia's first Protestant missionary. *Ethiopia Observer* 10(3): 215-219.

Paulos Tzadua, 1971 The ancient law of the kings - the *Fetha Nagast* - in the actual practices of theestablished Ethiopian Orthodox Church. *Kanon. Jahrbuch der Gesellschaft für das Recht der Ost-Kirchen* (Vienna), Acta Congressus, vol. 1, pp. 112-145.

Paulos Tzadua, 1973 The Catholic Church in Ethiopia, *Äthiopien.* Special issue of the *Zeitschrift für Kulturaustausch* (Bonn), pp. 64-69.

Paulos Tzadua, Abba (transl.), 1968 *The Fetha Nägäst. The Law of Kings,* Addis Ababa: Haile Selassie I University, Faculty of Law.

Paulos Tzadua,1986 Le diverse forme del matrimonio e li loro carattere dissolubile nella tradizione della chiesa d'Etiopia. *Quaderni di Studi Etiopici* 6-7: 5-30.

Pawlikowski, J.T., 1973 The Judaic spirit in the Ethiopian Orthodox Church: a case study. *Journal of Religion in Africa* 4(3): 178-199.

Payne, E., 1972 *Ethiopian Jews. The Story of a Mission,* London: Olive Press, 105 p.

Pedersen, K. Stoffregen, 1980 *Ethiopian Institutions in Jerusalem* (Second edition). Jerusalem: Tantur Oecumenical Institute for Theological Research.

Pedersen, K. Stoffregen, 1994 Les moniales éthiopiennes à Jérusalem - *Mahbär* et *Qurit.,* In: C. Lepage, *et al.,* eds., *Études Éthiopiennes. Actes de la Xe Conférence Internationale des Études Éthiopiennes, Paris, 24-28 août 1988,* vol.1, pp. 383- 390. Paris: Société Française des Études Éthiopiennes.

Pedersen, K. Stoffregen, 1995 *Traditional Ethiopian Exegesis of the Book of Psalms,* Wiesbaden: Harrassowitz.

Pedersen, K. Stoffregen,1983 *The History of the Ethiopian Community in the Holy Land from the Time of Emperor Tewodros II till 1974,* Jerusalem: Tantur Oecumenical Institute for Theological Research; 1986 The historiography of the Ethiopian monastery in Jerusalem, G. Goldenberg & B.

Pedersen, K. Stoffregen,1990 *Les Éthiopiens.* Turnhout: Éditions Brepols.

Pedersen, K. Stoffregen,1995 *Die Äthiopische Kirche von Afrika bis nach Jerusalem.* Trier: Aphorisma.

Pennec, H. 1994 La mission jésuite en Ethiopie au temps de Pedro Paez (1583-1622) et ses rapports avec le pouvoir éthiopien, *Rassegna di Studi Etiopici* 36: 77-116.

Pennec, H., 2000 *Des Jésuites au Royaume du Prêtre Jean (Éthiopie). Stratégies, Rencontres et Tentatives d'Implantation (1495-1633).* Paris: Université de Paris I (Thèse de Doctorat).

Pennec, H.1998 La correspondence royale éthiopico-européenne de 1607, traduite et réinterpretée, *Cahiers du CRA* 9: 91-111.

Persoon, J., 2002 The Ethiopian monk: a changing concept of masculinity. *Journal of Ethiopian Studies* 35(1): 43-66.

Pétrides, S.P., 1961 *La Présence Éthiopienne à Jérusalem. Son Statut Juridique et ses Droits de Propriété sur le Monastère de Dar-es-Sultan,* Addis Ababa.

Pétrides, S.P., 1969 The wonderful world of Ethiopian crosses, *Ethiopia Mirror* 7(2-3): 66-77.

Pétrides, S.P., 1972 Sur l'évangélisation le de l'Éthiopie, sa date, et son protagoniste., Abba *Salama* 3: 208-232.

Petros Haylu, Abba, 1968 *Il Canto Sacro Etiopico,* Quaderni dell'Istituto Italiano di Cultura, no. 3.

Picken, L., 1957 A note on Ethiopian church music, *Acta Musicologica* 29: 41-42.

Piechocinski, M.N., 1989 The iconography of Ethiopia: a review of the styles, themes, techniques, and influences in an historical perspective, *The Sacred Art Journal* 10 (3): 95-112.

Pieraccini, E., 1963 Per l'Egitto all'Etiopia. *La Voce del Nilo* 22: 222-232.

Pilkington, H., 1978 *A Critical Edition of the Book of Proverbs in Ethiopic.* Oxford: Oxford University (D.Phil. thesis).

Piovanelli, P., 1985 Il testo e le traduzioni dell'Enoch etiopico, 1976-1987, *Henoch* 10: 85-95.

Piovanelli, P., 1986 *La Traduzione Etiopica dei Paralipomeni di Geremia: Testo Critico con Introduzione e Commento,* Firenze: Università di Firenze (M.A. thesis).

Piovanelli, P.,1990 Un nouveau témoin éthiopien de l'Ascension d'Isaïe et de la Vie de Jérémie, *Henoch* 12: 347-363.

Piovanelli, P.,1993 Les aventures des apocryphes en Éthiopie *Apocrypha* 4: 197-224.

Piovanelli, P.,1993 Les aventures des apocryphes en Éthiopie, *Apocrypha* 4: 197-224.

Piovanelli, P.,1994a Les controverses théologiques sous le roi Zar'a Ya'qob (1434-1468) et la mise en place du monophysisme éthiopien, A. le Boullec, ed., *La Controverse Religieuse et ses Formes,* pp. 189-228, Paris: Éditions du Cerf.

Piovanelli, P.,1994b Nouvelles perspectives dans l'étude des "apocryphes" éthiopiens traduits du grec, C. Lepage, *et al.*, eds., *Études Éthiopiennes. Actes de la Xe Conférence Internationale des Études Éthiopiennes, Paris, 24-28 août 1988*, vol.1, pp. 323-330. Paris: Société Française des Études Éthiopiennes.

Pirenne, J., 1988 La signification symbolique des églises de Lalibela, Taddese Beyene, ed., *Proceedings of the VIIIth International Conference of Ethiopian Studies, Addis Ababa; 1984*, vol.2, pp. 137-146. Huntingdon, U.K.: ELM Publications.

Playne, B., 1957 *St. George for Ethiopia*, London: Constable.

Pramar, V.S., 1983 Discovering architectural links between ancient Gujarat and Abyssinia. *Marg* (India) 36(1): 82-83.

Raineri, O., 1980 Le relazioni fra chiesa etiopica e chiesa romana, *Nicolaus. Rivista di Teologia Ecumeno-Patristica* 2: 351-364.

Raineri, O., 1985-86 Mons. Pietros Hailu da Hebo (1899-1985), *Quaderni di Studi Etiopici* 6-7: 186-187.

Raineri, O., 1986 Libri di uso prevalentamente liturgico tra i mss. "Cerulli etiopici" della Vaticana, *Ephemeridas Liturgicae* 100(2): 171-185.

Raineri, O.,1993 Il *Pastore* di erma nel secondo testimone etiopico, *Orientalia Christiana Periodica* 59(2): 427-464.

Raunig, W., 1975 Zwei Ikonen aus der Äthiopien-Sammlung des Völkerkunde-Museum Wiens, *Ethnologische Zeitschrift* 1: 151-179;

Raunig, W.,1989 Ethiopian folk art painting, *Proceedings of the First International Conference on the History of Ethiopian Art*, pp. 69-71. London: Pindar Press.

Reminick, R.A., 1975 The structure and functions of religious belief among the Amhara of Ethiopia, In: H.G. Marcus, ed., *Proceedings of the First United States Conference of Ethiopian Studies, Michigan State University, 2-5 May 1973*, pp. 25-42. East Lansing: African Studies Center, Michigan State University.

Ricci, L., 1961 *Arte dell'Etiopia*, Roma: Gherardo Casini Editore, 66 p; 1986 In margine a una mostra di dipinti etiopic i tradizionali, *Annali dell'Istituto Universitario Orientale* 46(2): 277-290.

Ricci, L., 1966-68 Le Vite di 'Embaqom e di Yohannes, abbati di Däbrä Libanos di Scioa, *Rassegna di Studi Etiopici* 22: 75-102 and 23:75-102.

Ricci, L., ed., 1989 *Pittura Etiopica Tradizionale*, Roma: Istituto Italo-Africano, Rothemund, H.J.; 1956 *Äthiopische Malerei*, Munich: Slavisches Institut.

Ricci, L.,1970 *Vita di Walatta Pietros*, Tradotta da L. Ricci; Louvain: Peeters (Corpus Scriptorum Christianorum Orientalium vol. 316).

Ricci, L.,1980-81 Ad "Zar'a Buruk", *Rassegna di Studi Etiopici* 28: 61-76; 1982-83 Yasiniana, *Rassegna di Studi Etiopici* 29: 139-174.

Rodinson, M., 1960 L'homélie sur la foi et la Trinité de Sévérien de Gabala, *Atti del Convegno Internazionale di Studi Etiopici (Roma, 2-4 Aprile 1959)*, pp. 387-396. Roma: Accademia Nazionale dei Lincei.

Rodinson, M., 1964 Sur la question des 'influences juives' en Éthiopie. *Journal of Semitic Studies* 9: 11-19.

Rodinson, M., 1969 Les interdictions alimaentaires éthiopiennes, *Proceedings of the Third International Conference of Ethiopian Studies, Addis Ababa 1966*, vol.3, pp. 48-50. Addis Ababa: Institute of Ethiopian Studies.

Rønne, F.A., 1997 Christianity in the dynamics of South Ethiopian societies and cultures:Kambbaatta-Hadiiyya, In: K. Fukui, E. Kurimoto & M. Shigeta, eds., *Ethiopia in Broader Perspective Proceedings of the XIIIth International Conference of Ethiopian Studies, Kyoto, 12-17 December 1997*, vol.3, pp. 133-148. Kyoto: Shokado.

Rossini, C. C. 1928. Storia d'Etiopia. Milano and Bergamo: Instituto Italiano D'Arti Grafiche.

Rubenson, Sven; 1998 The interaction between the missionaries and the Orthodox: the case of Abune Selama, Getatchew Haile, A. Lande & S. Rubenson, eds., *The Missionary Factor in Ethiopia*, pp. 85-100. Frankfurt/M.: Peter Lang.

de Sacy, Silvestre. 1818. Mémoires d'histoire et de littérature orientales. *Mémoire de Acadademie des Inscriptiones*. Vol. Xlix.

Saeveras, O., 1974 *On Church - Mission Relations in Ethiopia 1944-69 with Special Reference to the Evangelical Church Mekane Yesus and the Lutheran Missions*. Lund: Forlag og Bokhandel A/S, 79 p. (Studia Missionalia Uppsaliensa, 27).

Samuel Wolde-Yohannis, 1996 *Il Fondo Umanistico dei Modelli e degli Ideali dei Gadl. Ricerca linguisticafilosofica su alcuni testi del XV secolo etiopico*, Roma: Università Pontificia Salesiana.

Samuel Wolde-Yohannis,1997 The *Gadl* as a basis for reconstructing the notion of the human person in Ethiopian philosophy, K. Fukui, E. Kurimoto & M. Shigeta, eds., *Ethiopia in Broader Perspective Proceedings of the XIIIth International Conference of Ethiopian Studies, Kyoto, 12-17 December 1997*, vol.3, pp. 211-218. Kyoto: Shokado.

Samuel, V.C., 1976 Christianity and indigenization, Abba *Salama* 7: 60-92.

Sato, R., 2002 Evangelical Christianity and ethnic consciousness in Majangir, W. James *et al.*, eds., *Remapping Ethiopia: Socialism and After*, pp. Oxford: James Currey.

Sauget, J.-M., 1974 Un exemple typique des relations culturelles entre l'arabe-chrétien et l'éthiopien un *Patericon* récemment publié, *Atti del IV Congresso Internazionale di Studi Etiopici (Roma, 10-15 Aprile; 1972, Atti del Convegno 2)*. Roma: Accademia dei Lincei, vol.1, p. 321-388.

Schneider, M., 1970 Deux actes de donation en arabe. *Annales d'Éthiopie* 8: 79-87.

Schneider, M., 1971 *Vie de Zä Yohannes, fondateur du couvent de Kebran, et textes relatifs à Kebran,* Paris: École Pratique des Hautes Études, Sorbonne (Thèse).

Schneider, M., ed., 1972 *Actes de Za -Yohannes de Kebran,* Louvain: Peeters (Corpus Scriptorum Christianorum Orientalium, vol. 332-333).

Schneider, R., 1972 *Actes de Zä -Yohannes de Kebran,* Louvain: Peeters (Corpus Scriptorum Christianorum Orientalium, vol. 330-331), 2 volumes.

Schneider, R., 1985 Les Actes d'Abba Afse de Yeha, *Annales d'Éthiopie* 13: 105-118.

Schneider, R., 1988 Nouveaux témoins du texte éthiopien des Règles de l'Église. *Journal Asiatique* 276: 71-86.

Scholler, H., 1986 The Ethiopian community in Jerusalem from 1850 to the conference of Dar- el- Sultan 1902 – the political struggle for independence, G. Goldenberg & B. Podolsky, eds., *Ethiopian Studies. Proceedings of the Sixth International Conference, Tel Aviv 1980,* pp. 487-500. Rotterdam: A.A. Balkema.

Scholz, P., 1989 Bemerkungen zur Ikonologie der sogenannten "Vier apokalytischen Wesen" an dem Steinaltar der Dreifältigkeitskapelle zu Lalibela, *Proceedings of the First International Conference on the History of Ethiopian Art,* pp. 23-29. London: Pindar Press.

Schultz, H.,1968 Reform and reaction in the Ethiopian Orthodox Church. *Christian Century* 85(31): 142-143.

Schultz, H.J., 1968 Reform and reaction in Ethiopia's Orthodox church. *Christian Century* 85: 142-143.

Schwarzbaum, H., 1962 Jewish, Christian, Moslem and *Falasha* legends of the Death of Aaron, the High Priest, *Fabula* (Berlin) 5: 185-227.

Sebhatleab Ayele, 1989 *Analisi di 'A'madä Mist'ir (Le Cinque Colonne del Mistero), Catechismo della Chiesa Ortodossa d'Etiopia.* Rome: Università Pontificia Salesiana.

Seip, G.A., 1974 Die Orthodoxe Kirche in Äthiopien. *Afrika Heute* 12(3) 25-28.

Sergew Hable Sellasie, 1964 New historical elements in the *"Gedle Aftse",* C.F. Beckingham & E. Ullendorff, eds., *Ethiopian Studies. Papers read at the Second Conference of Ethiopian Studies, Journal of Semitic Studies* 9(1): 200-203.

Sergew Hable –Sellassie, 1971 Die äthiopische Kirche. Abba *Salama* 2: 43-75.

Sergew Hable –Sellassie, 1992 The monastic library of Däbrä Hayq, *Orbis Aethiopicus* 1: 243-258.

Sergew Hable –Sellassie, 1993 Sources for the history of Dabra Libanos. *Journal of the Archives of Ethiopia* 1(2): 1-107.

Sergew Hable –Sellassie,1974 Introduction of Christianity to Shewa. *Bulletin of Ethiopian Manuscripts* 1974/1: 1-5.

Seyoum Wolde, 1988 The profile of writings on Ethiopian medieval Christian art, Taddese Beyene, ed., *Proceedings of the VIIIth International Conference of Ethio-*

pian Studies, Addis Ababa 1984, vol.2, pp. 165-172. Huntingdon, U.K.: ELM Publications.

Shack, W.A., 1968 The Mäsqal-pole: religious conflict and social change in Gurageland. *Africa* 38(4): 457-468.

Shelemay, K.K. & P. Jeffery, eds; 1994 *Ethiopian Christian Liturgical Chant. An Anthology*. 3 volumes, Madison: A-R Editions.

Shelemay, K.K., 1980 'Historical ethnomusicology': reconstructing *Falasha* liturgical history,15 *Ethnomusicology* 80: 233-258; 1986 *Music, Ritual and Falasha History*. East Lansing: African Studies Center, Michigan State University.

Shenk, C.E., 1972a *The Development of the Ethiopian Orthodox Church and its Relationship with the Ethiopian Government, from 1930 to 1970*, New York: New York University (Ph.D. thesis).

Shenk, C.E., 1972b The Italian attempt to reconcile the Ethiopian Orthodox Church: the use of religious celebrations and assistance to churches and monasteries, *Journal of Ethiopian Studies* 10(1): 125-136.

Shenk, C.E., 1988 The Ethiopian Orthodox Church: a study in indigenization, *Missiology* 16(3): 259-278.

Shenk, C.E., 1994 Church and state in Ethiopia: from monarcy to Marxism, *Religion in Communist Countries* 22(2): 203-226.

Shepperson, G., 1968 Ethiopianism, past and present. In: C.G. Baeta, ed., *Christianity in Tropical Africa*, pp. 249-268. New York: Oxford University Press.

Sileshi Mengiste 1998 *A History of the Monastery of Dima Giorgis*. Addis Ababa: Addis Ababa University, Department of History (BA thesis).

Sindima, H.J., 1991 Africa's Christian heritage: some notes on Christianity in Ethiopia. *African Theological Journal* 20(2): 109-122.

Six, V., 1975 *Die Vita des Abuna Tadewos von Dabra Maryam im Tanasee*, Hamburg: Universität Hamburg (Dissertation, Orientalistik).

Six, V., 1989 Kategorien der äthiopischen Zaubertexte, *Zeitschrift der Deutschen Morgenländischen Gesellschaft* 139(2): 310-317.

Six, V.,1999 Water - the Nile - and the *Täamrä Maryam*: miracles of the Virgin Mary in the Ethiopian version, *Aethiopica* 2: 53-68.

Stan, L., 1971 L'église d'Éthiopie. Abba *Salama* 2: 119-150.

Staude, W. 1958 Die ikonischen Regeln in der äthiopischen Kirchenmalerei, *Archiv für Völkerkunde* 13: 236-308.

Staude, W.; 1957 Iconographie de la légende éthiopienne de la Reine d'Azieb ou de Saba. *Journal de la Société des Africanistes* 27(1): 139-181.

Staude, W.1959a Étude sur la décoration picturale des églises Abba Antonios de Gonder et Däbrä Sina de Gorgora, *Annales d'Éthiopie* 3: 185-250.

Staude, W.1959b Une peinture éthiopienne datée dans l'église de Beta -lehem (région de Gaynt, province de Begemder), *Revue de l'Histoire des Religions* 156(1): 65-110.

Staude, W.1971 Les cinq clous du Christ et l'icone impériale éthiopienne, *Ethnologische Zeitschrift* 1: 4-26.

Stedman, S., 1979 Ethiopia: the Christian art of an African nation, *African Arts* 12: 82-83.

Stiehl, R., 1967-68 Christliche Mission beiderseits des Roten Meeres. *Welt des Orients* 4: 108-127.

Stierlin, H, 1977 En Afrique Orientale troublée: monuments de l'Abyssinie chrétienne. *Oeuil* (Switzerland) 268: 6-13.

Stitz, V., 1975 Distribution and foundation of churches in Ethiopia. *Journal of Ethiopian Studies* 13(1): 11-36.

Stjärne, P., 1960 Missionary work in Ethiopia, *Ethiopia Observer* 4(3): 77-82.

Strebel, B., 2001 Leben auf dem Missionsfeld. Chrishona-Pilgermissionäre in Äthiopien(1856-1868), *Aethiopica* 4: 121-157.

Strelcyn, S., 1973 La chrétienté dans la région de la Mer Rouge. *Journal of Religion in Africa* 5(3): 161-170.

Strelcyn, S., 1978 Le Psaume 151 dans la tradition éthiopienne, *Journal of Semitic Studies* 23(2).

Strelcyn, S.,1979 L'action de grâce de N.-D. Marie" et l' Anaphore de N.-D. Marie dite Ma'aza Qeddase dans la liturgie éthiopienne, *Journal of Semitic Studies* 24: 241-249.

Strelcyn, S.,1981 Les mystères des psaumes, traité éthiopien sur les psaumes (amharique ancien), *Bulletin of the School of Oriental and African Studies* 44(1): 54-88.

Strelcyn, S.,1984 Un poème satanique éthiopien, Fusella L., S. Tedeschi & J. Tubiana, eds., *Trois Essays sur la Littérature Éthiopienne*, pp. 83-116. Antibes: Ed. ARESAE.

Sumner, Claude. 1963 The Ethiopic liturgy: an analysis, *Journal of Ethiopian Studies* 1(1): 40-46.

Sumner, Claude. 1986. *The Source of African Philosophy: the Ethiopian Philosophy of Man*. Stuttgart, Wiesbaden: Franz Steiner Verlag.

Sumner, Claude. 1998. Ethiopia, Philosophy. In E. Craig (Ed.). *Routledge Encyclopedia of Philosophy*. London: Routledge.

Taddesse Tamrat, 1959 The *mateb*, *Ethnological Society Bulletin* (University College Addis Ababa) 9: 38-42.

Taddesse Tamrat, 1966 Some notes on the fifteenth-century Stephanite heresy. *Rivista di Studi Orientali* 22: 103-115.

Taddesse Tamrat, 1970 Hagiographies and the reconstruction of medieval Ethiopian history, *Rural Africana* 11: 12-18.

Taddesse Tamrat, 1985 A short note on the Ethiopian music, *Annales d'Éthiopie* 13: 137-143.

Taddesse Tamrat, 1993 Church and State in Ethiopia: the early centuries, In: R. Grierson, M.E. Heldman, & S. Munro-Hay, eds., *African Zion: the Sacred Art of Ethiopia*, pp. 33-42. New Haven - London: Yale University Press.

Taddesse Tamrat, 1998 Evangelizing the evangelised: the root problem between missions and the Ethiopian Orthodox Church, Getachew Haile, A. Lande & S. Rubenson eds., *The Missionary Factor in Ethiopia*, pp. 17-56. Frankfurt/M.: Peter Lang.

Taddesse Tamrat,1970 Persecution and religious controversies.In: Sergew Hable Selassie, ed., *The Church of Ethiopia. A Panorama of History and Spiritual Life*, Addis Ababa: The Ethiopian Orthodox Church.

Taddesse Tamrat,1972a *Church and State in Ethiopia, 1270-1535.* Oxford: Clarendon Press.

Taddesse Tamrat,1972b A short note on the traditions of pagan resistance to the Ethiopian Church (14th and 15th centuries). *Journal of Ethiopian Studies* 10(1): 137-150.

Tedeschi, S., 1964 Profilo storico di Dayr as-Sultan, *Journal of Ethiopian Studies* 2(2): 92-160.

Tedeschi, S., 1983 Les débuts de la politique religieuse de Yohannis IV, 1868-1876, In: M. Genoino Caravaglios, ed., *L'Africa ai Tempi di Daniele Comboni: Atti del Congresso Internazionale di Studi Africani, Roma, 19-21 Novembre 1981*, pp. 161-178. Roma: Istituto Italo-Africano.

Tedeschi, S., 1990 Un prelato armeno nell'Etiopia del Seicento, *Africa* (Roma) 45(1): 1-21.

Tedeschi, S.,1991 Ethiopian prelates, A.S. Atiya, ed., *The Coptic Encyclopedia*, vol. 4: 999-1044. New York, Macmillan International Tervuren: Koninklijk Museum voor Midden-Afrika / Berlin: Gordon & Breach Arts International [in Dutch].

Tedla da Hebo, A., 1994 Il *Tabot*: la sua importanza religiosa e giuridico-culturale nella Chiesa etiopica. *Orientalia Christiana Periodica* 60(1): 131-157.

Tedros Abraha, 2001 *La Lettera ai Romani. Testo e Commentari della Versione Etiopica.* Wiesbaden: Harrassowitz (Äthiopistische Forschungen, no. 57).

Teisohn, J., 1975 *Der auserwählte Richter: Untersuchungen zum traditions geschichtlichem Ort der Menschensohn-gestalt der Bilderreden des äthiopischen Henoch*, Göttingen: Vandenhoeck & Ruprecht.

Tekeste Negash, 1998 The Catholic mission and the Catholic community in Eritrea, 1894-1950, Getatchew Haile, A. Lande & S. Rubenson, eds., *The Missionary Factor in Ethiopia*, pp. 121-134. Frankfurt/M.: Peter Lang.

Tekle-Tsadik Mekouria, 1967 *L'Église de l'Éthiopie*. Paris: Promotion et Édition.

Tekle-Tsadik Mekouria,1994 L'influence du roi David et de son Psautier en Éthiopie. In: C. Lepage, *et al.*, eds., *Études Éthiopiennes. Actes de la Xe Conférence Internationale des Études Éthiopiennes, Paris, 24-28 août 1988*, vol.1, pp. 145-153. Paris: Société Française des Études Éthiopiennes.

Teodros Kiros, 2001 Zär'a Yacob: a seventeenth-century Ethiopian philosopher of modernity in Africa. In: Teodros Kiros, ed., *Explorations in African Political Thought*, pp. 69-80. New York - London: Routledge.

Terening Poladian, Bishop, 1964 Doctrinal position of the Monophysite churches. *Ethiopia Observer* 8(3): 257-265 (Also in: *Bulletin de la Société d'Archéologie Copte* 17: 157-175).

Tervuren: Koninklijk Museum voor Midden-Afrika/ Berlin: Gordon & Breach, Arts International [in Dutch].

Tescarole, G., 1970 La chiesa in Etiopia. *La Nigrizia* 88(2): 12-16.

Tesfagzhi Uqbit, 1973 *Current Christological Positions of Ethiopian Orthodox Theologians*, Roma: Pontificum Institutem Studiorum Orientalium (Orientalia Christiana, Analecta 193).

Tesfaye Gebre-Mariam, 1997 A structural analysis of the *Gädlä Täklä Haymanot*, *African Languages and Cultures* 10(2): 181-98.

Tewolde Beiene, 1983 *La Politica Cattolica di Seltan Sägäd I (1607-1632) e la Missione della Compagnia di Gesù in Etiopia. Precedenti, Evoluzione e Problematiche, 1589-1632.* Rome.

Tito Lepisa, Abba, 1963 *The Cult of Saints in the Ethiopian Church*, Rome: Università Gregoriana (Doctoral dissertation).

Tito Lepisa, Abba, 1969 The three modes and the signs of of the songs in the Ethiopian liturgy. In: *Proceedings of the Third International Conference of Ethiopian Studies, Addis Ababa 1966*, vol.2, pp. 162-187. Addis Ababa: Institute of Ethiopian Studies, Haile Selassie I University.

Tourny, O. 2000 Le support de l'écrit, la part de l'oralité dans la psalmodie de l'Église chrétienne orthodoxe de l'Éthiopie: l'exemple du psaume 62, *Annales d'Éthiopie* 17: 375-386.

Tourny, O., 2002 Abba Bayene, le dernier moine juif éthiopien. *Cahiers de Musiques Traditionelles* 15: 98-96.

Trucca, B., 1973 Gli antichi culti etiopici precristiani. *Sestante* 8(2): 23-31; 1980 Il culto delle pietre ritte (*ansâb*) in terra etiopica. *Quaderni di Studi Etiopici* 1: 66-78.

Tsegaye Berhane, 1989 *The Holy Trinity Cathedral, Addis Ababa (c. 1930 to 1974)*, Addis Ababa: Department of History, Addis Ababa University (B.A. essay).

Tsegaye Gebre-Medhin, 1967 L'art dans la vie des Éthiopiens, *Colloque sur l'Art Nègre*, volume I, pp. 91-98. Paris: Présence Africaine

Tubiana, J., 1960 A propos du "Livre des Mystères du Ciel et de la Terre", *Atti del Convegno Internazionale di Studi Etiopici (Roma, 2-4 Aprile 1959)*, pp. 403-408, Roma: Accademia Nazionale dei Lincei.

Tubiana, J., 1963 Le frère de Saint Lalibela (peinture éthiopienne), *Objets et Mondes* 3(3): 221-228.

Turaev, B., ed., 1955a *Acta S. Aaronis et Philippi* (Translation), Louvain: Imprimerie Orientaliste L. Durbecq (Corpus Scriptorum Christianorum Orientalium, vol. 31).

Turaev, B.,1955b *Vitae Sanctorum Indigenarum: Acta S. Fere Mika'el et S. Zar'a Abreham*, Louvain: Imprimerie Orientaliste L. Durbecq (Corpus Scriptorum Christianorum Orientalium, vol. 35-36, reprint of 1905 edition).

Turaev, B.,1961a *Acta S. Aaronis et Philippi*. Louvain: Peeters (Corpus Scriptorum Christianorum Orientalium,vol. 30).

Turaev, B.,1961b *Vitae Sanctorum Indigenarum Acta S. Eustathii*, Louvain: Peeters (Corpus Scriptorum Christianorum Orientalium, vol. 31-32).

Uhlig, S. & H. Maehlum, 1993 *Novum Testamentum Aethiopice: die Gefangenschaftsbriefe*, Stuttgart: Steiner.

Uhlig, S., 1983 *Hiob Ludolf's „Theologia Aethiopica"*, Wiesbaden: Steiner Verlag, 2 volumes.

Uhlig, S., 1993 Ethiopian manuscripts and paleography, R. Grierson, M.E. Heldman, & S. Munro-Hay, eds., *African Zion: the Sacred Art of Ethiopia* , pp. 57-61. New Haven - London: Yale University Press.

Ullendorff, E. & C.F. Beckingham, 1982 *The Hebrew Letters of Prester John*. London, etc.: Oxford University Press.

Ullendorff, E., 1960 An Aramaic "Vorlage" of the Ethiopic text of Enoch? *Atti del Convegno Internazionale di Studi Etiopici (Roma, 2-4 Aprile 1959)*, pp. 259-267, Roma: Accademia Nazionale dei Lincei.

Ullendorff, E., 1968 *Ethiopia and the Bible*. London: Oxford University Press for the British Academy.

Ullendorff, E., 1980 Hebrew, Aramaic, and Greek: the version underlying Ethiopic translations of the Bible and intertestamental literature, G. Rendsburg, *et al.*, eds., *The Bible World: Essays in Honor of Cyrus E. Gordon*, pp. 259-257. New York: Ktav Publishing House.

Ullendorff, E., ed.1987 *The Ethiopian Book of Enoch. A New Edition in the Light of the Aramaic Dead Sea Fragments*, 2 volumes, Oxford: Oxford University Press.

Ullendorff, E.,1983 Hebrew elements in the Ethiopic Old Testament, *Jerusalem Studies in Arabic and Islam* 9: 42-50.

Ullendorff, E.,1987 The *confessio fidei* of King Claudius of Ethiopia. *Journal of Semitic Studies* 32(1): 159-176.

Vanderkam, J.C., ed.,1987 The textual base for the Ethiopic translation of 1 Enoch, *Working with No Data. Semitic and Egyptian Studies to Th. O. Lambdin,* pp. 247-262, Winowa Lake: Eisenbrans.

Vanderkam, J.C.,1989 *The Book of Jubilees,* Louvain: Peeters (Corpus Scriptianorum Christianum Orientalium, vol. 510-511, Scriptores Aethiopices 87-88).

Voigt, R., 1999 Die äriträisch-orthodoxe Kirche. *Oriens Christianus* 83: 187-192.

Wasungu, P., 1977 Le "timket" ou l'épiphanie éthiopienne. *Ethno-Psychologie* 32: 313-320.

Wehlte, K.,1959 Rettung einer äthiopischen Wandmalerei, *Maltechnik* (Munich) 65(1): 1-17.

Weihs, F., 1974 Some technical details concerning Ethiopian icons, *Religious Art of Ethiopia*, pp. 298-318. Catalogue Linden Museum Exhibition, Stuttgart: Linden Museum.

Weyer, R. van de, 1973 The monastic community of Ethiopia. *Ethiopia Observer* 16(1): 8-14.

Willmott, H.M., 1961 *The Doors Were Opened: the Remarkable Advance of the Gospel in Ethiopia,* London: Sudan Interior Mission.

Winninge, I. and C. Winninge, 1976 *The International Church Worker: Investigations in Ethiopia,* Uppsala: Swedish Institute of Missionary Research.

Winssen, G.A.C. van,1965 L'église catholique en Éthiopie. *Neue Zeitschrift für Missionswissenschaft* 21(2): 118-131.

Winssen, G.A.C. van,1974 Ethiopian Christianity. *Zeitschrift für Missionswissenschaft und Religionswissenschaft* 58(2): 124-133.

Wisloff, F., 1966 *Holidays in Ethiopia*. Oslo: Lutherstiftelsen, 137 p. [in Norwegian].

Witakowski, W., 1956 Une ambassade éthiopienne à Rome en 1450. *Orientalia Christiana Periodica* 21: 286-298.

Witakowski, W., 1989/90 Syrian influences in Ethiopian culture. *Orientalia Suecana* 38-39: 191-202.

Wondyifraw Ambaye, 1988 Classical Ethiopian philosophy and traditional attitude. In: A.N. Gromyko, ed., *Proceedings of the IXth International Conference of Ethiopian Studies, Moscow, August 1986,* vol.6, pp. 222-234. Moscow: Akademia Nauk, for Institut Afriki.

Wright, S. & O. Jäger, 1961 *Ethiopia: Illuminated Manuscripts,* New York: Graphic Society (UNESCO World Art Series, no.15).

Wudu Tafete, 1989 *The Twin Churches of Raguel (1887 to 1985).* Addis Ababa: Department of History, Addis Ababa University (B.A. essay).

Yakob Beyene, 1975 Un manoscritto cattolico in tigrino del XIX secolo, *Annali dell'Istituto Universitario Orientale* 35(1): 1-20.

Yakob Beyene,1976 Un opuscolo cattolico di polemica teologica in tigrino del XIX secolo, *Annali dell'Istituto Universitario Orientale* 36(1):1.

Yaqob Beyene, ed., 1990 *Giyorgis di Sagla: Il Libro del Mistero (Mäs'hafä Mestir),* Louvain: Peeters (Corpus Scriptianorum Christianum Orientalium, vol. 515-516).

Yekunno-Amlak Gäbrä-Selasse, transl., 1966 Early Ge'ez Qene, *Journal of Ethiopian Studies* 4(1): 75-119.

Yeshaq, *Abuna* (L. Mandefro), 1997 *The Ethiopian Orthodox Tewahedo Church: an Integrally African Church,* Nashville: Winston [First edition published in 1989 in New York].

Yiheyisi Worqi, *Memhir,* 1969 Reading and translation of Qene: hidden meaning, *Journal of Ethiopian Studies* 7(2): 119-225 [in Amharic].

Yoftahie Kabede, 1958 *Genbot lidäta Ethnological Society Bulletin* (University College Addis Ababa) 8: 77-82.

Yonas Adao, 1999 *The History of Ziway Seminary School and Hamere Birhan Qidus Gebrael Monastery.* Addis Ababa: Holy Trinity Theological College (Senior Essay).

Young, M.J.L., 1973 A letter in Arabic to Pope Clement XI from Emperor Iyasu I of Ethiopia, *Orientalia Christiana Periodica* 39(2): 408-418.

Zanetti, U., SJ, 1992 Amulettes éthiopiennes chez les Bollandistes, *Analecta Bollandiana* 110: 28-30.

Zanetti, U., SJ, 1996 Christelijk Ethiopië. In: X. van der Stappen, ed., *Aethiopia. Volkeren van Ethiopië*, pp. 160-180.

Zanetti, U., SJ, 1999 Moines et ermites: des Pères du désert d'Egypte à ceux de l'Éthiopie contemporaine. In: C. Cannuyer, F. Mawet & J. Ries, eds.)., *Le Ciel dans les Civilisations Orientales*, pp. 89-104. Bruxelles - Louvain-la-Neuve - Leuven: Acta Orientalia Belgica, XII.

Zär'a Ya'kob, 1962-63 *Mäshafä Milad (Liber nativitatis) and Mäshafä Sellase (Liber trinitas).* Edited and translated by K. Wendt, Louvain: Peeters (Corpus Scriptorum Christianorum Orientalium, no.221-222, 235-236); 1964-65 *Il Libro della Luce del Negus Zär'a Ya'qob.* Edito da C. Conti Rossini, Louvain: Peeters (Corpus Scriptorum Christianorum Orientalium, vol. 250-251).

Zawdie Berhane, 1988 A note on the history of traditional building materials of Ethiopia, Taddese Beyene, ed., *Proceedings of the VIIIth International Conference of Ethiopian Studies, Addis Ababa 1984,* vol.2, pp. 725-731. Huntingdon, UK: ELM Publications.

Zuurmond, R., 2001a *Novum Testamentum Aethiopice, Part III. The Gospel of Matthew,* Wiesbaden: Harrassowitz.

Zuurmond, R., ed., 1989 *Novum Testamentum Aethiopice, Parts I and II. The Synoptic Gospels,* Wiesbaden: Harrassowitz.

Zuurmond, R.,2001b The textual background of the Gospel of Matthew in Ge'ez, *Aethiopica* 4: 232-241.

Index

❖